Economics, Anthropology and the Origin of Money as a Bargaining Counter

For many decades economists have disputed with economic anthropologists over the origins of money. Economists claim that money emerged from barter exchange; anthropologists claim that it originated as a 'unit of account' in the temples and palaces of ancient Mesopotamia. This book argues that money originated as a bargaining counter in a system of money-bargaining, emerging almost seamlessly from barter-bargaining. This is not the 'money' of mainstream economic conception – a 'veil' cast over a system of resource allocation defined in mathematical terms.

Confidence in the bargaining counter is sustained through 'support-bargaining,' a process in which individuals seek the support of their associates but seek at the same time to advance their own interests. A comprehensive 'Introduction to Support-Bargaining and Money-Bargaining' is provided by the work. The arrival of coin-money is recognised by many as a crucial event in the history of mankind, and it is argued here that the distinctive character of support-bargaining in ancient Greek city states made possible the introduction of coin-money. The dependence of coin-money on a particular form of support-bargaining also suggests the reason why coin-money was not introduced much earlier, given that the technology for producing coins was available long before their adoption.

This book will be of great interest to researchers in the history and origins of money, banking and economic theory more broadly.

Patrick Spread graduated from Trinity College, Oxford, UK and received a PhD from the London Business School. This is his ninth book based on the theory of support-bargaining and money-bargaining. In his career he has mixed theoretical research with work as an economic adviser and consultant to governments and economic development agencies.

Routledge Frontiers of Political Economy

China, Trust and Digital Supply Chains
Dynamics of a Zero Trust World
Warwick Powell

Macroeconomic Modelling, Economic Policy and Methodology
Economics at the Edge
Edited by Mikael Randrup Byrialsen, Hamid Raza and Finn Olesen

Economics, Anthropology and the Origin of Money as a Bargaining Counter
Patrick Spread

Bernard Schmitt's Quantum Macroeconomic Analysis
Alvaro Cencini

Blockchain and the Commons
Vangelis Papadimitropoulos

Globalization and the Decline of American Power
The Political Economy of the American Fall
Cyrus Bina

Marx and *Le Capital*
Evaluation, History, Reception
Edited by Marcello Musto

Permanent Economic Disorder
Shahzavar Karimzadi

Temporary Economic Crises
Shahzavar Karimzadi

For more information about this series, please visit: www.routledge.com/Routledge-Frontiers-of-Political-Economy/book-series/SE0345

Economics, Anthropology and the Origin of Money as a Bargaining Counter

Patrick Spread

Routledge
Taylor & Francis Group
LONDON AND NEW YORK

First published 2023
by Routledge
4 Park Square, Milton Park, Abingdon, Oxon OX14 4RN

and by Routledge
605 Third Avenue, New York, NY 10158

Routledge is an imprint of the Taylor & Francis Group, an informa business

British Library Cataloguing-in-Publication Data
A catalogue record for this book is available from the British Library

Library of Congress Cataloging-in-Publication Data
Names: Spread, Patrick, 1944– author.
Title: Economics, anthropology and the origin of money as a
bargaining counter / Patrick Spread.
Description: New York, NY: Routledge, 2023. |
Series: Routledge frontiers of political economy |
Includes bibliographical references and index.
Identifiers: LCCN 2022020422 (print) | LCCN 2022020423 (ebook) |
ISBN 9781032322278 (Hardback) | ISBN 9781032322308 (Paperback) |
ISBN 9781003313472 (eBook)
Subjects: LCSH: Money–Origin. | Barter.
Classification: LCC GN450.5 .S67 2023 (print) |
LCC GN450.5 (ebook) | DDC 332.4–dc23/eng/20220716
LC record available at https://lccn.loc.gov/2022020422
LC ebook record available at https://lccn.loc.gov/2022020423

ISBN: 978-1-032-32227-8 (hbk)
ISBN: 978-1-032-32230-8 (pbk)
ISBN: 978-1-003-31347-2 (ebk)

DOI: 10.4324/9781003313472

Typeset in Bembo
by Newgen Publishing UK

To My Wife, Evelyn

Contents

Introduction

The origins of money lie back in the ancient world. The facilitation of exchange seems one likely origin, favoured by economists. Money emerged to resolve inconveniences of barter, as described by Adam Smith.[1] Economic anthropologists have scorned the economic account on the grounds that there is no evidence for the emergence of money in this way. They have instead argued that the origin lies in designation of a 'money of account' in the temples and palaces of ancient Mesopotamia.

In both accounts the origin of money depends on the social and economic behaviour of people in ancient societies. Anthropologists have the advantage of being specialists in the study of such societies. They have to hand such evidence as is available about them. Their conclusions are potentially more 'scientific,' in the sense of empirically based, than those of economists, who rely more on a mathematical 'neoclassical model' of economic behaviour, supposedly universal, but involving numerous assumptions about human society that are recognised as unrealistic even in relation to the modern world, and even more so with regard to the ancient world. Karl Polanyi argued in *The Great Transformation* that 'markets' in the neoclassical economic sense did not exist in the ancient world, and consequently could not have been the origin of money.[2] Polanyi is the modern inspiration for the work of a group of 'economic anthropologists' who have pursued earlier theories identifying the origin of money in a 'money of account' established for administrative purposes in ancient Mesopotamia. According to David Schaps, writing on *The Invention of Coinage and the Monetization of Ancient Greece*,[3] 'the substantivist frame of reference [i.e. that deriving from Polanyi] has become a major and perhaps the dominant approach to the subject.' He refers to 'Polanyi and the economic anthropologists who have followed and deepened his work.'[4] Writers from other disciplines, including sociologists and historians, have pursued similar theory, so that the phrase 'economic anthropologists' is used here to designate a group of theorists that has drawn inspiration from Polanyi to develop the idea of the origin of money in a 'money of account.' For all such theorists, anthropological evidence is of fundamental importance. Whilst Schaps rates this group as 'perhaps dominant' amongst anthropologists, he recognises also that, 'it has not succeeded in driving other models from the field.'[5] Not all anthropologists are persuaded by Polanyi and the 'money of

DOI: 10.4324/9781003313472-1

account.' Yet the 'money of account' idea has become more significant since it forms the theoretical basis for 'Modern Monetary Theory.' The idea of a 'money of account' has a long history. John Maynard Keynes affirms such an origin in the opening of his *Treatise on Money,* published in 1930.[6]

Accepting that the origin of money lies in the social and economic behaviour of people in ancient times, the first requirement is a theory by which such behaviour can be consistently understood. It requires a socio-economic theory applicable not just to modern Western societies, but to societies of all kinds, industrialised and developing, around the world, and most importantly in the present context to societies of the ancient world. In recent decades, the idea of support-bargaining and money-bargaining has been developed to provide a broad theory of the functioning of societies. This book explains the emergence of money through the processes of support-bargaining and money-bargaining.

The idea of 'support-bargaining' was first set out in *A Theory of Support and Money Bargaining* in 1984.[7] It remains, however, little known. An 'Introduction to Support-Bargaining and Money-Bargaining' follows this Introduction, giving a basic general account of the theory. The first four chapters of the book provide further account of support-bargaining in contexts that make apparent its application across the ages and elaborate on important aspects relevant to the subsequent arguments of the book. A more extensive introduction to the theory is available in book form: *A Starter on Support-Bargaining and Money-Bargaining in Twenty-Eight Digestible Bites*.[8]

One major feature of the theory of support-bargaining and money-bargaining is that it conceives political, social, intellectual and economic affairs as all involving a similar dynamic of bargaining. 'Bargaining' is well understood in popular parlance – it is negotiated exchange. Conflicts of interest are resolved with outcomes acceptable to both parties, or they are not resolved and no exchange takes place. Either matters are let lie, or there is some form of enforcement of the interests of one against the other. Political, social and intellectual affairs are dealt with through support-bargaining. People assemble support for the interests they are promoting, and the faction with the greatest support is accorded the right to have its way. 'Support' functions as a bargaining counter. People engage in the pursuit of support, knowing that obtaining large volumes of support will ease the advance of their interests.

'Intellectual support-bargaining' involves the formation of theories or 'frames of reference,' which influence the observations people make and the interpretations they put on them. These frames of reference assemble support for the interests of their creators. The understanding of frames of reference is of particular importance when, as with the origin of money, it is necessary to deal with societies of very different types. It is also important as a means of understanding the role of theories in societies. Theories are constructed to advance interests in societies – to assemble the support necessary to advance interests. They encourage people to observe and interpret in ways conducive to the interests of the theory makers. Support assembled around theories can be readily employed in political support-bargaining. Both economists and economic anthropologists interpret observations of past societies for the advance of current interests. Economists of the neoclassical school are inclined to select and interpret with an emphasis on the advance of individual freedom, whilst economic anthropologists select and interpret more by reference to group interest.

Economic affairs are conducted through money-bargaining. Money functions as an alternative and supplementary bargaining counter to support. The similar dynamics of both support-bargaining and money-bargaining make it possible to understand the interlinking of the two bargaining processes in a way that consistently accounts for what is observed of political and economic interactions. The origin of money as bargaining counter is tied up with this interlinking. The adoption of coin-money for widespread use in the society of ancient Greece in the sixth century BCE was notably dependent on harmonious interlinking in a way that had not previously been possible.

'Money' is so naturally associated with 'economics' that it would be expected that economic theory would have a clear idea of what money is. But the basic 'neoclassical' or mainstream economic theory is concerned with 'resource allocation,' a process defined largely in mathematical terms. Products are valued in relation to other products, as in barter exchange, rather than directly in monetary terms. Money has no essential part in the neoclassical model. But it does not go unrecognised that money is prominent in economic exchange. Before the formulation of the neoclassical model in the late nineteenth century, money was identified as a medium of exchange adopted to circumvent the inconveniences of barter. With the formulation of the neoclassical model, it was explained as a 'veil' over underlying transactions that are essentially barter exchanges. Arthur Pigou ponders the issues in a book with the title *The Veil of Money*.[9] Paul Samuelson, in his highly influential textbook, describes money as an 'obscuring layer' which when peeled away reveals that trade, 'largely boils down to barter.'[10] Money emergent from barter was understood as a 'commodity' so widely acceptable as to be part of many exchanges, so that the awkwardness of 'barter' was displaced by a particular commodity as 'money.'

Nor has it escaped notice that 'money' is now put into circulation as credit provided by banks. The understanding of money as 'credit,' as opposed to 'commodity,' has been accepted with some reluctance by economists. The reluctance was partly prompted by pragmatic concerns. If money is put into circulation purely as credit, there is no natural constraint on its supply, as there is with a commodity money such as gold. The likely consequence of credit money could be a rapid expansion of supply and a rapid rise in prices. Credit money might lose its purchasing power and become inoperative as money. Examples of just such occurrences are not hard to find. A 'commodity' concept of money seemed safer than a 'credit' concept for the management of money.

The weakness of the explanations of money in neoclassical, or mainstream, economic theory gives scope for alternative theory. Economic anthropologists insist that the 'veil' theory of money is inadequate explanation of what is a central phenomenon of economic life. They contest the idea that money arose from barter on empirical grounds, arguing that there is no evidence from ancient societies for the existence of pure barter societies, let alone the emergence of 'money' from them. Societies were principally concerned with social relations; their material interests were met in the context of a process of 'reciprocity and redistribution' principally concerned with the maintenance of social relationships.

Economic anthropologists argue that money is appropriately conceived as credit, in accordance with theory first promulgated by Mitchell Innes in 1913.[11] Innes showed how credit notes could be used as money. Innes's theory was largely ignored or dismissed by economists. Economic anthropologists also refer extensively to Georg Friedrich Knapp's account of *The State Theory of Money*, published in 1905 in German but only published in English in 1924.[12] Knapp's work is cited in support of the contention that the origin of money lies not in exchange but in the decrees of states. In the economic anthropological account, the origin of money lies in the designation of a 'money of account' by state authorities, given value through acceptance by the state, principally in payment of taxes, and hence passing into use for private trade.

The mainstream economic preference for a commodity theory of money may have been influenced by the development of 'economics' as a distinct field of study. The ideal was a social science with intellectual rigour comparable to that of physics. Mathematics would describe economic exchanges, as mathematics describes the relationships of physical science to such effect. Social and political factors present particular difficulties with regard to mathematical codification, so a theory of material exchange developed as a distinct field. This makes difficult the incorporation of credit and debt, as creditors and debtors have contended since ancient times. Credit involves long-term relationships of a social as well as material nature. Being social, they inevitably become political. Interventions of the state are necessary to establish the obligations of creditors and debtors to each other and enforce their fulfilment. They drag economic theory away from the instantaneous transactions of the 'market' and make them transactions that require political engagement. They involve support-bargaining as well as money-bargaining. Hence added reason for the economic preference for a 'commodity' theory of money.

Credit and debt bridge disparities in time between expenditures and the receipt of incomes. All agents of money-bargaining systems experience these disparities. The earliest farmers had to finance sowing before they had revenues from sale of their crops. Today, people borrow to expend on houses, cars and holidays, expecting to repay their debts from future revenues. People save from current revenues to meet living expenses in later years, when they are no longer able to earn income. Companies must invest before they have products to sell. Governments also experience time disparities – revenues from taxation are seasonally irregular, whilst expenditures have to be maintained on a regular basis. Governments also need to make investments in communal facilities that will promote economic growth and generate tax revenues.

These time disparities between revenues and expenditures are universally managed through budgeting. Expenditures are made in advance of revenues by the use of credit; revenues received are saved in anticipation of future expenditures. The credit derives from the savings and the savings go to those who need credit. Credit is invariably an important part of the budgetary management of companies. For companies, being specifically concerned with the achievement of surpluses of revenues over expenditures, budgets are the essential registers of their performance. Some individuals are careful in their budgeting, assessing what they can afford to spend immediately on the basis of likely future income. Some are more casual, governing their expenditure by little more than 'money-in-the-pocket.' Budgets, more or less refined, are used by the agents of money-bargaining systems to deal with disparities between income and expenditure. Credit and savings are the means of bridging time disparities. The basic mathematical model of mainstream microeconomic theory involves immediate transactions, without mathematical or social complications of credit and debt, and consequently lacks any concept of accommodation of time disparities through budgeting. If mainstream economic theory included the idea of budgeting for the reconciliation of time disparities, economic anthropologists might have recognised in their 'money of account' nothing more than a money of budgeting.

The dissension between creditors and debtors can be attributed to the change in bargaining positions that takes place following release of funds under a credit agreement. To acquire credit, a borrower will give assurances of readiness to repay on an agreed time schedule. But once the loan is received, the borrower will not make precisely the same calculation. If the borrower neglects to repay, the options open to the creditor are unsatisfactory. Legal action is potentially costly and time-consuming. Collateral provision may not be easily realised. At best, there is delay in receiving back what has been lent. Meanwhile, the borrower has use of the money for an extended period. Creditors find themselves significantly dependent on the good faith of the borrower. Bargaining positions are changed.

Being aware of this feature of their business, lenders have been inclined to restrict their lending to people known personally to them. Within a small community, communal support-bargaining, threatening loss of social support, can be made to bear on repayment of debts. But for all the arrangements that creditors can make to protect themselves, the general provision of credit requires the establishment of laws setting out the obligations of creditors and debtors and the means of enforcing the repayment of credit. 'Debtors prisons' featured prominently in the penal systems of many nations in the nineteenth century. Politics, or a support-bargaining system, is a necessary part of credit provision.

Though it is almost universally recognised that provision of credit is essential to the growth of economies, the conflicting interests of creditors and debtors have been the source of much social and political dissension. Debtors, whether delinquent or genuinely unfortunate, are perennially at odds with their creditors. Creditors are necessarily those who have accumulated money in sufficient volume as to make it possible to lend out significant sums. Creditors are regarded as 'rich,' whilst those they lend to can often be classified as 'poor.' Debtors assemble support for their cause by identifying themselves with the struggle of the 'poor' against the 'rich,' or of 'the people' against 'the privileged.' This makes the conflict part of what is, in the understanding of support-bargaining, the fundamental social and political contention. For the 'bargaining' of support-bargaining is concerned with conflicts between the interests of individuals and the interests of the group, albeit in a context in which each needs the other.

The dispute between economists and economic anthropologists mirrors the same contention. In the neoclassical economic frame of reference, it is to the benefit of society if governments do not interfere with the free enterprise of individuals. Transactions are immediate, so credit provides no rationale for government engagement. Anthropologists and sociologists emphasise the importance of social relationships, and hence tend to see the primary interests of society as lying in the primacy of the group, or the primacy of socially determined interests. They see the pursuit of material interests outside of the social relationships as disruptive of social harmony.

The disruption arises because 'money' constitutes an alternative bargaining counter to 'support.' People will do things for money as well as for support, and sometimes will do things for money in disregard of support. Money strengthens the bargaining positions of individuals in relation to the group. The alternative undermines the bargaining positions of those who have established themselves with support – the ascendant groups, the rulers. Money-bargaining diverts from social relationships. The dissension between economists and economic anthropologists is thus a matter of political tendencies. Mainstream economists tend to the right, economic anthropologists to the left.

The central contention can be seen further in the 'anti-capitalist' sentiment prominent in economic anthropological theory. The ubiquitous incidence of time disparities between expenditures and incomes in economies has led to the development of financial services companies, many of which have grown to immense size. The essential nature of their services gives them strong bargaining positions and wide influence over the evolution of economies. Because of the 'rich versus poor' and 'people versus privilege' tenor of debates over credit and debt, they can be presented as agents of an elite oppressing ordinary people. They are the definitive institutions of 'capitalism.' Economic anthropologists, from their position on the left, naturally oppose their impositions on the rest of society. Polanyi describes capitalism as undermining people-friendly systems of 'reciprocity and redistribution.'[13] Subsequent economic anthropological and sociological writers condemn capitalism as the source of the social injustice they see as characteristic of modern society. David Graeber provides a forceful and popular anti-capitalist statement based on anthropological evidence, though so much 'over the top' as perhaps to discredit its message for all but the committed.[14]

The conflict between economists and economic anthropologists is no hand-to-hand encounter. Economic anthropologists are eloquent in their condemnation of economic theory for its lack of consistency with ancient empirical evidence regarding the origins of money. But the economic response is muted. David Schaps remarks that economists have shown little interest in the invention of coinage.[15] Money is not essential to the neoclassical model, so its importance is easily missed. The anthropological criticisms are similar to those levelled against mainstream microeconomic theory by other sources – it is inconsistent with empirical evidence from any time, not just ancient times. The lack of response can be attributed to the lack of capacity of the neoclassical frame of reference to deal with such alien material as that brought to light by economic anthropologists. It is unfortunate that economists have not been able to provide a clear, consistent and convincing theory of the material side of human conduct for use in association with other social research. Neoclassical economists have preferred to cultivate their own impeccable formal garden in a corner well removed from the jungle of human affairs.

The importance of budgets has further bearing on the origins of money. Following Adam Smith, money has been understood as a common 'commodity' offsetting the difficulties of barter. Transactions remain, as in barter, immediately complete, without further necessary association of buyer and seller. There is apparently no need for credit. The 'commodity' used as money is used in further exchange transactions. But if the agents involved are conceived as managing budgets, the receipt of a 'commodity money' can be understood as receipt of a credit. A credit is received whose value can be realised at some future date with the acquisition of commodities of a desired kind from others in the community who accept the commodity money. It resolves a time disparity between sale of one commodity and later purchase of another. 'Commodity money,' understood in the budgetary context of money-bargaining, is credit money. It is like a credit note issued and accepted by members of the society who support the money as their bargaining counter. Acceptance of the commodity money ensures its purchasing power. It involves a continued relationship between buyers and sellers in their common membership of the group that supports the bargaining counter they use.

Notes

1 Smith, Adam, 1986/1776, *The Wealth of Nations, Books I–III*, London: Penguin Books, pp. 126–32.
2 Polanyi, Karl, 2001/1944, *The Great Transformation: The Political and Economic Origins of Our Time*, Boston: Beacon Press. First published 1944.
3 Schaps, David, 2004, *The Invention of Coinage and the Monetization of Ancient Greece*, Ann Arbor: University of Michigan Press, Kindle Edition, L726.
4 Schaps, 2004, L5590.
5 Schaps, 2004, L733.
6 Keynes, John Maynard, 1930, *A Treatise on Money*, London: Macmillan, p. 3.

7 Spread, Patrick, 1984, *A Theory of Support and Money Bargaining*, London: Macmillan.
8 Spread, Patrick, 2019b, *A Starter on Support-Bargaining and Money-Bargaining in Twenty-Eight Digestible Bites*, London: Palgrave Macmillan.
9 Pigou, A. C., 1949, *The Veil of Money*, London: Macmillan, p. 14. Quoted by Ingham, Geoffrey, 2004, *The Nature of Money*, Cambridge: Polity Press, p. 15.
10 Samuelson, Paul, 1973, *Economics*, 9th Edition, New York: McGraw-Hill, p. 55. Quoted by Ingham, 2004, p. 15.
11 Innes, Alfred Mitchell, 1913, 'What Is Money?' *Banking Law Journal*, May, pp. 377–408. Reprinted in Wray, R. (Ed.), 2004, *Credit and State Theories of Money, The Contributions of A. Mitchell Innes*, Cheltenham: Edward Elgar.
12 Knapp, Georg Friedrich, 1924, *The State Theory of Money*, Abridged edition, Trans. H.M. Lucas and J. Bonar, London: Macmillan for the Royal Economic Society. First published in German, 1905.
13 Polanyi, 2001/1944.
14 Graeber, David, 2010, *Debt: The First Five Thousand Years*, Brooklyn: Melville House.
15 Schaps, David, 2004, *The Invention of Coinage and the Monetization of Ancient Greece*, Ann Arbor: University of Michigan Press, Kindle Edition, L726.

References

Graeber, David, 2010, *Debt: The First Five Thousand Years*, Brooklyn: Melville House.
Ingham, Geoffrey, 2004, *The Nature of Money*, Cambridge: Polity Press.
Innes, Alfred Mitchell, 1913, 'What Is Money?' *Banking Law Journal*, May, pp. 377–408. Reprinted in Wray, R. (Ed.), 2004, *Credit and State Theories of Money, The Contributions of A. Mitchell Innes*, Cheltenham: Edward Elgar.
Keynes, John Maynard, 1930, *A Treatise on Money*, London: Macmillan.
Knapp, Georg Friedrich, 1924, *The State Theory of Money*, Abridged edition, Trans. H.M. Lucas and J. Bonar, London: Macmillan for the Royal Economic Society. First published in German, 1905.
Pigou, A. C., 1949, *The Veil of Money*, London: Macmillan.
Polanyi, Karl, 2001/1944, *The Great Transformation: The Political and Economic Origins of Our Time*, Boston: Beacon Press. First published 1944.
Samuelson, Paul, 1973, *Economics*, 9th Edition, New York: McGraw-Hill.
Schaps, David, 2004, *The Invention of Coinage and the Monetization of Ancient Greece*, Ann Arbor: University of Michigan Press.
Smith, Adam, 1986/1776, *The Wealth of Nations, Books I–III*, London: Penguin Books.
Spread, Patrick, 1984, *A Theory of Support and Money Bargaining*, London: Macmillan.
Spread, Patrick, 2019b, *A Starter on Support-Bargaining and Money-Bargaining in Twenty-Eight Digestible Bites*, London: Palgrave Macmillan.
Wray, R. (Ed.), 2004, *Credit and State Theories of Money, The Contributions of A. Mitchell Innes*, Cheltenham: Edward Elgar.

Introduction to Support-Bargaining and Money-Bargaining

Support-Bargaining...

Support-bargaining offers a theory of the way humans relate to each other in social, political and intellectual affairs. It is universally accepted that we influence each other. Support-bargaining explains the motivations and mechanism behind this 'influencing.'

It is suggested that all humans have a fundamental sense of insecurity which inclines them to seek the support of others. To get the support they need, individuals behave in a manner that they anticipate will be pleasing. They speak courteously and sympathetically. They offer opinions that they anticipate will be acceptable. They act in ways that are likely to elicit approval. Their prime interest lies in the assembly of the support that will dissipate their sense of insecurity and give them confidence.

But individuals also have interests that are not the same as the interests of those around them. In some cases interests conflict. If an individual wants to go to a Chinese restaurant, whilst his or her associates want to go to a pub, there is conflict. Discussion, even argument, may result in agreement that they will go to the pub immediately and go to a Chinese restaurant next week. The group stays together. Or no resolution may be found. The individual and the associates go their separate ways. The rejected individual has to seek support from a different group that is more inclined to Chinese food. Support-bargaining involves cooperation and conflict between groups and individuals, each assembling support. It involves the formation and breakup of groups.

Support and security are connected through the necessity of support for effective violence. A single individual is likely to be ineffective in the exercise of violence on anything but the smallest scale. Groups are necessary to the delivery of socially significant violence. Hence the formation and breakup of groups is significant with regard to potential for effective violence. In normal social life, support-bargaining is carried on harmoniously, or with minor verbal argument, but it can degenerate into violence. Gang violence is an indication of the failure of support-bargaining in a community. Effective violence is characteristic not just of groups, but of organised groups. Organisation gives a group leadership,

DOI: 10.4324/9781003313472-2

focal purpose and a hierarchy of command by which action can be coordinated in pursuit of the focal purpose.

The importance of support-bargaining to the formation of social groups, and the need for group formation for the conduct of effective violence, means that support-bargaining must have had a central role in the process of natural selection that made possible the survival of the human species. Charles Darwin recognised the importance of group formation, but was unable to explain how it came about, himself expressing dissatisfaction with the explanations he could offer.[1]

The strength of support is such that violence can be largely excluded from human societies through the establishment of formal support-bargaining systems. 'Democratic' political systems can be seen as artificial or formalised structures for support-bargaining. In these structures all the adults of a society can be involved in defined support-bargaining sets, or constituencies, in which candidates from different groups, normally constituted as political parties, are selected as members of a secondary group authorised by their election to formulate and establish rules for the benefit of the society. The political parties avail themselves of the advantages of organisation to advance their focal policies. Members of the secondary groups, or legislatures, engage in further support-bargaining amongst themselves to determine communal interest and legislate for its advance. In formal support-bargaining structures 'support' has to be countable, so it is common to assign a single 'vote' to each participating individual. The psychology of support – the fervour of support, or the fervour of opposition – is discounted to facilitate the functioning of a formal support-bargaining system by reference to countable support. Such systems are liable to break down when vital interests of particular sections of a community determine that their support is undervalued.

Support-bargaining thus offers an explanation of the mechanics of democracy.[2] Early acceptance of 'democratic' constitutions invariably involved restriction of the franchise to property owners. It was tacitly recognised that landowners and owners of substantial property would not accept arrangements whereby they could be dispossessed simply by votes of the very clear majority that did not own land or substantial property. Such ownership constituted the vital interests of a section of society which could not be governed by support-bargaining. People would fight for their land and property. 'Democracy' was thus introduced initially by confining the right to participate to those who had land and property. In Britain, it was only after the First World War, in which the adult population demonstrated its violent capacity in defence of the nation, that the significance of the support of every adult individual was recognised.

Formal support-bargaining systems can only operate when the great majority of the people are tolerant of the aspirations and interests of others, and where those aspirations and interests are not of a kind that have to be regarded as vital interests – the sort of interests that people will fight to defend, rather than relinquish in a support-bargaining process. Such vital interests are often the basis of groups so tightly cohesive in defence of their interests that they constitute rigid groups. High cohesion, to the point of rigidity, is necessary to effective violence but incompatible with support-bargaining systems, which require flexibility, so that support can move between groups in response to changing situations. Faith groups are often established as rigid groups. Rigid groups can form on the basis of ethnicity.

Formal support-bargaining systems depend on assembly of support on the basis of ideas about how a society should be advanced; ideas about what constitutes a communal interest. Ideas, as opposed to violent capacities, become the focus of attention. Communal interest, like individual interest, depends on situation. So much of the support-bargaining over ideas is concerned with establishing 'the situation,' so that interests can be properly discerned. The process requires that pertinent information is readily available. The media, those organisations providing a constant flow of information about current affairs, far from being appendages to democracy, as mere reporters of what is going on, are integral to the assembly of support for different interests and essential to the functioning of support-bargaining systems.

Support-bargaining over ideas permeates support-bargaining across societies that have made themselves support-bargaining societies. Politicians debate, ordinary people debate, organised media shape and debate ideas. This 'intellectual support-bargaining' is also formalised in specialist institutions specifically charged with the formulation of ideas conducive to the well-being of their societies. Academic study of social issues of all kinds has risen in tandem with the rise of support-bargaining societies.

The assembly of support on the basis of ideas, debate and intellectual support-bargaining makes information a vital part of support-bargaining. Information is of yet deeper significance, since human minds deal only with information. Whatever the subject, it must come to human attention as information, whether perceptual information or testimonial information. An information interface constitutes the immediate matter with which support-bargaining and money-bargaining are conducted. The idea of an information interface is less instinctively true in the more material context of money-bargaining, since we know things or objects from perceptual information and are inclined, such is the nature of perceptual information, to assume we know the reality behind our perception. But our minds can only process information. The information interface is built through dissemination of information by many agents seeking to advance their interests. Hence much of it is misinformation.[3] Information is codified for purposes of communication in language and mathematics, both of which offer opportunities for the manipulation of information. Film communicates with particular emotional force.

To describe the formulation of theory as a matter of pursuing interests through intellectual support-bargaining is contrary to the principles by which theory-makers understand their function. Theories are not conceived as dependent on support. Academic institutions are set up with the conscious intention of divorcing those engaged in theory-making from the interests that plainly bias the opinions of those engaged in the ordinary practices of a society. Those in academia are expected to provide disinterested accounts of the functioning of society and the natural world. They are conceived as establishing solid connections of cause and effect, as identifying what is true and not true, even identifying what is right and wrong. They are concerned with the establishment of evidence that must self-evidently be acknowledged by all as proving a point at issue.

Evidence itself, however, is selected and interpreted for the assembly of support and the advance of interests. Law courts provide everyday illustrations of the assembly and use of evidence in this way. Even in the natural sciences, where the nature of the matters at issue best lends itself to the replication of the phenomena from which evidence is derived, and hence to the establishment of disinterested evidence, group support remains the final arbiter of what is accepted as 'true.' In the social sciences the theorist is dealing with the diverse motivations and behaviour of humanity, so that selection and interpretation of evidence is easily subordinated, instinctively and unconsciously, to the assembly of support for the advancement of interest.

Group support as final arbiter is an essential of human understanding. Theories are part of the process of intellectual support-bargaining. They constitute frames of reference by which people are induced to focus on phenomena identified as relevant in the theory, and interpret the phenomena in accordance with the interests of the theory-makers. Every frame of reference identifies its own relevant evidence, or identifies what it will accept as evidence, and provides the interpretation for such evidence. Theories are formulated by support-bargaining and the formation of 'theory groups.' These groups maintain support for the theory through circularity within the group. The members 'see' what the theory, or frame of reference, disposes them to see, and what they see is interpreted as confirming the validity of the frame of reference. Theory and 'evidence' fit together to give a sense of understanding. These propensities are reflected in the formation of distinct 'schools' of academic theory. Faith groups similarly develop frames of reference which determine what they will regard as evidence and how it is to be interpreted. Faith groups have provided basic psychological security and a sense of understanding for virtually all members of the human race, at least until recently.

Natural scientists establish paradigms by which they observe and interpret relationships of the natural world. The ideal of 'objective' evidence is most closely approximated in the natural sciences, due to the potential for replication mentioned earlier. Natural scientists are more inclined than most makers of theory to revise their paradigms and reassemble theory groups when they encounter anomalies, but the shifts in theory, which involve reconstitution of theory groups, do not occur without the friction that is part of intellectual support-bargaining as much as it is part of social and political support-bargaining.[4] The final arbitration of the group does not, of course, reveal any absolute information regarding the nature of the universe or the state of human society; it acknowledges the limitations of what humans can know.

...and Money-Bargaining...

The use of money can be related to the deficiencies of 'support' as a bargaining counter. 'Support' is a psychological benefit. It is to a degree ephemeral. It cannot be seen, touched or held. It has overtones of violence. For all its psychological importance, it is easily withdrawn, denied or forgotten. People are not unfailingly loyal in their support. A bargaining counter that is durable, divisible, visible and countable, and has no implications of violence, has advantages, particularly when it will function in a bargaining system that shares characteristics with the familiar support-bargaining. We can bargain with money because we learn from an early age how to engage in social support-bargaining. The characteristics of money make it particularly convenient and effective in bargaining over material goods, which can also be seen, touched and counted. There can be less argument over transactions when both sides have a durable record of what they have exchanged.

Nevertheless, the sterility of money, its lack of the kind of emotional assertion that is present with support, means that money-bargaining is generally subordinate to support-bargaining. Support-bargaining determines human behaviour, moulding it in accordance with what the members of a community find desirable and acceptable. Money and money-bargaining are sustained by support-bargaining. Money functions as an alternative and supplementary bargaining counter. Money maintains its function as a bargaining counter because the people in the community, using whatever has come into use as money, all support its use, as a matter of practical convenience. The disadvantages of barter are readily overcome with the identification of some common counter that can be used again and again in multiple transactions. Communities can fix on a particular item, whether commodity or token, that can be used in this way.

Sustained communal support depends, however, on the adopted money maintaining a steady value, or stable purchasing power. This condition requires that the supply of money is maintained at a level commensurate with the volume of trade in which it is used. So communities require that their governments manage the supply of the communal money so that it remains compatible with the volume of exchange taking place. If a current communal money loses its purchasing power to any significant degree, then people will look for a better alternative, and if it can be found, the community will relinquish its support for the current communal money.

Money is sustained by common support, and is a matter of common and familiar usage. The theory of money-bargaining is an explanation of the dynamics of this common usage. It will be apparent that, although it is a medium of exchange, it has little to do with the 'resource allocation' dynamic of neoclassical economic theory. The neoclassical model of economic exchange provides only a stylised mathematical account, acutely limited by unrealistic assumptions necessary to the use of mathematics. Its longevity relates to its success in protecting the 'individual' interest, and its adoption as the approved frame of reference for teaching of economics in institutions of higher education. It is scarcely an exaggeration to say that, whilst the neoclassical model is the rallying point for mainstream economists, the main point is the rally. The neoclassical frame of reference is sustained by the support of its theory group. Money-bargaining has a quite different dynamic to that of mainstream economic theory – a dynamic consistent with empirical observation. Whilst mainstream economic theory and money-bargaining share the general concept of money as a medium of exchange, 'exchange' means something different in money-bargaining from the exchange portrayed in mainstream economic theory.

In the first place, the dynamic of money-bargaining sees people as pursuing interests that are determined by their situations. They buy what fits with their situations. They buy houses that are convenient to their work, and of a size that fits their families, subject, of course, to a budget situation that permits the accommodation of such characteristics. They may fancy a Scottish castle or a French chateau, but very few find such acquisitions will fit well with their established situations. As regards minor purchases, people buy clothes that fit their bodies, and tools suited to the tasks they wish to perform. They will not buy a wheel that does not fit their car. That is to say, people judge their 'utility' or 'preferences' by reference to their situations.[5] People in different situations will have different utilities and preferences.

In recognition of this, companies design products that will fit the situations of buyers, both large groups of buyers, in similar situations, with limited budgets, and smaller groups, with larger budgets. Products are endowed with features that fit the situations of potential buyers. They are moreover offered for sale at locations and at times that correspond to the spatial and temporal situations of potential buyers. They are not the homogeneous supply, universally present in both space and time, that can interact with demand from buyers and permit the construction of the diagrams of supply and demand that are the basis of price formation in neoclassical economic theory.

Companies design and market their products in this way in order to ensure that their revenues cover their costs. As a basic essential of their continued existence, they seek to meet a viability criterion that 'Revenue > Costs.' Companies select locations that are most likely to enable them to fulfil this condition. The viability condition can be written as 'Sales × Price > Unit Cost of Provision × Volume of Provision.' Companies will normally locate in places where they can sell a large enough volume at a price exceeding the unit cost of provision, so that they meet or exceed the viability condition. Much effort is expended in reducing unit costs, as a means not only of meeting the viability condition, but providing a good surplus of revenues over costs. Productivity improvements are a means of reducing unit costs. The neoclassical representation of the 'firm' as a diagram of cost curves with the greatest surplus of revenues over costs arising where the marginal cost of production is equal to the market price determined by those aggregate supply and demand curves gives way to companies as the specialist money-bargaining agencies of money-bargaining systems formatting to ensure that their revenues are greater than their costs.[6]

Companies are specialists in money-bargaining, but all organisations require money for their effectiveness as bargaining agencies. Organisations run money budgets that enable them to take advantage of the motivations of money-bargaining in their operations. Staff must be paid with money to enable them to acquire the necessities of life. The payments also compensate for acceptance of hierarchical bargaining positions.

Prices in a money-bargaining system are set principally by reference to the unit cost of provision. They are, however, adjusted by reference to the availability of similar products in relation to the demand for them. 'Supply and demand' is thus not irrelevant, but it has none of the universality of the neoclassical concept. It is supply of products differentiated by features designed to fit the products to different situations of buyers, and provided so as to fit in with spatial and temporal situations of buyers. Bargaining position depends on the 'fit' of products to the situations of potential buyers. A tight fit enhances the value of a product over rivals with less appropriate products. A good fit is likely to be reflected in a good price. But bargaining position depends perhaps most importantly on the availability of alternatives for both provider and buyer. Besides the differentiation of product features and location, providers may eliminate an alternative source of what they provide by taking over a rival company.

For all engaged in money-bargaining there are time disparities between outlay of expenditures and receipt of revenues. These are dealt with through budgeting. Budgets retain money receipts until needed for expenditure. The money functions as a credit, redeemed at the time of its expenditure by the provider of whatever is acquired. The money-bargaining system involves a network of budgets, each budget controlled by an agent of the system. This includes the budgets of governments, making governments an integral part of a money-bargaining system. To be effective as a budgetary money-of-account, the money used must be the money used for money-bargaining in the community.

Whilst money itself functions as credit, a kind of 'social credit' arranged by societies to cover the time disparities of ordinary buying and selling, there is also a requirement for more specific credits deriving from specific lenders to specific borrowers. If 'money' is 'social credit,' the specific credits are like 'bespoke credits.' They are usually provided for purposes agreed between lender and borrower, for specific periods. They involve, moreover, the charging of interest. Time disparities are an integral part of money-bargaining. Consequently, credit is an integral part of money-bargaining – the system will not work without it. Farmers must acquire seed before they can raise crops for sale. Businesses must invest before they can produce. The provision of credit involves extended relationships between agents of money-bargaining systems. The relationships involve conflicts of interest, which can lead to damaging confrontations if not conducted in accordance with rules established through support-bargaining. Credit requires the regulatory intervention of states. The neoclassical economic model was formulated with an underlying intent to demonstrate the advantages of a purely private system of transactions, with no state involvement, for the allocation of resources. Accommodating credit means losing private autonomy. The neoclassical model does not take account of time disparities.

State budgets are used for the accommodation of communal interests, including matters of defence, climate change and pandemics. What constitutes a communal interest is determined by support-bargaining within the community and through the formal support-bargaining system described earlier. Support-bargaining and money-bargaining interlink most conspicuously in the accommodation of communal interests.

...their Interlinking...

The interlinks of politics and business are more comprehensible when each is conceived as operating under a similar dynamic, albeit with different bargaining counters. People will act to acquire support; they will also act to acquire money. Interlink is apparent in the ordinary course of life, in that people seek support in expectation that it may later open opportunities for employment and money revenues, and everyone expends money to enhance their popularity. We function both socially and financially.

Interlinking of a more formal kind is necessary to the provision of credit. Credit transactions are normally conceived in monetary terms. A sum of money is lent, to be repaid at a later time with interest. But, as noted earlier, such transactions involve longer-term relationships between debtor and creditor. The management of this relationship requires communal engagement to ensure that commitments on both sides are fulfilled. The conflict between lenders and borrowers, brought to high intensity today in the antagonism between 'capitalists' and 'anti-capitalists,' reflects the importance of credit in resolving time disparities in money-bargaining.

Interlink of a less visible kind is apparent also in the conduct of companies. They are the specialist money-bargaining organisations of money-bargaining systems, but their management and control, at least in larger companies, involves support-bargaining to establish the organisational focus that will be pursed through a company hierarchy.

Of more pervasive importance is the interlinking of support-bargaining and money-bargaining that arises with the provision of information. Numerous sources of information are required if people are to receive the necessary range of information. The sources must be independent of governments, since governments will inevitably provide information conducive to their own interests. News media have to operate as companies, pursuing as a priority the viability condition described earlier. Information, the life-blood of support-bargaining systems, has to be provided by agencies operating primarily as money-bargaining agencies. News media provide much of the information interface accessible to participants in the political life of a nation. By virtue of that provision, and the opportunities for manipulation of information for the advance of interests, media organisations move support. Without diverse news media, support-bargaining societies cannot function.

Money can also be used directly to thwart outcomes set up through support-bargaining. At its simplest, this is straightforward person-to-person bribery, but more systematic payments may be set up that divert the course of support-bargaining. Donors, for example, influence the policies of political parties. In Britain, trade unions created and finance the Labour Party.

...and their Evolution

It is characteristic of support-bargaining and money-bargaining systems that they evolve over time. A situation-based bargaining process provides a natural evolutionary dynamic. People pursue their interests by reference to their situations, and in doing so they change their situations, which in turn give rise to new interests, and so on. The standard historical pattern of economic evolution is of initial predominance of agrarian activities, then growth of manufacturing, then the emergence of service industries. In the present era, technological innovation, especially in information technology, plays a prominent role. Technology has played a major part in the overall evolution of money-bargaining systems. The introduction of railways in the nineteenth century and the internet in the present age have both had major impacts on the evolution of money-bargaining. Many companies are formatted on the basis of characteristics of technology. This involves not just new products and services, but reductions in unit costs of provision of already familiar products and services.[7]

This evolutionary dynamic gives money-bargaining a sense of history that is lacking in neoclassical economic theory, which anticipates only 'equilibrium.' Societies, including their money-bargaining systems, have evolved from the earliest times. The idea of money-bargaining thus facilitates an approach to earlier times, and in particular the ancient times in which money first made its appearance.

Back in that ancient time, it is argued, the conditions for determination of market prices through interaction of 'supply and demand' as understood in neoclassical economic theory did not exist, and hence 'money' could not have emerged from such 'markets.' But money-bargaining could and did take place in ancient times. People have met to exchange goods from the earliest times. That is all that is needed for the emergence of a bargaining counter. The money-bargaining of today can be seen as evolved from the exchanges of the ancient world.

The idea of support-bargaining and money-bargaining underpins the arguments of this book, with further elaboration of its dynamic where relevant to the matter under discussion. Previous books and articles on the subject are listed in the References.

Notes

1 Spread, Patrick, 2013, *Support-Bargaining, Economics and Society: A Social Species*, London and New York: Routledge, Chapter 2: 'Natural Selection and Support-Bargaining.' See also Spread, Patrick, 2019b, *A Starter on Support-Bargaining and Money-Bargaining in Twenty-Eight Digestible Bites*, London: Palgrave Macmillan, pp. 7–8, 34–9.

2 Spread, Patrick, 2008, *Support-Bargaining: The Mechanics of Democracy Revealed*, Sussex: Book Guild.
3 Spread, Patrick, 2019a, *Economics for an Information Age: Money-Bargaining, Support-Bargaining and the Information Interface*, London and New York: Routledge.
4 Spread, 2013, Chapter 6: 'The Evidence for Support-Bargaining.' See also Spread, 2019a, pp. 57–63.
5 Spread, Patrick, 2011, 'Situation as Determinant of Selection and Valuation', *Cambridge Journal of Economics*, Vol. 35, No. 2. Reprinted in Spread, Patrick, 2015b, *Aspects of Support-Bargaining and Money-Bargaining*, E-Book, World Economics Association.
6 Spread, Patrick, 2016b, 'Companies and Markets: Economic Theories of the Firm and a Concept of Companies as Bargaining Agencies', *Cambridge Journal of Economics*, Vol. 40, No. 3, pp. 727–53. Reprinted in Spread, 2015b.
7 Spread, Patrick, 2016a, *The Evolution of Economies: Money-Bargaining, Economic Change and Industrial Revolution*, London and New York: Routledge.

References

Spread, Patrick, 1984a, *A Theory of Support and Money-Bargaining*, London: Macmillan.

Spread, Patrick, 1984b, 'Blau's Exchange Theory, Support and the Macrostructure', *The British Journal of Sociology*, Vol. 35, No. 2. Reprinted in Spread, 2015b.

Spread, Patrick, 2004, *Getting It Right: Economics and the Security of Support*, Sussex: Book Guild.

Spread, Patrick, 2008, *Support-Bargaining: The Mechanics of Democracy Revealed*, Sussex: Book Guild.

Spread, Patrick, 2011, 'Situation as Determinant of Selection and Valuation', *Cambridge Journal of Economics*, Vol. 35, No. 2. Reprinted in Spread, 2015b.

Spread, Patrick, 2013, *Support-Bargaining, Economics and Society: A Social Species*, London and New York: Routledge.

Spread, Patrick, 2015a, 'Asymmetric Information, Critical Information and the Information Interface', *Real-World Economics Review*, Issue 70, pp. 121–40. Reprinted in Spread, 2015b.

Spread, Patrick, 2015b, *Aspects of Support-Bargaining and Money-Bargaining*, E-Book, World Economics Association.

Spread, Patrick, 2016a, *The Evolution of Economies: Money-Bargaining, Economic Change and Industrial Revolution*, London and New York: Routledge.

Spread, Patrick, 2016b, 'Companies and Markets: Economic Theories of the Firm and a Concept of Companies as Bargaining Agencies', *Cambridge Journal of Economics*, Vol. 40, No. 3, pp. 727–53. Reprinted in Spread, 2015b.

Spread, Patrick, 2019a, *Economics for an Information Age: Money-Bargaining, Support-Bargaining and the Information Interface*, London and New York: Routledge.

Spread, Patrick, 2019b, *A Starter on Support-Bargaining and Money-Bargaining in Twenty-Eight Digestible Bites*, London: Palgrave Macmillan.

1 Support, Support-Bargaining and Social Debt

The idea of support-bargaining rests on recognition that individuals are dependent for their psychological well-being on the support of those around them. A fundamental sense of insecurity inclines all individuals to seek support. People modify their behaviour and opinions to gain or retain the support of their associates. People may adopt opinions that seem absurd to those not involved in order to gain acceptance in a community. Individuals fearing loss of support from those they depend on are likely to redress rapidly the behaviour that is giving offence. If that is not possible, they will seek friends elsewhere. In ordinary social life, people tend to have circles of friends – neighbours, other parents taking children to the same school, customers at the same pub – but will change their social circles as circumstances change. There may be a 'falling out' that causes someone to drop one set of friends and find another.

The protagonists in support-bargaining are individuals, who need support, and their associates, or those with whom they might become associated. Individuals have their own inclinations and interests, and will pursue them as far as they can. But their paramount psychological interest lies in the continued assembly of support from those around them. To get that support they will compromise their own interests. Their associates shape a group interest through the support-bargaining that incorporates individuals into association. A group wishing to expand its membership will adapt its group interest so as to be acceptable to new members. There is continuous 'bargaining' over how far individuals can follow their own inclinations and how far they must modify those inclinations to accord with the requirements of those with whom they wish to associate. Individuals highly valued by their associates, because of the qualities they offer the group for advance of its interests, will find themselves obliged to make fewer and lesser modifications to their opinions and behaviour than those who are reckoned to have little to offer the group. As a condition of group membership, the latter will be obliged to conform more or less closely to the settled requirements of the group. They will 'tag along' as the group pursues its interests, whether it be a matter of which café they go to, or which mountain they climb. If the terms are unacceptable, their option is to seek an alternative group that finds their opinions and behaviour more consistent with its established interests.

DOI: 10.4324/9781003313472-3

People need constant reassurance of support, so they strive to build durable relationships of support with those around them. Long-standing membership of an established group confers a sense of confidence, a sense of harmony, above all a sense of security, in that if difficulties arise, there will be people around to help. The group forms a 'store' of support that can potentially be drawn on in times of stress. Families, neighbours, informal friendships, sports clubs, work places, charitable organisations, faith groups and nation states all provide reassurance to their members of protection in times when it is required. People support their group and are supported by it. Through membership of such groups individuals build what can be seen as social 'credit.' Their associates have commitments to them that involve ongoing support. In times of special need the group can be expected to provide any necessary support. They acknowledge at the same time obligations to support others in the groups with which they are associated.

Transgression against the requirements of a group can be harshly punished. In the informal context of social support-bargaining, a person who slights the interest of the group may be 'expelled' from the group, 'boycotted' or 'ostracised' by group members. In British middle-class society in the nineteenth century, strict moral observance was required, and women in particular who breached the code of sexual morality could be expelled from 'society.' In some circumstances people may be physically assaulted for contravening social conventions. Expressions of communal disapproval can be brutal. Ducking stools and stocks were used in the Middle Ages in Britain to express communal disapproval. Imprisonment can be seen as the formalised expression of communal rejection of behaviour, imposed in accordance with formal support-bargaining procedures for the governance of communal affairs. People are made to 'pay their debt to society' by serving time in prison.

Support-bargaining is, as the name suggests, competitive. Individuals compete for maximum incorporation of their own interests in the formulation of group interests, for maximum influence on the determination of group interests. It is a competition for social ascendancy. Individuals seek to concede as little as possible of their own interest in acquiring the support of their associates. One individual may make demands on a group which are incompatible with those of another. 'Negotiations' may be broken off with acrimony. One of the individuals concerned may accept erosion of his or her interests, whilst the other advances in influence over the group. The individual with lesser support may seek accommodation elsewhere. The departing individual may take with him or her some members of the group that see their interests as more akin to those of the departing individual than to the individual that retains the greatest support in the initial group. A rival group is established.

An individual emerging as ascendant in a group will require that group members fulfil the commitments to action made in the support-bargaining process that formed the group and gave the individual ascendancy. Members are expected to be loyal and responsive to the directions of their leader, or move out of the group.

While support-bargaining can be amiable and instinctive at the personal level, it becomes fractious, calculating and intemperate, a matter of 'hard bargaining,' when overall social ascendancy and government are contested. Leaders will demand the loyalty of their followers and denigrate in forceful terms whatever propositions are put up by their opponents for the assembly of support against them. At the national level, large groups command the majorities that entitle them to advance their interests in formal support-bargaining systems, so that the leader of such a group can accommodate the interests of loyal followers. Power lies in the leadership of a large and organised supportive group. Leaders call in the credits they have earned in service to their parties. Party members 'owe them support.'

Childhood and the Assumption of Social Debt

Groups are formed through support-bargaining for the advance of interests, social or political, in the normal course of adult life. But the strongest group bonds are those formed in childhood. Children assimilate the ideas, beliefs, behaviour and attitudes that are regarded as appropriate by their parents and others close to them. Through familial relationships children assimilate the 'culture' of their society. Their own dependence causes them to accept instruction and respond positively to affirmations of parents and others. Children plainly seek support and are loath to lose the support of those around them. Yet at the same time their capacity for 'bargaining' is limited, to the extent that 'bargaining' seems not such a good term for the processes of childhood assimilation of appropriate behaviour as it is for the engagement of adults in the formation of groups. Nevertheless, a 'bargaining' element is sometimes explicit – an ice cream for good behaviour. The ice cream is the tangible expression of support for the child, the counterpart to good behaviour. It can be seen as a bargaining process in which the options of children are so limited that they have very weak bargaining positions. As children get older, they take stock of their position, recognise that they have something to offer and begin to assert their interests. Teenagers are notoriously rebellious. They become aware of their own interests and the dependence of others on their goodwill.

Instruction received in childhood imprints ideas in minds that endure into adulthood. Such ideas invariably include a sense of indebtedness to parents, teachers and the society in which a child is raised. Religious and philosophical beliefs form a prominent part of the ideas that are assimilated in childhood, and these commonly form the basis for an acceptance of social debt. Christian faith commands, 'honour thy father and mother.' Confucian teaching sets out obligations to family and rulers. Secular patriotism cultivates the idea of debt to a fatherland that nurtures each individual. Self-sacrifice will potentially be expected in settlement of the debt.

David Graeber identifies the philosophical and sociological origins of the idea of individual obligation in the work of the early-nineteenth-century French philosopher and political pamphleteer Auguste Comte.[1] He quotes Comte:

> We are born under a load of obligations of every kind, to our predecessors, to our successors, to our contemporaries. After our birth these obligations increase or accumulate before the point where we are capable of rendering anyone any service.[2]

Graeber notes that the idea of such obligations was developed in France as an idea of 'social debt,' becoming a common slogan for some political movements. He notes also that it was used by the Soviet Union to justify the interdiction on Soviet citizens from emigration to other countries. The Soviet Union had nurtured, educated and trained its people; they could not renege on such debts by migration.[3]

The idea of all individuals having social obligations has been particularly cultivated in Japan. Ruth Benedict describes the subtleties of *on*, the obligations that every Japanese owes to emperor, parents, teachers and others.[4] *On* has to be repaid either in the form of *gimu*, with a concept of repayments that are eternal and can never be fully repaid, or through *giri*, which are repayments precise in both form and time. *Giri* repayments may be made to others in the context of obligations arising from *on*. But *Giri* is also required, 'outside the circle of *on*,' in the protection of one's own reputation.[5] *Giri* in this sense is associated with the Western notion of 'honour,' including a sense of necessary vengeance and vendetta. It is not a matter of social debt incurred by virtue of social inclusion, but more a sense of maintaining parity with regard to offences against oneself and kindnesses received. Benedict presents the sense of obligation and the ongoing need for repayment as fundamental to Japanese behaviour, pervasive in all aspects of Japanese life, including military affairs and corporate employment. Such obligations take precedence over any inclinations arising from individual human sentiment. The individual is subject to communal obligations imposed by the group. 'To the Japanese it is sufficient reward to be respected in his world and "a man who does not know *giri*" is still a "miserable wretch." He is scorned and ostracized by his fellows.'[6]

Before we are useful we need nurture, care, teaching and training. We need the support of the community before our own support becomes of value to others. The only way we can get this is by 'borrowing' from those who provide such services, with an implicit undertaking to repay in the course of time. Thus, we acquire early on an obligation to support the society that has raised us to a condition in which we can provide useful support. In social support-bargaining, we run up a deficit early on. The idea of 'credit,' 'obligation' and 'debt' in support-bargaining involves distinct considerations of time disparities between benefits received and repayments at a later date.

This understanding of social debt in support-bargaining is easily recognised as duplicated in our understanding of debt in the monetary context. Time disparities of monetary expenditures and revenues, analogous to the dependent intake of children and the later contributions of adults to their societies, are apparent in money-bargaining. Benedict relates *giri* in the form of repayments relating to *on* specifically to the recognition in America of obligations to repay monetary credit.[7] Support is extended in credit and repaid, as money also is extended and repaid. Credit and debt are part of the shared dynamic of bargaining in both support-bargaining and money-bargaining.

Situation and Interests

Group membership acquired involuntarily through childhood experience involves support-bargaining of a particular kind, in which the child is scarcely in a position to engage in any serious bargaining with parents and other adults. Support-bargaining amongst adults has rather different qualities. Groups form spontaneously amongst people who share interests, and shared interests arise from shared situations. The shared situation of having children of school age creates shared interests in the safety of journeys to school and the quality of the school. Village people share the situation of residence in their village and will have interests connected with the amenities of the village. Employees of a business share a situation and will have shared interests associated with their conditions of work. Such shared interests in a factory setting were the basis for the formation of trade unions, leading in Britain to the establishment of one of the major political organisations, the Labour Party, contesting the governance of the country through formal support-bargaining systems.

Some interests relating to situation are advanced through the assembly of support and through support-bargaining. Other interests are pursued through money-bargaining. People buy houses that fit in with their situation. They must have access to their place of work. The house must be of a size to accommodate their family. Clothing and shoes must fit the person for whom they are acquired. What people buy at a supermarket is determined in part by the stocks they hold at home.[8] The requirement that acquisitions should fit to a situation makes all transactions distinct, since although agents may have certain aspects of situation in common, their situations are also in important respects unique. It also means that bargaining positions are different, since situation determines when, where, with what degree of urgency, with what degree of precision and with what options interests are to be fulfilled. Situation dictates interests, but also imposes constraints. If a wound is such that it needs a bandage immediately, the interest is constrained to the immediate. A bandage available tomorrow is of no account. It may be necessary to pay more for a bandage immediately available than one that would be available tomorrow or next week. If there is to be a 'level playing field' for all participants in an economy, all have to be under the same constraints of situation.

The dependence of interests on situations has no place in the neoclassical economic model. The fit of interests to situation is difficult to model mathematically. In the economic model, consumers have merely to express preferences, without any concern for how they come to have their preferences. Yet it is surely plain that our interests depend on our situations. It is one of the major sacrifices of realism made by neoclassical economists to ensure that economic theory is mathematically tractable. People are able to assess the fit of interests to situations, and the fit of whatever might accommodate interests, because natural selection has equipped the species with a sense of symmetry.[9]

Loyalty and Rigidity

Support is a psychological benefit of great strength in the control of human behaviour and the maintenance of human belief. It can act as a kind of social 'superglue,' the 'glue' being strongest when set in childhood. But at the same time, being a psychological benefit, support can in certain contexts be forgotten, or ignored. The flexible support-bargaining systems of democracies depend for their efficacy on the movement of support from group to group. Changing situations change interests and affiliations. People changing their affiliations and commitments must break old compacts of support. Support and all the credits and obligations involved with it are sustained only to the extent that they are sustained in the minds of those involved. Over time, they can be eroded away and replaced by others. A sudden change of situation can bring about rapid changes in patterns of group support. Those who gain support will move ahead with confidence, but those who lose support may feel deprived of what is owed to them. Many words of condemnation are associated with such changes: betrayal, treason, treachery, disloyalty, opportunism.

Obligations of loyalty to a group often give rise to dilemmas of conflicting loyalties, since people are invariably members of more than one group. Loyalty to a group of primary affiliation may be challenged by obligations to a broader group with different interests. Some staff of Volkswagen in the early twenty-first century would have known that their company had introduced software that permitted the company to breach legislation on emissions, setting the company's interest in profit above the interest of the broader community in clean air. The staff owed silence in loyalty to their company, but owed disclosure to the broader community. When President Trump pronounced climate change to be a hoax, members of the Republican Party were expected to deny the reality of changing climate, whatever their private thoughts on the matter. When President Trump pronounced that his defeat in the presidential election of 2020 was a result of electoral malpractice, Republicans were expected to endorse his opinion. An independent enquiry into child sexual abuse, reporting in November 2020, concluded that the Catholic Church had protected the reputation of the Church rather than protecting the victims of abuse. In Britain, senior staff of the Post Office, including legal staff, would have known that the Horizon software supplied to sub-postmasters was prone to error, but allowed prosecutions of sub-postmasters to proceed, and some to be imprisoned, to protect the Post Office. Conflicts arise between loyalty to a particular group and the 'facts' that are certified in a different group. Protagonists manipulate information to consolidate support for their positions.

These conflicts may be scarcely apparent when a group commands very extensive loyal support. Religious groups sustain by faith positions that are untenable on any reasonable assessment of known facts. But when a whole society is committed to a particular faith, the commitments are easily propagated as indisputable facts. People often set loyalty to family, gang, group, faith, company, government, party or organisation above loyalty to any wider but less well-defined, less organised and less prominent group, above any commitment to groups that seek to assemble support on the basis of impartial evidence. People pursue their interests, but their overriding interest is in the security that derives from support. They are inclined to follow the directives of the group that offers the most pertinent support.

Loyalty is most strongly promoted in military organisations. Effective military action requires that each person can rely on the backing of others. Combat groups need to stick together. Loyalty is so important to military success that the concept probably originated in the context of tribal warfare. The sense of loyalty gives groups strong cohesion, often to the point where they are rigid groups – groups held together so tightly that very few can ever break away from the group.[10] People adhere without question to the ideas and behaviour approved in the group. Rigidity is often characteristic of group ideals inculcated in childhood. The shared indebtedness of a whole people to a leader, such as the indebtedness to an emperor in the Japanese understanding of *on*, is conducive to loyalty and rigidity.

But the counterpart to such rigidity is that it is incompatible with the sort of tolerance and flexibility that is necessary to the support-bargaining of democracy. If support cannot move to different groupings in response to changing situations, then democracies cannot function. Rigid groups provide security for their members, but their capacity to adapt to changing circumstances is limited. Authoritarian states whose ascendancy is based on the exercise of violence tend to cultivate rigid codes of behaviour and rigid belief in deities. 'Democratic' forms of government can only emerge when people are free to assemble information about their circumstances, and can tolerate the formation of different ideas regarding the appropriate actions to be taken. The transition from autocracy to democracy can be long and slow because of the radical changes in group attitudes that are required.

Rigid groups provide a kind of security. When only one kind of information is allowed circulation, people come to believe it, for lack of alternatives to take up. But even that internal security is achieved at the cost of external insecurity. While rigidity is most commonly related to ideas inculcated in childhood, it can also be induced by insecurity arising from external threats. The internal support-bargaining of a group becomes more intense with the perception of external threats. When individuals are scared, they seek more intensively the protective support of those around them. Leaders commonly identify 'enemies' to enhance the cohesion of their own followers. Antagonistic alien groups are identified, even invented, to promote the cohesion of a home group. President Putin causes the public information media under his control in Russia to portray the West as threatening to Russian interests. Russians cannot assess situations for themselves without the considerable effort required to obtain the information necessary to do so. President Trump built rigid and tumultuous support from the cultivation of enemies. Because rigidity is characteristic of groups engaging in violence, the perception of rigidity in other groups gives rise to a sense of threat, and the cultivation of rigid positions to counter the threat. Rigidities build up, making violence more likely, and offsetting any security that derives from membership of a rigid group.

The idea of a 'home' society as trustworthy and nurturing, imbued with beliefs of incontestable veracity, whilst threatened by alien societies of malicious disposition and shockingly heretical beliefs, has resulted in incessant violence between nations around the world. Societies find it necessary to maintain readiness for war, both with regard to weaponry and mental dispositions. Chapter 2 considers further aspects of violence and its relation to support and support-bargaining. The subject has a significant bearing on the extent and growth of money-bargaining. Money-bargaining is always severely constrained by violence. But economic anthropologists have been inclined to see the desire for material advantage, especially when associated with the use of money, as the origin of violence in otherwise peaceable societies.

Notes

1 Graeber, David, 2012, *Debt: The First 5,000 Years*, Brooklyn and London: Melville House, pp. 69–71.
2 Comte, Auguste, 1891, *The Catechism of Positive Religion*, tr. by R. Congreve, 3rd Edition, London, p. 295. Quoted in Graeber, 2012, p. 70.
3 Graeber, 2012, p. 71.
4 Benedict, Ruth, 1954/1946, *The Chrysanthemum and the Sword*, Rutland, VT and Tokyo: Charles E. Tuttle Company, pp. 98–176.
5 Benedict, 1954/1946, p. 145.
6 Benedict, 1954/1946, p. 176.
7 Benedict, 1954/1946, pp. 141–3.
8 Spread, Patrick, 2011, 'Situation as Determinant of Selection and Valuation', *Cambridge Journal of Economics*, Vol. 35, No. 2, pp. 335–56.
9 Spread, Patrick, 2013, *Support-Bargaining, Economics and Society: A Social Species*, London and New York: Routledge, Chapter 10: 'Social Symmetries.'
10 Spread, Patrick, 2008, *Support-Bargaining: The Mechanics of Democracy Revealed*, Sussex: Book Guild, pp. 27–31, 377–84, 439–52, etc. See also Spread, Patrick, 2015, 'The Political Significance of Certain Types of Group', in *Aspects of Support-Bargaining and Money-Bargaining*, E-Book, World Economics Association.

References

Benedict, Ruth, 1954/1946, *The Chrysanthemum and the Sword*, Rutland, VT and Tokyo: Charles E. Tuttle Company.

Comte, Auguste, 1891, *The Catechism of Positive Religion*, Trans. R. Congreve, 3rd Edition, London.

Graeber, David, 2012, *Debt: The First 5,000 Years*, Brooklyn and London: Melville House.

Spread, Patrick, 2008, *Support-Bargaining: The Mechanics of Democracy Revealed*, Sussex: Book Guild.

Spread, Patrick, 2011, 'Situation as Determinant of Selection and Valuation', *Cambridge Journal of Economics*, Vol. 35, No. 2, pp. 335–56.
Spread, Patrick, 2013, *Support-Bargaining, Economics and Society: A Social Species*, London and New York: Routledge.
Spread, Patrick, 2015, 'The Political Significance of Certain Types of Group', in *Aspects of Support-Bargaining and Money-Bargaining*, E-Book, World Economics Association.
Spread, Patrick, 2015, *Aspects of Support-Bargaining and Money-Bargaining*, E-Book, World Economics Association.

2 Support, Violence, Homer, Malinowski

The psychological significance of support and its consequent effectiveness as an influence on human behaviour can be attributed to its association with violence. Giving 'support' suggests a commitment to protect someone, to stand by them, even to the extent of violent combat. Without support, people feel vulnerable, both physically and psychologically. The association with violence is at the same time an association with group membership, since effective violence is delivered in groups. Assembly of support implies establishment of a capacity for effective violence. It was argued in *Support-Bargaining, Economics and Society* that the formation of groups for effective violence through support-bargaining would have been necessary to the survival of the human species. Darwin saw the necessity for group formation but acknowledged his difficulties in identifying the mechanism.[1] The connection of support with violence is apparent in the national cohesion that emerges when a nation is threatened by an external enemy. Tight groups are formed under threat from real or imagined 'enemies.' The association of support with violence gives it potency across the whole range of human cooperative engagement, including the formulation of theories regarding the functioning of societies.

The connection of support with violence runs by degrees from a loose and largely mute connection in everyday support-bargaining, to communication by words or other means of the violent possibilities of support, to threats of violence, veiled or prominent, to demonstrations of the numbers that suggest significant violent potential, to support expressed in actual violence, delivered most effectively with the internal cohesion of armed forces. In violent societies the most compelling expressions of support are the phalanxes of armed men that can be assembled in the field.

Darwin presents natural selection largely as a matter of success in combat. The survivors are the courageous and the tough. They are also the sociable, because he recognises the necessity for group cohesion in combat. But he accounts the instinct for self-preservation as a trait to be overcome, an obstacle to fulfilment of obligations to the tribe. Fear leads to self-preservation. It blunts readiness for combat.[2] But the instinct for self-preservation is the basis of the insecurity which makes people seek support and form the groups that are effective in combat. What seems at first sight to be an obstacle to effective violence and

DOI: 10.4324/9781003313472-4

survival is the basis of the group formation necessary to survival. It is a paradox of human nature, made apparent in the theory of support-bargaining, that the instinct that seems most selfish is also the instinct that impels humans to group association and makes them such successful survivors.

Modern 'democratic' states operate under a support convention which substitutes support for violence. Instead of fighting for social ascendancy, support is recognised as proxy for violence, so that decisions can be reached without bloodshed. In analogy to violent combat 'majority support' is reckoned decisive in formal support-bargaining. As an acceptable rule of thumb, the larger army will win a violent encounter, and the faction with a majority of votes in a formal support-bargaining system is accepted as entitled to advance of its proposals. Formal support-bargaining structures are established through which support can be expressed and interests advanced on the basis of aggregated support. The equivocal psychology of support is set aside in favour of an identifiable and countable form of support. 'Votes' are allocated to all adult members of a state for participation in elections that form a legislature. The formal structures constitute artificial bargaining sets defined in terms of territories and participants. The structures are arranged so that through them groups can emerge with majorities, giving them entitlement to govern.

It has not so far been possible to establish an international support convention. The United Nations forms what can be seen as an embryonic international legislature, but it falls well short of the functions performed by national legislatures. Violence remains a prominent arbiter of the outcome of international disputes. States negotiate treaties and arrangements with each other based on balances of political and economic advantage. These, however, cover specific matters, rather than establishing general procedures for determining all issues. A breakdown of negotiations, in which one side insists on what another will not deliver, can result in armed conflict. Conflicting interests over vital issues, such as territorial sovereignty, and imbalances of violent capacity more generally, impede the emergence of any international support convention. Established nations with high violent capacity will not accept structural voting arrangements comparable to those of nation states that give all participants equal status. Such arrangements would potentially lead to overriding of vital interests of the powerful. The richer states, in particular, would resist arrangements that might, for example, establish a global right to free movement of people. Similar concerns, particularly over land and property, impeded the emergence of national democracies.[3] An international support convention perhaps requires the intervention of extra-terrestrial forces to provide an external threat sufficient to bring about the formation of a cohesive international earth alliance.

Into the nineteenth century violence played a prominent part in international trade. Merchants needed armed force to establish themselves in territories with which they sought to trade. Nations built empires to secure trade with territories that offered the best opportunities for trade development. In the seventeenth century hybrid 'companies' were formed that combined trade with the armed force necessary to its secure conduct. The Dutch East India Company (Vereenigde Oostindische Compagnie, or VOC) secured Dutch trade with the Spice Islands. The East India Company secured British interests in India. The British navy established itself as the 'police' of international waters, though not an impartial police. With changing attitudes to trade, arising partly from new economic theories and partly from new opportunities arising from the technical changes that drove the European industrial revolution, the element of violence in international trade was reduced through the nineteenth century. The East India Company was wound up in 1874.

The material returns from violence are most particularly apparent in institutionalised slavery. In the ancient world it was standard practice for conquered peoples to become the slaves of their conquerors. Slaves were part of the spoils of war. The children of slaves became themselves slaves. Slavery was not the violence of one armed faction fighting another, but of armed men imposing their will by violence on unarmed civilian groups. Russian noblemen owned serfs along with their estates up to emancipation in 1861. In the United States the use of slaves on southern cotton plantations divided support for and against into groups of such rigidity that no settlement through support-bargaining was possible. The southern states deemed their slaves to be property and of such vital interest that they would fight rather than relinquish it. The civil war of 1861–5 was fought with great intensity and heavy casualties. British enslavement took place outside the country, on sugar plantations in the West Indies, so that it was not so apparent to ordinary Britons. It seems to have been largely ignored until brought to public attention by the efforts of those who sought to abolish it. Beneficiaries of slavery presented it as tolerable, and even benign. Few could research first-hand the actual conditions of slavery, and those in a position to do so were mostly the major beneficiaries. Slave trading was ended by the British government in 1807; slavery in British colonies was abolished in 1833. The status of slaves as 'property' was officially recognised by payment of generous compensation to slave owners. The abolition of slavery did not result in widespread dissemination of information about slavery and its consequences. The importance of slavery to British economic wealth has only become apparent in recent decades. The lesson of slavery appears to be that, in the absence of vociferous ethical support ranged against it, religious or secular, groups with preponderant capacities for violence will coerce others to their material service.

In the most recent era, the use of violence has been tempered by the highly destructive nature of military technologies. Mutual annihilation was a real prospect if the cold war of the decades following the Second World War had become hot. As it was, the cold war gave rise to periodic crises, such as the Cuban Missile Crisis of 1963, and 'proxy' wars, such as the conflicts in North Korea and Vietnam, designed to halt what was seen in the West as Soviet and Chinese communist expansion across Asia. The use of local forces reduced the status of such confrontations. Home territories of the great powers were not threatened. So, the most destructive weapons were kept in their silos.

States still feel themselves obliged to maintain readiness for war. They can still count on raising armies for their 'defence.' Ordinary males will volunteer to fight in support of their national government, and many more will accept conscription readily enough if they are assured by their government that the national interest requires violent repulse of enemies. Concepts of social debt, with a duty to fight in defence of a home nation, are still maintained. High casualties and severe hardships will be endured in defence of national territory, and even in fighting over foreign territory, if it is recognised as essential to national security.

The military life is not all hardship and danger. It is renowned for its camaraderie. People under external threat naturally look to their immediate associates for the support they need, so those in combat groups tend to form tight psychological bonds of mutual support. The military life also relieves people of irksome civilian obligations to find work, find accommodation, prepare food and generally take responsibility for their own lives. The military life is sometimes characterised as mostly boring with bursts of high excitement. But for some, it is a relief from the boredom of everyday existence – you may be able to 'see the world' at the expense of someone else.

The readiness to fight is, however, more conditional in full support-bargaining societies than in societies of a more authoritarian type. In authoritarian states people are more inclined to follow the directives of their governments, for fear of the consequences of not doing so. People learn habits of submission from birth. Starved of information, they are in any case unable to formulate alternatives to the pictures painted by their governments of their situations. In democracies people expect to be well-informed, to debate issues, and have some say in the decision-making of their governments. Children are taught to think for themselves. Resistance of conscripts and people in general, and the unexpected military prowess of the enemy, made it necessary for the United States to withdraw from Vietnam. Commitments to reduce terrorism in the West, following the destruction of the World Trade Centre in New York in 2001, by fighting in Afghanistan proved difficult to sustain, and ultimately impossible, because democratic opinion did not thoroughly agree the justifications provided.

Support conventions of limited scope have been established in the West for many years, but the full support conventions commensurate with ideas of democracy are of fairly recent adoption. The 'Glorious Revolution' of 1688 in Britain took significant steps in constraining the authority of the monarch and advancing that of an elected parliament after the Civil War of 1642–9. But universal suffrage of adult males was only adopted after the First World War, and for all adult females in 1928. The introduction can be related to the demonstrations of individual capacities for violence in the First World War. People who fought so bravely clearly had a stake in their country. The Act of 1918 gave the vote to all adult men over 21, but those over 19 who had fought in the War also became entitled to vote. Women too made major contributions to the violent efforts of the First World War, but the grant of suffrage to women over the age of 30 in the 1918 Act was probably influenced also by the demonstrations of female capacity for violence in the suffragette movement before the War.

The historic exclusion of women from engagement in local and national affairs, and what amounted to the persecution of women in many states, ancient and modern, can be attributed to their lesser capacity for violence as compared to men, with the implication that their support could similarly be accounted of little significance. Warfare has become much less a matter of physical strength. Furthermore, the increased use of support conventions, the rise of education and the greater prominence of ideas in the conduct of public affairs have diminished the significance of personal capacities for violence, so that the support of women has become equivalent to that of men in affairs of government.

Material Aspects of Violence

Themistocles, the historian of the Peloponnesian War between Athenian and Spartan alliances in the fifth century BCE, was inclined even at that time to minimise the role of brute force in warfare. He remarked that 'in general, one is victorious in war by intelligence and by monetary superiority.'[4] While wars are waged with great intensity and high rhetoric, success is fundamentally contingent on information and the money necessary to supply of men and materials. James Macdonald echoes the monetary point. He argues that financiers played a critical role in the emergence of modern democracies by providing the credit necessary to their success in war. Democratic states are better able to raise finance for military action, and raise it on more advantageous terms, than authoritarian states. A French official expressed concern in 1774 that Britain's parliamentary government might make it easier for Britain to raise finance for war than was possible for despotic France.[5]

Finance is important because the time disparities apparent in all spheres of human activity are particularly prominent in the context of warfare. Armies have to be raised, clothed, equipped, trained, fed, housed, paid and transported before there can be any action, and before there can be any 'returns.' The risks attaching to such credit are higher than is common with finance for civil undertakings. Alexander the Great mortgaged his inherited estates to raise money for his campaigns. His later plunder of Persian treasure was apparently more than sufficient to secure his estates.[6] Mediaeval English monarchs borrowed from bankers in Lombardy. Britain borrowed world-wide to raise funds for the repulse of Hitler. The risks are not just the risks of failure in combat. Thrones and heads, notably of Charles I of England and Louis XVI of France, have been lost at least partly on account of the ruinous costs of war.

In the absence of credit, rulers are obliged to find other means of financing the early expenditures necessary to war. In ancient Mesopotamia palaces and temples stored treasure, mostly in the form of silver, contributed by or exacted from their people.[7] In ancient Egypt and in the Syrian and Hittite empires, stores and treasure houses were built.[8] In the eighth century BCE Greek states began to build monumental temples, for use as stores of wealth and as centres for sacrificial feasting.[9] Thucydides ascribes to Pericles, statesman and general, the enumeration in his speeches of the stored treasure available to wage war. Most of it was held in sanctuaries.[10] Athens had also, from 495 BCE, the silver mine at Laurion as a source of finance for its defence. Laurion silver was used to build the fleet that saved Athens from Persian invasion.[11]

The 'returns' from violence are not necessarily reckoned in material terms. States fight for their freedom or 'sovereignty.' They must raise and risk finance to achieve such objectives. Success may be achieved only at substantial material cost. The Second World War was uniquely destructive of property across the territories of the combatants. But for the Western alliance the material damage was a necessary price for repulse of Nazi Germany. In earlier ages, when weaponry was less destructive, the sovereignty or ascendancy attaching to territorial conquest often came with material returns. While a king might go to war as a matter of political expedience, his financiers would look rather at the earnings potential of their loan. Occupation of territory means occupation of land with rental value, built property, agricultural potential, livestock and mineral wealth. Levies can be imposed on the people of conquered territories. Conquered people may be enslaved. Wars may be fought primarily with an eye to such returns, though such motivation is seldom acknowledged. Fritz Heichelheim records that the New Kingdom in Egypt, the Hittite and the Assyrian kingdoms were true robber states, gaining much of their wealth from wars and conquests.[12] Of the Classical age he writes, 'If possible, the campaign expenses for soldiers' pay and all other outlay were now more or less carefully balanced against income from booty, tributes, Persian and other subsidy payments, and other such income.'[13] States analysed invasions of other territories as business analysts evaluate their investments. William the Conqueror invaded England in 1066 on the grounds that he was the rightful king of England. His leading supporters gained landed estates for themselves at the expense of the native Anglo-Saxons. Britain's empire would have been much smaller if its major colonies had not offered such opportunities for material gain. Governments today use land as a potent form of control over their people. State-owned land can be withheld from those who criticise government policies or head movements opposed to government. Dissidents are allocated the worst land, or none at all.

Material returns may also be independent of any enjoyment of sovereignty. Common soldiers have been attracted to 'the flag' not just by the prospect of a regular wage – not always realised – but in expectation of loot from conquered territories. British naval officers and men fighting Napoleon's fleets saw the prospect of wealth through the capture of French and Spanish ships as 'prizes.' Mediaeval armies in Europe did not necessarily set out to kill their adversaries; better to take aristocratic prisoners and demand a ransom for their release.

Military Organisation

Military matters, with their attendant risks to life and limb, tend to concentrate minds. From the earliest times, violence and the prospect of violence have been central to people's fears and ambitions. It is, as has been seen, a major impulse to the formation of groups. Effective violence, however, requires something more than the formation of groups. It requires the assembly of finance and the coordination of all those aspects of military affairs that are essential to overall success. In the idea of support-bargaining and money-bargaining, groups are given focus and defined purpose through organisation. A brief account of organisations is in the *Starter*, covering both their use in support-bargaining and in money-bargaining.[14]

There are two essentials of organisation. Firstly, it involves arranging people in hierarchies, with each level of a hierarchy having a subordinate position to the one above. The hierarchies are defined with constrained bargaining positions at each level, such that each must conform to instructions provided from higher levels. Through such hierarchies, leaders can ensure that the particular purpose of the organisation, as defined by its leaders, is pursued at all subordinate levels.

The second essential is the use of a money budget. To achieve its purpose, an organisation has to pay staff and buy goods and services necessary to the advance of its interests. The motivations of support-bargaining by which groups are formed have to be supplemented by the motivations of money-bargaining. Money-bargaining is effective in the accommodation of everyday material needs. Payments also induce people to accept the inconveniences of hierarchies. As was seen in the Introduction, budgets are used also by all agents of money-bargaining systems to manage time disparities between expenditures and revenues.

The clear purpose, 'victory,' in the military context, and the need for coordination of action towards that objective, means that groups intending violence would have been amongst the first to adopt the hierarchies and budgets of organisation. The importance of hierarchy, the 'chain of command,' is seen at its most striking in the military context. Success invariably depends on soldiers fulfilling their obligations in precise coordination with others. The heavy costs involved in putting an army in the field was noted in the previous section. Budgets are needed to ensure that payments to soldiers are made at the appointed time and supplies of military equipment are available when needed. MacDonald's emphasis on finance reflects the importance of budgeting to the effectiveness of military organisation.

Military organisation is in many cases the organisation of a state. Violence has been the common arbiter of 'sovereignty,' the determinant of who governs a territory and its people. State and military have often been all but inseparable. Armies are organised for self-sufficiency. They cover employment, the essentials of education, in the form of military training, the essentials of health, in the provision of military medical personnel, and the provision of transport and engineering services. The armies of modern democratic countries expect to be provided with orders from their governments, so that their responsibility is confined to implementation. But army officers have quite commonly been ready to take on the overall control of societies themselves. Kings have generally seen themselves as being the leaders of their armed forces, as well as leaders of their society. The British monarch is today the formal head of the armed forces; similarly, the President of the United States is the head of the country's armed forces. Military organisation and state organisation have historically been closely linked if not coterminous.

Military budgets and the budgets of military regimes played an important role in the evolution of money-bargaining. Military garrisons stationed in occupied territory frequently constituted substantial settlements, presenting opportunities locally for supply of food, building materials, tools, weapons, furniture, kitchen utensils, clothing and footwear. They also required various services, such as laundry, construction services, domestic services and entertainment. A garrison spending budgetary revenues from its central authority would introduce money into circulation in its surrounding community. In some circumstances the population surrounding a garrison would find security in moving close to the garrison. The defensive walls protecting a garrison could become the walls of a city. Many cities in England have their origins in Roman garrisons in the period of Roman occupation. Across Europe, cities retain the remains of fortifications originally built to protect citizens from external attack. Cities provide the confluences of people that are most conducive to the evolution of money-bargaining.[15] Retail services, in particular, benefit from confluences of people, and the success of retailing leads to the development of supply chains. The internal security of cities made it easier for people to go about their businesses. Demonstrable success of money-bargaining in cities has set in train a long historical process of urbanisation.

The association of military organisation with state organisation is apparent in the sense of hierarchy that is apparent in many civil societies. Populations become structured on the model of military hierarchies. Everyone is accorded a place in a social hierarchy that mirrors the ranks of a military system. Those breaking out of their allotted place may be ostracised by their fellow citizens; that is, social support is withdrawn.

Different levels of a civilian hierarchy are commonly allocated different roles. An 'aristocracy' tops the civilian hierarchy, conferring titles on themselves to identify their status. They tend to be prominent in governance and in the upper ranks of military hierarchies. Their children inherit titles and privileges. Habits of command and deference become settled across the civil hierarchy. Hereditary aristocrats still sit by constitutional right in the influential 'House of Lords' of the United Kingdom parliament. France abolished such civilian hierarchy in the revolution of 1789, dispensing rather brutally with its aristocracy, as a matter of 'enlightenment.' In 1804, Napoleon crowned himself emperor. The founding fathers of the United States ruled out civil hierarchies for those of European origin, in accordance with the same 'enlightenment.'

The tendency to class formation on the model of military hierarchies is strengthened by the acquisition of land by military conquest and its allocation to those most prominent in the military action that acquires it. As was noted above, ownership or control of land gives extensive control over the population dependent on that land for its livelihood. Thus, classes originating in military hierarchies become more strongly established in civil society through their control of land. The children of the landed classes inherit the land of their parents and through it sustain ascendancy.

Karl Marx simplified the social hierarchies in accordance with his purpose. He identified just two critical social groups, the bourgeoisie and the proletariat, the former owning capital and the latter without capital, each with interests related to its situation.[16] The essential situation of Western society was, according to Marx, the conflict of these interests. Bourgeois ownership of capital enforced the subordination of the proletariat. The potential for conflict is heightened by giving the groups involved the appearance of rigidity. As was seen in Chapter 1, rigid groups are prone to conflict. In the idea of support-bargaining, the basic contention is between individuals and groups, rather than between groups preconceived as established with assigned interests. Groups formed through support-bargaining do not automatically become rigid. People judge their interests by reference to their circumstances. The fluidity of social groups in a support-bargaining system provides the flexibility that reduces or even eliminates violence in democratic systems of government. Marx defines his protagonists in a way that disposes them to violence, so that his theory implies the necessity for violence. He defines in accordance with his own preconception: the necessity of violent revolution to bring about social justice. The theory was formulated and its protagonists defined to assemble support for the revolutionary cause.

The Homeric Code and Material Intrusions

Though there are communal and material attractions to military life, it comes with the major drawbacks that people get killed and their dependents suffer. People have a 'first instinct' for self-preservation. The instinct seems essential to the survival of all animate species. As was seen above, Darwin emphasises the importance of aggression in his account of the origin of species, but the idea of support-bargaining implies that survival of the human species depends also on the instinct for self-preservation, since it is that instinct that gives rise to the sense of insecurity, which, in turn, drives people to seek support and form groups. Requirements for group cohesion in the face of danger have given rise to the establishment of elaborate codes of 'honour' cultivating such military virtues as courage, loyalty and self-sacrifice. Such codes, enforced through the support of their associates, cause individuals to suppress their own interest in self-preservation in order to achieve group purposes. The 'camaraderie' of military life accords each individual the support of the group contingent on their adherence to the military codes. Each individual is obliged to recognise his dependence on the success of the group. The extraordinary heroism displayed by many soldiers is in part testimony to the strength of the support established amongst fighting men.

The 'warrior code' is cultivated in some of the earliest surviving literature. It is commonly cultivated most intensely amongst the leaders of a society, since it is leaders who must inspire others by persuasion and example to suppress fear and fight even to the sacrifice of their lives. Richard Seaford interprets Homer's *Iliad* and *Odyssey* in the context of his theory that the epics display the evolution of Greek thought that made Greek city states the first to adopt coins for use in common trading throughout their societies. Seaford's title, *Money and the Early Greek Mind*, suggests a connection between mental attitudes and the emergence of money, just as it was suggested above that the support convention, and hence the conduct of 'democratic' political systems, depends on attitudes developed within a society. Attitudes of early Greek minds produced both a form of 'democracy' and the widespread use of coins.[17]

In Seaford's account of the *Iliad*, Achilles is the epitome of the heroic warrior in pursuit of the honour that comes from selfless commitment to a communal cause. But Achilles' falls out with his leader, King Agamemnon, over the sharing of booty after battle.[18] The exploits and attitudes of Achilles and his associates have gripped the imagination of people in subsequent eras. European culture has drawn heavily on Greek and Roman culture, with the epics of Homer central to the tradition and an inspiration for the conduct of war. The mediaeval exploits of King Arthur and his Knights of the Round Table echo the heroic endeavour of Achilles in the *Iliad*. Homer's epics are treated, in default of better evidence, as depicting, albeit imperfectly, the Greek society of the early first millennium BCE. The accuracy of the depiction is, of course, open to question. The Arthurian legends, on their own, would certainly give a misleading impression of mediaeval society.

The Homeric ideal includes a disdain for material interests. The heroes exchange gifts of artefacts of precious metal or fine cloth, unworked precious metal, women and chariots with horses.[19] These items are recognised as 'valuable' within their community. Silver and gold are highly prized, but there is no indication of their being valued above everything else, or as representing wealth in general.[20] The value of traditional relationships is elevated by contrast with the scorn cast on material wealth.[21] The use of gold in payment is connected with 'nefarious purpose' or has other negative connotation.[22] Barter trade is incidental, conducted almost exclusively with non-Greeks.[23]

While gift exchange is concerned with the establishment and maintenance of personal relationships, with no implication, at least superficially, of anything like 'trade' for material advantage, there is nevertheless attention to relative values. On occasions, this becomes significant. When Glaucus gives Diomedes a gift of golden armour and receives from Diomedes bronze armour, an exchange equivalent in value to 100 cattle for 9, the narrator, Homer, comments that Zeus stole the wits of Glaucus.[24] The exchange is being evaluated in different contexts: in the context of gift-giving for the sealing of friendship, and in an alternative context of trade for material advantage. Seaford notes, 'It is a reminder that trade, despite its marginality in the Homeric narratives, was surely an important part of the world in which the narratives were produced.'[25] A wider world is allowed by Homer to intrude into the heroic culture he promotes, and allowed to cast doubt on the integrity of the heroic culture. Gift-giving was designed to seal personal relationships, but its conventions would necessarily have offered scope for other messages through their breach. It might be regarded as insulting to reciprocate a gift worth 100 cattle with a gift worth 9.

Gift-giving is a way of assembling support; hence a matter of support-bargaining. The practice of 'reciprocity,' of gift-giving, central to anthropological theory, is intended to generate 'interpersonal relationships.' It can be seen as part of a process of assimilating potential rivals or enemies into friendship, or at least creating sufficient mutual support to reduce or eliminate any progression to violence. The leaders of the Greek states that form Homer's coalition against Troy exchange gifts to ensure support for the maintenance of their campaign. The gifts constitute visible and tangible evidence of the loyalty they express to each other in a context of oral support-bargaining. The 'redistribution' of food in Homeric culture can similarly be seen as the assembly of support from the general populace for their social arrangements. Looking after the food requirements of people elicits their support and reduces the potential for unrest or insurrection.

Seaford identifies a fissure in the stability of Homeric society, and by implication in the Greek society of the time, in that Achilles disputes with King Agamemnon the right of the King to control for his own interests the division of the booty from war. For all his heroic protestations, Achilles complains that there is no gratitude for exceptional performance – good and bad fighters get the same rewards.[26] Seaford remarks: 'Reciprocity between leader and warrior, the form of centralised reciprocity known as redistribution, has been destroyed by the leader's selfish control of the process.' The breakdown is marked by Achilles' rejection of the visible expression of their friendship and alliance: 'Hateful to me are his gifts.'[27] Agamemnon opts for equality of shares, without recognising any obligation to match honour with wealth.

The dispute suggests the erosion by money-bargaining of a system geared to the assembly of support. 'Economics' is disrupting the 'politics.' Notions of 'honour' and 'heroism' and the impulse to act in accordance with them are outcomes of support-bargaining. A group or society organises itself to repel violence, or in the case of the *Iliad*, to recover the beautiful Helen, who is held by the Trojans. But material reward, the rewards of money-bargaining, can divert people away from the ideals of behaviour they are expected to fulfil as members of their community. Achilles refuses to fight, but asserts his indifference to 'trade' by refusing placatory gifts from Agamemnon, and later resumes his heroic commitment to the Greek cause. The impulses to pursue both support and money split the Greek force. Seaford comments, 'It illustrates how the breakdown of the interpersonal relations of reciprocity might favour the development of the impersonal equivalence inherent in trade and of a universal measure of value.'[28] Equally, and perhaps with greater import, the development of trade and the use of money might break down the interpersonal relations of gift-giving and support-bargaining. Money potentially detaches the individual from the group, to the detriment of group interests. In Homer, however, the ascendancy of the group is maintained. Trade and monetisation are marginalised beside a mainstream preference for the support-bargaining of reciprocity.[29] The ambiguous undertow of material interest is apparent in what is superficially the noble intercourse of friendship and esteem. Money-bargaining is entwined almost imperceptibly with support-bargaining. The pressures of support-bargaining are such as to discourage any acknowledgement of material interest.

While Homer's elite warriors redistribute booty and cultivate cohesion through gifts of 'treasure,' the custom of sacrificial feasting provides a further form of redistribution in their society. This is redistribution from the wealthy to the ordinary people. Animal sacrifice is central to Homeric society, with an emphasis on communality and an 'equal feast.' The distribution of booty is private, individual and irregular, while feasting is an open and regular public ritual distribution of food. Sacrifice is important to the cohesion of the state, or 'polis.'[30] Seaford sees the communal feasting ritual as a further aspect of the rifts in Homeric society:

> Tension between individual appropriation and communal distribution in Homer occurs not within the animal sacrifice but rather in the narrative as a whole – both within the distribution of booty and between it and sacrificial distribution. This is because, in sharp contrast to sacrificial distribution, the heroic individualism that forms so much of the Homeric ethos has disturbed or even marginalised the principle of equal distribution.[31]

The conflict between the individual and the group, the fundamental contention of support-bargaining, is apparent even in a context in which individualism is expressed in terms of heroic military service to the community. The individual wants a share of the booty that reflects his individual contribution to advance of communal interests, and wants that mode of redistribution that can allocate reward on an individual basis to be elevated above that mode of distribution that insists on equal shares to all.

Seaford notes that the social arrangements for feasting in Homeric epic, and hence by supposition the arrangements that pertained in Greek states of the period, were different from those portrayed in the epics of the Near East. The Greek mind, Greek attitudes, were different to those of the Near East. Seaford notes that there have been recent advances in the identification of similarities between Greek social practices and those of Mesopotamia in the late Bronze Age, but he is concerned to make clear the distinctiveness of the Homeric world.[32] The societies shared most fundamentally the redistributive function.[33] Temples in both regions redistributed the goods and services donated to them, 'donation' evolving in Mesopotamia to enforced collection. There were, however, significant differences. In ancient Mesopotamia the food assembled was for the god, even if, behind the scenes, the food was consumed by temple staff.[34] In Homeric Greece the sacrificial animals were a feast for the people, not for the gods. The gods ate ambrosia, so would not be interested in meat.[35] The temples of Mesopotamia were set up on a grander scale than those of Greece, and engaged in a wider range of activities. Seaford writes:

> Generally speaking, in Mesopotamia the massive temple owns much land, and is a centre for the collection, distribution and storage of food, vast amounts of which are regularly supplied for the god, to be consumed in fact by the other members of his household, the temple personnel.[36]

Michael Hudson also comments on the scale of Mesopotamian temples: 'Mesopotamia's temples and palaces were endowed with their own land, herds of cattle and dependent labour to make them self-supporting.'[37] In contrast, there is no evidence from classic Attica of the public ownership of herds and flocks.[38] Land ownership and a degree of self-sufficiency meant that the practices of Mesopotamian temples were different from those of Greek temples. The former were redistributing food, but their chief concern was the provision of food for the god. The Mesopotamian temples appear as agents of social administration on a substantial scale, dominated by a privileged section of their community. Greek temples were smaller and more dependent on their people, and consequently more responsive to the interests of common people. In Mesopotamia 'the motor of the system is divine demand,'[39] as interpreted by the temple priests, whereas in Greece the community had more influence on the proceedings of the temple. Thus Seaford writes: 'The polis...performs some of the social, economic and legal functions that in Mesopotamia were performed by the temples, and it finances public sacrifice so as to provide a feast not for an elite but for itself.'[40] There are then markedly different attitudes prevalent in Greek society from those of ancient Mesopotamian society.

The rifts in Homeric society suggested by the *Iliad* and the contrast with epic material from the Near East lead Seaford to conclude that while the Near Eastern epics portray societies that are relatively stable under authoritarian control, Homer's society is undergoing transition. He writes:

> Central to the Homeric epic, by contrast, is the *failure* of redistribution – redistribution among mortals and on a small scale. Homer, in contrast to the Mesopotamian epics, is the epic of a society in transition.[41]

In the terms of evolutionary support-bargaining, the current situation described by Homer is felt to be unsatisfactory by important social groups. Those of individualistic mind are contesting the distribution of rewards with the group. They can be expected to seek changes to advance their interests, through which their society will evolve.[42] In Mesopotamia, dominant organisations are unchallenged. Temples and palaces rule with military and intellectual supremacy. Part of the evolutionary outcome of these tensions in Greek society is the introduction and widespread usage of coin-money.

A Pacific Alternative: The *Kula* Code

Most societies have found it necessary to cultivate a 'warrior code' akin to the Homeric code for their protection in an uncertain and threatening world. If people are not prepared to fight for the survival of their society, with development of the mental attitudes necessary to fighting, then they are liable to lose their society to violent external invaders. But such arrangements may not be the only option. Bronislaw Malinowski studied a group of islands, the Trobriand Islands, populated by people of Melanesian race, just to the West of the Papua New Guinea mainland, with the Western tip of the mainland also part of the study group, which had developed a system of gift exchange within and between the components of the group. The *Kula* system of gift exchange has provided anthropologists and sociologists with empirical evidence for the existence of an alternative system from that which what is operative in the West for the cultivation of social harmony and, integral to that process, the fulfilment of material needs.

Malinowski describes the *Kula* as operating both within small inner *Kula* communities and between more distant *Kula* communities, with *Kula* expeditions launched between distant communities on an annual basis.[43] The economic relations within an inner *Kula* group are described as: 'a state of affairs where production, exchange and consumption are socially organised and regulated by custom, and where a special system of traditional economic values governs their activities and spurs them on to efforts.'[44] Chiefs and sorcerers, or magicians, are the central figures in the arrangements. A chief has an over-right on land, but sub-chiefs and others have other rights related to the land. A garden magician exercises authority in land matters since certain rituals must be performed at each stage of gardening.[45] Garden produce is distributed according to customary rules, which, as Malinowski puts it, 'enmeshes the whole community into a network of reciprocal obligations and dues, one constant flow of gift and counter-gift.'[46] Malinowski interprets this as giving a 'constant economic undertow to all public and private activities – this materialistic streak which runs through all their doings…'[47]

The chief receives by dues and tributes about 30 per cent of the whole food production of his district, which he stores and displays.[48] The chief transforms part of this food wealth into objects or tokens of permanent wealth. These are axe-blades, necklaces of red shell discs and arm-shells.[49] Through his accumulated wealth the chief can direct activities in the community, though Malinowski emphasises that he is obliged to pay for the services he requires in valuable tokens, food, pigs, coconuts or betel nuts. Malinowski describes the role of chief as in some respects like a 'tribal banker,' though he is concerned that the title should not be taken too literally.[50] The chief takes deposits and distributes what is deposited. The role of chief involves organisation of communal festivities in which the distribution of food plays a prominent part.[51] Barter is well developed in the community, including resort to haggling.[52] But at the same time, Malinowski records that there is no room for any free exchange.[53] He also records that there are no deferred payments, and hence there is no need for money, though the treasured objects serve as a means of 'condensing wealth.'[54] Further, acceptance of a treasured object as gift implies acceptance of an obligation to reciprocate at some later date, so time delays are integral to gift exchange. Gifts are given with expectation of later reciprocation for what might be regarded as the express purpose of maintaining a friendly connection over time, renewed at the time of reciprocation.

The *Kula* rituals of the annual expeditions to people in other islands of the group involve gift-giving and an obligation to reciprocate in accordance with established custom. The *Kula* round necessitates long sea voyages between islands in specially built canoes designed for safe passage on open seas. The gifts of inter-island exchange are ornamental, but seldom used as ornaments.[55] They comprise arm-shells and necklaces of shell discs; no other products are acceptable. Necklaces are gifted in a clockwise direction around the islands of the group, while arm-shells are gifted in an anti-clockwise direction.[56] Circulation of a gift in the wrong direction is unacceptable. The gift-giving is undertaken between agreed partners, forming long-standing relationships. People develop numerous *Kula* partnerships over the years. An important and elderly person, such as a chief, can have perhaps three hundred *Kula* partners. A *Kula* partner is obliged to trade with his partners and to offer protection, hospitality and assistance whenever needed.[57]

Magic plays a prominent part in *Kula* custom. Ceremonies have to be performed at all stages of a *Kula* expedition, starting with rituals performed when a *Kula* canoe is under construction. Spells are cast to ensure the safety of the expeditioners and incline their *Kula* partners to act with generosity towards them. Sorcerers and magic are prominent in the sense of adventure surrounding the *Kula* expeditions. Those involved are braving the elements and the whims of supernatural powers. Acts of heroism, encounters with fabulous sea-monsters and narrow escapes are celebrated in stories of the *Kula*.[58]

The *Kula* rounds involve plenty of subsidiary trading.[59] The subsidiary trade is carried on through gifts and reciprocation with a *Kula* partner, but by barter with others.[60] The gift exchange of the *Kula* system is recognised by Malinowski as establishing foundations on which barter can be safely conducted between people who might otherwise fall out over the terms of trade. Instead of using military force to establish secure environments for trade, as was the practice in the era of imperial expansion, the Trobriand Islanders establish security through gestures of friendly support. Investment in peacekeeping is the prelude to material trade.

Malinowski interprets the internal gift-giving of islands as giving a 'constant economic undertow to all public and private activities.'[61] In the understanding of the theory of support-bargaining, the gift-giving is more a matter of assembly of support – creating connections, making friends, promoting communal cohesion and reducing the potential for violence amongst islanders. The gifts can be seen as tangible expressions of support. They bestow support and solicit reciprocal support. They relieve the sense of insecurity. The expeditionary gift-giving serves the same function between the island populations of the *Kula* group. The gifts exchanged between islands under *Kula* custom have negligible material value. Their significance rests entirely on the way they are interpreted by givers and receivers. They are tokens of regard, respect, affection, friendship – tokens of support. *Kula* partners and the interlocking relationships established by multiple *Kula* partnerships form groups whose members are actively in support of one another, and consequently unlikely to engage in violence. The expeditionary gift exchanges, even more than those of Homeric gift exchange, involve very precise specification of the items, very minor in themselves, that can be given and received, thus ruling out any implications of trade. Barter trade for mutual material advantage is made possible by the establishment of friendly relations through gift-giving. Material trade is an appendage of the support-bargaining, so that no independent material exchange emerges that might endanger social cohesion. 'Politics' lays the foundations for peaceable 'economic' transactions.

The *Kula* round assembles support in the same way as Homeric gift exchange. The potential for violence between the islands is apparent, since isolation tends to breed insecurity and suspicion. The potential for violence is apparent also from the violence of head-hunting expeditions launched by Melanesians of the Roviana Lagoon in the Solomon Islands, about three hundred miles to the West of the *Kula* group. These raids died out in the early twentieth century, only shortly before Malinowski carried out his research on the *Kula* round in the period 1914–20. Concerns over self-preservation in an environment of dire threats seem mostly to have given rise to the emergence of warrior codes, the cultivation of violent ideologies and consequent common outbreaks of violence. The fear of violence generates ideas of counter-violence, which escalate to actual violence. The *Kula* custom seems designed to maintain peace by creating a sense of mutual support across the communities of the Trobriand Islands.

The parallels with Homeric custom are irresistible, even though the two societies are more than two and a half thousand years apart in time and half a globe apart in space, and one is fiction and the other fact, or at least an interpretation of empirical observations. Gift exchange is a means of maintaining cohesion in both societies, understood here as support-bargaining. Both have a strong materialist element, though both prefer that it remain largely covert. The gift exchange is in both cases more 'honourable' – that is, more openly approved in the community – than the material concerns. Material accumulation is scorned in both Homeric and Kula ideology, except in the context of communal distribution.[62] Both recognise the potential for violence in material exchange unalloyed by some established social affinities. Certain objects are in both regarded as being of special value, even though they are for the most part not useful. They are valued for their symbolism of status, dignity and desirability, and even because they excite feelings of envy. These items of value are administered differently from that which is of essential use – the food. Both societies have a centralised system for provision of significant amounts of food, the one through its temples and the other through its chiefs, the latter operative in particular islands, rather than through the *Kula* group as a whole. In both societies supernatural beings – gods or sorcerers – play a central role in communal life. Rituals honouring the supernatural beings and seeking their helpful intervention in the lives of the supplicants are felt to be of fundamental importance in both societies. Both societies also create a sense of epic adventure and heroism in their activities, the Homeric society seeking the defeat of Troy and the *Kula* Islanders success in overcoming the hazards of long sea passages and the unpredictable interventions of malicious spirits. While the sense of epic adventure is common to both societies, the different aims pursued in such adventures constitute a significant difference between the two societies. The Homeric Greek society is contriving a unified alliance to conduct its war against Troy, while the Trobriand Islands society is pursuing regional harmony in the face of natural and supernatural threats. Both societies, as implied by the present analysis, are trying to establish the goodwill and cohesion amongst themselves that is required for the successful pursuit of their objectives.

There are parallels also with modern Western societies. Gift-giving is important in Western societies, even if it is not regarded as crucial to the functioning of societies. Reciprocation is normally expected. At Christmas, Christians extensively exchange gifts, creating notable peaks in retail sales of consumer goods. People value objects, most often ornaments of no utilitarian value, though often of aesthetic merit, particularly when received as gifts. Objects can be assessed as 'valuable' for their aesthetic qualities or their associations, without reference to their utility or value in money-bargaining. Children told that something, like a tea service, or a book, is 'valuable,' do not necessarily think in terms of a monetary value; rather they assume it is 'valuable' because those around them recognise it as valuable. People display their valued objects in glass-fronted cases. Objects in museums are regarded as valuable, without necessarily having monetary value. If someone knows 'the price of everything but the value of nothing,' there is an implication that the person is devoid of the sense of true value that arises from honourable social sympathies. Some things are valuable because of the support accumulated around them; other things have values assigned in money-bargaining. In Western society items of 'sentimental value' are commonly kept for long periods, but in Homeric society gifts might be passed on quite rapidly, while in *Kula* society no one keeps gifts for any length of time.[63]

There exist also today distinctions between what is appropriately exchanged in money-bargaining and what is appropriate to support-bargaining, or politics. Members of legislatures are not expected to sell their services as members of a legislature for money. Civil servants should not provide favours for those who pay them privately. In many Western societies provision of health and education services are provided wholly or mainly under the aegis of support-bargaining rather than money-bargaining. It is still regarded as improper in many social groups to introduce considerations of money in any but the most discrete terms into issues of friendship and hospitality. There is a 'material undertow' to discussions of social rituals such as funerals and weddings. People may spend large sums of money, much more than necessary on a simple utilitarian reckoning, to acquire certain goods that are reckoned to confer social status – cars, houses, clothes, jewellery are prominent amongst such goods. Diamonds have gained a distinct role as expressing personal valuation in connection with betrothal and marriage.

The behaviour of people in Homeric legend and the *Kula* Islands is different from modern society not so much in kind as in prominence. Gift exchange and the following of rules about what is appropriate in a social context and what is acceptable in a monetary context are present in modern societies. The development of both support-bargaining and money-bargaining has meant that much more can be delivered, particularly in the way of services, through redistribution by a central government as an agent of both support-bargaining and money-bargaining. But gift exchange and the various social considerations attaching to private transactions have been overshadowed by the growth of money-bargaining as the essential means of advancing material interests, both utilitarian and cosmetic. The 'economic undertow' has risen to the surface.

Malinowski is wary of deriving any great theoretical conclusions from his study of the *Kula*. He expressly remarks that he 'cannot enter into any theoretical speculations' himself.[64] He emphasises the importance of economic considerations, in the sense of material or utilitarian interests, in the whole set of *Kula* customs. His main contention is that Western theorists have provided a wholly erroneous account of the behaviour of people in pursuit of material well-being. He remarks, 'While the significance of the *Kula* is obscure, it is clear in dissipating ideas that man is entirely materialistic.'[65] The economists' concept of 'economic man' is untenable in the light of *Kula* custom. Crude, rationalistic concepts of primitive mankind do not survive empirical investigation.[66] Malinowski insists that primitive people are not coldly egotistic, but have a deep and universal tendency to create social ties through exchange of gifts.[67]

The interpretation of *Kula* in the theory of support-bargaining and money-bargaining is that the Kula gift exchanges are expressions of support by which security is established across an island group. It is not so much that humans treasure social relationships; more that they try to avoid violence. *Kula* exchange minimises risks of violence. Individuals are not, as Malinowski affirms, coldly egotistic. Their priority is the acquisition of support to alleviate their sense of insecurity. In doing so, they form social groups. But the result is not necessarily the social harmony described by Malinowski. People engage in support-bargaining to advance their interests, and interests will inevitably conflict, sometimes to a point beyond resolution through support-bargaining. Nevertheless, support-bargaining can establish sufficient group security for the safe conduct of material exchange.

The *Kula* seems designed to provide a peaceable alternative to the 'warrior code' of Homeric heroism. It promotes friendship and peace through group formation and harmonisation of group interests. It provides a basis for peaceful trade. The Homeric code promotes a warrior ideal around which a group can cohere to wage war against Troy.

But the *Kula* custom may not bear the full weight of peacekeeping. At the time of Malinowski's research (1914–20), the *Kula* group was part of the Territory of Papua, under Australian administration. Thus, primary responsibility for law and order in the group was in the hands of a foreign agency, deriving its authority from a formal support-bargaining process. Malinowski, being little concerned with the political content of the *Kula* custom, gives no account of this wider context, though there are occasional hints. When participating in a *Kula* expedition, he approaches a village by canoe and remarks, 'Now, after the White man's influence has rendered unnecessary all precautions against raiding parties, the village has come down to the narrow strip of foreshore...'[68] The implication is that the *Kula* custom is not itself the basis of peace between the islands. Something Homeric may be required. Chris Gregory confirms the limitations of *kula* custom:

> The fact is that the Milne Bay area of PNG [Papua New Guinea] was one of the first regions colonised at the end of the last century. Gold miners, planters and missionaries poured into the area and, over the years, thousands of migrant labourers and students have flowed in and out. Kula is to a large extent an artefact of this history; like many other indigenous exchange systems in PNG it flourished when the colonial state suppressed clan warfare.[69]

The absence of the *Kula* kind of custom in anything more than the traces identified above in modern societies suggests that the cohesion it promotes is not sufficiently strong as to offset the impulses which cause societies to develop codes of behaviour that make them effective in combat. Formal support-bargaining systems, such as governed the Australian administration in Papua, have been extensively effective in reducing violence, though at the time of Malinowski's research on the *Kula* custom, they had notably failed to keep the peace in Europe. Nevertheless, the complexity of the *Kula* suggests development over many decades, even centuries, so that prior to the arrival of the white man's politics, *Kula* custom may have played a role in promoting peace across the islands.

Malinowski's study of *Kula* custom is recognised as a major insight into the behaviour of human societies and a groundbreaking innovation in ethnographic technique. But it is also an example of the way preconceived ideas can influence the phenomena identified for attention and the interpretation put on them. The political status of the Territory of Papua falls outside the enthnographic frame of reference. The influence of theory, or 'frames of reference,' is considered further in Chapter 4, with further consideration of Malinowski's theory in Chapter 5. Malinowski's diaries, published in 1967, confirm the selectivity of Malinowski in identifying phenomena for evaluation in his ethnographic study and the possibility of alternative interpretations of *Kula* custom and Trobriand Islands society.

Notes

1 Darwin, Charles, 2004/1871, *The Descent of Man, and Selection in Relation to Sex*, London: Penguin, pp. 152, 155–8. First published 1871. On the implications of support-bargaining for the survival of the human species, see Spread, Patrick, 2013, *Support-Bargaining, Economics and Society: A Social Species*, London: Routledge, Chapter 1: 'The Problem with Natural Selection,' and Chapter 2: 'Natural Selection and Support-Bargaining.'

2 Darwin, 2004/1871, pp. 128, 134, 154–6. For comment, see Spread, 2013, pp. 20–4, 40–1.

3 Spread, Patrick, 2019b, *A Starter on Support-Bargaining and Money-Bargaining in Twenty-Eight Digestible Bites*, London: Palgrave Macmillan, p. 40; Spread, Patrick, 2008, *Support-Bargaining: The Mechanics of Democracy Revealed*, Sussex: Book Guild, pp. 386–90; Spread, Patrick, 2016, *The Evolution of Economies: Money-Bargaining, Economic Change and Industrial Revolution*, London and New York: Routledge, pp. 183–5.

4 Quoted by Schaps, David M., 2004, *The Invention of Coinage and the Monetization of Ancient Greece*, Ann Arbor: University of Michigan Press, Kindle Edition, L627.

5 MacDonald, James, 2006, *A Free Nation Deep in Debt: The Financial Roots of Democracy*, Princeton and Oxford: Princeton University Press, pp. 3–4.

6 MacDonald, 2006, pp. 23–4, 43.

7 Schaps, 2004, L1170.

8 Heichelheim, Fritz, 1958, 1964, 1970, *An Ancient Economic History, from the Palaeolithic Age to the Migrations of the Germanic, Slavic and Arabic Nations*, Trans. Joyce Stevens, Leiden: A. W. Sijthoff, Vol. 1, 1958; Vol. 2, 1964; Vol. 3, 1970; 1958, pp. 178–9. First published 1938.

9 Seaford, Richard, 2004, *Money and the Early Greek Mind*, Cambridge: Cambridge University Press, p. 53.

10 Seaford, 2004, pp. 95–6.

11 Schaps, 2004, L3602–15.

12 Heichelheim, 1958, 1964, 1970; Vol. 1, p. 178.

13 Heichelheim, 1958, p. 93.

14 Spread, 2019b, pp. 20–4, 83–6. See also Spread, Patrick, 2016, 'Companies and Markets: Economic Theories of the Firm and a Concept of Companies as Bargaining Agencies', *Cambridge Journal of Economics*, Vol. 40, No. 3, pp. 727–53.

15 Chapter 5: Locational Format in Spread, 2008. See also the section 'Markets as Confluence' in Chapter 5 of this book.

16 Marx, Karl and Engels, Friedrich, 2005/1848, *Manifesto of the Communist Party*, 1888 Edition, Project Gutenberg, Kindle Edition, L12–200. First published 1848.

17 Seaford, 2004. Seaford's main theory is that the concept of money influenced the development of pre-Socratic philosophy. The lead-in to this main theory is the idea that Greek adoption of money, and the concept of money, arose from Greek social custom and the thinking behind it.

18 Seaford, 2004, pp. 37–8.

19 Seaford, 2004, p. 42.
20 Seaford, 2004, p. 31.
21 Seaford, 2004, p. 31, inc. Note 59.
22 Seaford, 2004, pp. 32–3.
23 Seaford, 2004, pp. 26–7.
24 Seaford, 2004, p. 34.
25 Seaford, 2004, p. 34.
26 Seaford, 2004, p. 37.
27 Seaford, 2004, p. 37.
28 Seaford, 2004, p. 37.
29 Seaford, 2004, pp. 26, 37.
30 Seaford, 2004, p. 50.
31 Seaford, 2004, p. 45.
32 Seaford, 2004, p. 68.
33 Seaford, 2004, p. 69.
34 Seaford, 2004, p. 74.
35 Seaford, 2004, p. 73.
36 Seaford, 2004, p. 74.
37 Hudson, Michael. 2004, 'The Archaeology of Money: Debt versus Barter Theories of Money's Origins', in R. Wray (Ed.), *Credit and State Theories of Money: The Contribution of A. Mitchell Innes*, Cheltenham: Edward Elgar, pp. 99–127.
38 Seaford, 2004, p. 77.
39 Seaford, 2004, p. 74.
40 Seaford, 2004, pp. 86–7.
41 Seaford, 2004, p.73. Original emphasis.
42 On the evolution of societies and economies, see Spread, 2016, Chapter 1: Support-bargaining and the evolution of human societies.
43 Malinowski, Bronislaw, 1920, 'Kula: The Circulating Exchange of Valuables in the Archipelagoes of Eastern New Guinea', *Man*, Vol. 20, July, pp. 97–105.
44 Malinowski, Bronislaw, 1921, 'The Primitive Economics of the Trobriand Islanders', *The Economic Journal*, Vol. 31, No. 121, pp. 1–16, p. 15.
45 Malinowski, 1921, pp. 3–5.
46 Malinowski, 1921, p. 8.
47 Malinowski, 1921, p. 8.
48 Malinowski, 1921, p. 8.
49 Malinowski, 1921, p. 9.
50 Malinowski, 1921, pp. 11–12.
51 Malinowski, 1921, p. 11.
52 Malinowski, 1921, p. 13.
53 Malinowski, 1921, p. 14.
54 Malinowski, 1921, p. 13.
55 Malinowski, 1920, p. 98.
56 Malinowski, 1920, p. 98–9.
57 Malinowski, 1920, p. 98. For further description of the *Kula* see Malinowski, Bronislaw, 2002/1922, *Argonauts of the Western Pacific: An Account of Native Enterprise and Adventure in the Archipelagoes of Melanesian New Guinea*, London: Routledge, pp. 81–104. First published 1922.
58 Malinowski, 1920, pp. 103–4.

59 Malinowski, 1920, pp. 98,105.
60 Malinowski, 1920, p. 105.
61 Malinowski, 1921, p. 8.
62 Malinowski, 1922, p. 189.
63 Malinowski, 1921, p. 100.
64 Malinowski, 1922, p. 515.
65 Malinowski, 1922, p. 516.
66 Malinowski, 1922, p. 516.
67 Malinowski, 1922, p. 175.
68 Malinowski, 1922, p. 268.
69 Gregory, C. A., 1997, *Savage Money: The Anthropology and Politics of Commodity Exchange*, Amsterdam: Harwood Academic Publishers, p. 45.

References

Darwin, Charles, 2004/1871, *The Descent of Man, and Selection in Relation to Sex*, London: Penguin, pp. 152, 155–8. First published 1871.

Gregory, C. A., 1997, *Savage Money: The Anthropology and Politics of Commodity Exchange*, Amsterdam: Harwood Academic Publishers

Heichelheim, Fritz, 1958, 1964, 1970, *An Ancient Economic History, from the Palaeolithic Age to the Migrations of the Germanic, Slavic and Arabic Nations*, Trans. Joyce Stevens, Leiden: A. W. Sijthoff, Vol. 1, 1958; Vol. 2, 1964; Vol. 3, 1970. First published 1938.

Hudson, Michael, 2004, 'The Archaeology of Money: Debt versus Barter Theories of Money's Origins', in R. Wray (Ed.), *Credit and State Theories of Money: The Contribution of A. Mitchell Innes*, Cheltenham: Edward Elgar, pp. 99–127.

MacDonald, James, 2006, *A Free Nation Deep in Debt: The Financial Roots of Democracy*, Princeton and Oxford: Princeton University Press.

Malinowski, Bronislaw, 1920, 'Kula: The Circulating Exchange of Valuables in the Archipelagoes of Eastern New Guinea', *Man*, Vol. 20, July, pp. 97–105.

Malinowski, Bronislaw, 1921, 'The Primitive Economics of the Trobriand Islanders', *The Economic Journal*, Vol. 31, No. 121, pp. 1–16.

Malinowski, Bronislaw, 2002/1922, *Argonauts of the Western Pacific: An Account of Native Enterprise and Adventure in the Archipelagoes of Melanesian New Guinea*, London: Routledge. First published 1922.

Marx, Karl and Engels, Friedrich, 2005/1848, *Manifesto of the Communist Party*, 1888 Edition, Project Gutenberg, Kindle Edition. First published 1848.

Schaps, David M., 2004, *The Invention of Coinage and the Monetization of Ancient Greece*, Ann Arbor: University of Michigan Press, Kindle Edition.

Seaford, Richard, 2004, *Money and the Early Greek Mind*, Cambridge: Cambridge University Press.

Spread, Patrick, 2008, *Support-Bargaining: The Mechanics of Democracy Revealed*, Sussex: Book Guild.

Spread, Patrick, 2013, *Support-Bargaining, Economics and Society: A Social Species*, London: Routledge.

Spread, Patrick, 2016, 'Companies and Markets: Economic Theories of the Firm and a Concept of Companies as Bargaining Agencies', *Cambridge Journal of Economics*, Vol. 40, No. 3, pp. 727–753.

Spread, Patrick, 2016, *The Evolution of Economies: Money-Bargaining, Economic Change and Industrial Revolution*, London and New York: Routledge.
Spread, Patrick, 2019b, *A Starter on Support-Bargaining and Money-Bargaining in Twenty-Eight Digestible Bites*, London: Palgrave Macmillan.
Wray, R. (Ed.), 2004, *Credit and State Theories of Money: The Contribution of A. Mitchell Innes*, Cheltenham: Edward Elgar.

3 Support and the Organisation of Faith

The exercise of violence on any significant scale involves the formation of groups through support-bargaining. Groups, whether tribes, factions or nations, form for the advance of shared interests, including defence of territory. But support assembles with similar spontaneity around beliefs in the role of supernatural beings in controlling the affairs of human societies. Such beliefs very often constitute 'vital interests' which people see as non-negotiable, which they will fight to defend. The beliefs are sustained by the intensity of support for them in their supporting groups. Adherents attach little importance to empirical evidence for their validity; observations are selected and interpreted in accordance with their preconceptions. Adverse empirical evidence is neutralised as misconceptions arising from a lack of the vision that comes with true belief. Properly understood, all is consistent, though such understanding is exclusively that of supernatural beings. Extensive evidence in 'anecdotal' form – parables, stories, myths, revelations, miracles – suffices as authentication of the control exercised by the deities. The beliefs tend to be specific to particular societies, so that within a society there may be little or no challenge to the prevalent belief. India and Pakistan split on independence in 1947 into a Muslim Pakistan and a Hindu India. It is easier to sustain supernatural beliefs of a particular kind when no one questions their veracity. That different societies hold different and incompatible beliefs with similar conviction is not regarded as evidence calling into question the validity of all beliefs. The support generated within each group makes all believe that their own is the one true faith.

The impulse to adopt religious beliefs can be seen as arising from the individual sense of insecurity and consequent impulse to seek support. It is the same impulse described in Chapter 1 that causes people to engage in support-bargaining. They find that the support of human associates falls short of what they crave. Associates prove to be fickle, disloyal, unreliable and sparing in their love. People then invent supernatural sources of support that will look after them. The deities are set up as participants in a support-bargaining process with humans. They provide succour in times of trouble and can direct events in accordance with the interests of their adherents. In return they are understood as requiring certain behaviour, including worship, material offerings and conformity to instructions regarding personal conduct. There is no possible

DOI: 10.4324/9781003313472-5

way of knowing what the requirements of a supernatural being would be, so the attributed requirements can only be fabrications of human minds, and reflections of the fears and aspirations of human minds. Faith involves participation in support-bargaining systems created within human minds to offset a sense of insecurity and satisfy a craving for support.

Religious groups form on the basis of a need for supernatural support, but they also actively provide the human support that is necessary to all. Religious groups at a local level are usually welcoming, friendly and helpful to their members, giving reassurance and encouragement to each other. Support derived in imagination from the attentions of supernatural beings created by group teaching is supplemented by the actual human support forthcoming within the group. The more outrageous the beliefs seem to outsiders, the more solidarity required of those insiders who maintain the faith, and the more dependent each becomes on the reassuring support of their associates. 'Martyrs' who died in defence of their faith are presented as examples of the strength of support that is expected of the faithful.

With support thus assembled, the way is open for its direction for advance of various interests not specifically related to the deities but readily assigned to their oversight. Those that can harness to themselves the support of a large religious group in a society, preferably the dominant religious group of their society, can advance their own interests in that society. Secular rulers around the world have always sought to ensure that they either control or have the support of the dominant religious group. European history records incessant friction between churches and monarchs as the latter sought freedom of action unconstrained by behavioural requirements of the deity, in the form of moral obligations. Historians and anthropologists describe the societies of Mesopotamia and the Near East in ancient times as ruled from 'temples' and 'palaces.' Ancient Egyptian society was dominated by Pharaohs and priests. The Mayans of Central America have left testimony to the importance of religious faith in their culture in the ruins of great pyramids. The remains of temples, pyramids and fortresses around the world suggest the joint exercise of governance, however fractious, by secular and religious leaders from the earliest times.

Religious groups invariably ensure that all children born to group members are initiated into the group through intensive instruction in the tenets of the faith. The great majority of members of faith groups follow the faith in which they were initiated and instructed as children. The beliefs take on an incontestable status that arises from association with early parental and communal care. People are loyal to their faith group as they are loyal to their parents. Faith groups in many parts of the world were responsible for the establishment of schools for the instruction of children in the ways of the faith. Christian faith-based institutions later played a major role in the extensive secular education systems of modern times. Schools of religious foundation, bearing still the names of saints, play a major part in modern education systems in Christian countries. Madrassas still instruct Muslim children in the tenets of their faith.

In Europe, Christian teaching and Christian institutions have provided comfort and support for countless ordinary people amidst the hardships of their lives. Countless priests have dedicated their lives to the support of others. Deprived of the most basic material comfort, many people have been lifted in spirit by affirmations of a caring deity and the assurance of happiness in an afterlife. At a local level, the shared certainty of god and salvation, communal worship, familiar texts and stories, and 'God bless you,' have integrated the humblest people in their communities.

Yet on a broader stage, such teaching and institutions have maintained the subordination of people to the advantage of ascendant groups. The need to maintain order by threats of violence, or the actual exercise of violence, is diminished if those most likely to create disorder can be persuaded that their circumstances accord with the will of supernatural powers, and that those same supernatural powers will see that they are recompensed if they show appropriate faith, humility and obedience. If the ruler of a society is appointed by the acknowledged deity, there is every reason for obedience. Faith groups have been important buttresses of civil power. The support that sustains faith groups has been universally applied to the maintenance of civil power. Human credulity and the craving for support have been used, whether the users acknowledged it to themselves or not, to facilitate the imposition of government. The linkage is sharply apparent in the way Christian missionaries unwittingly facilitated the subordination of people in less developed societies to the rule of colonising powers.

People affiliated to religious groups feel they receive the support of the supernatural beings recognised in their group. But the price they pay can be high. The deities are often portrayed as highly demanding and even bloodthirsty. The gods may exact vengeance in brutal forms. They may demand bloody sacrifices of animals and even in some cases of human beings. Those who transgress against the teachings of their group may be subject to torture or execution. Similar brutality is apparent in the secular conduct of human beings, but in the religious context it can contrast sharply with qualities of compassion and love that are presented, especially to children, as the definitive characteristics of their deities. Religion has endorsed inclinations of secular rulers to cruelty and inhumanity. These darker characteristics of deities are of necessity, as noted above, reflections of the impulses of human minds. Only the adherents of particular faiths will understand such characteristics as being qualities of entities existing independently of human thought.

The soft element in the teaching of religious groups elevates social ideals of peace, compassion and social harmony. Such groups might be expected to provide the sort of ideological commitment to social harmony that was sought through the *Kula* links around the Trobriand Islands. But other teachings of faith groups, and their history, are suffused with hatred and violence. Religious groups have clashed across history. Christians launched crusades against Muslims in the 'Holy Land.' After the Reformation in Europe, the Roman Catholic Church fought protestant churches over doctrinal issues and ascendancy in different territories. Divine origin of teaching gives the adherents of different faiths a sense of certainty and with it an obligation to concede nothing to those expressing different ideas. Any default is an offence to the divinities, and subject to their divine retribution. Adherents have formed groups of great rigidity in their theological teaching, their prescriptions for social conduct, and in their hostility to outsiders. In violent times, which are most times in human history, such steadfastness has been regarded as supremely virtuous, and has been assiduously cultivated. It is the sort of commitment honoured in the Homeric 'warrior code.'

But in societies concerned to minimise violent conflict by accommodating different interests, the rigidity is disadvantageous to the point of incompatibility. Faith groups are in large measure, in their raw state, incompatible with the support-bargaining systems, or 'democratic' societies, in which movements of support between groups result in accommodation of many interests, though subjecting most to some degree of compromise. Movements of support arise from changes in information available. The aversion of faith groups to any information not recognised in their teaching, particularly if challenging to their teaching, means that movements of support are suppressed. Some nations determined that religious groups in positions of secular power would impede the development of support-bargaining systems for government. Separation of church and state has been seen as important to freedom of religious choice and essential to the operation of democracy. The First Amendment to the Constitution of the United States guarantees freedom of religion and prohibits any laws that establish a national religion. The French Revolution rounded on the power of the Catholic Church, taking extreme anti-clerical measures. The Civil Constitution of the Clergy, a law passed in 1790, placed the Church under the control of the revolutionary government established the previous year.[1] The French state remained secular by law, though tolerant of extensive Church influence.

Religious Organisation

Religious groups gain much of their effectiveness from the rigidity inherent in the nature of their beliefs, but the projection of group bargaining strength requires the focus that derives from organisation. It was seen in Chapter 2 that requirements for violence provided an early impulse to organisation of groups. A further early impulse lay in the formation of religious groups. Religious leaders recognised the power that was within their grasp if they could properly harness the support their teaching attracted. Considering the advantages of supplementing support for secular causes with the intense support connected with supernatural beliefs, the impulses to military organisation and organisation of faith groups would have been interlinked. Physical strength allied to powerful motivation is a potent mix. If an organised military and an organised faith group made common cause, the combined force could dominate a society, and potentially its neighbours as well, unless the neighbours looked to their own organisation. 'Soldiers of God' can be a fearsome prospect.

The most successful of the Christian churches is the Roman Catholic Church, whose membership constitutes about half of all Christians. Protestants, in many different denominations, constitute nearly 40 per cent of Christians.[2] The authority of the Pope, the head of the Roman Catholic Church, is understood as deriving from that of St. Peter, the leading apostle of Jesus Christ. The doctrine of 'papal infallibility' gives the Pope authority to determine the focal doctrinal tenets of the Church, and a large hierarchical bureaucracy gives him the means of concerted pursuit of his purpose. The Pope heads the Roman Curia, with responsibilities allocated like those of government departments. He appoints a College of Cardinals to advise him and to elect a new Pope when necessary. Archbishops, Bishops and Priests mainly have territorial responsibilities in the hierarchy.[3] The Catholic hierarchy has a more collegiate approach to decision-making than the command hierarchies of military organisations; the difference easily related to the temporal situations in which the two organisations commonly expect to operate.

The supernatural beings created as the foci of religious groups are invariably understood as requiring 'offerings' as a condition of their benevolence to humans. These offerings provide the second essential of organisation – finance. The need for finance is awkward for many religious organisations. *The Holy Bible*, the sacred book of Christianity, includes the comment that, 'the love of money is the root of all evil.'[4] People should do what is needed, and what they have capacity to do, from commitment to the cause, not for love of payment. Religious teaching generally deplores the pursuit of material riches, so that the requirements of religious organisations for funds can seem at variance with their own teaching. The offerings most doctrinally acceptable are donations such as those to 'mendicant' friars or to monks vowed to poverty and dependence on charitable offerings – they apparently provide no more than the most basic material necessities. But religious organisations of any size have to sustain substantial hierarchies whose constituent officials have to be paid at least sufficient to sustain the energy to work and engage with their communities. Numerous ancillary staff are required to administer church property and the logistics of church activities. Religious organisations have to engage in money-bargaining adjunctive to their support-bargaining. 'Sufficient' is a matter of judgement. Some religious organisations have found it necessary to project a sense of material power alongside their spiritual power. Large budgets have been used to ensure that their material status is commensurate with the support they derive from doctrinal commitments. Christian bishops live in 'palaces.' Even priests in the Church of England, in charge of parishes, near the bottom of the organisational hierarchy, could mostly expect to reside in substantial vicarages, even if their monetary incomes were small. An imposing residence gave them the status to maintain social relations with the squire and other local dignitaries.

Diarmaid MacCulloch in *A History of Christianity* records the introduction of tithes by the Catholic Church, following the transformation of farming production in Western Europe around 1000 AD and the introduction of parishes as the basis of pastoral care. MacCulloch writes:

> As parishes were organized, it became apparent that there were new sources of wealth for churchmen as well as for secular landlords. The parish system covering the countryside gave the Church the chance to tax the new farming resources of Europe by demanding from its farmer-parishioners a scriptural tenth of agricultural produce, the tithe. Tithe was provided by many more than the old aristocratic elite, and was another motive for extending the Church's pastoral concern much more widely.[5]

The passage suggests that rising agricultural incomes offered opportunities for new revenues and an expansion of influence, as distinct from the church acquiring revenues necessary to its already established work. Revenue might be the primary impulse, rather than merely needed for pastoral care of communities. Tithes were available as a consequence of agricultural improvements, and the church's mission was expanded to take advantage of them. As with the *Kula* round described by Malinowski, an 'economic undertow' sometimes threatens to become the main stream.

The passage suggests also a strategic manoeuvre by the mediaeval church to reduce its financial dependence on the aristocratic landowners who had financed the church and, because of that, had been able to shape its teaching and behaviour. Tithes left the church financially beholden to a much larger number of people. Such a large number, in the absence of any organisation specifically concerned with the advance of its interests, would find it difficult to exercise any concerted influence on the activities of the church. Diversifying its sources of finance strengthened the authority of the Church hierarchy.

The above quotation continues immediately as follows:

> This had a large number of consequences, not least in the church's attitude to sin. It certainly did not denounce as sinful the movement to enserf a large section of the population, any more than it had challenged slavery in the ancient world; that was hardly surprising, since very often great monasteries like Cluny were in the forefront of imposing serfdom on their tenants.

The passage suggests the commitment of the Church to advance of its material interests even at the expense of the well-being of the poor whose care was ostensibly a primary obligation. The Church itself, teacher of moral probity, was ready to impose serfdom on its people for its own material advantage. Some nominally religious foundations might be regarded as unambiguously crossing the line separating primary purpose in the advance of Christian principle and primary purpose in generating revenues.

The quotation further continues:

> But the clergy also became more alert to the possibilities of sin that wealth produced, and sought to protect their people from the consequences. It was during the twelfth century that avarice and the taking of interest on money (usury) became major themes for the church's moralizing alongside the most basic of human sins, pride.

The temptations of the Church itself made it aware of the temptations facing its people, and led to doctrinal innovation that influenced the evolution of economic enterprise and created tensions within Western society. 'Usury,' lending at interest, was the primary means by which time disparities between revenues and expenditures could be accommodated. If good Christians could not engage in usury, the practice had to be undertaken by non-Christians. The Jews were restricted in the range of activities they were permitted to undertake, so the opportunity to provide credit was readily taken up. Lending at interest inevitably involves conflict between creditors and debtors. The Jews attracted social odium as usurers and became isolated in European society as enemies of conscientious Christians. The rigidity of groups based on religious belief was intensified. Jews became the pariahs of Western society, held responsible for many social misfortunes and persecuted. The common animosity against Jews in Europe played a part in making possible the mass murder of Jews in Nazi Germany.

MacCulloch describes also the use of the concept of Purgatory to expand the revenues of the Church. Purgatory was a middle stage between Heaven and Hell. People could shorten the time of their deceased relatives in Purgatory and smooth their subsequent entry into Heaven by commissioning masses from priests.[6] The purchase of 'indulgences' was a further means by which time in Purgatory could be abbreviated. Doctrine seems to have been created for the raising of revenues. MacCulloch writes of indulgences:

> There were good reasons to cherish indulgences and their sale; they were very useful for fund-raising for good causes, such as the rebuilding of churches or the support of the charitable homes for the elderly and infirm called hospitals (themselves a part of the Purgatory industry, since their grateful inmates were expected to pass their time praying for the welfare of the souls of their benefactors). Indulgences were as ubiquitous as the modern lottery ticket…'[7]

The 'good causes' have become vehicles for the raising of funds, rather than primary commitments that require budgetary support. Even when a 'cause' is conspicuously the primary commitment, it is not a pastoral cause, but a means of displaying the wealth and power of the Church through the splendour of its edifices. Indulgences were marketed with particular vigour to raise funds for the construction of St Peter's Basilica in Rome. The sales were particularly resented in Germany, where they aroused the ire of Martin Luther and prompted his doctrinal assault on the Catholic Church.[8]

In the nineteenth century the financial needs of the Vatican were more plainly related to the maintenance of its spiritual ministry. MacCulloch notes that the introduction, or revival, since it had been a mediaeval tradition, of 'Peter's Pence' in 1871 was comparable in financial importance to the introduction of tithes. It followed the loss of the Papal States and the refusal of Pius IX, as a matter of principle, to accept monetary compensation from the Italian government for their loss.[9] 'Peter's Pence' was given directly to the Vatican, while other offerings were made to parishes and dioceses.

The modern financial circumstances of the Catholic Church have their origins in the Lateran Treaty of 1929 which established the Vatican State and provided a large sum of money in compensation for the earlier losses of land. In the hands of Bernardino Nogara this money was invested profitably, though not necessarily ethically, in various enterprises, earning the Church, from a Soviet journalist, endorsed by MacCulloch, the title of 'the greatest financial trust in the world.'[10]

The 'evil' attaching to money in Christian scripture has made churches reluctant to associate their work with money, so that they tend to be secretive about financial matters.[11] MacCulloch's history is of amazing scope, but while he refers to financial events of particular significance, there is no systematic account of the part played by finance and budgeting in the building by Christian organisations of the largest following of any religion. The custom of discretion over financial matters seems to influence even MacCulloch. Or it may be that the necessary information has been so effectively concealed that no satisfactory account of the evolution and influence of budgets is feasible. The Christian way of thinking does not prompt attention to monetary matters. But given the role of the churches, their budgetary fortunes are an essential part of their histories and the histories of the states in which they have operated. 'Offerings' included large amounts of land through wills. It was noted above that land confers power and wealth in agricultural communities, and the churches and their monasteries were major landowners, amassing great wealth. In the mediaeval period in England appointments to lucrative ecclesiastical posts were part of the patronage through which monarchs maintained their rule. While Christian teaching tends to divert attention from financial matters, the importance of organisation in support-bargaining and money-bargaining necessarily draws attention to the role of finance in churches and all other organisations.

Religious organisations were the main employers of the learned. Some indication of the economic significance of clergy in Britain in the seventeenth century, though not inclusive of 'associated services,' is provided by Gregory King's compilation of occupations and incomes relating to 1688. At that time, according to his tentative estimates, there were 10,000 families headed by clergymen, accounting for 0.9 per cent of the population, on a level of affluence similar to that of farmers, artisans and shopkeepers. For comparison, there were 9,000 families of naval and military officers, comprising 0.7 per cent of the population, with about double the annual family incomes of the clergy.[12] As might be expected, the military outgunned the churches in affluence, even if they were defeated in numerical strength.

The crucial turning point in the fortunes of the Christian church might have been as much financial as spiritual. According to MacCulloch, the Emperor Constantine, after becoming emperor with, as he supposed, the support of the Christian god, reckoned, 'his side of the bargain was to turn Christians from a harried, suppressed cult, accused of ruining the empire, into the most favoured and privileged of all Roman religions.' With the adoption of Christianity by the Emperor, it would no longer be potentially subversive to make 'offerings' to the Christian church; on the contrary, they would be seen as expressions of loyal support for the Emperor, and hence good investments for the future. It never hurts to contribute to the ruler's favourite charity. With those revenues, the Christian church would have the budget to embark seriously on its mission.

John Pollard summarises the development of Vatican finances from the mid-nineteenth century to the mid-twentieth century in fairly dramatic terms:

> The Vatican's financial journey from being based on a localised feudal/territorial state, heavily fiscally dependent on the revenue from a landed economy of an essentially rural agrarian society, to being a capitalist 'holding company' with Italian-wide and world-wide financial interests parallels the rise of the modern papacy as we know it and in part helps to explain that development.[13]

The comment implies not simply that finance was important to fulfilment of the focal purpose of the Catholic Church, but that financial matters came close to displacing pastoral issues as the focal purpose of the Church. Certainly, they had a major impact on the way the Church developed its pastoral care and the degree to which it was able to impose its preferences on the world-wide Catholic Church. The Church was able to employ a large bureaucracy to advance its interests around the world.[14] Doctrinal matters, inescapably of pure invention, sustained only by the support of the faithful, can easily evaporate in the insistent realism of material interest.

In the later twentieth century the financial activities of the Catholic Church were extraordinary. The Vatican used its rights of diplomatic confidentiality and special taxation arrangements with the Italian government to engage in illegal financial transactions through the Institute for the Works of Religion, known as the 'Vatican Bank,' and Banco Ambrosiana, in which the Vatican Bank held shares. The chairman of Banco Ambrosiana was found hanging from scaffolding under Blackfriars Bridge in London in 1982, probably murdered. Richard Bosworth claims that because of its financial structures the Vatican is little more than a multinational company.[15]

In 2020, both the Vatican Bank and the Roman Curia were the subject of investigations by Moneyval, an organisation set up to combat money-laundering and the finance of terrorism.[16] 'Money is the root of all evil,' and the Church has been unable to resist its allure. The full verse from Timothy is: 'For the love of money is the root of all evil: which while some coveted after, they have erred from the faith, and pierced themselves through with many sorrows.' Church leaders and followers presumably feel great sorrow not only for the damage done by the transactions they engaged in, but also at the damage to the reputation of the church as guardian of spiritual values.

Religious faith has attracted great support and the communal influence that goes with extensive support. To enhance and exercise the influence arising from the support, religious groups have organised themselves, involving the establishment of hierarchies and budgets. Material interests have in some cases all but overwhelmed the spiritual purposes of religious groups. Religious organisations have been able to use the power inherent in their support to control information that circulates about their affairs. Adverse information is suppressed; those who try to propagate it are stopped. Control of the information interface gives churches freedom to pursue purposes incompatible with their proclaimed missions. Ancient societies of the Near East were governed by 'palaces' and 'temples.' The temples would have had the bargaining strength in domestic affairs attendant on the concentration of large volumes of support on the supernatural beliefs they upheld. As dominant organisations, they would operate budgets for control of their material affairs, no doubt prone, like their modern counterparts, to put material considerations from time to time above the spiritual commitments that they proclaimed as their prime purpose. People are inclined to give money to causes they see as integral to their well-being, and the recipients may exploit such propensity for purposes other than the approved causes.

Notes

1 Pollard, John F., 2005, *Money and the Rise of the Modern Papacy: Financing the Vatican, 1850–1950*, Cambridge: Cambridge University Press, p. 4.
2 Pew Research Center: Religion and Public Life. Online at: www.pewforum.org/2011/12/19/global-christianity-traditions/#defining. Accessed 27 August 2019.
3 Wikipedia contributors, 'Papal infallibility'; 'Roman Curia'; 'Hierarchy of the Catholic Church', *Wikipedia*. Accessed 18 November 2020.
4 *Holy Bible, The*, Authorised Edition, I Timothy 6, v. 10.
5 MacCulloch, Diarmaid, 2010, *A History of Christianity: The First Three Thousand Years*, London: Penguin Books, p. 369. MacCulloch's reference: Swanson, R. N., 1999, *The Twelfth-century Renaissance*, Manchester: Manchester University Press, p. 8.
6 MacCulloch, 2010, pp. 369–70.
7 MacCulloch, 2010, p. 556.
8 Pollard, 2005, p. 3.
9 MacCulloch, 2010, pp. 931–2.
10 MacCulloch, 2010, p. 937. MacCulloch's reference: Pollard, 2005, esp. 143–9, 162–7, 205 (quotation).
11 Pollard, 2005, p. 1.

12 Spread, Patrick, 2016a, *The Evolution of Economies: Money-Bargaining, Economic Change and Industrial Revolution*, London: Routledge., p. 115, Table 5.1. The table is derived from Mathias, Peter, 2001, *The First Industrial Nation: The Economic History of Britain 1700–1914*, Abingdon and New York: Routledge.

13 Pollard, 2005, p. 1.

14 Pollard, 2005, p. 1.

15 Bosworth, R., 1996, *Italy and the Wider World, 1860–1960*, London: Routledge, p. 159. Referenced by Pollard, 2005, p. 216.

16 Anon, 2020, 'A Holy Mess: Has the Vatican Cleaned up Its Finances', *The Economist*, 26 September.

References

Anon, 2020, 'A Holy Mess: Has the Vatican Cleaned up Its Finances', *The Economist*, 26 September.

Bosworth, R., 1996, *Italy and the Wider World, 1860–1960*, London: Routledge.

Holy Bible, The, Authorised Edition.

MacCulloch, Diarmaid, 2010, *A History of Christianity: The First Three Thousand Years*, London: Penguin Books.

Mathias, Peter, 2001, *The First Industrial Nation: The Economic History of Britain 1700–1914*, Abingdon and New York: Routledge.

Pew Research Center: Religion and Public Life. Online at: www.pewforum.org/2011/12/19/global-christianity-traditions/#defining. Accessed 27 August 2019.

Pollard, John F., 2005, *Money and the Rise of the Modern Papacy: Financing the Vatican, 1850–1950*, Cambridge: Cambridge University Press.

Spread, Patrick, 2016a, *The Evolution of Economies: Money-Bargaining, Economic Change and Industrial Revolution*, London: Routledge.

Swanson, R. N., 1999, *The Twelfth-century Renaissance*, Manchester: Manchester University Press.

Wikipedia contributors, 'Papal infallibility'; 'Roman Curia'; 'Hierarchy of the Catholic Church', *Wikipedia*. Accessed 18 November 2020.

4 Intellectual Support-Bargaining and Frames of Reference

Religious faith provides ready understanding of the world and its people. Instead of a mass of confusing phenomena in the natural world and strange, sometimes frightening, human behaviour, all is explained as the work of a god, or gods, or similar supernatural beings. All such phenomena are under their control and subject to their purposes. It is an understanding accessible to virtually anyone, in that it requires no great mental prowess. People are asked only to have faith, to adopt the ideas of those around them. Religious faiths provide frames of reference by which people can live their lives with tolerable intellectual security, bolstered by the support of similar-minded people around them.

The sense of 'understanding' arises from a sense of all phenomena fitting together in a unitary whole. People form groups based on a shared frame of reference. Inside a group, members confirm for each other the truth of their frame. Confidence grows within the group in the veracity of the frame and the justice of the causes it sustains. The support assembled in the formation of such groups provides a foundation for advance of their interests. This political dynamic of frames of reference means that positive efforts are made to establish frames of reference and attract support into the groups that sustain them. Religious groups have been amongst the most successful in assembling support around frames of reference, and advancing group interest by deployment of such support in political support-bargaining.

Other frames of reference have had similar impact. Academic and other 'theories' that explain various phenomena, or give understanding of them, constitute frames of reference. Theories are shaped to advance certain interests through the assembly of support in what constitute 'theory groups.' The support assembled can be transferred for political purposes. The process by which these theories and theory groups are formed is closely akin to the ways in which support is assembled for more specifically political purposes. Ideas are evaluated in groups and modified to expand the group or intensify the commitment of its members. It is a process of intellectual support-bargaining, closely associated both theoretically and practically with political support-bargaining.

This link between theory and political action has eluded many social theorists, prominent amongst them those seeking to establish how the philosophical 'Enlightenment' of the eighteenth century had such political consequences.

DOI: 10.4324/9781003313472-6

Joel Mokyr records in a footnote: 'Whether the work of intellectuals criticizing political structures from Rousseau to Marx can actually inspire political revolutions remains controversial.'[1] Mokyr describes the process through which theories become established and influence political change through an analogy with the dynamics of economic exchange. He identifies modern economic growth as the consequence of radical changes in a culture of 'beliefs, values and preferences' brought about through a 'market for ideas,'[2] led by 'cultural entrepreneurs'[3] in a 'Republic of Letters.'[4] In the market for ideas: 'people try to persuade an audience of the correctness of their beliefs and the merit of their values...'[5] In other words, they assemble support. The dynamic of exchange is right, but the bargaining counter is support.

Mokyr apparently reckons that an economic analogy to explain a key part of his cultural thesis will assemble support from economic theory groups. But early in his book he rejects the support of economists. He queries the relevance of economic theory to matters of cultural change:

> ...we must understand how culture changes and why societies have different cultures. If economists cannot contribute to this literature, they should leave it to other social scientists, but in that case they must concede much of the explanation of modern economic growth to others.[6]

He warns economists off the cultural patch, but then courts their support in his explanation of cultural change.

Jonathan Israel, in his thesis regarding the impact of the 'Radical Enlightenment,' makes a similar comment to that of Mokyr: 'In recent years, scepticism as to whether "books cause revolutions" has proved both influential and pervasive in university history teaching.'[7] Israel is similarly pressed to provide an explanation of how theory influences political practice, though the question seems fundamental to his thesis regarding the impact of the Radical Enlightenment on democracy in the West. Israel argues that without the surge of egalitarian literature from the Radical Enlightenment there would have been no 'grounding' for the surge of revolutionary ideas in North America and Europe in the late eighteenth century.[8]

It is commonly assumed that the formation of theory is directed at the identification of 'the truth' about human society, but assembly of support tends to take precedence over the pursuit of truth. That is partly because truth is elusive and in strict account unobtainable. But it is also because support determines what theory takes hold and has effect. It is also because, psychologically, we can do without truth, but we cannot do without support. The best chance of genuine pursuit of truth arises when such pursuit poses no conflict with the assembly of support – when the truth is of such importance that people will only support the pursuit of truth. The closest approach to truth derives from tests of consistency. Consistency is a matter of how phenomena are seen and interpreted, or understood, and consequently a matter itself of group support. People gain the conviction that they have encountered truth when they find all phenomena encountered consistent with their frame of reference. Those of religious faith find such conviction. Convictions are strengthened when associates confirm or support the identified truth. If no one questions the group understanding, it will be taken as truth.

But the consistency of a single frame of reference may provide the sensation of truth without adequately fulfilling the necessary tests of consistency. Consistency has to be established across different frames of reference. If people using different frames of reference understand phenomena in the same way, assent to the same interpretations, then the likelihood that the observations correspond to something more than idiosyncratic group interpretation is increased. Nevertheless, 'truth' in the strict sense, either about the world or human behaviour, is beyond reach.[9] We know only the information that our minds can deal with, so that while we are connected to a possible world beyond our minds through our senses, we can know only the information they convey to our minds.

People for the most part will not bother with such apparently pedantic scruple, but the elusiveness of truth has become a prominent issue in recent years as some political leaders have presented as fact what is plainly inconsistent with widely available evidence, and contributors to social media routinely and maliciously post misinformation. The acknowledgement that access to absolute truth is impossible seems to accord to all the freedom to say and write whatever they please. The response to critics is, 'Can you prove me wrong?' But if there is no access to absolute truth, there are still distinctions to be made between what is probably true and what is probably false. The accord of multiple sources of information provides the consistency that is the best test of truth. Misinformation is not a new phenomenon. It is surely as old as information itself. But its incidence seems to have increased markedly in public life in recent decades. Leaders say what suits them, with less heed to the obligation that used to be inculcated in all children: to 'tell the truth.' Nor do distinguished academic theorists necessarily refrain from similar indulgence.[10]

'Truth' is, in effect, displaced for the assembly of support and the advance of interests. The intellectual support-bargaining process is directed at the advancement of interest. Claims to pursuit of 'truth' signify at best a conscious and conscientious aspiration, but may be no more than what is effective in assembly of support. Nevertheless, if certain 'truths' or 'facts' can be accepted amongst all those involved in a support-bargaining process, they establish limits to a bargaining process, and may facilitate agreement on otherwise disputed matters.[11]

As with the religious frames of reference, secular theoretical frames of reference determine what is picked out as significant from the multiple phenomena open to human observation, and dictate how such phenomena are interpreted. Clearly, if a theoretical frame of reference favourable to certain interests can be established in the minds of a wide population, those certain interests will be supported and advanced. The competition for political ascendancy thus has a parallel in competition for intellectual ascendancy – competition to establish certain theories as predominant in the minds of people. If such theories can be established in the minds of children, they are likely to be the more firmly fixed and more habitually used, thus generating a propensity in the population so imbued to advance interests associated with the theory.

The 'understanding' provided through frames of reference necessarily involves simplification. The mind is required to 'understand' through a single mental 'take' on phenomena selected from the great variety that is open to observation. The frame of reference constitutes the core or skeleton of a theory; those elements held in common as fundamental by the members of the theory group. Many members of a theory group are likely to adhere to distinctive variations on the underlying theme, and these will often be disputed within the theory group. Nevertheless, it is the core frame of reference that gives the immediate sense of comprehension and becomes the focus of support. Further simplifications of a frame may be formulated with a view to facile assembly of support, extending its appeal outside the core theory group responsible for its original formulation. It is, in effect, adapted to political support-bargaining. The establishment of the frame of reference is an important part of intellectual support-bargaining, since it determines the support accruing to the group and its potential influence outside the group.

The above analysis conceives theory formation as an autonomous process, generating frames of reference or theories in accordance with the interests of the formulators. But the process is far from autonomous. The formulators are necessarily part of the societies in which they work and are involved with the political issues of their times. Their interests will very often be political interests, or linked to political interests. Hence while the support assembled around theories may be used also in the advance of political interest, the support assembled for the advance of political interest may be applied also in theory formation. Support will be most easily assembled for theories that have resonance and accord with political interests. Processes of theory formation may be institutionally set apart and shielded from political interests, but still theory formation is necessarily undertaken in a political environment. Support is the bargaining counter of both political support-bargaining and intellectual support-bargaining, and it is consequently difficult to separate the two processes in any definitive way.

The 'Frames of Reference' Idea

This use of frames of reference is well established in psychological and sociological contexts, though without the idea of political and intellectual support-bargaining it is not possible to understand fully the part they play in the dynamic of social change. Bronislaw Malinowski notes that a necessary part of the mental approach to primitive societies is the recognition that they all have different ways of looking at life and interpreting their experience: 'Every human culture gives its members a definite vision of the world, a definite zest for life.'[12] He emphasises the importance of deriving from the *Kula* custom an understanding of native *weltanschauung*, or world view. The details matter only in so far as they are used to develop the overview. He writes:

> It is in the love of the final synthesis, achieved by the assimilation and comprehension of all the items of a culture and still more in the love of the variety and independence of the various cultures that lies the test of the real worker in the true Science of Man.[13]

He presents the *Kula* customs as an inseparable whole, encompassing what people from other cultures might distinguish as social relationships, economic relationships and religious faith.[14] The idea of frames of reference is apparent also in his comment that science, 'has to analyse and classify facts in order to place them in an organic whole, to incorporate them in one of the systems in which it tries to group the various aspects of reality.'[15] 'Frames of reference' are the 'systems' within which phenomena are integrated and understood.

Muzafer Sherif describes the human pursuit of nutrition, shelter and mating as bounded by customs, traditions, values, laws, standards, etiquette and other social products. These are what he treats as 'social norms,' and his book seeks to identify how social norms are formed.[16]

In a chapter on 'The Frame of Reference in Psychological Phenomena,' Sherif describes psychological tests indicating the use of frames of reference. The psychological tests relate mainly to laboratory tests, and consequently relate mainly to tests on individuals that show how individuals make their decisions on the basis of predispositions or preconceptions. He notes that objects can seem hot or cold, heavy or light, depending on what they have immediately experienced.[17] He refers to the ambivalent picture, known as the 'Rubin vase,' that may be seen either as a vase or two faces in profile, depending largely on what the viewer is prepared to see. The alternation of perceptions influenced the Gestalt school of psychology. Gestalt psychologists emphasise the importance of 'anchoring,' the interpretation of experience by reference to an organised field.[18] Individual interpretations are invariably made by reference to what the individual has already established. 'Experience appears to depend always on *relations*.'[19] His analysis extends also to social groups. An 'anchor' that is used for reference may be a frame of reference, 'of which the most important part is the social group to which one belongs.'[20] Through social contacts people 'interiorize' social norms. 'These interiorized social norms enter as frames of reference among other factors in situations to which they are related, and thus dominate or modify the person's experience and subsequent behavior in concrete situations.'[21] Sherif notes that if a person is a member of a certain church and a certain businessman's organisation, there is a fair chance of predicting his reactions to certain situations.[22] When Swazi chiefs visited London, their abiding memory was that of policemen directing traffic with waves of their arms; the same gestures that Swazis were accustomed to use when greeting each other, and hence amongst the collection of norms that formed their frame of reference.[23] For them, the phenomenon that stood out in London was the gesture already established in their minds as part of their frame of reference.

Sherif's identification of the essential human pursuits as nutrition, shelter and mating means that his quest to identify the origins of social norms is jeopardised from the start. Humans seek first of all their security, their self-preservation, and for their security they seek support, engage in the support-bargaining that forms groups.[24] He describes psychologists as conceiving individual psychology in opposition to social psychology, and comments, 'If there is ever to be a psychology attaining scientific generality and comprehensiveness in its principles, it will furnish us with general principles that will apply equally to the individual in any situation, individual or social.' Sherif makes the link between individual use of references or 'anchors' and the social expression of common norms a matter of 'internalizing.' The basic dynamic of support-bargaining, as described in Chapter 1, lies in the conflict and cooperation of individuals and their associates. Support-bargaining identifies the link between individual and group psychology. The existence and importance of frames of reference is thus established as a consequence of strong human instincts for self-preservation and communal security.

Erving Goffman stresses the role of 'frames' in generating understanding. In his Introduction he states: 'My aim is to try to isolate some of the basic frameworks of understanding available in our society for making sense out of events and to analyze the special vulnerabilities to which these frames of reference are subject.'[25] He is concerned with the organisation of individual experience, not the organisation of society: 'This book is about the organization of experience – something that an individual actor can take into his mind – and not the organization of society.'[26] He maintains the individual emphasis, even an emphasis on more off-beat individual behaviour, but can still note that: 'the primary frameworks of a particular social group constitute a central element of its culture.'[27] Goffman applies 'frame analysis' in a wide range of circumstances, from the important to the trivial, with interaction of different frames. But the preoccupation with the individual psychology of frames distances his analysis from the concept of frames of reference that is part of support-bargaining. Goffman did not elide his concept of individual frames with that of social frames, as did Sherif. Goffman's analysis is peripheral to the much more socially significant role of frames apparent in the dynamic of intellectual support-bargaining.[28] But one point is notable: the frame of reference is taken in the present context as something wide-reaching and substantially constructed, like economic theory or socialism, but much less complex constructs can serve at least as kin to frames of reference, as the spring of perception and interest, such as discourtesy in a shop or a sore toe.

The idea of a frame of reference, in the terminology of the 'paradigm,' gained great prominence through Thomas Kuhn's extension of it to natural scientific theory formation.[29] In Kuhn's account, paradigms are very strongly associated with a group – the 'scientific community' shares a paradigm and is defined by its paradigm. That paradigms, or frames of reference, could be used by natural scientists, normally considered to be 'objective,' gave them greater standing than arose from their conception in social science. Natural scientists had 'a way of looking at things' that influenced their investigations. That was merely 'bias' in social scientists. Paradigm change, as described by Kuhn, occurs as a result of the build-up of anomalies to an existing paradigm. Phenomena cannot be understood, interpreted or reconciled with the existing paradigm and a 'scientific revolution' occurs, introducing a new paradigm that better explains the anomalous observations. The Copernican revolution, the Newtonian revolution and the displacement of Newtonian physics by quantum mechanics and general relatively are the archetypal paradigm changes of physical science.[30]

The absence of the idea of support-bargaining is as problematic to Kuhn's analysis as it is to Goffman's. Kuhn cannot explain the relationship of scientists to their paradigm. Scientists, like everyone else, want to be recognised by their associates as valuable to their group. They seek support. Of necessity, support is most easily assembled by conforming to group expectations, the received opinion within the group. Hence a received paradigm becomes established within a scientific community, and is defended as best is possible against anomalies arising from information gathered through empirical observation. Efforts are made to explain away the anomalies until some individual, a 'non-conformist,' one of the 'awkward squad,' takes a quite different approach and proposes a different way of understanding the phenomena. The fundamental dynamic of support-bargaining is the conflict between individuals and their associates for advance of their interests. For the most part, the group is ascendant over ordinary individuals. But an individual exceptionally endowed with skills, such as skills of enquiry, experiment and intellectual synthesis, recognised as of particular value to the group, can turn the group to his or her point of view. A violent group will support great fighters like Alexander and Napoleon; a scientific group will support great scientists like Newton and Einstein. Natural science is 'special' amongst theory groups in that it deals with material things, or things with material associations, that lend themselves to replicative empirical testing. Information can be derived about the behaviour of materials from replicative empirical testing that is minimally affected by the non-truth interests of testers. Such 'facts' gain acceptance in the theory group. Such testing is not so easily conducted in the social sciences, so that accepted 'facts' are not so readily established and the requirement for authentication shifts by default to assembly of support in the process of intellectual support-bargaining.[31]

Theories, Frames and Situations

Neoclassical economic theory was created in the late-nineteenth century with the ambition to eliminate the 'bias' that was apparent in social science and give economics something of the 'objectivity' that was accorded the natural sciences. In physics, mathematics had revealed remarkable facts about the physical world, and given physical science distinctive status as a means of reaching beyond the subjectivity of human minds to reveal something like eternal truths. Economists envisaged that by adopting mathematical codification for the exposition of their theory they would acquire similar status.

Neoclassical theory was born of such high purpose, and became the mainstream of microeconomic theory. The model was formulated by economists of different nationalities, though Leon Walras, a Frenchman, is the acknowledged instigator.[32] The high hopes for objectivity rested in part on the recognition that economics deals with material phenomena, like sacks of grain, grinding wheels and locomotives. Their qualities, including their existence itself outside human minds, were hardly open to question. They could be counted. For these reasons, mathematical codification seemed promising. However, economics involved human beings, whose idiosyncrasies were difficult to tie down in mathematical codification. Even the idea that humans derive their interests and values from their situations is difficult to model in mathematical terms, and becomes virtually impossible when it is recognised that concepts of situation are shaped by social influences. If economics was to have the objectivity of mathematics, then it would have to be constrained to the sort of phenomena that were suited to mathematical codification, or could be plausibly understood in such form. Hence neoclassical economic theory was developed with an array of assumptions that positively distort economic processes to permit mathematical codification. The major stumbling block of humanity was accommodated by an assumption of rationality. Humans would do whatever was necessary to reach the objectives established for the model – the maximisation of output and incomes. 'Economic man' acts with predictable rationality to reach the established objectives. 'Reason' was the Enlightenment ideal, so that the assumption of a rational 'economic man' would repel only those who had not been enlightened. This reduction of mankind to the rational precluded any idea that human interests might be dependent on human situations, still less situations that depended on opinions of associates. 'Economic man' acted and thought independently of the group.

The formulation of the model means also that settlements are immediate. There are no time disparities, and consequently there is no concept of budgeting to accommodate time disparities. Credit and savings for budgetary accommodation of time disparities are not required. Adam Smith's initial account of a model involving natural prices was an attempt to demonstrate that individual pursuit of material advantage was conducive to the well-being of society. His 'natural price' model involved no time disparities. Smith's account of the emergence of money from barter similarly portrayed transactions as being completed instantaneously. Hence the formulators of the neoclassical model had no difficulty in assuming that the transactions of the model were completed immediately. Smith's idea that the free play of 'natural prices' would be conducive to the well-being of society was apparently vindicated when the mathematical model, in its most basic form, was revealed to generate an 'optimal allocation of resources.' There seemed a remarkable harmony of natural science, mathematical precision, moral integrity and individual freedom. Those using religious frames of reference saw evidence of supernatural design.

What economists produced, however, under the guise of disinterested, unbiased and objective theory, was a frame of reference. As a frame of reference, it assembled support. Such support transferred readily into political support-bargaining. Being derived from academic institutions, it provided a dependable volume of 'responsible' support for the efficacy, in terms of social advance, of policies of individual freedom, free enterprise and minimal government regulation of economic affairs.

The mainstream economic model has provided a foundation for more specifically political ideologies designed to assemble support in the political support-bargaining process that determines government. The process involves constant efforts of rival parties to establish their understanding of 'the state of the nation' as the nationally accepted understanding, with the consequences that their interests gain support, their party is elected, and their policies are implemented. They try to establish frames of reference, derived from more theoretical expositions, that will have the practical consequences of drawing people to their understanding of the social situation and the actions necessary to its improvement. Parties of the right argue that their society is flourishing under freedom of individual enterprise that generates employment and incomes across society, generating also tax revenue for government that enables it to provide the infrastructure necessary to business enterprise and the health, education and other services that are so important to the well-being of people.

Such frames of reference fulfil the 'anchorage' function recognised as psychologically essential. They are analogous to the 'situations' proposed in Chapter 1 as the references by which individuals identify their interests and needs. Both frames of reference and 'situations' are formulated by reference to group support and group interests, though the latter, presented in the context of economic preferences, has more of an individual emphasis.

It is possible that the development of a 'mainstream' institutionalised economics after the Second World War based on the neoclassical mathematical model of economic behaviour was given impetus by the particular situation at that time. With the emergence of a 'Cold War' between the West and the Soviet Union, Senator Joseph McCarthy led a House Un-American Activities Committee in the early 1950s designed to root out communist subversion. The approach was aggressive and intimidating. Many economists may have instinctively favoured a mathematical model broadly supportive of patriotic positions as offering greater political security than any that might have suggested left-leaning positions. The suggestion is unflattering to economists, but it at least helps to explain the adoption of a model that is so far removed from actual economic practice. The survival of such theory into more tolerant times can be explained as the consequence of the career advantages to be derived from membership of a dominant institutionalised theory group. As noted above, support assembled around political interests can be utilised also in the formulation of theory. In the Soviet Union, theory making was confined to elaboration of the Marxist–Leninist theory by which the regime justified its rule. There is still a tendency to sideline all economists who do not at least pay lip service to the mainstream model as 'lefties.'

The idea of the frame of reference extends further. Ordinary people need 'anchorages' beyond what is necessary merely for economic selection. They have to make decisions or express preferences over a great range of family, marital, social, political, educational, health, entertainment and other issues. They use what might be conceived as a 'common frame of reference,' the sort of 'common theory' that commands support across a wide range of ordinary people. It constitutes their 'culture.'[33]

'Theory' is generally thought of as formulated by people of unusual intelligence in institutions of higher education established for the purpose. But in the understanding of intellectual support-bargaining, theory is a matter of the accumulation of support for certain understandings of phenomena. In that context, it becomes clear that there is a 'common theory,' sustained by the support of ordinary people, for the conduct of their everyday lives.[34] The idea of a common theory is apparent in Douglass North: 'But while we think of our everyday lives as guided by "common sense," such knowledge is at base theoretical.'[35]

Common theory, or a common frame of reference, tells people that they live under the constraint of time; that they are confined to one place at any one time; that acting agreeably to others is likely to elicit an agreeable response; that insulting others is likely to elicit insults in return; that the sight of a tree means that a tree exists in the place where it is seen, independently of the mind that registers it; that money is needed for food, shelter and clothing; that it is necessary to ensure circumstances, such as employment, by which money can be acquired; that people manipulate information for their own advantage, and may tell lies; that the sun, moon and stars move predictably in the sky.

For nearly all societies, common theory includes a notion that supernatural beings in some form oversee the affairs of humans, and much time and effort have to be spent in ensuring their favourable disposition to humanity. Punishment awaits those who fail to perform the appropriate rituals. Common theory thus connects with what might be termed 'high theory,' the sort of theory developed in socially isolated institutions of learning.

'High theory' can for the most part be recognised as dealing with issues that are in their inception concerns of common theory. 'High theory' has grown out of common theory, though elements may be absorbed back into common theory. 'High theory' is inescapably connected with common theory, since it is of necessity formulated in language that embodies understanding of common theory. 'High theory' always makes reference to common theory, even when it might be thought most distant from it. Early 'high theory' was mostly devoted to discerning more clearly the characteristics of the supernatural beings that feature in common theory. Ready acceptance in common theory of ideas of supernatural control made possible the elaboration of the qualities of supernatural beings in 'high theory,' without the 'high theory' becoming irrelevant. Other 'high theory' has not avoided that fate. *The Economist* newspaper once remarked that, 'In the popular mind, economics is bunk…'[36]

Socialism, Polanyi and Economic Anthropologists

Mainstream economic theory has received extensive support, intellectual and political, from those on the right of the political spectrum. It has not, however, carried everyone away. The plight of those less able to come to terms with industrial society has also exercised minds. Individual freedom involving mistreatment of employees and disregard for the impact of business activities on society as a whole raises support for greater communal control of individual activity. Ideas of socialism and communism, based on the ascendancy of communal interest, have assembled large volumes of support, so that societies in the West have developed on a theoretical basis of both economic and socialist theory. They have developed as support-bargaining societies, the divisions sharply apparent in terms of the interests of individuals and the interests of the group that are the fundamental contention of support-bargaining.

While on the right of the political spectrum, concepts of socio-political situation emphasising the advantages of individual freedom, as portrayed above, have been presented, on the left the situation has been presented in terms of the subordination of ordinary people to the interests of a small elite that owns and controls productive capacity, with consequent disparity between the wealth of a few and the poverty of many. Social justice requires a redistribution of material wealth and greater opportunities for poor people. Only by concerted popular effort has it been possible to wrest from the elite the money needed to provide health, education and welfare services.

This contention between right and left is reflected in the contention between economists and economic anthropologists over the origins of money. Karl Polanyi is a pivotal figure. Many economic anthropologists see *The Great Transformation* as the key indictment of economic theory and a cogent expression of the idea that humans are not primarily materialistic. Material interest was historically embedded in the conduct of human relationships and should be re-embedded.[37] The resort to economic 'markets' in the nineteenth century in Europe was destructive of human societies. Economic anthropologists have agreed that Polanyi's analysis makes plain that economic theory has no application to the ancient world, where there were no 'markets.' Ancient societies operated a system of 'reciprocity and redistribution' which cultivated social relationships and met the material needs of everyone. These ideas make Polanyi a central figure in the anti-capitalist movement. *The Great Transformation* is considered further in Chapter 5.

Polanyi described his account of ancient societies as 'substantivist,' a means of meeting material requirements through social interactions, as opposed to the 'formalist' account of economic theory, involving optimisation of output. As quoted in the Introduction, David Schaps notes that:

> For the primitive economies studied by modern anthropologists, the substantivist framework has become a major and perhaps the dominant

> approach to the subject, changing permanently the terms of the discussion even by those who reject Polanyi's most dogmatic assertions. [38]

Moses Finley drew on Polanyi's theory in *The Ancient Economy*, recognised as a basic and authoritative text on the economies of ancient Greece and Rome.[39] Schaps remarks that substantivism 'has not succeeded in driving other models from the field, largely because by the classical period the existence of markets in Greece is, as Polanyi knew, incontrovertible.'[40] Much depends on what constitutes a 'market,' an issue taken up in Chapter 5. While anthropologists have divided over 'substantivism' and 'formalism,' historians have divided more between 'primitivists' and 'modernists,' the former approaching ancient economies as characterised by the predominance of subsistence household arrangements, while the latter see more parallels with modern industrial economies, with significant domestic exchange and engagement in international trade. Finley is regarded as an advocate principally of the 'primitivist' viewpoint. Schaps suggests that there is potential in the modernist approach, which has to date 'been ploughed only lightly.'[41] There is, however, Fritz Heichelheim's study, *An Ancient Economic History*, which covers economic change in a broadly conventional macroeconomic frame of reference from the Palaeolithic period through to about the sixth century AD.[42] Heichelheim's approach, first published in 1938 and published in English in 1958–70, seems to have lost traction in the modern debate. Since slaves were prominent in the workforces of the ancient world, the class-based analysis of Karl Marx has application.[43] The difficulties of analysis, and the relevance of the idea of frames of reference, are apparent in Schaps's assessment that:

> Disagreements between primitives and modernists; among substantivists, formalists, and Marxists; among historians, economists, philologists, and anthropologists made problematical the interpretation of even the simplest item of economic evidence.[44]

Support-Bargaining and Money-Bargaining as Frame of Reference

The idea of support-bargaining and money-bargaining itself constitutes a frame of reference. It draws attention to certain phenomena and interprets them in a certain way. It necessarily shares the characteristics of frames of reference. The importance attached to 'support' is a matter of interpretation. It is an understanding of human psychology, so that it is abstract, invisible, intangible. At a personal level it is communicated by words, gestures, signs, body language, gifts and behaviour. Even so, the presence and effects of support have to be largely inferred from outcomes. Support brings about certain events, but the occurrence of the events is taken to imply support. There is that element of tautology or 'echo' that is inseparable from the idea of a frame of reference.

Kuhn noted the element of tautology in scientific paradigms.[45] We are confined to what our minds can deal with, so that there are no totally secure anchorages outside our own invention. Acceptance of the role of support as a bargaining counter in the process of support-bargaining is predicated on the consistency of such explanation across a great range of human thought, actions and outcomes.

The acceptance of individual expressions of support, in the form of votes, in formal support-bargaining structures and on other occasions when formal expressions of support are required, suggests that support does have the underlying psychological significance identified in the theory of support-bargaining and money-bargaining. Without the associations of support in people's minds, votes would not be accorded the weighty significance they have.[46]

The idea of support-bargaining and money-bargaining identifies the similarities in the dynamics of political and economic processes. We normally think of human relationships and 'politics' as operating in accordance with different motivations from those of economic exchange, the first a matter of human feeling and the second a matter of negotiated exchange for material advantage. The 'democratic' understanding of politics conceives everyone as engaged in pursuit of a 'general good,' while in economic transactions people are conceived as looking after themselves. In support-bargaining and money-bargaining, both seek accommodation of their interests through bargaining, the one using support as a bargaining counter and the other money.

This common dynamic draws attention to the interlinking of politics and economic exchange as the interlinking of support-bargaining and money-bargaining. Social, political, intellectual and monetary matters interlink and affect each other. The two systems may reinforce each other, or may conflict. The nature of support, particularly its association with violence, means that it will normally prevail over money-bargaining in the determination of outcomes. People will nevertheless act for money as well as, or alternatively to, support. The friction is relevant to the use of money in a community, since those ascendant through support-bargaining may find their positions eroded by the use of money and money-bargaining. Coin-money is especially likely to diminish the influence of those ascendant through support. The interlinking of support-bargaining and money-bargaining is a vital part of the dynamic of bargaining societies and played an important part in the emergence and evolution of money.

The idea of support-bargaining provides also an interpretation of violence as the 'backing' of support. Support in groups implies violent capacity, so that the interests of well-supported groups are normally advanced. Rigid groups have violent potential. Money-bargaining is made possible through the establishment of the alternative bargaining counter 'money,' for use mainly in material exchange, where the abstract and imprecise nature of support is disadvantageous. But since money functions as an alternative bargaining counter to support, and may carry little direct implication of support, money-bargaining strengthens individual bargaining positions. This is further reason for an ascendant faction to look with suspicion on the spread of money-bargaining.

The idea of support-bargaining and money-bargaining is notably different from other theories in that it constitutes a multi-frame theory. Established theories present their unique 'truth' about society, jostling with other unitary frames of reference for the support they need to advance the interests incorporated in their formulation. Support-bargaining and money-bargaining is a theory that incorporates the idea of multiple frames of reference constructed through intellectual support-bargaining. It functions as a 'frame of frames.' It draws attention to the different frames of reference as a phenomenon of prime importance, and interprets them as outcomes of intellectual support-bargaining. This multi-frame character means that support-bargaining and money-bargaining provides its own approach to 'truth.' Although, given the qualities of our minds, any absolute truth is beyond our reach, yet we can build probabilities of truth by assessing the consistency of interpretations of phenomena in multiple frames.

Drawing attention to certain phenomena implies that everyone should pay attention to them; it unavoidably implies that they are important. It elevates them above other phenomena, and diverts attention from other phenomena. It assembles support for their significance and value. It thus promotes the sort of society in which such phenomena are prominent. It influences the concept of the 'ideal' society and assembles support for the concept, so that it helps to realise that concept.

While many theories engage with partisan interest in the conflict between individuals and the group, the theory of support-bargaining and money-bargaining suggests that the conflict is a fundamental part of human psychology; individuals want to be independent, but their first priority is the support of others. Individuals are addicted to the support of their associates, but contest the terms on which they get it. Support-bargaining and money-bargaining sustains neither the individual nor the group interest. It recognises the innovation and energy that emerges with individual freedom, but recognises also the importance of communal interests identified through support-bargaining. It sustains a process of mediation between different interests. It is a frame of reference conducive to an open support-bargaining society dependent for its peaceable conduct on movements of support between interests. It is a 'constitutional' type of theory, establishing a framework for the conduct of societies in which competing interests can be peaceably resolved.

It identifies rigid groups as associated with violence, hence as a threat to the necessary processes of compromise, and consequently something to be shunned in the ordinary conduct of affairs. It marginalises violence as an acceptable means of resolving social conflict. That has always been a partisan position. Autocrats with armies have sought to dominate societies for millennia. They have sought to establish the sort of rigidity amongst their supporting groups that assures loyalty and is effective in violence. Democracy has evolved slowly in the face of long traditions of loyalty and selfless commitment to a single group. Periods of destructive violence have led people to change their attitudes and recognise the potential of societies based more on secular ideas than violence. Full formal support-bargaining was established only in the twentieth century in most Western nations. It is now challenged by those who see in the emergence of China as a global political and economic power a model for the successful advance of the interests of a people by an authoritarian state. Such states depend on the exercise of violence, minimising the extent of actual violence by controlling access to information. They confine their people to a single frame of reference, so that people only assimilate information fitting to the frame and can interpret that information only in accordance with the interests of the ruling authority. Those that escape such confines are removed from the society by imprisonment or other means. China is 're-educating' a whole ethnic group in the Xinjiang region of north-western China.

To the Western intellectual elite, who have been the main architects of democratic order in the West, such intolerance is incompatible with the well-being of a society. In its own societies, the Western elite has been disturbed by the mass support expressed for leaders of intolerant 'populist' factions and support for the suppression of information and opinion in arenas of democratic debate.[47] It has been disturbed also to find itself designated 'the enemy' by influential factions in Western societies. Ideals of loyalty and moral virtue have been co-opted to the support of authoritarian interests, whilst the freedom of ideas that is essential to open support-bargaining is condemned. The threat posed by such thinking was apparent in the assault on the United States Capitol on 6 January 2021 by protestors alleging that the 2020 presidential elections was 'stolen' from Donald Trump, and determined to prevent the ratification of the result. Western intellectuals have assembled support for theory groups advancing both individual and group interests, and nurtured through the idea of democracy the support-bargaining processes by which such conflicting interests can be accommodated. They have assisted the development of societies with the most successful material, social, intellectual, artistic and humanitarian living conditions ever experienced.

Historical Frames

The idea of the frame of reference has particular application in dealing with historical societies. Such societies formed their own frames of reference, in accordance with their contemporary interests. We are far from the ancient world, but the supposition is that those ancient people thought by reference to their situations and formed frames of reference through which they could advance their interests in their world. The inscriptions, monuments, written records, buildings and artefacts of the ancient world were all made with reference to the frames established in those societies. Those who study them in a different era will have their own frames of reference, deriving from their own current interests, by which to understand ancient times..The difficulties of reaching any firm conclusions are apparent from Schaps's comment, quoted above, that the different interpretations of the various theory groups engaged in research on ancient societies have 'made problematical the interpretation of even the simplest item of economic evidence.'

The ancient Greeks have long been recognised in Western European societies as of special significance. They were the first in the West to write copiously about their societies and debate in writing what are still recognised as key questions concerning the conduct of human societies. Their minds seem more accessible to modern minds than those of other ancient societies because they first formulated the frames of reference covering large areas of social conduct and organisation that are identifiably the forerunners of frames of reference used today. Richard Seaford's thesis regarding the emergence of coinage in ancient Greek society under the influence of early Greek minds reflects this status.[48]

While the frames of reference of those ancient times were formulated to assemble support in those times, the frames of reference formulated in modern times are formulated to assemble present support. The idea of frames of reference identifies the problem. To understand historical societies, it is necessary to evaluate their different viewpoints, to adopt the outlooks of historical persons or groups. But it also suggests the impossibility of doing so in anything more than a superficial way. It identifies the problem and provides a framework within which it can be approached, but does not resolve it. To embrace a culture, it is necessary to live it, to share the situation and interests that created it. The problem is the temporal counterpart to the cultural gap that Malinowski tried to cross in the Trobriand Islands.

The multi-frame character of support-bargaining and money-bargaining gives it a better chance of dividing the true from the false than single frame theories. It has also the quality, identified in the Introduction, arising from its multi-frame character, of being applicable across the ages. It rests on the principle that people are insecure and seek the support of others to alleviate that sense of insecurity. This sets up the ageless contention between individuals and the societies which are essential to them. It suggests also that interests derive from immediate situations, both in a material and social sense. Situations are defined through the support-bargaining of their times.

The multi-frame character of support-bargaining and money-bargaining makes apparent also why it is that mainstream economic theory has such difficulty in dealing with past societies. It is presented as a unitary frame of reference, illuminating a unique truth about certain social conduct. It is based on an idea of equilibrium, so that through price adjustments and volume adjustments, economic systems revert to equilibrium positions. There is no scope for historical development in the understanding of economists. Geoffrey Hodgson elaborated on the lack of historical dimension in economic theory in *How Economics Forgot History*.[49] The difficulties are compounded when the history in question is that of a remote ancient world. In the idea of money-bargaining, economies unfold from situation to situation in an evolutionary process. It is thus intrinsically a theory that can take account of social change, even over long periods.

Part of the 'unique truth' of mainstream economic theory is its concept of 'economic man,' designed, as suggested above, to ensure the rational and hence predictable decisions necessary to a mathematical account of economic exchange. The idea of 'economic man' rules out the process envisaged in support-bargaining through which societies develop their ideas of contemporary 'situation' and identify their interests. It is not people of their time deploying frames of reference that influence their understanding of the world and make possible interpretation of their experience. Using the economic frame of reference makes it difficult to comprehend the decision-making of societies distinctly different from those of modern Western society, such as those of the ancient world. Economists have no comprehension of the societies of the ancient world in which money evolved.

The propensity of theorists to interpret the past by reference to modern frames of reference is apparent in *The Great Transformation*. Polanyi's book is formulated as a critique of modern Western society, drawing selectively on evidence about earlier societies, but attributing to them also a process of 'reciprocity and redistribution' that is essentially Polanyi's prescription for improvements to modern societies. He favours a society in which the group interest is predominant, and attributes to earlier societies the social harmony and easy prosperity that might arise from 'reciprocity and redistribution.' Economic anthropologists have taken up Polanyi's frame of reference. They view the ancient world through his frame of reference, assembling evidence that is consistent with his views. Their account of the origin of money as a 'money of account' accords with a society engaged in 'reciprocity and redistribution,' without the conflicts of monetary exchange. They see in the ancient world phenomena that tend to confirm the validity of their modern frame of reference.

The anthropological frame of reference nevertheless makes apparent an important inconsistency in the neoclassical frame of reference. It was seen above that in the neoclassical model transactions are concluded immediately. With no time disparities between receipts and payments, there is no need for credit, and no need for budgets. Economists have conceived money largely in terms of a particularly popular 'commodity.' Anthropologists point out that much of the trade of the ancient world, as now in the modern world, was carried on with credit. Outstanding balances were settled when a harvest was sold, or at some other propitious time. Dissension between creditors and debtors gave material exchange a crucial social dimension. Adam Smith described money as an expedient arising from the inconvenience of barter, but he assumed that barter and the monetary transactions that replaced it are matters of immediate settlement.[50] The economic model is thus incapable of explaining a central phenomenon of the ancient world. Smith's account of the emergence of money from barter is the immediate focus of the economic anthropologists' case that economic theory is inconsistent with empirical evidence. Chapters 5 and 7, in particular, deal further with these issues.

Notes

1 Mokyr, Joel, 2018, *A Culture of Growth: The Origins of the Modern Economy*, Princeton and Oxford: Princeton University Press, p. 120, fn. 1.
2 Mokyr, 2018, pp. 62, 83 and see Index.
3 Mokyr, 2018, pp. 59–69.
4 Mokyr, 2018, pp. 179–224.
5 Mokyr, 2018, p. 62. Mokyr's references on a 'market for ideas': Polanyi, Michael, 1962, 'The Republic of Science: Its Political and Economic Theory', *Minerva*, Vol. 1, pp. 54–73; Stigler, George, 1965, 'The Intellectual and the Market Place', *Kansas Journal of Sociology*, Vol. 1, No. 2 (Spring), pp. 69–77; Coase, Robert, 1974, 'The Market for Goods and the Market for Ideas', *American Economic Review*, Vol. 64, pp. 384–9; Gans, Joshua S. and Stern, Scott, 2003, 'The Product Market and the "Market for Ideas": Commercialization Strategies for Technology Entrepreneurs', *Research Policy*, Vol. 32, pp. 333–50; Mokyr, Joel, 2007, 'The Market for Ideas and the Origins of Economic Growth in Eighteenth Century Europe', (Heineken Lecture), *Tijdschrift voor Sociale en Economische Geschiedenis*, Vol. 4, No. 1, pp. 3–38.
6 Mokyr, 2018, p. 8.
7 Israel, Jonathan, 2010, *A Revolution of the Mind: Radical Enlightenment and the Intellectual Origins of Modern Democracy*, Princeton and Oxford: Princeton University Press, p. 87.
8 Israel, 2010, p. 87.
9 For further comment, see Spread, Patrick, 2019a, *Economics for an Information Age: Money-Bargaining, Support-Bargaining and the Information Interface*, London and New York: Routledge, pp. 45–6.
10 Spread, 2019a, 'Introduction'.
11 See Spread, Patrick, 1984, *A Theory of Support and Money Bargaining*, London: Macmillan, pp. 110–5, 168–85; and Spread, 2019a, pp. 185–90.
12 Malinowski, Bronislaw, 2002/1922, *Argonauts of the Western Pacific: An Account of Native Enterprise and Adventure in the Archipelagoes of Melanesian New Guinea*, London: Routledge, p. 517. First published 1922.
13 Malinowski, 2002/1922, p. 517.
14 Malinowski, 2002/1922, p. 515.
15 Malinowski, 2002/1922, p. 509.
16 Sherif, Muzafer, 1966/1936, *The Psychology of Social Norms*, New York: Harper & Row, pp. 1–3.
17 Sherif, 1966/1935, pp. 34–6.
18 Sherif, 1966/1935, p. 37.
19 Sherif, 1966/1935, p. 32.
20 Sherif, 1966/1935, pp. 39–40.
21 Sherif, 1966/1935, pp. 43–4.
22 Sherif, 1966/1935, p. 27.
23 Sherif, 1966/1935, pp. 40–1.
24 On social norms and support-bargaining, see Spread, Patrick, 2013, *Support-Bargaining, Economics and Society*, London and New York: Routledge, pp. 116–7.
25 Goffman, Erving, 1986, *Frame Analysis*, New York: Northeastern University Press, by arrangement with Harper & Row, p. 10
26 Goffman, 1986, p. 13.
27 Goffman, 1986, p. 27.

28 For further comment on Goffman's frame analysis, see Spread, Patrick, 2008, *Support-Bargaining: The Mechanics of Democracy Revealed*, Sussex: Book Guild, Chapter 11: 'Frames and Echoes'.
29 Kuhn, Thomas S., 1970, *The Structure of Scientific Revolutions*, Chicago: Chicago University Press. First published 1962.
30 For further comment on Kuhn's account of paradigms, see Spread, 2008, Chapter 11: 'Frames and Echoes'.
31 Spread, 1984a, pp. 3–7; Spread, 2019a, pp. 14–5, 45–51, 59–63, 206–10.
32 Walras, Leon, 2003/1874, *Elements of Pure Economics: Or, the Theory of Social Wealth*, London: Routledge. First published 1874.
33 On support-bargaining and culture, see Spread, 2013, pp. 44, 98–103, etc.
34 Spread, 2013, Chapter 8: 'Common Theory and Personification', pp. 160–99; and 'Symmetry and Common Theory', pp. 235–8; Spread, 2019a, pp. 26, 71–2.
35 North, Douglass C., 1981, *Structure and Change in Economic History*, New York: Norton, p. 48.
36 Anon, 1999, 'Economics Focus: Unfinished Battle', *The Economist*, 10 April.
37 Polanyi, Karl, 2001/1944, *The Great Transformation: The Political and Economic Origins of Our Time*, Boston: Beacon Press. First published 1944.
38 Schaps, David, 2004, *The Invention of Coinage and the Monetization of Ancient Greece*, Ann Arbor: University of Michigan Press, Kindle Edition, L720.
39 Finley, Moses, 1973, *The Ancient Economy*, London: Chatto & Windus.
40 Schaps, 2004, L735.
41 Schaps, 2004, L650–5, 671
42 Heichelheim, Fritz, 1958, *An Ancient Economic History*, Trans. Joyce Stevens, Leiden: A. W. Sijthoff, Volume 1, 1958; Volume 2, 1964; Volume 3, 1970. First published in German, 1938; Revised Edition 1958, 1964, 1970.
43 Schaps, 2004, L667–73.
44 Schaps, 2004, L39–45.
45 Kuhn, 1970, pp. 183–4. See also Spread, 2008, p. 338.
46 See also Spread, 2013, Chapter 6: 'The Evidence for Support-Bargaining'.
47 Spread, 2019a, pp. 308–11.
48 Seaford, Richard, 2004, *Money and the Early Greek Mind*, Cambridge: Cambridge University Press.
49 Hodgson, Geoffrey, 2001, *How Economics Forgot History: The Problem of Historical Specificity in Social Science*, London and New York: Routledge.
50 Smith, Adam, 1986/1776, *The Wealth of Nations*, Books I–III, London: Penguin Books, pp. 126–32.

References

Anon, 1999, 'Economics Focus: Unfinished Battle', *The Economist*, 10 April.

Coase, Robert, 1974, 'The Market for Goods and the Market for Ideas', *American Economic Review*, Vol. 64, pp. 384–9.

Finley, Moses, 1973, *The Ancient Economy*, London: Chatto & Windus.

Gans, Joshua S. and Stern, Scott, 2003, 'The Product Market and the "Market for Ideas": Commercialization Strategies for Technology Entrepreneurs', *Research Policy*, Vol. 32, pp. 333–50.

Goffman, Erving, 1986, *Frame Analysis*, New York: Northeastern University Press, by arrangement with Harper & Row.

Heichelheim, Fritz, 1958, *An Ancient Economic History*, Trans. Joyce Stevens, Leiden: A. W. Sijthoff, Volume 1, 1958; Volume 2, 1964; Volume 3, 1970. First published in German, 1938; Revised Edition 1958, 1964, 1970.

Hodgson, Geoffrey, 2001, *How Economics Forgot History: The Problem of Historical Specificity in Social Science*, London and New York: Routledge.

Israel, Jonathan, 2010, *A Revolution of the Mind: Radical Enlightenment and the Intellectual Origins of Modern Democracy*, Princeton and Oxford: Princeton University Press.

Kuhn, Thomas S., 1970, *The Structure of Scientific Revolutions*, Chicago: Chicago University Press. First published 1962.

Malinowski, Bronislaw, 2002/1922, *Argonauts of the Western Pacific: An Account of Native Enterprise and Adventure in the Archipelagoes of Melanesian New Guinea*, London: Routledge. First published 1922.

Mokyr, Joel, 2007, 'The Market for Ideas and the Origins of Economic Growth in Eighteenth Century Europe', (Heineken Lecture), *Tijdschrift voor Sociale en Economische Geschiedenis*, Vol.4, No. 1, pp.3–38.

Mokyr, Joel, 2018, *A Culture of Growth: The Origins of the Modern Economy*, Princeton and Oxford: Princeton University Press.

North, Douglass C., 1981, *Structure and Change in Economic History*, New York: Norton.

Polanyi, Karl, 2001/1944, *The Great Transformation: The Political and Economic Origins of Our Time*, Boston: Beacon Press. First published 1944.

Polanyi, Michael, 1962, 'The Republic of Science: Its Political and Economic Theory', *Minerva*, Vol. 1, pp. 54–73.

Schaps, David, 2004, *The Invention of Coinage and the Monetization of Ancient Greece*, Ann Arbor: University of Michigan Press, Kindle Edition, L720.

Seaford, Richard, 2004, *Money and the Early Greek Mind*, Cambridge: Cambridge University Press.

Sherif, Muzafer, 1966/1936, The Psychology of Social Norms, New York: Harper & Row.

Smith, Adam, 1986/1776, *The Wealth of Nations*, Books I–III, London: Penguin Books.

Spread, Patrick, 1984a, *A Theory of Support and Money Bargaining*, London: Macmillan.

Spread, Patrick, 2008, *Support-Bargaining: The Mechanics of Democracy Revealed*, Sussex: Book Guild.

Spread, Patrick, 2013, *Support-Bargaining, Economics and Society: A Social Species*, London and New York: Routledge.

Spread, Patrick, 2019a, *Economics for an Information Age: Money-Bargaining, Support-Bargaining and the Information Interface*, London and New York: Routledge.

Stigler, George, 1965, 'The Intellectual and the Market Place', *Kansas Journal of Sociology*, Vol. 1, No. 2 (Spring), pp. 69–77.

Walras, Leon, 2003/1874, *Elements of Pure Economics: Or, the Theory of Social Wealth*, London: Routledge. First published 1874.

5 Polanyi, Gifts and Markets

The quest for the origins of money starts with investigation of the place of material interests in human societies. If money emerged from barter, then economic exchange might be seen as largely independent of social and political considerations, and money likewise might be considered largely independent of politics. But if material interests are met incidentally to the conduct of social relations in a society, then economic affairs are matters of social and political determination, and the anthropological contention that money originated as a 'money of account' designated by the state becomes more plausible.

Harry Pearson notes that debate over the integration of economic affairs into the social life of ancient societies, ranging 'primitivists' against 'modernists,' dates back at least into the mid-nineteenth century. The primitivists saw such societies as characterised by subsistence or household production, whilst the modernists recognised more a trading or 'market' character. The debate was at its height at the turn of the twentieth century.[1] Bronislaw Malinowski's ethnographic research, conducted in the period 1914–20, into *Kula* practices, described in Chapter 2 as presenting an alternative 'code of conduct' to the 'warrior code' portrayed in the Homeric epics, provides a sharp account of a society integrating its material satisfactions with conduct designed to ensure harmonious social relations. Malinowski concludes that the evidence of the *Kula* customs disproves any notions that man is almost exclusively materialistic; it dispels 'crude, rationalistic conceptions of primitive mankind.'[2] The evidence does not support the notion that natives live only for their own household. Those holding such a notion, 'ignore the deep tendency to create social ties through exchange of gifts.' Malinowski submits that such tendency, 'is a universal feature of all primitive societies.'[3] He contends that, rather than the operation of markets based on competitive exchange and the interplay of supply and demand, 'we find a state of affairs where production, exchange and consumption are socially organised and regulated by custom…'[4] The idea of an economic system detached from obligations to social harmony is dismissed as untenable for all primitive societies. Economic anthropologists, following Karl Polanyi's endorsement of Malinowski's conclusions, infer that ancient societies would have closely integrated their economic affairs with their social and political arrangements.

DOI: 10.4324/9781003313472-7

Malinowski is, nevertheless, far from denying the motivation of material interest. In his article 'The Primitive Economics of the Trobriand Islanders' he emphasises, as noted in Chapter 2, a 'constant economic undertow' in the conduct of *Kula* societies and refers to 'the materialist streak that runs through all their doings.'[5] In another article on *Kula*, he comments, 'We have here a very interesting form of tribal enterprises. In a sense they are *economic*, for the natives carry out their organised purposeful work under the stimulus of a desire for wealth, for ownership.'[6]

Malinowski's observations and interpretations are nevertheless dictated by the thesis which he wishes to establish, or the frame of reference in which he operates. Malinowski presents his assessment of economic and social motivations as conclusions derived from his research, but they are plainly part of the frame of reference that guides his research. The conclusions are only 'echoes' of the predispositions. He argues that the *Kula* culture is probably typical of primitive societies in general. But he records also that most Pacific islanders made voyages for trade in the ordinary sense.[7] The *Kula* culture then appears as the exception rather than the rule – Malinowski himself refers to it as 'an exchange of an entirely novel type.'[8]

The *Kula* society is small. Malinowski emphasises in his account of research techniques the importance of providing statistical documentation of the society being researched.[9] But he provides no demographic data on the Trobriand Islands. Such data were probably not officially available, but estimates would have been feasible. Malinowski gives the impression of a large society, but records only 'thousands': 'Again, the *Kula* presents a type of intertribal relationship of unprecedented magnitude, the standing partnership linking together thousands of people scattered over an immense area.'[10] But it was probably not many thousands. The population of the Trobriand Islands at the beginning of the twentieth century is estimated at about 8,000.[11] The long-distance *Kula* exchanges which give *Kula* its most salient character were annual events. There were no external threats to the *Kula* group that necessitated provision for defence against external attack. The *Kula* society is perhaps better conceived as a cult protected by an externally imposed political system, rather than an independent and generally operable social order. Not all were members. Some men in *Kula* villages did not take part, and some entire villages did not take part.[12] The ceremonial exchange of necklaces and armlets is a more subtle and attractive cultish trait than the common run of cultish belief, but it does not suggest an alternative socio-political order to that of Western nations. Western nations at the time of Malinowski's research were in extreme conflict, but in normal times, their internal affairs, material, social, political and spiritual, were conducted through the complex debates and affinities of support-bargaining.

A frame of reference is formulated to advance the interests of the theory group that creates the frame. Thus Malinowski's thesis is not only that an economy can be 'socially organised and regulated by custom' but that such organisation is effective and rewarding to those involved. He wants it to be attractive. He selects and interprets his observations in accordance with his thesis. 'Gift-giving' of garden produce, 'enmeshes the whole community into a network of reciprocal obligations and dues, one constant flow of gift and counter-gift.[13] The words 'gifts' and 'gift-giving' imply the nature of the provision. A 'gift' is necessarily a kindness and a society based on gift-giving is necessarily an admirable society – the words are used to imply such character. The words probably confuse ethnographers as much as their readers. But gifts are not necessarily so well-meant. Gift-giving is not necessarily an expression of harmonious social relationships. People may give for fear of the consequences of not giving. In which case, gift-giving is something like extortion. Chiefly edicts, backed by the society, are irresistible, and if attempts are made to resist them, the resisters are punished. The chiefs in the Trobriand Islands have 'special henchmen' who can enforce the orders of the chief with capital punishment.[14] Malinowski notes that the preference was for enforcement by evil magic rather than capital punishment, but that was no great mercy to islanders with 'an enormous dread' of such magic. Jonathan Parry and Maurice Bloch note that 'Those who write in the Marxian tradition ...tend...to treat the world of gift-giving as non-exploitative, innocent and even transparent.'[15] Church leaders in the West used popular fear of eternal damnation to enforce certain modes of behaviour. Authoritarian states and criminal gangs commonly enforce their authority through fear of the consequences of disobedience. There are examples in recent history of cult leaders making extreme demands on their followers. 'Gifts' and 'gift-giving' have to be understood in the context of the social organisation of the people involved.

Malinowski records also that 30 per cent of what is produced is handed to the chief in dues and tributes.[16] The chief acts as something like the 'tribal banker.' He collects a considerable portion of tribal yield 'by the accumulation of which he gives himself a still bigger fund of power.' The society is ruled by 'power,' not necessarily with the assent of 'the people.' It may be conceived that people assent freely to such impositions, but in the tribal context, 'freedom' is sharply constrained by tribal opinion. Tribal support and the consequences of losing it dominate the behaviour of tribal people. People might protest if they did not fear the consequences of doing so. Malinowski interprets what he observes as evidence for his alternative system, and as evidence that the alternative is benign. But much of the argument can be construed as euphemism, a placatory gloss on underlying tensions. Authoritarian systems of suppression and enforcement are visible, as it were, through the cracks. The pursuit of 'gain' in the form of power or political dominance is as strong a motivation as the pursuit of material advantage, and perhaps stronger.

The 'economic undertow' is then, in important part, the fear that breaking from the social organisation that provides material necessities will result in ostracism and loss of the essential means of livelihood. The system is sustained through its control of economic necessities. The chiefs and notables have a primary interest in ensuring that all material interests are fulfilled through the social organisation which they control. Hence they would not welcome intrusions, like pearl fishing, which threatened their ordering of society. Malinowski acknowledges the help he receives from Western pearl traders settled in the Trobriand Islands, both related to his research and personal, without elaboration of their significance to the people of the region.[17] If the people could look after themselves independently by earning money, chiefly control of the society would be under threat. The King of Tonga recognised the same consequences if money were introduced into his kingdom.[18] The presence of pearl traders implies that at least some islanders took opportunities to look after their material requirements by earning money outside the traditional arrangements.

The argument here, pursued in later chapters, is that means of material provision outside the traditional social order would pose a threat to those ascendant in the existing social order. Chiefs and other rulers would try to keep their people dependent on their dispensation. While barter, under ceremonial communal supervision, would be tolerable, the use of money would suggest a system outside the control of rulers. Even clumsy forms of money, used by specialist traders with means of weighing and assaying, would be manageable. Merchants could be monitored and supervised to ensure that they paid proper deference to their rulers. But money in the hands of ordinary people, with the ready convenience of coins, could be seen as a potentially serious threat to an existing ruling group. Through money-bargaining, numerous people could get rich, and would potentially use their money for political purposes. Money constitutes a second bargaining counter. Its use implies reduction in the value of support, the primary bargaining counter and the counter on which, in so far as they did not depend on violence, the rulers were dependent. In this view, social order without coin-money was not benign and sufficient, as economic anthropologists tend to imply, but a matter of social ascendancy and privilege, which would come under threat with the introduction of coin-money. The widespread use of coinage was delayed until a society emerged that could tolerate the use of a very convenient second bargaining counter.

Thus the question raised in the opening paragraph of this chapter regarding the integration or separation of material provision from social and political affairs has to be understood in the context of competition for social and political ascendancy through support-bargaining and money-bargaining, involving the two bargaining counters, 'support' and 'money.' Those gaining ascendancy by virtue of the support they have assembled may try to integrate material provision with their political control. They are likely to limit the use of money, and resist its most convenient form – coinage – which gives rise to extensive money-bargaining. The alternative bargaining counter constitutes a threat to their continued rule. Use of inconvenient money might be tolerated, but not encouraged. Coinage could only be adopted for extensive use when political circumstances permitted.

Malinowski's animosity towards the pursuit of material gain outside social relationships is apparent in his account of the natives of the Amphlett Islands.[19] These Islands do not provide the same natural bounty as the other islands of the Trobriand group. They are rocky and difficult to live on. Of necessity, their inhabitants developed alternative means of survival. They developed unique skill in pottery, and traded their pots to neighbouring islands. Malinowski notes that they had a near monopoly of the trade and adds:

> They have also the main characteristics of monopolists: grasping and mean, inhospitable and greedy, keen on keeping the trade and exchange in their own hands, yet unprepared to make any sacrifice towards improving it; shy, yet arrogant to anyone who has any dealings with them.

Users of Malinowski's frame of reference, insisting on social relationships as more benign than those of economic exchange, would interpret trading monopoly as offensive. But the above interpretation seems beyond even what might be inspired by the technical frame of reference. It seems a matter of more fundamental prejudice. It brings to mind the demonisation of Jews and usury in Europe, as described in Chapter 3.

Malinowski's technique of anthropological research requires the assembly of information on *the imponderabilia of actual life*. The researcher has to assemble material on how life is actually lived, requiring that the researcher becomes closely involved with the life of the society under investigation.[20] In getting close to the natives of the other Trobriand Islands, Malinowski seems to have lost any sympathy for the Amphlett Islanders, who do not share the attitudes of his preferred group.

Malinowski forcefully condemns people who do not conform to the behaviour which his frame of reference demands. People should be exchanging gifts in pursuit of social harmony; but the Amphlett Islanders are trading with hard bargaining. Adam Smith similarly condemns a 'third order' of people engaged in economic transactions, the businessmen, who impede the emergence of 'natural prices.' Their behaviour is inconsistent with the behaviour approved in his frame of reference, which brings individual interest into alignment with social interest.[21] If a certain group does not conform to the frame of reference, the rest of society must be persuaded to ignore them as immoral and beyond the consideration of decent people.

Speaking Frankly

The influence of Malinowski's frame of reference is apparent from his diaries, published in 1967. The ethnographic frame of reference is concerned with the social relationships of Trobriand society and the integration of material concerns in the network of social relationships. It is concerned also with the empirical or scientific approach to ethnographical research. Malinowski is a skilled and conscientious investigator, but with an intense personality. The diaries reveal substantial disparity between the presentation of the ethnographic findings and Malinowski's experience and private opinions of Trobriand society.

The impression given by the ethnographic reporting is of a unitary and ordered society, at ease with the presence of a stranger enquiring into its ways. The diaries tell of considerable difficulties for the researcher, and assessments of Trobriand people that are sharply at odds with what is presented in the reports. The diaries use what may be seen as a 'common' frame of reference, deriving from common theory, or common experience. In that frame, especially if its interpretations are not to be public, you say straightforwardly what you experience and whether you like it or not. The support of others may be of little account. It is honest, but does not observe the same phenomena or follow the same interpretations, nor does it advance the same interests, as a formal theoretical frame of reference. If word gets out, as the diaries did, it can be damaging to both personal and professional reputation. But it also makes apparent the artificiality of formal research using an identifiable frame of reference. It makes apparent the exigencies of intellectual support-bargaining. The *Kula* society is a society on paper, constructed to assemble support for a particular frame of reference and advance the interests of a particular theory group.

The diaries make apparent the element of 'social construction' in scientific endeavour. Malinowski's report on the *Kula* culture is shaped by interests of himself, his subjects and the wider ethnographic theory group. It is a similar process to that described by Bruno Latour and Steve Woolgar in the construction of scientific theories, though in the ethnographical context there is more scope for selective perception and interpretation than there is with the impersonal and largely material matter of investigation in the natural sciences.[22] The empirical approach in the social sciences allows more scope for the selection and interpretation of the phenomena encountered by reference to group interests, and the omission of inconvenient phenomena, than is typically feasible in the natural sciences.

James Clifford compares Malinowski's *Argonauts of the South Pacific* and his *Diaries* with Joseph Conrad's novel *Heart of Darkness*, seeing similar crises of personality for Malinowski and the characters of the Conrad novel. In the diaries, 'what is visible, a pronounced ambivalence toward the Trobrianders, empathy mixed with desire and aversion, is nowhere in *Argonauts*, where comprehension, scrupulousness, and generosity reign.'[23] Clifford concludes:

> In any event what Malinowski achieved in writing was simultaneously (1) the fictional invention of the Trobrianders from a mass of field notes, documents, memories, and so forth, and (2) the construction of a new public figure, the anthropologist as fieldworker…[24]

The treatment of Malinowski's study of *Kula* society alongside Homeric mythology in Chapter 2 is not so inappropriate as might at first appear. Homer is writing fiction, drawing on reality; Malinowski is ostensibly recording reality, but veers into fiction. Our minds are always selecting and interpreting information, so that we can never grasp reality as it is.

Polanyi: Reciprocity and Redistribution

Malinowski sought to establish that people are not necessarily or primarily motivated by prospects of material gain. The *Kula* system is presented as displaying alternative motivations involving social relationships and cooperation which result in effective material provision. Polanyi uses Malinowski early in *The Great Transformation* as prime evidence for alternative motivation. But Polanyi seriously misrepresents the *Kula* system as described by Malinowski. It was seen above that Malinowski was selective in the characteristics of the *Kula* society that he chose to record and interpreted them in accordance with his thesis. Polanyi takes interpretation a stage further to establish the principle of 'reciprocity and redistribution.' Polanyi argues that, on the basis of Malinowski's research, modern ethnographers are agreed on the basic economic characteristics of early societies:

> ...the absence of the motive of gain; the absence of the principle of laboring for remuneration; the absence of the principle of least effort; and, especially, the absence of any separate and distinct institution based on economic motives.[25]

He continues:

> But how, then, is order in production and distribution ensured? The answer is provided in the main by two principles of behavior not primarily associated with economics: *reciprocity* and *redistribution*. With the Trobriand Islanders of Western Melanesia, who serve as an illustration of this type of economy, reciprocity works mainly in regard to the sexual organization of society, that is, family and kinship; redistribution is mainly effective in respect to all those who are under a common chief and is, therefore, of a territorial character.[26]

Under a system of reciprocity and redistribution:

> ...institutional patterns and principles of behaviour are mutually adjusted. As long as social organization runs in its ruts, no individual economic motives need come into play; no shirking of personal effort need be feared; division of labor will automatically be ensured; economic obligations will be duly discharged; and, above all, the material means for an exuberant display of abundance at all public festivals will be provided. In such a community the idea of profit is barred; higgling and haggling is decried; giving freely is acclaimed as a virtue; the supposed propensity to barter, truck, and exchange does not appear. The economic system is, in effect, a mere function of social organization.[27]

Yet Malinowski makes clear that economic motivations are in play. As was seen above, he gives considerable emphasis to the economic aspects of the exchanges between people of the Trobriand Islands. Malinowski recognises an 'economic undertow' in all the conduct of the *Kula* people. The sharper edges to trade are reduced by customary notions of equivalence, as the need for too much haggling is obviated in Western societies by widespread trading at fixed prices. But Malinowski makes clear that the Trobriand Islanders engage in bargaining over material things:

> Exchange of useful articles against one another does exist in Kiriwina [the main island of the Trobriand group] both in internal and external trade. Indeed, barter among the natives is very well developed. Their exchange sometimes takes the form of free gift and following counter-gift – always repaid according to definite rules of equivalence. Sometimes it is real barter (for which they have a term – *Gimwali*), where one article is traded against another, with direct assessment of equivalence and even with haggling.[28]

And further, in another article:

> It must also be emphasised that all these natives, and more especially the Trobrianders, have both a word for, and a clear idea of, barter (*gimwali*) and that they are fully aware of the difference between the transactions at the *Kula* and common barter.[29]

Malinowski not only recognises the economic motivations of engagement in barter, but recognises that the Trobriand Islands make a distinct separation between the 'gifting' transactions that are conducive to social relationships and the 'barter' that is motivated by economic concerns. The Trobriand Islanders distinguish politics and social order from an economic order. Malinowski records, 'many squabbles, deep resentments and even feuds over real or imaginary grievances in the *Kula* exchange.'[30]

Kula was a process of support-bargaining that smoothed the way to trade. Envoys still bear gifts to foreign governments when they want to negotiate treaties on trade. While academic economists do not recognise motives beyond that of material self-interest, business people recognise that friendship is helpful to the conclusion of business transactions. Businesses give 'free gifts' to drum up sales. Salesmen charm their customers so that the customers will see them as friends and be reluctant to disappoint. Businessmen entertain each other to ensure that important deals go through.

Polanyi claims that 'the alleged propensity of man to barter, truck, and exchange is almost entirely apocryphal.'[31] He is consequently inclined to deny any appearance of such mechanisms. He claims in the above quotation that 'barter, truck and exchange do not appear,' but Malinowski makes them prominent. Polanyi claims that higgling and haggling is 'decried,' and claims later that 'no higgling and haggling, no truck, barter, or exchange enters.'[32] Yet Malinowski specifically refers to haggling as part of the conduct of exchange transactions. He stresses motivations regarding wealth and ownership. Malinowski recognises, even if he does not approve, the hard-bargaining of the Amphlett Islanders. The Amphlett Islanders may be nasty, but that does not mean they can be discounted as representative of human behaviour.

To press home his claim that the *Kula* society constitutes a full and viable alternative to the pursuit of material gain, Polanyi exaggerates its scale: 'The Kula ring, in western Melanesia, based on the principle of reciprocity, is one of the most elaborate trading transactions known to man.'[33] Yet it was elaborate only in its preparations and ceremonial; in numbers it was inconsiderable. Geoffrey Hodgson notes that there are serious difficulties in accepting that what is possible within a small *Kula* society is possible within a society of millions.[34]

The idea in 'reciprocity' that gift-giving is motivated by the desire to form social relationships, and owes nothing to considerations of material advantage, is not born out by Malinowski's research. Malinowski certainly dismisses ideas of any predominance of 'cold egotism.'[35] In the quotations above he refers to the capacity of islanders to distinguish between social transactions and economic exchange. But he nevertheless acknowledges that the distinction between 'gift-giving' in the context of social custom and 'barter' for material gain is not clear-cut:

> I have on purpose spoken of forms of exchange, of gifts and counter-gifts, rather than of barter or trade, because, although there exist forms of barter pure and simple, there are so many transitions and gradations between that and simple gift, that it is impossible to draw any fixed line between trade on the one hand, and exchange of gifts on the other. Indeed, the drawing of any lines to suit our own terminology and our own distinctions is contrary to sound method.[36]

Malinowski identifies seven gradations of interaction, ranging from 'Pure Gifts' to 'Trade, pure and simple.'[37] Pure gifts, he notes, are rare and, in terms of the purest meaning of a 'gift,' not even rare. It is a social obligation, and hence not purely a matter of gifting.[38] There are penalties for not giving a gift. 'Gifts' are given as what is effectively payment for services such as sex, mourning, magic, canoe-building and carving.[39] There is 'Ceremonial barter with deferred payment.'[40] This is formalised barter in which a 'gift' is always accepted, but must be repaid by an equivalent counter-gift at a later date. The *Kula* circulating exchange of bracelets and armlets comes into this category. The *Kula* involves permanent partnerships involving gifts and counter-gifts. This 'Ceremonial barter' is the sixth category of interaction, only one short of 'Trade, pure and simple.' The latter is seen as exchange for mutual advantage. Each side acquires what is needed and parts with what it regards as a less valuable article. Equivalence of value in exchange is agreed by haggling or bargaining.[41]

The distinction between gift-giving and trade is largely a matter of 'how you see it,' of the operative frame of reference. Malinowski recognises this in his comment quoted above (at Note 35) that we should not draw lines 'to suit our own terminology,' meaning to suit our own frame of reference. If the 'hard-bargaining' of plain barter is going to make people angry and aggrieved, to the extent of a breakdown in relationships, then it is better for all concerned that they view the transactions as manifestations of communal generosity and friendship. There is a preference for the psychological balm of gift-giving over the potentially divisive idea of barter trade. If it is understood also that the cohesion of the society depends on gift-giving, then gift-giving is not only balm to individual psychology, but balm to the society as a whole and its rulers. If a chief and his notables are to retain social control, they must control the material welfare of their people.

Polanyi, like Adam Smith before him, is assembling support for his frame of reference on the basis of support already assembled behind notions of morality relating to communal advantage. Smith wanted to show that individual interest led to fulfilment of communal interests, and presented the idea of 'natural prices' to make it appear so. Polanyi portrays in *Kula* society a community in which ideas of individual gain have been eliminated by natural propensities to work for the common good. In *Kula* society there is no shirking, economic obligations are met and there is communal abundance, because people act under the shared motivation to advance the well-being of their community. 'Reciprocity' and 'redistribution,' based on motivations of communal obligation and generosity, cement a society together and at the same time generate production and distribution of material necessities. The way societies actually function, as observed and experienced, is of lesser importance, important primarily in maintaining the credibility of the main contention. Smith's system of 'natural prices' was only plausible if people were prepared to avert their gaze from the actual observable behaviour of those engaged in business. Polanyi's creation works only if people are prepared to avert their gaze from the rougher side of conformity in authoritarian societies.

The tensions in *Kula* society are apparent in Malinowski's references to the use of 'henchmen,' the terror of magic and aspirations to 'renown.' The valuables of the *Kula* are valuable because they are 'objects of competitive desire and renown.'[42] The accumulation of wealth in the hands of the chief supplements his power.[43] 'Redistribution' may be motivated by genuine concerns for the well-being of the people, but it may also be interpreted as a matter of 'buying off' the populace, lest they should grow weary to the point of violence of the impositions put on them. Violence and support-bargaining, the latter substituting for the former to a greater or lesser extent, are used in competition for social ascendancy. As noted above, rule is generally provided by an ascendant group. In violent societies, such groups are coercive. People know that if they act in a manner that threatens the ascendant group, particularly if they challenge its ascendancy, they are likely to be damaged, in forms ranging from damage to material interests up to and including execution. On the other hand, those who speak and act in favour of the ruling group are likely to gain reward and advancement. Hence authoritarian states create for themselves an appearance of virtue, whilst controlling their people through fear. In such circumstances, the emergence of money-bargaining independent of central control poses a threat to the ruling group and is likely to be suppressed.

Polanyi is harnessing support already assembled for group interests in the political context to a theory of 'reciprocity and redistribution.' He is, in Mokyr's terminology, a 'cultural entrepreneur' operating in the 'market for ideas.' Mokyr references Douglass North's idea of 'ideological entrepreneurs' as close to his concept of 'cultural entrepreneur.'[44] But North's ideological entrepreneurs are not persuasive. They are driven rather by a desire for rationalisation and simplification of decision-making: 'Ideologies are intellectual efforts to rationalize the behavioral pattern of individuals and groups.'[45] Ideology is a matter of coming to terms with what is experienced rather than any attempt to influence the way societies evolve.[46] In the present view, the 'ideological entrepreneur' is more persuasive than the 'cultural entrepreneur,' with a distinctly political persuasive intent. Polanyi is persuasive, and also manipulative, even to the extent of misrepresentation for ideological advantage. The treatment of evidence is the accessible distinction between the scientist and the 'ideological entrepreneur.' In the broadest terms, Polanyi is engaged in the ongoing conflict between individuals and groups that is support-bargaining.

Polanyi insists that, 'The outstanding discovery of recent historical and anthropological research is that man's economy, as a rule, is submerged in his social relationships.'[47] He makes no reference to the Soviet Union, the contemporary society in which material provision was integrated into a political and social system. All the goodwill and social sentiment that is supposedly found in *Kula* society was in the Soviet Union enforced by state decrees, surveillance, control and violent coercion. The Soviet Union is an illustration of the illusions that can be propagated by ideological entrepreneurs, perhaps also an illustration of the difficulties of transposing small-scale notions of social goodness into a population of millions.

Polanyi: Embedding and Interlinking

Polanyi's account of *The Great Transformation* includes the idea that economic processes in nineteenth-century Europe became detached from socio-political control. Rather than being 'embedded' in society through reciprocity and redistribution, material interests became more and more detached as a distinct 'economic' system.

The notion of 'embeddedness' has been taken up by economic anthropologists, with a prominent role in arguments over the origins of money. It seems appropriate that a 'money of account' is designated by the state if material affairs are wholly embedded in the socio-political organisation of a society. 'Reciprocity and redistribution' is the institutional embodiment of embeddedness. Gift-giving is taken as directed towards the establishment and maintenance of social relations, whilst also accommodating material interests. 'Redistribution' involves political allocation of material goods. The 'money of account' is a matter of administrative convenience.

The word 'embedded' gives no clear idea of any relationship between what is economic and what is socio-political. A bullet may 'embed' in a wall, but it remains a bullet and the wall remains a wall. A plastic pipe may be 'embedded' in concrete, but both remain distinct as pipe and surrounding material. Fred Block, in his Introduction to *The Great Transformation*, records that Polanyi's inspiration for 'embeddedness' is not known for sure, but Polanyi researched English coal mining at one period, where coal mining technology was required to extract coal embedded in rock, providing possible inspiration for the political-economic notion of 'embeddedness.'[48] Polanyi might be inclined to reject such a provenance, since it suggests advantages in disembedding.

The problem, as Polanyi sees it, is that:

> The market pattern, on the other hand, being related to a peculiar motive of its own, the motive of truck or barter, is capable of creating a specific institution, namely, the market. Ultimately, that is why the control of the economic system by the market is of overwhelming consequence to the whole organization of society: it means no less than the running of society as an adjunct to the market. Instead of economy being embedded in social relations, social relations are embedded in the economic system.[49]

The threat is that the economic system will throw off social control and become dominant in society, to the advantage of those who dominate economic affairs, and to the detriment of those ill-equipped to take advantage of economic opportunities. Polanyi describes practices under the English guild system, as in all other economic systems in previous history, as embedded in the general organisation of society. Relationships, including the terms of apprenticeships and wages, were all regulated by the custom of the guild and town.[50]

Polanyi's understanding of a 'market' is the 'self-regulating market' of neoclassical economic theory: 'Prices must be allowed to regulate themselves. Such a self-regulating system of markets is what we mean by a market economy.'[51] He comments that 'the most startling peculiarity of the system lies in the fact that, once it is established, it must be allowed to function without outside interference.[52] Because of this requirement, economics is separated from politics; material gain is pursued beyond the reach of governments. Polanyi argues that self-regulating markets emerged for the first time in history in nineteenth-century Britain.[53] He accounts them a 'unique development' of the nineteenth century and the institutional origin of modern social disaffection.[54] The 'Great Transformation' of the nineteenth century was, according to Polanyi, a consequence of the advance of the idea of self-regulating markets to domination of society. He comments:

> Neither under tribal nor under feudal nor under mercantile conditions was there, as we saw, a separate economic system in society. Nineteenth-century society, in which economic activity was isolated and imputed to a distinctive economic motive, was a singular departure.[55]

'Self-regulating markets' are a concept of economic theory, originally proposed by Adam Smith through the idea of 'natural prices' and given mathematical form by neoclassical economists in the later nineteenth century with 'market prices.' Polanyi implies that the theory became the reality, or very close to the reality. He makes no distinction between market theory – the way economists think an economy works, or the way they think it should work – and the way economies actually work. It is only the neoclassical understanding of markets that is unique to our time. Markets in practical form, in the sense of gatherings of people for purposes of trade, have existed forever. At least, scholars have claimed that markets and prices had a substantial economic influence in ancient civilisations such as Rome and Babylonia.[56]

Polanyi describes Tudor and Stuart regimes as regulating change so as to make it bearable, then affirms:

> But nothing saved the common people of England from the impact of the Industrial Revolution. A blind faith in spontaneous progress had taken hold of people's minds, and with the fanaticism of sectarians the most enlightened pressed forward for boundless and unregulated change in society.[57]

But only a few paragraphs later he acknowledges:

> While the organization of world commodity markets, world capital markets, and world currency markets under the aegis of the gold standard gave an unparalleled momentum to the mechanism of markets, a deep-seated movement sprang into being to resist the pernicious effects of a market-controlled economy. Society protected itself against the perils inherent in a self-regulating market system—this was the one comprehensive feature in the history of the age.[58]

It is recognition that in practice society was not given over to self-regulating markets. Along with the new economic enterprise a socialist movement gained support, devoted to the interests of the common people, and requiring that economic affairs should be regulated by governments.

Nor was it socialists alone that saw the need for regulation of markets, or whatever went under that name. Polanyi recognises that some economists, whilst advocating markets, also advocated their regulation:

> Fourthly, there is the significant fact that at various times economic liberals themselves advocated restrictions on the freedom of contract and on *laissez-faire* in a number of well-defined cases of great theoretical and practical importance.[59]

Polanyi's ideological frame of reference requires that economists should be viscerally supportive of 'self-regulating markets.' The above statement is, on the face of it, contrary to his argument. But the statement is used not to establish favour for regulation amongst economic liberals, but rather to prove that there was no 'anti-liberal conspiracy theory' hatched amongst those opposing 'self-regulating markets.' According to Polanyi, those promoting 'self-regulating markets' alleged an 'anti-liberal conspiracy' against them.[60] Pro-regulation comment by economic liberals can then be interpreted more as evidence that there is no conspiracy against liberals, rather than as their support for regulation. The above quotation is followed immediately by the comment that, 'Antiliberal prejudice could, naturally, not have been their motive.' The absence of a conspiracy against liberals is confirmed by the statements of liberals aligning themselves with the supposed perpetrators of the conspiracy. As Polanyi recognises, there was no need for conspiracy – the opposition to economic liberalism arose spontaneously among many people, including the economic liberals who, whilst recognising the benefits of free market ideas, could also see adverse consequences.

'Conspiracies' are useful for the reconciliation of behaviour to a favoured frame of reference in the face of awkward evidence. They are employed to establish that the most straightforward evidence is contrived. Donald Trump alleges a conspiracy to deprive him of victory in the presidential election of 2020. The devil has been conspiring for centuries to sow doubt in the minds of Christians. Polanyi neutralises evidence against his ideological cause by accounting it evidence against a conspiracy that would damage his cause.

The developments of nineteenth-century Europe exemplify the interaction of support-bargaining and money-bargaining and the underlying conflict between individual interest and group interest. The individual interest was allowed expression in the expansion of money-bargaining, but group interest established extensive controls through support-bargaining over the operation of money-bargaining. The interlinking of support-bargaining and money-bargaining makes apparent what it is for an economy to be embedded in a political system. The support-bargaining system predominates by virtue of the association of support with violence. As was seen in Chapter 2, The connection of support with violence runs by degrees from largely mute connection in everyday support-bargaining through to actual violence. It was seen also in Chapter 2 that foreign trade was widely 'embedded' in actual violence, or more or less explicit threats of violence, when violence had been pushed more to the margins in the internal conduct of Western nations. Money-bargaining gains acceptance because of the efficacy of 'money' as a bargaining counter, particularly in transactions involving material goods and well-defined services.

Polanyi emphasises the very distinct nature of 'self-regulating markets' and their necessary independence of any political control. His position is based on the neoclassical model of market processes, in which the optimal allocation of resources depends on the free play of private interest, without interference from governments. The practice is plainly different – Polanyi himself recognises the gallant efforts of society to protect itself (at Note 57). He confuses theory with practice. Sitta von Reden notes that 'Polanyi's concept of market exchange clearly refers to the market principle; nevertheless, he sought the origins of it in market places and ports of trade *(emporia)*.'[61]

The link between theory and political practice was identified in Chapter 4. Support established in a theory group can be transferred to political programmes; or support established for political programmes can form the basis of theory groups. Intellectual support-bargaining and political support-bargaining are intertwined. Since they use the same bargaining counter, they are entwined often to the point of being indistinguishable. 'Theory formation' is well embedded in political practice. Any separation is largely dependent on institutional arrangements made to isolate those engaged in theory formation from immediate political interest. Isolation has, however, caused theory-makers in some cases to lose track of the actual behaviour of the societies in which they are embedded. Economic processes are more easily understood as distinct from political processes because they use a different bargaining counter.

Theory and Practice: Microeconomics and Macroeconomics

Polanyi's preoccupation is with the theoretical market of neoclassical economics, much less with the realities of nineteenth-century society. That Polanyi should confuse theory with practice is to some extent understandable, since economists do the same. The neoclassical microeconomic approach is limited to a highly artificial understanding of economic transactions, bounded by the assumptions necessary to codification in mathematical terms. It assumes only the involvement of private agents in the form of 'suppliers' and 'consumers,' or at least tractable constructs held to represent 'suppliers' and 'consumers.' Actual economies are observably and obviously quite different. A wholly different 'economics' has been developed in which all the assumptions of the neoclassical model are invalid. People operate in time and space; transport is prominent; there are time disparities, requiring budgets, and requiring credit and debt; products are systematically differentiated for bargaining advantage; information is manipulated for bargaining advantage; there are governments with large budgets to advance communal interests; there are organisations; large companies dominate many sectors; large financial services companies provide credit; technological innovations drive growth; labour divides in accordance with technological requirements; humans act like humans; companies behave like companies.

Macroeconomics is concerned with the actual functioning of economies and their management. It relies heavily on statistical series that record quantifiable aspects of economic endeavour. In aggregate the series become a system of national accounts, incorporating a certain understanding of economic relationships. The accounts form a frame of reference for the monitoring and management of economic affairs, and for international comparisons of economic structures and performance.[62]

Macroeconomics is, as the above comments imply, incompatible with neoclassical microeconomic theory. This incompatibility has been an important concern of economists,[63] although few have drawn the obvious conclusion that the microeconomic model is fallacious. Kenneth Arrow, an arch-exponent of mathematical modelling, in an article on the accomplishments of Paul Samuelson, the author of the leading economics textbook of the second half of the twentieth century, comments that, 'Samuelson has not addressed himself to one of the major scandals of current price theory, the relation between microeconomics and macroeconomies.'[64] The fault is not confined to Samuelson. Arrow made the comment in 1967, but the scandal has not been resolved, only sublimated. It is perhaps regrettable that Arrow himself did not address the problem in greater depth, since his own work displays the inconsistencies very prominently.

The theory of support-bargaining and money-bargaining explains macroeconomic performance. It is based on observed patterns of behaviour in economies. It is both microeconomic and macroeconomic theory. Macroeconomic money-bargaining is microeconomic money-bargaining in aggregate; the two seamlessly linked. In the macroeconomic sphere, as portrayed in support-bargaining and money-bargaining, money is the bargaining counter with which money-bargaining is conducted. In macroeconomic theory money is described as a medium of exchange. As was noted in the Introduction, there is no place for money in the neoclassical model, so that money as a 'medium of exchange' is descriptive of macroeconomic behaviour, without fitting into any microeconomic explanation. It is readily understood as a matter of common observation, a matter of common theory. People see how money is used in their everyday transactions, and easily recognise it as a medium of exchange. In the theory of money-bargaining, money is the bargaining counter integral to the dynamics of money-bargaining. It is also, like the 'medium of exchange,' a matter of common observation. People well understand a bargaining process, as distinct from simple 'this-for-that' exchange, in connection with their use of money, and money as a 'bargaining counter' is an integral part of that understanding. The theory of money-bargaining is an elaboration of the concept of bargaining with money that is part of common theory.

It suited the politics of individualism in the nineteenth century that it should be thought that markets were self-regulating. Some counter to the tide of mass interest was inevitable. But it was perhaps not inevitable that intellectual support-bargaining should have been so deeply 'embedded' with political support-bargaining as to produce economic theory so conducive to a particular partisan cause. It would have been quite feasible, especially having regard to the role of machines, to develop an empirically based account of the behaviour of economies. The theory of money-bargaining could have emerged in the nineteenth century if the formulation of economic theory had been divorced from political interest and focussed on empirical evidence, as in the science on which it was modelled. Mathematical codification could then have been used, as in physics, in the service of empirical understanding, rather than as an end in itself. The use of the bargaining counter 'support' in both intellectual support-bargaining and political support-bargaining proved fatal to the emergence of realistic economic theory. The political interest dominated the theoretical formulation.[65] The establishment of the neoclassical model of economic behaviour was a result of the subordination of empirical enquiry into social affairs to concerns over the advance of mass political movements in the intellectual support-bargaining of the nineteenth and twentieth centuries.

It is understandable that Polanyi should confuse economic theory with economic practice, given the confusion amongst economists. But hardly excusable. Polanyi claims to be making original observations about the conduct of human society, so might reasonably be expected to take account of the observable performance of economies, as opposed to the ideas held about them. It suited Polanyi's ideological interest that economics should be the individualist thesis of the 'self-regulating market' rather than the observable functioning of macroeconomies. Polanyi's anthropological followers have been misled into the idea that economic exchange had no part, or very little part, in the conduct of ancient economies. If Polanyi is not to be excused, still less are economists.

Rather than acknowledge the incompatibility of microeconomics with what is observed of macroeconomic behaviour, economists have mostly preferred to argue reconciliation between them. These attempts at reconciliation give economic theory much of its elusive character. Economists imbued with the 'core' neoclassical frame of reference avert criticism by reference to the modifications that supposedly reconcile it with empirical observation. The modifications are held to be no more than modifications; insufficient to nullify the basic import of the core model regarding the optimal allocation of resources. But the integrity of the core is vital to the economists' cause, since the quality of 'optimal allocation of resources' applies only to the most basic model. The differences listed above are surely sufficient to demonstrate that macroeconomic processes are wholly different to the conception of the neoclassical model, involving both different participants and a different dynamic.

Early modifications to the neoclassical economic model aimed at reconciling it with macroeconomic observation addressed the tendency of companies to form monopolies and oligopolies. In the 1930s two analyses appeared in the same year using the mathematical techniques of the neoclassical model.[66] Monopolistic ambitions of suppliers are a major snag to the supposed 'self-regulating' character of markets. Later, government engagement in economies was partially reconciled with the principles of the economic model through the idea of 'public goods.'[67] Companies have been explained as necessary to the minimization of 'transaction costs.'[68] In a recent book, George Akerlof and Robert Shiller, both winners of the Nobel Memorial Prize for Economics, seek to reconcile neoclassical theory with the distortions of consumer selection arising from manipulation of information through advertising and other dissemination of information. They acknowledge that information is so manipulated to promote sales that it effectively treats people as fools.[69] Hence their title *Phishing for Phools*. They, nevertheless, claim that the 'market' still provides an optimal allocation of resources, no matter it is an allocation based on misinformation – that it is, in effect, an optimal allocation for fools.[70] This example carries a lesson that applies to all such attempts to reconcile the neoclassical microeconomic model with macroeconomic observation: they effect no reconciliation, but rather prove the micro-model wrong.

Transformation by Companies

Polanyi's preoccupation with the iniquities of 'self-regulating markets' blinds him to the real dynamics of economic systems. The 'transformation' that took place in Europe in the nineteenth century appears in the idea of money-bargaining to rest heavily on the activities of companies operating as specialist money-bargaining agencies. The idea of markets based on 'natural prices' and the 'market prices' of the neoclassical economic model, which embodies the idea of the 'self-regulating market,' was primarily of theoretical interest. Mathematicians particularly enjoyed the economic model. They are, however, easily adapted to the practical purpose of providing support for ideas of free engagement in economic enterprise. This support helped to convince politicians of the expediency of giving companies greater freedom to operate. Political support for enhanced freedom of companies gave rise in mid-century to the passage of legislation giving companies the option of 'limited liability.' This distinct legal character established unambiguously their status as specialist money-bargaining agencies. Investors were liable only for the money they invested, rather than to the full extent of their personal wealth. 'Companies' expanded their role as the dominant agencies of economies.

In the neoclassical microeconomic model, 'products' are undifferentiated within product groups, so that supply and demand relate to a uniform product and the 'price' relates to that uniform product. Supply and demand at different prices are commonly represented as curves on a graph, with the intersection of the two lines identifying the 'market' price, the equilibrium price at which supply is equal to demand. Such curves can only be drawn if products are homogeneous and transactions are coincident in space and time. 'Consumers' buy a product up to the point where its marginal utility is equal to the market price they must pay for it. A 'firm' increases its production up to the point where its marginal cost of production is equal to the market price. The 'firm' is defined in this way to accommodate mathematical codification. This mode of price formation is central to the neoclassical model and the basis of the idea of economic 'markets' as taken up by Polanyi. It is markets of this kind that are held not to have existed in the ancient world.

But as a matter of empirical observation and experience, firms, or companies, act quite differently and prices are set quite differently. The continued existence of a company depends on its meeting a viability condition: that revenues are greater than costs. This condition can be written as: 'sales × price > unit cost of provision × volume of provision.' Companies set their prices by reference to their unit costs. So long as their prices are above their unit costs, their revenues will exceed their costs, assuming they can sell all, or nearly all, their volume of provision. So they direct their efforts to the minimisation of unit costs and to achievement of sales at or above the price dictated by their unit costs. They will seek to minimise their unit costs through choice of technologies, locational selection and other means. They will try to ensure sales by differentiating their products from those of rivals. Technology will help them differentiate.[71]

The setting of a minimum price, or 'base price,' is then a matter for the producer or provider. It is related to unit costs, but is adjusted in accordance with the level of sales achieved, which is related, in turn, to what other providers can offer. So 'supply and demand' is not irrelevant, but it is not relevant in the way presented in the neoclassical economic model. Supply depends on the format of companies, or similar agencies. Demand depends on the situations of potential buyers. Prices can be established by providers anywhere at any time, by reference to their unit costs. Even in the ancient world, any agent engaging in exchange using money, of whatever kind, could have put a product up for sale at a base price, and adjusted it in accordance with the number of buyers who came forward.

Polanyi argues that the introduction of machinery into Western economies made inevitable the emergence of self-regulating markets: 'we insist that once elaborate machines and plant were used for production in a commercial society, the idea of a self-regulating market system was bound to take shape.'[72] But technology influences unit costs. Machinery can produce large volumes of goods at low unit cost. Hence a user of machinery can offer lower prices than companies without comparable machinery, and develop a monopolistic position. Far from the introduction of machinery making inevitable the establishment of self-regulating markets, such innovation positively obstructs the operation of self-regulating markets. The company with the lowest unit costs will potentially monopolise the market. 'Machinery' is more the basis for a theory of money-bargaining.

These 'economies of scale,' and the broader unit cost implications of technology, constitute a major flaw in the argument that free markets produce an optimal allocation of resources. It is a further incompatibility of the microeconomic model with macroeconomic practice, or empirical observation. The emergence of monopoly under 'free enterprise' is a major part of the anticapitalist case. Mergers and takeovers increase the size of companies and reduce unit costs, or help to gain economies of scale. They are thus conducive to the emergence of monopoly. Anti-trust law aimed at impeding the development of monopolies was introduced in the United States in 1890, with other countries subsequently introducing similar measures. Instead of self-regulatory markets returning economic systems to equilibrium, the systems are evolutionary, with companies and their technologies playing a major part in their evolution.

Companies behave like companies by seeking to advance their bargaining positions. Buyers often benefit from better products and better service at lower prices, but they may suffer when a company achieves a bargaining position of such strength that it can impose prices well above its unit costs of provision.

Disparities in time between revenues and expenditures are prominent in macroeconomic practice. All agents operate budgets to deal with them. Companies operate budgets that are, by virtue of their specialism in money-bargaining and the importance of the viability condition, of central importance to the monitoring and assessment of their performance. They use substantial credit. Ordinary people also use credit and savings to reconcile time disparities. Amongst their most important requirements for credit is that relating to the purchase of houses. The highest priority for savings is that for the finance of retirement.

These requirements have brought about the format of many companies to provide financial services. Banks play a major role in the conduct of business and the management of economies. They play a major role in the management of money. Credit provision by banks and its subsequent repayment is the major means by which money is put into circulation and withdrawn from circulation in an economy. The stability of the purchasing power of money depends on control of its supply, so that bank provision of credit has to be regulated. Central banks have been established in virtually all nations to supervise bank provision of credit so that companies and individuals get the credit they need, whilst ensuring price stability and protecting borrowers and savers against bank failures.

The need for credit is so widespread that the financial institutions providing it can grow to great size, with their revenues far in excess of what is needed to meet the viability condition. They become highly influential in money-bargaining networks. 'Capitalism' derives much of its character from these institutions, and they have become targets of a global 'anti-capitalist' movement. 'Anti-capitalist' sentiment is apparent in the work of economic anthropologists and sociologists dealing with ancient societies. Their antipathy, and their preference for the ascendancy of interests based on group support, is analogous to the antipathy of ancient rulers to the emergence of independent systems of material provision involving the use of a rival bargaining counter to 'support' in the form of 'money.'

Polanyi stresses the significance of what he refers to as *haute finance* in the great transformation, but makes no reference to the essential services the banks and other financial institutions provide in overcoming the time disparities that are integral to the conduct of economic affairs. *Haute finance* is seen principally as the link between international political and economic life by which peace in Europe was maintained up to the First World War. *Haute finance* was unable to sustain this function amidst the economic and social disintegration leading up to the First World War.[73]

Companies must, as a minimum condition for their survival, meet the viability condition. Many companies fail to meet the viability condition, but some go on to exceed it handsomely. Owners can become rich, and being rich they are potentially in a position to assemble support, and being in that position they become a potential threat to support-bargaining agencies. Money-bargaining will potentially impinge too sharply on support-bargaining for the interests of rulers. One bargaining counter threatens the other. Hence companies can only operate and grow independently where they are tolerated by rulers. This commonly means societies in which rulers feel secure in the support of their people. The introduction of limited liability legislation in Europe marked social acceptance of companies as independent specialist money-bargaining agencies and stimulated growth in their activities. Practical companies rather than theoretical self-regulating markets were the agents of the 'Great Transformation.'

Polanyi affirms that society protected itself against the perils inherent in a self-regulating market system (at Note 57). Through support-bargaining, sufficient support was assembled to identify a communal interest in the regulation of economic affairs for communal advantage. Support-bargaining makes possible this assembly of support for ideas of communal interest. Today, support is assembled to combat climate change, a covid pandemic, poverty and a host of other interests. In the concept of a support-bargaining and money-bargaining society, there is not only individual interest, as in neoclassical theory, but also communal interest. Macroeconomic enquiry similarly recognises communal interest and the major role in economies of governments and their budgets. Through formal support-bargaining systems, governments gain authority to raise revenues for budgets, and make expenditures to advance what has been identified as communal interest. This 'communal interest,' identified through support-bargaining, is glossed in the reconciliation of neoclassical theory with macroeconomic conduct in terms of 'public goods.' The notion of 'public goods' does not explain the range or qualities of the services, and they are invariably services, provided by governments. 'Public services' are created through support-bargaining to meet communal interests, and provided by the state as agency of communal interest. The stronger the private money-bargaining, the more funding can be made available through government budgets for provision of these public services. Today, governments are more inclined to see private money-bargaining as advantageous to their continued rule, by virtue of the revenues that can be derived from it, and the employment it creates, rather than, as in previous eras, as threatening their ascendancy.

Markets as Confluence

The above understanding of companies and the conception of interests and values as related to situation implies a different understanding of markets to that of microeconomic theory. A company controls the unit cost of provision and the volume of provision. It also determines the base price at which it can offer goods for sale, related to its unit cost of provision. The one part of the viability condition that it does not control is 'sales.' It has to find means of making sales at the base price, or above, that will bring revenues sufficient to fulfil the viability condition. Its products are designed to accommodate certain consumer situations, so to make the necessary sales, it has to link up in some way with consumers in the relevant situations.

'Markets' can be understood as the confluences of people that make achievement of sales and fulfilment of the viability condition most likely, whilst at the same time giving buyers the best chance of finding products that fit their situations, including their budgetary situations. Markets as confluences of people for purposes of trade must, as suggested above, have been used 'forever.' Coastal fishermen in the earliest times would have had reason to arrange confluence with inland gardening people for purposes of exchange. Market gardeners will see people gathered in cities as their primary markets. Sheep farmers will see the weekly gatherings in their local market town as the place to achieve necessary sales of their flocks. Retailers of jewellery will want to be in high streets or shopping malls with well-heeled footfalls. Confluence on the internet today widely substitutes for physical confluence in the making of sales, so that jewellers, for example, will want to be prominent amongst the 'finds' of search engines on the internet. Producers of motor vehicles will ship their vehicles around the world to find people with the need for transport and the budgets to buy motorised transport. Transport makes possible the physical shipment of goods from sellers to buyers, in whatever forum a sale is negotiated. Many products will move through supply chains, ending up in the confluences of people where sales of individual items are made to their final buyers.

Markets as conceived in money-bargaining will still adjust; or at least, the agents involved, in pursuit of viability, will adjust what they offer and accept as circumstances change. Companies will redesign their products to fit better the situations of consumers. They will design cheaper or more expensive products according to the revenue figures derived from their current sales of products, or sales of similar products by other companies. They will develop and utilise new technologies that produce a better fit of product to situations, including budgetary situations. Consumers will adjust their requirements in accordance with their understanding of their situations. Opinions change, like fashions, with regard to what is fitting. But the agents of money-bargaining make their adjustments in accordance with their interests, and their interests will change with changing situations, with none of the apparently impersonal mathematical inevitability of the neoclassical model. The adjustments of money-bargaining are part of an evolutionary process, not movement towards equilibrium, as in the neoclassical model.

The advantages of confluence to trade of all kinds are apparent in the development of cities and towns. Broadly, any changes that bring people together, that give rise to group formation and settlement in a particular location, will generate conditions advantageous to business development. Military garrisons are the origin of many towns and cities across Europe. A garrison, funded by the state that imposes its presence, provides opportunities for sales of food, clothing, entertainment and much else in potentially sufficient volume to provide a viable return to a company, or an agent operating like a company, in pursuit of 'viability.' Similarly, a large manorial community can stimulate trade. Towns become centres of governance and administration and the influx of personnel creates opportunities for sales. Ecclesiastical centres present opportunities for sales. Trade between city people and surrounding farmers has been and is still a common pattern of trade.

Governments responded to movements of support in the nineteenth century in Europe by giving greater freedom for the operation of companies. This freedom was enlarged in Britain to facilitate the introduction of railways. The introduction of limited liability legislation in Britain in the 1840s, mentioned above, was driven in part by desire to facilitate investment in railway construction and operation. Railways, along with companies, brought about the 'transformation' in nineteenth-century Europe. They connected settlements far more effectively than canals and made it possible for companies to sell across a whole country, greatly facilitating the meeting and surpassing of the viability condition. The people of whole countries became more or less confluent, or at least sufficiently confluent to be treated by companies as targets for their sales. Connections were then built internationally through the development of shipping and associated services.[74] It became possible to conceive of a global 'market,' with people from around the world in confluence.

Some companies, such as Alibaba, Facebook and Twitter, have recently grown to enormous size, with returns that amply fulfil the viability condition, through what may be seen as the provision of 'confluence' itself. They offer people connections to each other. The more connections they can offer, the more attractive it is to buyers to join the confluence. Connections attract connectors. But those taking up the opportunities for connection do not pay the companies for the service. The confluences created are valuable for the opportunities they create for companies to make sales. Advertising agencies pay to disseminate information in the confluences on behalf of their clients, expecting to generate sales. The convenors of traditional town markets offered confluence to the farmers around the towns. 'Bazaars' created confluence in the ancient Middle East.

Notes

1 Pearson, Harry W., 1957, 'The secular debate on economic primitivism', in Karl Polanyi, Conrad M. Arensberg, and Harry W. Pearson (Eds.), *Trade and Market in the Early Empires: Economies in History and Theory*, Glencoe: Free Press and Falcon's Wing Press, pp. 3–11, pp. 3–4.

2 Malinowski, Bronislaw, 2002/1922, *Argonauts of the Western Pacific*, London: Routledge & Kegan Paul, p. 516.

3 Malinowski, 2002/1922, p. 175.

4 Malinowski, Bronislaw, 1921, 'The Primitive Economics of the Trobriand Islanders.' *The Economic Journal*, Vol. 31, No. 121, pp. 1–16, p. 15.

5 Malinowski, 1921, p.8.

6 Malinowski, Bronislaw, 1920, 'Kula: The Circulating Exchange of Valuables in the Archipelagoes of Eastern New Guinea', *Man*, Vol. 20, pp. 97–105, p. 105.

7 Malinowski, 1920, p. 97.
8 Malinowski, 2002/1922, p. 511.
9 Malinowski, 2002/1922, pp. 12–7, 24.
10 Malinowski, 1920, p. 105.
11 Source: Countries and their Cultures. www.everyculture.com/Oceania/Trobriand-Islands-Orientation.html. Accessed 10 October 2019.
12 Malinowski, 1920, p. 98.
13 Malinowski, 1921, p. 8.
14 Malinowski, 1921, p. 10.
15 Parry, Jonathan and Bloch, Maurice, 1989, 'Introduction'. *Money and the Morality of Exchange*, Cambridge and New York: Cambridge University Press, p. 9.
16 Malinowski, 1921, pp. 8, 12.
17 Malinowski, 2002/1922, pp. xvii, xix.
18 Spread, Patrick, 2013, *Support-Bargaining, Economics and Society: A Social Species*, London: Routledge, pp. 200–3.
19 Malinowski, 2002/1922, pp. 46–7.
20 Malinowski, 2002/1922, pp. 18–9, 24.
21 Smith, Adam, 1986/1776, *The Wealth of Nations*, Books I–III, London: Penguin Classics, pp. 356–9. Smith, Adam, 2009/1776, *An Inquiry into the Nature and Causes of the Wealth of* Nations, Project Gutenberg E-book, Adobe Digital Editions, pp. 189–91. First published 1776. See also Spread, Patrick, 2019a, *Economics for an Information Age: Money-Bargaining, Support-Bargaining and the Information Interface*, London and New York: Routledge, pp. 103–4.
22 Latour, Bruno and Woolgar, Steve, 1986, *Laboratory Life: The Construction of Scientific Facts*, Princeton: Princeton University Press. See also Spread, 2019a, pp. 35, 49–51.
23 Clifford, James, 1986, 'On Ethnographic Self-Fashioning: Conrad and Malinowski', in Thomas C. Heller, Morton Sosna, and David Wellberg (Eds.), *Reconstructing Individualism: Autonomy, Individual and the Self in Western Thought*, Redwood City CA: Stanford University Press, p. 98.
24 Clifford, 1986, p. 98.
25 Polanyi, Karl, 2001/1944, *The Great Transformation: The Political and Economic Origins of Our Time*, Boston: Beacon Press, p. 49.
26 Polanyi, 2001/1944, pp. 49–50.
27 Polanyi, 2001/1944, p. 52.
28 Malinowski, 1921, p. 13.
29 Malinowski, 1920, p. 100.
30 Malinowski, 2020, p. 100.
31 Polanyi, 2001/1944, p. 46.
32 Polanyi, 2001/1944, p. 52.
33 Polanyi, 2001/1944, p. 51.
34 Hodgson, Geoffrey, 2017, 'Karl Polanyi on Economy and Society: A Critical Analysis of Core Concepts', *Review of Social Economy*, Vol. 75, No. 1, pp. 1–25, pp. 8–9.
35 Malinowski, 2002/1922, p. 175.
36 Malinowski, 2002/1922, p. 176.
37 Malinowski, 2002/1922, pp. 177–89.
38 Malinowski, 2002/1922, p. 177.
39 Malinowski, 2002/1922, pp. 181–3.
40 Malinowski, 2002/1922, p. 187.
41 Malinowski, 2002/1922, p. 189.

42 Malinowski, 2002/1922, p. 511.
43 Malinowski, 2002/1922, pp. 12–13.
44 Mokyr, 2018, p. 59. Mokyr's reference: North, Douglass, 1981, *Structure and Change in Economic History*, New York: W. W. Norton, p. 65.
45 North, 1981, p. 48.
46 North, 1981, pp. 48–9.
47 Polanyi, 2001/1944, p. 48.
48 Block, Fred, 2001, 'Introduction' to Polanyi, 2001/1944, *The Great Transformation*, p. xxiv, fn. 10.
49 Polanyi, 2001/1944, p. 60.
50 Polanyi, 2001/1944, p. 73.
51 Polanyi, 2001/1944, p. 44.
52 Polanyi, 2001/1944, p. 44.
53 Polanyi, 2001/1944, pp. 41–2.
54 Polanyi, 2001/1944, pp. 4, 70.
55 Polanyi, 2001/1944, p. 74.
56 Hodgson, 2017, p. 2.
57 Polanyi, 2001/1944, p. 79.
58 Polanyi, 2001/1944, pp. 79–80.
59 Polanyi, 2001/1944, p. 154.
60 Polanyi, 2001/1944, p. 151.
61 Reden, Sitta von, 1995, *Exchange in Ancient Greece*, London: Duckworth, p. 105.
62 On macroeconomics and money-bargaining, see Spread, Patrick, 2016a, *The Evolution of Economies: Money-Bargaining, Economic Change and Industrial Revolution*, London and New York: Routledge, Chapter 3: 'Macroeconomics and Money-Bargaining'.
63 Rizvi, S. Abu Turab, 1994, 'The Microfoundations Project in General Equilibrium Theory', *Cambridge Journal of Economics*, Vol. 18, No. 4, pp. 357–77; see also Spread, 2016a, pp. 44–6.
64 Arrow, Kenneth, 1967, 'Samuelson Collected', *Journal of Political Economy*, Vol. 75, pp. 730–7, p. 734.
65 On the theory of Frederick List, empirically based but with more overt political implications than neoclassical theory, see Spread, 2016a, pp. 269–72. See also: List, Frederick, 1856, *National System of Political Economy*, Trans. G. A. Matile, Philadelphia: J. B. Lippincott. First published in German 1841.
66 Robinson, Joan, 1969/1933, *The Economics of Imperfect Competition*, London: Macmillan. First published 1933. Chamberlin, E. H., 1962/1933, *The Theory of Monopolistic Competition*, Cambridge: Harvard University Press. First published 1933.
67 For comment see Spread, Patrick, 2004, *Getting It Right: Economics and the Security of Support*, Sussex: Book Guild, pp. 23–6.
68 Coase, Ronald H., 1937, 'The Nature of the Firm', *Economica*, New Series, Vol. 4., No. 16, pp. 386–405. For comment see Spread, 2016a, pp. 83–5; see also Spread, 2019a, p. 20.
69 Akerlof, George and Shiller, Robert, 2015, *Phishing for Phools*, Princeton: Princeton University Press.
70 Akerlof and Shiller, 2015, p. 6. For further comment, see Spread, 2019a, pp. 18–9.
71 Spread, Patrick, 2016b, 'Companies and Markets: Economic Theories of the Firm and a Concept of Companies as Bargaining Agencies', *Cambridge Journal of Economics*, Vol. 40, No. 3, pp. 727–53. See also Spread, 2016a, pp. 29–33.

72 Polanyi, 2001/1944, p. 43.
73 Polanyi, 2001/1944, p. 18–22.
74 Spread, 2016a, pp. 133, 141–5, 251–8.

References

Akerlof, George and Shiller, Robert, 2015, *Phishing for Phools*, Princeton: Princeton University Press.

Anonymous, Countries and their Cultures. *World Culture Encyclopedia*, www.everycult ure.com/Oceania/Trobriand-Islands-Orientation.html. Accessed 11 March 2021.

Arrow, Kenneth, 1967, 'Samuelson Collected', *Journal of Political Economy*, Vol. 75, pp. 730–7.

Block, Fred, 2001, 'Introduction' to Polanyi, 2001/1944.

Chamberlin, E.H., 1962/1933, *The Theory of Monopolistic Competition*, Cambridge: Harvard University Press. First published 1933.

Clifford, James, 1986, 'On Ethnographic Self-Fashioning: Conrad and Malinowski', in Thomas C. Heller, Sosna Morton, and David Wellberg (Eds.), *Reconstructing Individualism: Autonomy, Individual and the Self in Western Thought*, Redwood City, CA: Stanford University Press.

Coase, Ronald H., 1937, 'The Nature of the Firm', *Economica*, New Series, Vol. 4., No. 16, pp. 386–405.

Hodgson, Geoffrey, 2017, 'Karl Polanyi on Economy and Society: A Critical Analysis of Core Concepts', *Review of Social Economy*, Vol. 75, No. 1, pp. 1–25.

Latour, Bruno and Woolgar, Steve, 1986, *Laboratory Life: The Construction of Scientific Facts*, Princeton: Princeton University Press.

List, Frederick, 1856, *National System of Political Economy*, Trans. G.A. Matile, Philadelphia: J. B. Lippincott. First published in German 1841.

Malinowski, Bronislaw, 1920, 'Kula: The Circulating Exchange of Valuables in the Archipelagoes of Eastern New Guinea', *Man*, Vol. 20, pp. 97–105.

Malinowski, Bronislaw, 1921, 'The Primitive Economics of the Trobriand Islanders.' *The Economic Journal*, Vol. 31, No. 121, pp. 1–16.

Malinowski, Bronislaw, 2002/1922, *Argonauts of the Western Pacific*, London: Routledge & Kegan Paul.

North, Douglass, 1981, *Structure and Change in Economic History*, New York: W.W. Norton.

Parry, Jonathan and Bloch, Maurice, 1989, 'Introduction'. *Money and the Morality of Exchange*, Cambridge and New York: Cambridge University Press.

Pearson, Harry W., 1957, 'The Secular Debate on Economic Primitivism', in Karl Polanyi, Conrad M. Arensberg, and Harry W. Pearson (Eds.), *Trade and Market in the Early Empires: Economies in History and Theory*, Glencoe: Free Press and Falcon's Wing Press.

Polanyi, Karl, 2001/1944, *The Great Transformation: The Political and Economic Origins of Our Time*, Boston: Beacon Press. First published 1944.

Reden, Sitta von, 1995, *Exchange in Ancient Greece*, London: Duckworth.

Rizvi, S. Abu Turab, 1994, 'The Microfoundations Project in General Equilibrium Theory', *Cambridge Journal of Economics*, Vol. 18, No. 4, pp. 357–77.

Robinson, Joan, 1969/1933, *The Economics of Imperfect Competition*, London: Macmillan. First published 1933.

Smith, Adam, 1986/1776, *The Wealth of Nations*, Books I–III, London: Penguin Classics.

Smith, Adam, 2009/1776, *An Inquiry into the Nature and Causes of the Wealth of Nations*, Project Gutenberg E-book, Adobe Digital Editions. First published 1776.

Spread, Patrick, 2004, *Getting It Right: Economics and the Security of Support*, Sussex: Book Guild.

Spread, Patrick, 2013, *Support-Bargaining, Economics and Society: A Social Species*, London: Routledge.

Spread, Patrick, 2016a, *The Evolution of Economies: Money-Bargaining, Economic Change and Industrial Revolution*, London and New York: Routledge.

Spread, Patrick, 2016b, 'Companies and Markets: Economic Theories of the Firm and a Concept of Companies as Bargaining Agencies', *Cambridge Journal of Economics*, Vol. 40, No. 3, pp. 727–53.

Spread, Patrick, 2019a, *Economics for an Information Age: Money-Bargaining, Support-Bargaining and the Information Interface*, London and New York: Routledge.

6 Words, Maths and Money

In the understanding of support-bargaining and money-bargaining, people identify their interests by reference to their situation. Their understanding of situation has a large element of the physical. They have families to care for, houses to look after, vehicles, furniture, gardens and villages to which they are attached, and employment, which normally has strong physical associations. But their understanding has also a large element of abstraction. They have a certain position in the society of their location, and in the society that is their nation. They understand the 'culture' and follow the 'morality' of their society.

These more abstract elements are prominent in the formulation of the 'frames of reference' described in Chapter 4 as directing attention to certain phenomena and determining the interpretation given to those phenomena. The frames of reference perform a similar function to that of situation, though the 'situation' may be conceived as something more familial and physical, whilst the 'frame of reference' is more abstract and intellectual.

Both these crucial references depend on information for their construction. Much of the information that goes into the construction of a concept of situation is perceptual information, deriving from what are assumed to be 'real' things that exist independently of the observation of them. Houses, furniture and vehicles are all known from visible and other perceptual information. While we 'know' that houses, furniture and vehicles exist as independent objects, we have no direct knowledge of anything independent of our mental cognition. We tend to embellish the basic objects with additions deriving from mental preoccupation with advantage. Houses are 'fine houses' or 'small houses'; furniture is 'old,' 'elegant' or 'rickety'; vehicles are 'stylish,' 'luxury' or 'old bangers.' Objects necessarily have locations and presence at certain times, which may or may not suit our interests. Whatever the object, our conception of it will include characteristics related to its compatibility with our circumstances and interests. In support-bargaining, where advance of interests depends heavily on establishing a particular frame of reference in widespread usage, it is clearly essential that the information necessary to that particular frame of reference is freely and attractively available, to facilitate adoption of it.

It was suggested in *The Economics of Information* that, since information is peculiar to our minds, we live and work in an 'information interface.'[1]

DOI: 10.4324/9781003313472-8

Support-bargaining and money-bargaining are carried on using a great range of information about things, ideas, affiliations, social status, friendships, families, political ideals and so on. Strictly, we 'know' nothing other than this information interface, because we are confined to our minds. Because of the interests at stake in use of the information interface, the content of the information interface is manipulated for the advance of interests. Information that is conducive to the interests of certain agents will be intensively posted to the information interface, whilst those agents will endeavour to suppress or limit attention to information that is not conducive to their interests. In political support-bargaining, rulers will purvey information that is advantageous to them, and suppress information that is likely to erode their support. Companies engaged in money-bargaining will emphasise the ready fit of their products to the situations of potential buyers, whilst trying to suppress information that suggests they are unsuited. Those operating in the information interface, which is everyone, are faced with the task of identifying the information that is relevant to them and sufficiently dependable to be accepted as a basis for decisions as to how they should act.

This question of what is 'dependable as a basis for decisions' is the question of evidence. In a court of law prosecutors seek to assemble information that will 'prove' that an accused person committed the crime of which he or she is accused. The accused will be trying to suppress information that might count against him or her. The prosecutor will be endeavouring to establish that those providing information supporting the case are honest and dependable, whilst equally the defence will be providing information that suggests they are liars and dissemblers. The prosecutor will be trying to corroborate information. Judges and juries are more likely to accept information as 'true' if it comes from more than one witness.

In the wider context of the information interface people perform a similar routine in trying to establish what information is sufficiently well substantiated to form the basis of decisions. They will try to assemble comprehensive information relative to the decisions they are facing. They will evaluate the reliability of sources. They will seek corroborative information. This evaluation is in general ongoing, in that people are incessantly assimilating information relevant to their interests. But it is also more specific when particular decisions are necessary. In the specific context, the process is inevitably constrained by the situation of the person concerned. There are time constraints, budget constraints and potential constraints on access to information. People may depend on one source which they think and hope is reliable, rather than seeking corroborative information. In some cases, they will only have one source of specialist information to rely on.

This process of assembling, selecting and corroborating information is refined and systematised in 'scientific method.' Natural science is mostly concerned with material things, or phenomena connected with material things, hence with durable states, so that the same phenomena can be subjected to systematic testing by different individuals and groups under conditions that are the same, or very nearly so. Replication is a cornerstone of scientific method. By isolating particular information and with repeated tests in conditions that are as like as possible, scientists identify what is consistent across the range of their testing. Within the limitations of such testing, they can derive durable 'truths' about the nature of the phenomena involved. Some phenomena, such as the phenomena of quantum mechanics, seem contrary to previously accepted principles by which consistency is assessed. What seems 'impossible' is apparently not so at quantum level. Traditional notions of scientific testing have had to be revisited.

Science and scientific method nevertheless remain the best that can be done in sorting what is true from what is false in the information interface. Scientific method owed much to the procedures established in law courts in the mid-seventeenth century, when scientific method was being formulated.[2] The techniques are applied in principle, if not in detail, in the different circumstances encountered outside the laboratory. Information is assembled, as comprehensive as possible, and from multiple sources, and subjected to analysis to identify what is consistent across all sources, and hence may be taken as 'truth' or 'fact,' and used as a basis of decision.

Yet the court proceedings indicate clearly that whatever the hypothetical yearning for truth and justice, the common bent of minds is to the advance of their own interests. Scientific method goes against the natural grain of our minds. If people want something, they think of any number of reasons why they should have it. They assemble information to establish a situation which plainly implies that the claim they make is worthy of support. If a group wants their friend in the team for a football match, they will extol his skills as a player and denigrate the skills of his rivals. 'Disinterested' analysis is likely to be ignored or derogated. Political parties are established to advance group interests and depend on the loyalty of their members for the support necessary to create majorities in a legislature. Those who think the party is 'wrong' on wider group considerations are required to suppress their opinions and support the party. The overriding importance of support means that loyalty to the group takes priority over questions of 'truth' and 'falsehood,' and even over 'probability and 'improbability.' Information is assembled that justifies the position taken by the group.

Those who wanted the United Kingdom to leave the European Union sought to establish in the lead-up to the referendum of 2016 the failures of the Union and the opportunities that would arise outside it. Such evidence was claimed to justify support for departure. Those who wished to remain identified the advantages of being in the Union, with the plain implication that British people should support remaining in the Union. Much of the 'expert' analysis – analysis by those formally qualified in and intimately acquainted with the issues involved – suggested that leaving the Union would be economically damaging. But such opinion was widely derogated and ignored as the failure of an intellectual elite to recognise the new opportunities that would arise from leaving. Support was committed to leaving regardless of any expert opinion.

The priority accorded to group interests over recognised 'truth' and 'facts' is often prominent in the context of religious groups. Such groups cultivate their own group-supported 'truths' which can be at odds with what is understood as 'truth' amongst those who do not share the faith. In 2019 the Roman Catholic Church canonised several people, each of whom was found to have performed at least two verified miracles. Large crowds applauded the canonisations in St. Peter's Square.

When people see their advantage as lying in a particular direction, they give support to actions that will take their group, and if necessary, other groups, in that direction. Support is assembled for that course of action, using whatever information is available as 'evidence' for the benefits of the advocated direction. Given support, action will be taken, justified by whatever evidence can be presented, or without evidence, or even in defiance of solid evidence that the action will be damaging not only to others but to the group itself. People see by reference to their frames of reference, and they adopt those frames of reference that advance their interests. Evidence is cited or rejected in accordance with its fit to the frame of reference.

Such processes appear as the assembly of factional support against sober analytical evidence. Social advantage trumps science. The tribe is more important than any amount of analysis. As Aaron Wildavsky found, it can be difficult to 'speak truth to power.'[3] But the sober analytical evidence is itself an outcome of support-bargaining, even if it is intellectual support-bargaining based as far as possible on scientific method. If it is a clearly discernible fact that a particular course of action cannot be pursued, then it is unlikely to be pursued. People will fear the consequences. If a particular course of action requires that a certain person moves from Sydney to London within an hour, then that course of action will be ruled out without contention. If a boulder is blocking a road, then any transaction involving delivery of supplies along that road is ruled out. But analysis often supports 'probabilities,' rather than incontestable 'facts,' and such support is readily outweighed by the support assembled for group interest.

Moreover, while it is possible to distinguish a scientific or analytical approach to the discernment of truth, there is no escaping the factional interests of the scientists and analysts. Where they look for information, and the interpretation they give to it, are conditioned by their own interests and affiliations, their own frames of reference. Thus in intellectual support-bargaining, as well as political and social support-bargaining, the normal approach is to adopt a particular frame of reference, or theory, or hypothesis, and assemble evidence likely to attract support to it, to argue for the theory. It is factional rather than scientific, interested rather than disinterested. Given the ethics surrounding academic enquiry – the group-approved 'best-practices' – it is tempting to claim that those engaged in intellectual support-bargaining are more likely to abandon their hypotheses when confronted with evidence against them, but intellectual theory groups can be stubborn in their defence of interests embodied in theory that runs contrary to empirical evidence. Evidence is more commonly assembled to advance a cause than to establish which cause is worthy of support.

This is the behaviour that makes frames of reference into 'echo chambers,' as described in Chapter 4. People assemble support for advance of their interests by assembling support favourable to their understanding of situation. In academic intellectual support-bargaining, it is good practice to 'define' the phenomena under consideration. The phenomena are inevitably defined by reference to a preconceived frame of reference, and after due interpretation of the defined phenomena, it is concluded that they are consistent with the particular frame of reference by which they were defined, and consequently the frame of reference is validated for use by everyone, with consequent advance of the interests of the formulators. Since we are confined to what is in our minds, and our minds advance our interests, and our minds only deal with information, we are confined to this sort of 'echo chamber.' The only way out, not always practicable, is the conscientious adherence to evidence derived from multiple frames of reference.

Linguistic Codification of Information

Our minds deal exclusively with information, with an understanding of an external world, but no certain knowledge of it. But the complications of information do not end there. If information is to be communicated between people, it has to be codified in a form in which it can be transmitted and received. Many forms of codification are used, but the main form is language. All communities have languages in which they commonly communicate information, either in speech or in writing.

As would be expected in a system of support-bargaining developed for the advance of interests, the linguistic forms of codification include many characteristics apparently designed to assemble or deter support. Linguistic communication influences the assembly of support, over and above the neutral information that is conveyed. Words are given meanings by their user groups that convey approval or disapproval of the information conveyed, according to the interests of the group. Political and religious activists and advertisers of products for sale all use words designed to raise support in the minds of their audience for the interests they seek to advance. Language is used to advocate, approve, praise, flatter, persuade, promote and propagate, or to show disapproval and rejection. Certain words suggest that whatever they refer to or describe should be supported, whilst others suggest that they should not be given support. There are 'positive' and 'negative' words by reference to implications for support. 'Gifts' have positive implications; they imply friendship and respect. 'Extortion' is condemned. 'Terrorists' are not to be given support, but 'freedom' has positive implications; hence 'freedom fighters' are to be supported. 'Beggars' do not merit support, but 'the homeless' have a claim to our support. The word 'capitalists' is commonly used to imply that such people should not be supported, but the words 'self-made men' convey approval. Political parties of the left advocate 'compassion' and 'equality,' while those on the right advocate 'freedom' and 'enterprise.' To those on the right, the left are advocates for 'spongers' and the 'work-shy'; to those on the left, the right are advocates for the 'greedy' and 'selfish.' Enemies are demonised as 'murderous,' 'ruthless,' 'terrorist,' 'treacherous, 'dishonest,' 'lying' and 'deceitful.' Friends are 'amiable,' 'loyal' and 'trusty.' Even houses, cars and furniture, as noted above, are often coupled with epithets displaying our favour or disapproval of them.

Linguistic codification results in the development of distinctive vocabularies in different frames of reference. Every frame of reference tends to develop its own preferred vocabulary, with words associated by their members with favoured concepts of situation. The frame of reference adopted by a writer is normally apparent from the choice of words. Right-wing writers tend to use words such as 'self-reliance,' 'initiative,' 'innovation,' 'leadership' and 'industrious,' as well as the words 'freedom' and 'enterprise' mentioned above. Left-wing writers communicate using such words as 'social justice,' 'community,' 'solidarity,' 'under-privileged,' 'compassion' and 'equality.' Choice of words means that it is usually possible to identify the frame of reference preferred by a writer within a very few sentences.

Speech gives opportunities distinct from those of written language. Rhetoric, the choice of words and intonations that persuade, defy, reject and bring together, is an essential of political support-bargaining. Adolf Hitler rose to power through his talent for rhetoric, assembling support amongst the German people for actions that seem in retrospect indefensible. Fortunately, Winston Churchill was also an accomplished rhetorician, rousing the British and attracting allies to repel German attack. Rhetoric involves expression or projection of personality, often with overtones of threat along with its persuasion. Rhetoric brushes aside counter-argument with intimidatory words and phrases. Swear words mean nothing but convey aggression and threat. President Trump used 'Twitter' for a written form of rhetorical expression. Rhetoric tends to consolidate and extend group support based on factional loyalty and distract from considerations of wider and analytical interest. Joel Mokyr remarks of 'cultural entrepreneurs' that 'What determined their success was not only content but also rhetoric: the effective cultural entrepreneur needs to find a formulation and a language that resonates with his intended audience.'[4] Even in the sphere of intellectual support-bargaining, rhetoric is employed to assemble support, though in the case of written words, the 'rhetoric' may be designated 'polemic.'

There is more conveyed subconsciously through linguistic codification than is conveyed by choice of words alone. Michael Kraus and his colleagues, researching in the United States, report that decisions on the appointment of a manager from interviews with candidates can be made within a few seconds of the start of the interview on the basis of speech. From the socio-economic position of the candidates, as revealed by their accents, pronunciation and sentence structure, interviewers feel they are able to judge the suitability of candidates for a post.[5] Spoken language conveys information and persuades or dissuades in a way that transcends the substantive information conveyed through language. Support can be assembled and lost simply through unconscious modes of linguistic expression. From the speech of candidates, interviewers would discern, consciously or unconsciously, that the candidate was 'one of us,' whether conservative, radical, anarchic or amusing, and would fit into their group. Vocabulary reveals the frame of reference a person prefers; vocabulary, accent, sentence structure, habitual phrases and similar traits reveal social group affiliations.

Word Association in the Acceptance of Money

Since certain words prompt so strongly the giving or withholding of support, it is advantageous to associate activities or people whom it is desired to support with the words that prompt support and those who oppose with the words that have negative connotations. Enemies can be labelled as 'terrorists,' so that the negative support connotations of the word 'terrorist' apply to them. A criminal can be described as a 'lovable rogue,' so that the rogue is a least credited with the support due to someone who is 'lovable.' Economic anthropologists favour etymological evidence relating the names adopted for moneys to earlier usage of the words. Words for coins associate them with communal rituals or communal morality. Or coins may be understood as inheriting names previously applied to what might have been used as money. Whether pure association, or something more substantive, the words for the coins effectively assemble support, or deter support, from the new coins.

Amongst the Greeks of the sixth century BCE words were used to give money favourable associations with items that were part of communal sacrificial feasts. Richard Seaford notes that the Greek names for coins of low value, 'obol' (plural 'oboloi') and 'drachme,' took their names from the spits used for roasting at communal sacrificial feasts. An obol was the spit itself; the drachme was a 'handful,' or six spits. Receptacles have been found designed to hold six spits.[6]

Seaford argues, following Bernhard Laum, that the use of the words for roasting spits as words for money implies that animal sacrifice was an important factor in the genesis of coinage.[7] Seaford makes the case for spits actually being used as money. Spits have the portability, countability, durability, value range, standardisation and mass production that create the communal confidence and substitutability for other objects that are necessary to perform money functions. The portability, countability and durability are characteristics of the spits themselves, while the other qualities are conferred by social means. He concludes that iron spits could have performed the functions of money and this 'taken together with the etymology of obol and drachma makes it almost certain that the spits played a role in the development of Greek money.'[8]

David Schaps also gives the use of spits, along with tripods and cauldrons, and other utensils, similar credence as being used as money: 'Iron spits have been found in contexts that strongly suggest a use as currency.'[9] Schaps notes the etymological connections in oboloi and drachme.[10] According to Schaps, the moral philosopher Plutarch claimed that spits were once used as money.[11]

The potential for assembly of support through association of coins with the sacred ritual of communal feasting suggests that the Greeks would readily have promoted their innovation by that means. The new coins may have been given the same name as the items that had been used earlier as currency, giving both practical indications of how they were to be used, and an association with communal feasting. Or the new coins might have been given the name oboloi just for the association. In either case, the sanctity of communal feasting would usefully rub off onto the new-fangled coins. In this way, coins can fairly be seen as deriving from animal sacrifice. Seaford remarks that the etymological usage of 'oboloi' and 'drachme' for money may itself have strongly influenced the acceptance that spits were used as money.[12] He concludes that neither the examples he cites nor any other finds 'demonstrate that spits had any monetary function.'[13] But whether substantive or merely associative, the words link money with communal feasting.

A further useful linguistic connection for Greek coinage was made through the term '*nomisma*,' introduced to refer to coinage or currency in the fifth century BCE. Seaford records that the name derives from *nomisdein*, 'to acknowledge.' In its earliest usage, *nomisma* was the collective confidence that could unite an army. '*Nomisma*' gave confidence and dissolved the terror of battle. It was 'mysterious enough to be divinely inspired,' so that again, currency had uplifting and sacred connections.[14] It also promoted the recognition that the function of coins is a matter of collective confidence.

Sin, Debt and the Christian Church

Europe in the middle ages had a rather different culture, though still rooted in supernatural belief. Christian theology disapproved of money and money-bargaining, most especially the provision of credit necessary to deal with time disparities of budgetary expenditures and revenues. 'Usury' was sinful and no possible occupation for a Christian. 'Debt' was associated with the most censorious words of the Christian vocabulary.

Geoffrey Ingham argues that 'primordial debt' owed by the living to ancestors, deities and the cosmos had to be repaid by sacrifice and personal deprivation, with valuables and food given up to priests who mediated between society and the cosmos.[15] He regards the basis for such notions as 'conjectural,' but cites 'considerable indirect etymological evidence.'[16] Drawing on Hudson, he writes:

> In all Indo-European languages, words for 'debt' are synonymous with those for 'sin' or 'guilt,' illustrating the links between religion, payment and the mediation of the sacred and profane realms of 'money.'[17]

Thus 'debt' and 'money' are associated with Christian theology not positively, in a way that would assemble support for the money, but with implications of offence and obligations to atonement. The words for debt are described as 'synonymous' with those for 'sin' and 'guilt,' but the relationship seems more a matter of association than synonymity. 'Debt,' or the imposition of debt, is classified as 'sin.' Commercial debt is associated with religious debt, and hence with the 'sin' that underlies the obligation to make religious donations. The association brings credit and debt within the ambit of religious faith, but in such a way as to distance the provision of credit from what is regarded as acceptable, or deserving of support. Credit and debt, money and money-bargaining, are distanced from the dominant institutions established through support-bargaining. Credit and debt are distanced as 'usury' not only in a functional sense but also by confinement to a sub-group stigmatized on religious grounds as degraded. Jews became the specialist providers of credit, reinforcing their status as 'outsiders.'

Money and debt had to have a place in the order created by the deities, and an association with 'guilt' and 'sin,' with assignment to a sub-group guilty of a serious religious offence, would suit the interests of the religious authorities. Money, debt and commerce were potentially subversive of religious commitment, and hence threatening to religious leaders. Money will potentially distract people from their duties to their deity and to the church that is the chosen instrument of the deity on earth. For the church, money is an alternative bargaining counter that threatens to relieve people of their need for support from the church. The redistribution by which the church retains the support of the poor will potentially lose its importance. The poor will become less dependent. Church authorities would use their role in teaching and the formulation of doctrine to erode any inclinations amongst their people to the pursuit of money. The association of 'money' with 'sin' contributed to that objective. The church authorities might be recognised as the original anti-capitalists.

By Association: Compensation and Taxation

Ingham sees money as emerging through 'the process of progressive abstraction of money from a substantive fixed "payment," in the form of an offering of an institutionally specific sacred debt, to decontextualized symbolic tokens denominated in money of account.'[18] Ingham identifies two theories of the processes by which money arose, or by which what he calls 'moneyness' was established. The first theory is that money derived from compensation payments for personal injury. Penalties established for transgression of social values provided a scale of accepted values which were used as the basis of money values.[19] The second theory is that 'money' derived from the practices of ancient temples in Mesopotamia. The temples used clay tokens to represent agricultural products or work-time contributed in accordance with debt obligations to society and to deities. The clay tokens were then linked to gold and silver.[20] Ingham continues:

> Gold and silver and an accumulation of tokens of indebtedness were all symbols of sovereign and priestly power and status. The integration of the two – that is, precious metals and debt tokens – was probably a step in the development of forms of money that culminated in coinage.[21]

Michael Hudson uses the evidence of word associations to link debt and money to ideas of personal injury and restitution:

> The fact that the words for debt in nearly all languages are synonymous with 'sin' or 'guilt' reflects an origin in reparations for personal injury. German *Schuld* (debt, sin) bears the meanings both of offence and obligation to make restitution.[22]

This association is the basis of the first theory identified by Ingham for the origin of money – that it arose from compensation payments for personal injury. Standard payments in restitution for the infliction of personal injuries might have formed the basis of a scale of values from which the value of money was derived. Philip Grierson argues that money values could not have been generally attached to commodities before the advent of markets, and since money values were present in 'customary' and 'command' pre-market economies, money valuations must have originated independently of market mechanisms. He concludes that in such societies money valuations:

> provided a scale for evaluating personal injuries in the institution which the Anglo-Saxons termed the wergeld, and it is in this institution that the origin of money as a standard of value must, I believe, be sought.[23]

Ingham quotes another passage from Grierson:

> Behind the phenomenon of coin is the phenomenon of money, the origins of which are not to be sought in the market but in a much earlier stage of communal development, when worth and *wergeld* were interchangeable terms.[24]

The origin of money lies then in the standard values established in relation to personal injuries. The theory puts the origin of money firmly in the state domain, with the state as arbiter of appropriate compensation payments.

Grierson and economic anthropologists give too much credence to Polanyi's argument that markets, which he understands in the neoclassical sense, did not exist in the ancient world. As was seen in Chapter 5, pre-economic-market societies could still be money-bargaining societies. The character of companies in Chapter 5 is that of specialist money-bargaining agencies seeking to meet a viability condition. But informal agents can perform similar functions. Anyone can identify a rough base price, based on their assessment of the unit cost of provision, and look for sales. All that matters is that their revenues exceed their expenditures. The neoclassical market of 'standard products, traded between many small suppliers and many small buyers' is not the market of money-bargaining. People would derive from money-bargaining an idea of what money was worth in goods and services. The compensation payments of *wergeld* would then be calibrated with a view to penalizing the offender through material sacrifice, and bringing some comfort to the injured. Grierson raises queries about his own idea: 'That money as a standard of value may very likely have originated in the Wergeld is of course no proof that it in fact did so.'[25] And finally, 'That wergelds were the basis of all monetary systems one would not wish to affirm…'[26]

Hudson uses word associations also to link payments under mediaeval social institutions to modern money. Thus:

> The media for tax payments would seem to be the bridge concept. The German word for money, *Geld*, derives from Gothic *gild*, 'tax,' but an earlier connection to paying fines is indicated by Old Icelandic *gjald*, 'recompense, punishment, payment,' and Old English *gield*, 'substitute, indemnity, sacrifice.'[27]

'Money' is etymologically associated with payment of taxes. Contributions that were originally voluntary became standardised as 'fixed obligatory payments.'[28] Taxation is associated with notions of liability for offences committed or a general sense of social obligation. The quotation further associates money with compensation or *wergeld* payments. But Hudson seems to discount the *wergeld* idea, remarking that in ancient Mesopotamia injury payments were made to the victims or their families, and were paid in cattle or servant girls, not money.[29] This suggests the above argument, that wergeld payments punished the perpetrators of an offence by material deprivation and were of some comfort to the victims by receipt of such materials.

Money in the form of standardised weights of metal emerged, in Hudson's account, from large public institutions, temples and palaces, in Mesopotamia. Ingham derives his account of temple and palace practices in ancient Mesopotamia from Hudson.[30] The temples were endowed with their own land, herds of cattle and dependent labour, making them self-sufficient, rather than dependent on taxation. They operated alongside a family-based rural economy.[31] This suggests a lesser role for tax as a bridging concept. Nevertheless, authorities without independent sources of revenues but with sufficient dominance in their societies to raise levies would wish to justify the levies. The origin of money in the temples and palaces of ancient Mesopotamia and the part played by taxation are considered in Chapter 9.

Graeber's Word Association

David Graeber sees 'money' and 'debt' as something like 'the root of all evil' and associates them freely with all the worst of human society.[32] The pursuit of wealth is a powerful human motivation and has given rise to many crimes against humanity. But judgement must take account also of the positive advantages of the use of money and debt, and the feasible alternatives. Time disparities between outlays and returns are, as was seen in the Introduction, inescapable in both support-bargaining and money-bargaining, and debt of some kind is the only way they can be accommodated. The pursuit of money and the provision of credit have led to grave offences, but they have also given rise to the exercise of productive energy, enriching traders, their employees and their communities. Moreover, the abuses arising from the pursuit of money have been more than matched by the abuses that have arisen from the pursuit of power, or social ascendancy. Graeber adopts a simple and uncompromising anti-capitalist frame of reference that filters out almost all that is incompatible with his cause.

Graeber exploits word associations to the extreme. He never fails to associate money and debt with the words most likely to repel support from the users of money and the providers of credit. He is concerned at the reordering of obligations relating to social debt as debts of business transactions through the adoption of business vocabulary for credit and debt. Moral obligations are reduced to commercial debts.[33] Morality becomes a matter of business. 'If your daughter ends up in a mining camp working as a prostitute, well, that's unfortunate, but incidental to the creditor. Money is money and a deal's a deal.'[34] Debt is associated with the abuse of beloved daughters and the degradation of prostitution. Clearly, Graeber does not wish to see any support accorded to creditors.

Graeber similarly associates modern employment with 'debt peonage,' the entrapment of people in labour contracts through debt effectively forced upon them by tax obligations to governments or conditions of company employment. He remarks, 'and, increasingly, simply being able to go to college now almost necessarily means debt peonage for at least half one's subsequent working life.'[35] The word association is intended to create aversion to the idea of students being obliged to take loans to finance their university education. But the loans open the way for many students to education and the employment opportunities arising from education, which would otherwise be beyond their reach. The aim is to stigmatize graduate employment as 'debt peonage,' but the alternative interpretation is that if graduate employment is 'debt peonage,' then debt peonage is not so bad.

Graeber makes further associations of the idea of 'money' in an early passage:

> When the ancients thought about money, friendly swaps were hardly the first things that came to mind. True, some might have thought about their tab at the local alehouse or, if they were a merchant or administrator, of storehouses, account books, exotic imported delights. For most, though, what was likely to come to mind was the selling of slaves and ransoming of prisoners, corrupt tax-farmers and the depredations of conquering armies, mortgage and interest, theft and extortion, revenge and punishment, and, above all, the tension between the need for money to create families, to acquire a bride so as to have children, and use of that same money to destroy families – to create debts that lead to the same wife and children being taken away.[36]

Money is associated with tragic events, using words designed to alienate support from whatever may be connected with them. 'Slavery,' 'theft,' 'extortion,' 'punishment' are matters of revulsion; so too should be the origin of such conditions or acts. Wives and children are to be protected, so anything that threatens the family relationship is to be rejected. Graeber acknowledges that 'We just don't know what a political debate in a Syrian tavern in 750 BC was likely to be about.'[37] He is then blithe, to say the least, to impute to the minds of the ancients such sentiments regarding their attitudes to money.

Graeber uses an 'anarchist' or 'anti-capitalist' frame of reference formulated for the advance of current interests. In the sense adopted in Chapter 5, he is an 'ideological entrepreneur,' promoting an ideology of anarchism and anti-capitalism with little capacity to recognise and absorb what is beyond the purview of those ideologies. He uses word associations to fix historic phenomena firmly in a modern anti-capitalist frame of reference.

Language is so necessary a part of communication that it is scarcely possible to describe situations and ideas without using words that convey favour or antipathy towards them. That makes it easier, or more tolerable, or less obviously tendentious, to use words specifically selected to attract or alienate support by their associations. The acceptability of word selection is a matter of acceptance or rejection of the frame of reference in which the words are commonly deployed. Supporters of the anti-capitalist movement may endorse Graeber's analysis and his use of words, but those who look with favour, or at least more tolerance, on modern support-bargaining and money-bargaining systems will find them hard to swallow. Graeber's arguments, beyond the linguistic excess, are discussed further in Chapter 8.

Visual Codification in the Acceptance of Money

One important alternative to linguistic codification is visual codification. A painting such as Anthony Van Dyke's portrait of Charles I portrays 'majesty' in a visually striking and supportive image. In the one image, 'majesty' is associated with handsome, well-groomed appearance, military prowess, courage, elegance, taste, refinement, opulence and open-air integrity. Human minds assimilate perceptual information more easily and quickly than testimonial information[38] – our survival must in the past have depended on rapid reactions to perceptual information. So ideas conveyed in visual codification can be taken up more rapidly and with more conviction than ideas conveyed in linguistic codification. 'Majesty' portrayed by Van Dyke surpasses the most eloquent rhetorician. The natural limitations of the visual medium mean that it excludes much that might also be associated with the idea of 'majesty.'

Visual codification is used to establish the identity and nature of coin-money. Coins were stamped with the figures of deities and heroes, and later with the heads of rulers, for pictorial association with desirable, trustworthy or powerful beings.[39] They helped to assemble support for the coinage. Seaford asserts that the marks on coins were different from the seals used to identify ownership, in that, 'coin-marks create no imagined attachment between the coins and their source.' But in the next paragraph he acknowledges that 'this is not to say that the coin-mark could not evoke powerful associations (with a polis, a deity, a ruler, etc.), or that these associations were unimportant in establishing the acceptability of the coins so marked.'[40] Such positive associations for the assembly of support are important to the acceptability of a currency. The heads of rulers still appear on the coins of many countries, along with symbols associated with the countries. The images on coins serve to identify in particular the political jurisdiction within which the coin originates and is generally acceptable.

An Athenian coin, first minted in 510 BCE, was stamped with the head of Athena on one side and an owl on the other side. Athena was the patron deity of Athens, the goddess of wisdom and war. An owl was her mascot. Owls were, as now, associated with wisdom. Owl coins became recognised and widely traded around the ancient world. Like a modern trademark, the owl built confidence amongst users of the coin.

Visual codification, such as the marks on coins, is possibly more effective than linguistic codification in assembling support, though it has more limited range. Not all phenomena can be reduced to pictures. Abstract ideas in particular are in many cases difficult to communicate through visual codification. Political policies are difficult to communicate by visual means. Not so attitudes to politicians. The caricatures in cartoons persuasively misrepresent the appearance of politicians for the assembly of support for them or against them. Rather than handsome, elegant and refined, like 'majesty on horseback,' politicians are often represented as grotesque in appearance and delinquent in behaviour. The consequences of visual codification in maps and films for the understanding of society are considered in *Economics for an Information Age.*[41]

Mathematical Codification of Information

Economists in the late-nineteenth century adopted mathematics for codification of economic ideas. The preference was inspired by the remarkable advances in physics that had been achieved through the use of mathematics. But the preference was justified also by reference to the biases, preferences and persuasion that inevitably crept into debates using linguistic codification. Mathematics seemed to offer a purity of expression that freed it from the personal prejudices that could be expressed, wittingly and unwittingly, through language. It was potentially of particular value in a context in which personal prejudices of a political kind, leaning to left or right, were particularly likely to intrude. It would have seemed potentially of particular value also in a context that dealt extensively with physical things like grain, textiles, shoes, beer and kettles. The mathematical neoclassical model, referred to also as the 'marginal model' or the 'Walrasian model,' forms the core frame of reference of mainstream economic theory.

It has, however, all the limitations of pictures as a form of codification. It presents a caricature of the functioning of economies rather than an account consistent with empirical observation. Like caricatures, it omits extensive and important detail. And like caricatures, it has been extraordinarily persuasive. Though eliminating some of the personal prejudice that can be conveyed through language, it introduces the particular prejudices that arise from the selection necessary to mathematical codification. Mathematics requires that phenomena present themselves in a certain form. They have to be discrete, quantifiable, concrete and homogeneous. They have to behave in ways that are mathematically consistent. Phenomena that do not present in that form are either ignored or redefined so that they do. The codification requirement has been permitted to govern the registration of phenomena.

The commitment to mathematical codification affects the treatment of information in neoclassical theory. Since human minds can only deal with information, the adoption of a codification that rules out extensive information is a critical weakness. The development of an alternative macroeconomic account of economic performance was noted in Chapter 5. Macroeconomics uses linguistic codification to deal with a great range of phenomena and detail that is inaccessible to mathematical codification. It creates a great part of the information interface in which modern debate over social and economic affairs is maintained. But the information interface is made up of information deriving from different interest groups using different frames of reference, all competing for bargaining advantage. It is consequently a compendium of inconsistent and often conflicting information.

Mathematics cannot accommodate these conflicting opinions. People can only act rationally when the information they receive is plain and unambiguous. Neoclassical modellers have been obliged to assume that information is 'perfect.' So mainstream economic theory assumes that the information available to 'economic man' is information referent without ambiguity or question to actual phenomena existing independently of human minds. We know things as they are, independent of any perception or interpretation of them. Only on that assumption is the core model able to show an optimal allocation of resources. It was seen in Chapter 5 that George Akerlof and Robert Shiller have recently tried to sustain the notion of optimal allocation in the context of extensive manipulation of information, with results over the border to ridiculous. The presence of false and misleading information is not taken as evidence against the neoclassical assumption of perfect information, and hence against the validity of the core model. Neoclassical economists stand by their frame of reference and the theory group as stubbornly as any politician stands by his factional diagnosis of the ills of a nation.[42] Mathematics cannot deal with what 'appears to be,' or 'is made to look as if.' Only linguistic codification can deal with considerations of that sort.

The mathematical economic model eliminates some of the personal prejudice introduced by language, but all is restored when supplementary accounts in linguistic codification are provided to give the theory some semblance of consistency with empirical observation of the functioning of macroeconomies. As suggested in Chapter 5, these linguistic extensions serve not to reconcile the model with empirical observation, but only to demonstrate that the mathematical model is untenable.[43] So much more is apparent in linguistic codification as to make plain the insupportable omissions and misconceptions of the mathematical model. The neoclassical theory group has nevertheless sustained sufficient support to remain ascendant in leading academic institutions. The mathematical model has maintained its appeal, but just as 'majesty on horseback' and political caricatures are poor evidence for the nature of their subjects, the model is a fallacious guide to the working of economies.

This state of theoretical economic affairs seems to have kept practitioners of other social sciences from engaging with economic issues. Ingham quotes Randall Collins's view that sociologists have neglected money because 'it is not sociological enough.'[44] But given the confusion, and the immense academic effort put into the development of economic theory, both microeconomic and macroeconomic, it may seem daunting and superfluous to enter the debate. Better leave it to the specialists and follow what they provide. It may also be that some sociologists have been deterred by the codification of microeconomic theory in mathematical terms. Sociologists are generally less fluent than economists in mathematics, though their research often requires statistical expertise. Mathematics forms a useful barrier to intruders into the neoclassical theory group. For whatever reasons, sociologists have not until recently chosen to formulate a distinctive alternative theory of economic exchange. Sociologists and economic anthropologists have, as noted in Chapter 5, focused in recent decades on the weakness of the accounts of 'money' in neoclassical economic theory.

Ingham's Sociological Approach

Ingham mounts a systematic challenge to economists in his account of *The Nature of Money*. He expresses impatience in his Preface with the limitations on thought imposed by 'disciplinary boundaries of the social sciences in modern academia.'[45] After initiation into the 'sociological tribe' at Cambridge University, he found himself living for twenty-five years in the Economics Faculty surrounded by the 'economics tribe.' He became interested in the nature of money and approached 'elders' of the 'economics tribe' for enlightenment. He found it difficult to accept that money was not really very important; that it was just a 'neutral veil' covering what was essentially barter. Being unconvinced by the answers he received, he set out on his own quest.[46] His conclusion was that money originated as a 'money of account,' independent of any exchange processes, in the temples of ancient Mesopotamia. This is the basic alternative account of the origins of money established in opposition to the economic account of the emergence of money from barter.

Ingham argues that money, far from being unimportant, is the 'pivotal institution of modern capitalism.'[47] The mathematical model of economic exchange does not involve money, only relative values of different commodities and services. Ingham quotes Schumpeter's view that 'Money enters the picture only in the modest role of a technical device that has been adopted in order to facilitate transactions.'[48] It implies that money is 'neutral'; a 'veil' over the 'real economy' that is the true arbiter of allocations. Exchange ratios between commodities govern the real economy. Or money can be seen as a commodity developing its own ratios of value to other commodities and services. By acting as the common commodity, it functions as a 'lubricant' to the system of exchange, eliminating the difficulties inherent in barter and ensuring that exchange ratios settle rapidly to the levels appropriate to their supply and demand.[49]

Ingham notes that, in spite of money being conceived as a 'veil,' it has been accorded great importance in influencing the performance of economies. Thus, 'In the late 1970s and early 1980s, it was thought that regulating the quantity of money in circulation could control inflation, as it was believed occurred under the gold standard.'[50] Inflows and outflows of gold in consequence of imbalances in external trade were seen as regulating domestic price levels automatically. It was thought that control over the money supply could perform a similar function. According to Ingham, 'it failed.'[51] Economist could not agree on what 'money' was and how precisely it got into the economy. 'As a practical policy doctrine, monetarism was very short-lived…'[52]

Ingham's own account of money goes beyond the conventionally 'sociological':

> Moreover, by a 'sociology of money' I intend more than the self-evident assertion that money is produced socially, is accepted by convention, is underpinned by trust, has definite social and cultural consequences, and so on. Rather, I shall claim that money *is* itself a social relation; that is to say, money is a 'claim' or 'credit' that is constituted by social relations that *exist independently of the production and exchange of commodities*. Regardless of any *form* it might take, money is essentially a provisional 'promise' to pay, whose 'moneyness,' as an 'institutional fact,' is assigned by a description conferred by an abstract money of account. Money is a social relation of credit and debt denominated in a money of account.[53]

Money is a social relation of credit and debt, independent of any exchange of commodities. The designation of an abstract 'money of account' confers 'moneyness' as a matter of 'institutional fact.' The only agency with the authority to establish this 'money of account' as 'institutional fact' is the state.

Ingham requires that the state is involved in the creation of money as designator of a 'money of account' and guaranteed acceptor of the money in payment of tax debts:

> for money to be the most exchangeable commodity, it must first be constituted as *transferrable debt* based on an abstract money of account. More concretely, a state issues money, as payment for goods and services, in the form of a promise to accept it in payment of taxes.[54]

Money becomes exchangeable when it is issued by the state in payments for goods and services with a promise that it will be accepted in payment of taxes to the state. 'Money' is thus 'money' by state adoption and issue, and given value through the state's undertaking to accept it in payment of taxes. Ingham emphasises the authority involved in establishment of 'money': 'Money *is* a form of sovereignty, and as such it cannot be understood without reference to an authority.'[55]

Ingham distinguishes in money the quality of 'valuableness,' which he holds to be distinct from its 'value':

> Money possesses a specific quality of valuableness, or validity, as opposed to its particular value, or purchasing power. States confer the quality of valuableness by accepting the tokens as payment for taxation and using them to make their own purchases. The substantive value of money is a closely related, but, nonetheless, distinct question.[56]

The 'valuableness' of money is thus regarded as distinct from its 'value' in terms of purchasing power, though the two are acknowledged to be 'closely related.' Money is held to be, following Knapp,[57] dependent on its designation as an abstract unit of account, not tied necessarily to its efficacy in acquiring goods or services.[58]

Ingham sees the 'moneyness' of money as 'institutional fact' deriving from its designation by the state as 'money of account.' In strict terms, as noted in Chapter 4, 'facts' are established by evidence. Ingham's 'institutional fact' seems to be the kind of fact that can be established by a ruler by virtue of support for their rule. A state can have, or acquire, institutional authority to declare what shall be regarded as 'fact.'[59] People have not uncommonly looked to priests or rulers to define for them the nature of the universe and their society. 'Institutional facts' may, however, also be seen as arising from popular thinking. Rules, customs and beliefs become established in common theory and gain the status of facts for practical purposes and in the minds of ordinary people. The existence of a deity may become a matter of fact to large numbers of adherents. Through support-bargaining communities can form group understandings of the facts of their existence. Certain 'rights' may have the status of 'facts' by virtue of support accorded in a society. This understanding of 'institutional fact' suggests more a money deriving from a popular role, such as private exchange, rather than deriving from state fiat under the assumption of state establishment of 'institutional facts.' Both kinds of 'institutional facts' are outcomes of support-bargaining. The two might act together, reinforcing each other, or they might be discordant. The institutional authority might be concerned with establishing 'valuableness' in accordance with its own interests, while the communal support might be for a 'value' based on purchasing power in private exchange. The discord is apparent in modern practice. It is not unusual for governments to insist on an 'official' exchange rate for their national currency, while private citizens accord it quite different valuation.

Ingham makes a sharp distinction between the 'moneyness' or 'valuableness' of money and value by reference to purchasing power. His 'money' is given exchange value through the promise of acceptance in taxation. The apparent importance of the purchasing power of money is an illusion:

> Money may *appear* to get its ability to buy commodities from its equivalence with them, as implied by the idea of the purchasing power of money as measured by a price index. But this misses out a crucial step: the origin of the power of money in the promise between the issuer and the user of money – that is, in the issuer's self-declared debt, as outlined above.[60]

The 'promise' appears to be the acknowledgement by the state that the money constitutes a credit for its recipient. The 'credit' is apparently the 'self-declared debt' of the state – an obligation to accept the money in tax. But the 'self-declared debt' of the state comes with the state's self-declaration as creditor – a tax debt is imposed on the recipient. Only the principle of tax debt is established; the extent of the debt is apparently at the further discretion of the state.

Ingham confuses the valuations that arise from support-bargaining with the valuations that arise from money-bargaining. Without the theory of support-bargaining and money-bargaining, he is unable to disentangle the functioning of the two systems and identify the connections between them. He is aware that there are two systems of valuation, but assumes that money must be the operative valuator in both. He tries to redefine the nature of money so that it might be operative in both support-bargaining and money-bargaining. Taxation is reckoned to connect the two 'moneys.' Taxation is associated with 'primordial debt' and obligations to make donations to religious organisations (Note 15). In that context, a context of support-bargaining, people might be bound to accept taxes imposed on them as debts they must pay. But the concept of tax as debt in that context does not transfer readily as a concept of tax in a money-bargaining context. The debts of the 'sacred' realm are not readily accommodated in the 'profane' realm of money (Note 17).

In the idea of support-bargaining and money-bargaining, there are two operative bargaining counters, 'support' and 'money.' The bargaining process, with similar dynamic in both support-bargaining and money-bargaining, interlinks the political with the economic. Money-bargaining can reinforce support-bargaining, or it can run counter to support-bargaining. But the money-bargaining system is fundamentally dependent on support-bargaining, first because support-bargaining has implications of violence, so that the operation of a money-bargaining system depends on its acceptance through support-bargaining. The second reason for dependence is more immediately pragmatic. The stability of the bargaining counter 'money,' when used in a wide community, requires overall control of its supply. This is most effectively provided through a government – that is, through support-bargaining. The use of 'support' and 'money' in support-bargaining and money-bargaining, respectively, produces two kinds of valuation. The interlinking and interdependency of the two types of bargaining make it easy to confuse the valuations. Guided by a frame of reference that prefers group valuations to individual valuations, and inspired by Polanyi's account of ancient and modern societies, Ingham seeks to establish the state as the creator of money.

People value things, events, ideals, displays and beliefs through the assembly of support for their recognition as valuable. These are valuations arrived at through support-bargaining. The social relation that *is* money, according to Ingham, the 'claim' or 'credit' that is constituted by social relations (Note 53), independently of any monetary exchange, is coherent only in the context of support-bargaining. But valuation by communal support is not necessarily accordant with values established through money-bargaining. The problem with the linkage of 'sacred' and 'profane' taxation was noted earlier. A state taking upon itself to define a 'money' would define in accordance with its interests, including its need for ongoing support. Such definition would inevitably be different to valuations established through money-bargaining. As was seen in Chapter 1, the value and use of support in support-bargaining is related to its psychological nature, its dependence on the sense of insecurity which causes people to value support. 'Support' as a bargaining counter is qualitatively different from 'money.' But since support-bargaining generates a sense of value through a dynamic similar to that of money-bargaining, the different valuations are open to confusion.

Used as a money of account in an organisation trading outside the organisation, a state-defined money would potentially bring about serious financial dislocation. Budgeted values would not reflect the values recognised outside the organisation. Hudson notes that what he calls 'the value dimension' enabled temples and palaces 'to coordinate their internal resource flows and dealings with the rest of the economy.'[61] Coordination of dealings with the rest of an economy requires that the money of account be the money used in transactions with the rest of the economy. The money of effective budgeting is the money used in the rest of the economy. The differences between group valuations by support and valuations by reference to exchange are apparent in Homer's account of the transaction between Glaucus and Diomedes (Chapter 2). The gold suit of armour given by Glaucus to Diomedes is reckoned equivalent in expression of support to the bronze armour given by Diomedes to Glaucus. But Homer points out that the gold armour is worth more than ten times the bronze armour in money. If Glaucus values the armour he received from Diomedes as 100 cattle in his revenues – the same as the armour he gave to Diomedes – and plans to expend the 100 cattle on a fine sword and shield, his plans will be disrupted when he gets only 9 cattle for the armour.

It was seen in Chapter 2 that Malinowski finds it difficult to draw the line between 'gifts' given for the advancement of social relations, or the accumulation of social support through support-bargaining, and the exchanges of trade, or money-bargaining. Gifts commonly have a 'sentimental' value different from their monetary value. Homes and museums around the world contain objects that are highly valued through support, but which are often of modest value in money-bargaining. Many buildings and monuments are valued principally on account of the support they have amongst those using and viewing them. A state designated 'money of account' is likely to involve values that are misleading and potentially damaging with regard to the management of the financial affairs of the state when it is engaged in money-bargaining with non-state agents.

The distinction between the 'support' of support-bargaining and the 'money' of money-bargaining runs through the ambiguities of Ingham's idea of a 'money of account.' The 'moneyness' or 'valuableness' that he distinguishes from value can be seen as valuation based on communal support-bargaining. It is a matter of 'institutional' valuation. Ingham seeks to make this support-money effective in money-bargaining by associating it with acceptance for tax purposes. He conceives that people will accept payment in a state-defined money for goods and services when they know it will be accepted in payment of taxes (Note 54). But people will not accept such payment knowing only that it is good for paying taxes. The state designated money must, if it is to function as money, acquire purchasing power in money-bargaining. The state itself needs to receive money in taxes that has purchasing power, so that it can pay for goods and services in an acceptable money. The state can impose taxation, by virtue of its capacity for violence, or by virtue of support. But taxation, to be useful, must transfer purchasing power in money-bargaining to the state.

Ingham acknowledges the importance of this quality of money when, immediately following the above quotation (Note 53), he remarks, 'In the most basic sense, the possessor of money is owed goods.'[62] That is, money must have purchasing power in a money-bargaining system. Ingham maintains (Note 56) that the substantive value of money is closely related to the state designated value, but distinct from it. But the value of money depends on the goods that can be acquired with it, and the state will levy taxes on that basis. The substantive value is the value dictated by purchasing power, and the state will be concerned that its tax revenue has purchasing power.

A similar attempt to link the values of support-bargaining with those of money-bargaining is apparent in Hudson's idea of tax as a bridge concept between value deriving from support-bargaining in relation to sin, punishment and sacrifice and value in money-bargaining. The etymology of words suggests the connection. Taxation appears as a bridge because it involves prominent linkage of support-bargaining with money-bargaining. Support-bargaining, at least in support-bargaining societies, authorises the transfer of purchasing power in money-bargaining to the state for provision of communal services. In violent societies the transfer is an outcome of violence, or violent threat. In the mediaeval world, as in the ancient world, support-bargaining is intimately concerned not only with the violent capacity of the state, but with the mass commitment of support to religious organisations. But the obligations that come to be recognised through support-bargaining do not necessarily register as obligations in money-bargaining.

Ingham radically but unobtrusively changes his position mid-way through his book. He affirms that money underwent a transition from 'money of account' to 'medium of exchange' with the introduction of coins: 'In other words, early coins represented a transition between money (fixed by money of account) and a convenient medium of exchange with a variable exchange rate.'[63] The advent of coin-money sharpens the distinction between money-bargaining and support-bargaining, so that distinctive valuations by money-bargaining, largely independent of political valuations, are more easily recognised. The distinctive support-bargaining of the Greek *poleis* also makes it easier to see a distinction between politics, as support-bargaining, and money-bargaining. The dominance of both political and economic affairs by the temples and palaces of ancient Mesopotamia contributes to confusion between the two. Ingham may also have recognised that the valuation of money through taxation, thereby providing a mechanism by which a money of account becomes a money of exchange, is difficult to sustain. The 'money of account' is conceived as having, in its inception, no connection with exchange, so Ingham's recognition of a transition to 'medium of exchange' is transformative. It restores and acknowledges the central notion of value as purchasing power, displacing the notion of 'valuableness.' The distinction Ingham tries to make between the valuation of money through taxation and its 'substantive' value (Note 56) is lost. It becomes more likely that the origin of money lies in the selection of certain commodities for the accommodation of time disparities – a budgetary role – to avoid the inconveniences of barter.

Ingham's idea of money originating in designation of a 'money of account' by the state, with valuation derived from its acceptance in tax payments, suggests that purchasing power is of little or no relevance. Hence Ingham is at pains to deny any links between the supply of money and the level of prices in an economy. He discusses Irving Fisher's 1911 quantity theory of money set out in *The Purchasing Power of Money*,[64] concluding that, 'the transition mechanism from quantity to price was not demonstrated, nor was it supported by empirical data.'[65] He emphasises the failure of monetary policy in the 1970s and 1980s to control inflation in the way its proponents predicted was possible (Notes 50–52). But his comment (Note 62) that in the most basic sense the holder of money is owed goods implies that money must have purchasing power. And maintaining purchasing power requires some steady relationship between available money and available goods. Ingham's difficulties with purchasing power are apparent in his comment that 'A coherent and comprehensive answer to this question of the determination of the purchasing power of money scarcely exists.'[66] His later acknowledgement that the introduction of coin-money meant that money became a 'medium of exchange' amounts to an admission that purchasing power is of paramount importance. He does not, however, find it necessary to revisit his account of the relationship between money and prices. It is self-evident that if money is a 'medium of exchange,' its volume and value must bear closely on the volume of goods exchanged and the speed with which they change hands.

The idea of 'purchasing power' is central to macroeconomic analysis of the functions and valuation of moneys, with abundant empirical evidence to support a connection between money supply and the overall price level in an economy. Virtually all economics textbooks cover the purchasing power of money and its relation to inflation. John Maynard Keynes provides an account of 'The Purchasing Power of Money' in Chapter 4 of his *Treatise on Money*, covering ways of measurement and the problems involved in measurement.[67] *The Economist* newspaper, for amusement as much as enlightenment, uses a 'Big Mac' index of the purchasing power of different currencies to identify over- or under-valuations of currencies in relation to the United States dollar. MacDonald's 'Big Mac' hamburgers have roughly the same unit cost of provision, the same ingredients and labour input, in all countries, so their price should be the same in all countries. Any differences in the dollar prices at prevailing exchange rates imply divergence from 'true' exchange rates based on purchasing power. Instead of the laborious process of assembling and valuing a large 'basket' of goods to establish a price index, the 'Big Mac' alone serves as a useful ready reckoner. If nothing else, the index illustrates the importance attached by economists in macroeconomic analysis to the purchasing power of a currency. Ordinary people also seem to have a good idea of money having purchasing power. If people see prices rising, they know their money incomes, if unchanged, cannot buy so much. In times of hyperinflation, the loss of purchasing power in a currency becomes painfully apparent. Money is transferrable credit, which is transferrable purchasing power, so long as there are dependable debtors. The management of money is a matter of ensuring that social debtors remain dependable, thereby assuring the maintenance of purchasing power. The importance of 'dependable debtors' is explained in Chapter 7.

Notes

1 Spread, Patrick, 2019a, *Economics for an Information Age: Money-Bargaining, Support-Bargaining and the Information Interface*, London and New York: Routledge.
2 Goldman, Alvin I., 2003, *Knowledge in a Social World*, Oxford: Clarendon Press, p. 223. See also Spread, 2019a, pp. 203–10.
3 Wildavsky, Aaron, 1979, *Speaking Truth to Power: The Art and Craft of Policy Analysis*, Boston: Little, Brown.
4 Mokyr, Joel, 2018, *A Culture of Growth: The Origins of the Modern Economy*, Princeton and Oxford: Princeton University Press, p. 64.
5 Kraus, Michael W., Torres, Brittany, Park, Jun Won, and Ghayebi, Fariba, 2019, 'Evidence for the Reproduction of Class in Brief Speech', *Proceedings of the National Academy of Sciences*, 12 November, Vol. 116, No. 46, first published October 21, 2019 https://doi.org/10.1073/pnas.1900500116. Reported by Ball, Tom, 2019, 'Plummy Voices Get the Plum Jobs in Seven Words', *The Times*, 21 October, p. 13.
6 David, 2004, *The Invention of Coinage and the Monetization of Ancient Greece*, Ann Arbor: University of Michigan Press, Kindle Edition, L2192–201.
7 Seaford, Richard, 2004, *Money and the Early Greek Mind*, Cambridge: Cambridge University Press, p. 102. Laum, Bernhard, 1924, *Heiliges Geld*, Tübingen: Mohr.
8 Seaford, 2004, p. 104.
9 Schaps, 2004, L2192.

10 Schaps, 2004, L2187–202.
11 Schaps, 2004, L2192.
12 Seaford, 2004, p. 104.
13 Seaford, 2004, p. 103.
14 Seaford, 2004, pp. 142–3.
15 Ingham, Geoffrey, 2004, *The Nature of Money*, Cambridge: Polity Press. As the source of this hypothesis, Ingham cites Aglietta, M. and Orlean, A. (Eds.), 1998, *La Monnaie Souvereigne*, Paris: Odile Jacob; and Aglietta, M. and Orlean, A., 1982, *La Violence de la Monnaie*, Paris: PUF.
16 Ingham, 2004, p. 90.
17 Ingham, 2004, p. 90.
18 Ingham, 2004, p. 90.
19 Ingham, 2004, pp. 91–3.
20 Ingham, 2004, pp. 93–6.
21 Ingham, 2004, p. 94.
22 Hudson, Michael, 2004, 'The Archaeology of Money: Debt versus Barter Theories of Money's Origins', in R. Wray (Ed.), *Credit and State Theories of Money: The Contribution of A. Mitchell Innes*, Cheltenham: Edward Elgar, pp. 99–127, p. 102.
23 Grierson, Philip, 1977, *The Origins of Money*, London: Athlone Press, p. 19.
24 Grierson, 1977, p. 33. Quoted in Ingham, 2004, p. 92.
25 Grierson, 1977, p. 21.
26 Grierson, 1977, p. 28.
27 Hudson, 2004, pp. 103–4. Hudson cites Benveniste, Emile, 1973, *Indo-European Language and Society*, Coral Gables. First published 1969, Paris.
28 Hudson, 2004, p. 104.
29 Hudson, 2004, p. 99, p. 105.
30 Ingham, 2004, p. 93, p. 215 (Note 10).
31 Hudson, 2004, p. 104.
32 Graeber, David, 2012, *Debt: The First Five Thousand Years*, Brooklyn and London: Melville House.
33 Graeber, 2012, pp. 13–4.
34 Graeber, 2012, p. 14.
35 Graeber, 2012, p. 379.
36 Graeber, 2012, p. 85.
37 Graeber, 2012, p. 80.
38 See Spread, 2019a, p. 65, pp. 257–60, etc.
39 Seaford, 2004, p. 119.
40 Seaford, 2004, p. 119.
41 Spread, 2019a, pp. 210–30, 257–60.
42 For further comment, see Spread, 2019a, pp. 18–9. Pp. 15–29 discuss further aspects of 'Neoclassical economic theory and information'.
43 Spread, Patrick, 2016, *The Evolution of Economies: Money-Bargaining, Economic Change and Industrial Revolution*, London: Routledge, pp. 11, 89, 95, 98; Spread, 2019a, p. 24; Spread, 2019b, p. 107.
44 Ingham, 2004, p. 10. Collins, Randall, 1979, 'Review of M. Mayer, *The Bankers*', *American Journal of Sociology*, Vol. 85, pp. 190–4.
45 Ingham, 2004, p. viii.
46 Ingham, 2004, pp. viii–ix.
47 Ingham, 2004, p. 10.

48 Ingham, 2004, p. 17, quoting Schumpeter, J., 1994/1954, *A History of Economic Analysis*, London: Routledge, p. 277.
49 Ingham, 2004, p. 17.
50 Ingham, 2004, p. 8.
51 Ingham, 2004, p. 8.
52 Ingham, 2004, p. 9.
53 Ingham, 2004, p. 12. Original emphasis.
54 Ingham, 2004, p. 4.
55 Ingham, 2004, p. 12.
56 Ingham, 2004, p. 48
57 Knapp, Georg Friedrich, 1924, *The State Theory of Money*, Abridged edition, Trans. H. M. Lucas and J. Bonar, London: Macmillan for the Royal Economic Society. First published in German, 1905.
58 Ingham, 2004, p. 48.
59 Cf. Berger, Peter and Luckman, Thomas, 1991, *The Social Construction of Reality*, London: Penguin, pp. 134–8. See also Spread, 2019a, p. 184.
60 Ingham, 2004, p. 12.
61 Hudson, 2004, p. 122.
62 Ingham, 2004, p. 12.
63 Ingham, 2004, p. 99.
64 Fisher, Irving, 1922, *The Purchasing Power of Money*, New York: Macmillan.
65 Ingham, 2004, p. 21.
66 Ingham, 2004, p. 84.
67 Keynes, John Maynard, 1958, *A Treatise on Money*, London: Macmillan, pp. 53–64. First published 1930.

References

Aglietta, M. and Orlean, A. (Eds.), 1998, *La Monnaie Souvereigne*, Paris: Odile Jacob.

Aglietta, M. and Orlean, A., 1982, *La Violence de la Monnaie*, Paris: PUF.

Ball, Tom, 2019, 'Plummy Voices Get the Plum Jobs in Seven Words', *The Times*, 21 October, p. 13.

Benveniste, Emile, 1973, *Indo-European Language and Society*, Coral Gables. First published 1969, Paris: Éditions de Minuit; 1973, London: Faber.

Berger, Peter and Luckman, Thomas, 1991, *The Social Construction of Reality*, London: Penguin.

Collins, Randall, 1979, 'Review of M. Mayer, The Bankers', *American Journal of Sociology*, Vol. 85, pp. 190–4.

Fisher, Irving, 1922, *The Purchasing Power of Money*, New York: Macmillan.

Goldman, Alvin I., 2003, *Knowledge in a Social World*, Oxford: Clarendon Press.

Graeber, David, 2012, *Debt: The First Five Thousand Years*, Brooklyn and London: Melville House.

Grierson, Philip, 1977, *The Origins of Money*, London: Athlone Press.

Hudson, Michael, 2004, 'The Archaeology of Money: Debt versus Barter Theories of Money's Origins', in R. Wray (Ed.), *Credit and State Theories of Money: The Contribution of A. Mitchell Innes*, Cheltenham: Edward Elgar, pp. 99–127.

Ingham, Geoffrey, 2004, *The Nature of Money*, Cambridge: Polity Press.

Keynes, John Maynard, 1958, *A Treatise on Money*, London: Macmillan. First published 1930.

Knapp, Georg Friedrich, 1924, *The State Theory of Money*, Abridged edition, Trans. H. M. Lucas and J. Bonar, London: Macmillan for the Royal Economic Society. First published in German, 1905.

Kraus, Michael W., Torres, Brittany, Park, Jun Won, and Ghayebi, Fariba, 2019, 'Evidence for the Reproduction of Class in Brief Speech', *Proceedings of the National Academy of Sciences*, 12 November, Vol. 116, No. 46, first published October 21, 2019 https://doi.org/10.1073/pnas.1900500116.

Laum, Bernhard, 1924, *Heiliges Geld*, Tübingen: Mohr.

Mokyr, Joel, 2018, *A Culture of Growth: The Origins of the Modern Economy*, Princeton and Oxford: Princeton University Press.

Schaps, David, 2004, *The Invention of Coinage and the Monetization of Ancient Greece*, Ann Arbor: University of Michigan Press, Kindle Edition.

Schumpeter, J., 1994/1954, *A History of Economic Analysis*, London: Routledge.

Seaford, Richard, 2004, *Money and the Early Greek Mind*, Cambridge: Cambridge University Press.

Spread, Patrick, 2016, *The Evolution of Economies: Money-Bargaining, Economic Change and Industrial Revolution*, London: Routledge.

Spread, Patrick, 2019a, *Economics for an Information Age: Money-Bargaining, Support-Bargaining and the Information Interface*, London and New York: Routledge.

Wildavsky, Aaron, 1979, *Speaking Truth to Power: The Art and Craft of Policy Analysis*, Boston: Little, Brown.

Wray, R. (Ed.), 2004, *Credit and State Theories of Money: The Contribution of A. Mitchell Innes*, Cheltenham: Edward Elgar.

7 Barter, Credit and Money

In the neoclassical model resources are allocated mathematically, with implicit reference to relative values of commodities, so money is not essential to the model. Money is a concession to empirical realism, the neutral facilitator of allocative exchange, oiling the wheels so that the ratios of value of different commodities determined by the model are easily established and resources flow to the optimal allocation. Karl Menger gives this concept a historical context, noting that from the earliest times people have adopted certain commodities, such as salt, cattle, skins and cowrie shells as commodities in sufficient common demand and with sufficient common acceptance to perform the functions of money.[1] Menger argues that it is the 'saleability' of such commodities, their ready acceptance in a community, that makes it possible for them to function as money. 'Saleability' perhaps aligns them too closely with ordinary commodities, which are accepted for their usefulness, deriving from their own inherent qualities, whereas it is an essential feature of money that it is useful in exchange. Usefulness, other than usefulness in exchange, is not a necessary feature of money, as it is of ordinary commodities.

John Stuart Mill, writing 'Of Money' in his *Principles of Economics*, the standard nineteenth century textbook, emphasises the inconvenience of barter. A tailor might starve before he could find someone with bread to sell who wanted a coat. Even if he found a baker who wanted a coat, Mill still sees difficulties in that the coat cannot be subdivided into pieces of equivalent value to a desired measure of bread.[2] Money, for Mill, is merely an overlay to what is essentially barter: 'All interchange is, in substance and effect, barter; whoever sells commodities for money, and with that money buys other goods, really buys those goods with his own commodities.'[3] Money in this 'overlay' role is accepted as the means by which the 'mathematical' exchanges of the neoclassical economic model are accomplished. Paul Samuelson, in the textbook that dominated the latter half of the twentieth century, agrees with Mill, 'Even in the most advanced industrial economies, if we strip exchange down to its barest essential and peel off the obscuring layer of money, we find that trade between individuals or nations largely boils down to barter.'[4]

The idea of support-bargaining and money-bargaining suggests, like mainstream economics, that money probably emerged from a process of barter, though

DOI: 10.4324/9781003313472-9

the dynamic of money-bargaining is different. The standard presentations of barter, including those of Mill and Samuelson, suggest that a person having something to sell and wanting something else must find the exact counterpart person who wants the something and has for sale the something else. A tailor having a coat for sale and wanting bread must find a baker who has bread for sale and wants a coat. But a person trying to exchange, say, a surplus bag of grain, will enhance his bargaining position if he is willing to accept not just, say, a cooking pot, in exchange, but a variety of products. He may then be able to choose whether he accepts a cooking pot, a block of salt, a leg of mutton, a dozen fish or a wooden box. Caroline Humphrey sees barter as an innovative, accommodating process of this kind, involving negotiations:

> The word barter as I use it implies an open-ended, potentially innovative, negotiable, transaction, in which need not only answers need but can also create a new demand: 'If you don't want these potatoes, perhaps you would like this pair of scissors.'[5]

A 'package' of various commodities might be acceptable to establish parity of exchange value. Flexibility regarding the commodity or commodities to be received in exchange increases options and potentially improves the return. The 'double coincidence of wants,' suggested by Newlyn as the condition for barter, is more easily achieved if the 'wants' are varied.[6] It might then be that a few commodities become popular in such exchanges. Traders would not want to build up large stocks of products that other people wanted to get rid of. But if they found that stocks of a particular product were useful because others found them acceptable in barter transactions, then they would continue to accept them in barter deals, and be happy to maintain a stock of them. If 'standard cooking pots' were reasonably dependable as items accepted in barter exchanges, they would perform the function of money. They would become a bargaining counter accepted in a community for purposes of exchange. The choice of commodity for bargaining counter would be affected by considerations of durability, portability, appropriate supply and perhaps divisibility. The great variety of commodities that has been used as money is consistent with the selection of a favoured commodity in different communities for the practical purpose of getting round the inconveniences of barter. Glyn Davies lists twenty-five commodities that have been used as money, but notes that he lists only a 'minute proportion' of the commodities that have been used as money.[7] Paul Einzig identifies a great variety of commodities that have been used as money.[8] All such commodities, on the above analysis, are consequences of efforts in communities to circumvent the inconveniences of barter. Barter itself involves bargaining, so money-bargaining could emerge almost seamlessly from barter-bargaining.

We are accustomed to a single currency used across a particular community, mostly a national community. With that reference, we tend to look for a single currency in other societies, including ancient societies. But the above speculation on the emergence of money through a bargaining process might lead initially to the emergence of different commodities in use as money at the same time, or in close sequence, according to what was available and convenient to particular transactions. There would be a degree of 'makeshift' in what functioned as money. Then in the course of time a single 'most accepted' commodity might emerge as the dominant form of 'money.'

In a rural backwater, with people making perhaps one barter transaction per month, identification of 'most favoured commodities' that could serve as bargaining counters might be a prolonged process. A single commodity might never emerge as bargaining counter. But with a dense population, with a corresponding density of transactions, favoured commodities and even a single favoured commodity might emerge quite rapidly. Adam Smith notes that people would be likely to retain a certain quantity of a commodity that they expected to be generally acceptable in exchanges.[9] If cooking pots gained favour as bargaining counters, people might set up workshops to produce cooking pots to be sold for use in the community as bargaining counters. Or if blocks of salt became the favoured bargaining counter, transport inland of salt from coastal pans might be organised. People still receive 'salaries' because salt was the money in which their ancestors were paid.

The requirements of people in bargaining systems are understood as dependent on their situations (Chapters 1, 4). The emergence of a favoured commodity or commodities as money implies a change from the valuation, say, of a cooking pot by reference to its usefulness as 'something in which to prepare food' to its function as 'revenue for a budget,' with a view to subsequent expenditure from that budget. The value reference changes from usefulness in the context of a general household or family situation to budgetary situation. There could easily be a period when a commodity was valued both for its usefulness and for its performance of the money function. Usefulness as a cooking pot provides a back-up value for a cooking pot initially accepted for its value in exchange. With a budgetary role well established, a cooking pot would no longer have to be good for cooking. Its design might change so that, whilst retaining some features that identified it as a cooking pot, it becomes easier to use in its budgetary role. It becomes more of a 'token.' 'The knives that circulated as money in China were useless for cutting; the sickles that were hoarded in Germany in the early and middle Bronze Age ceased to be functional in the late Bronze Age…'[10] The adoption of stylised forms of useful objects opens the way for adoption of commodities such as cowrie shells as money, which are not 'useful' as requirements of a practical household.

Money as Credit

The neoclassical concept of money is scorned by economic anthropologists as lacking any empirical foundations (Chapter 5). Michael Hudson, for example, remarks that, 'There is no evidence that money evolved "naturally" out of barter…'[11] They claim that Adam Smith's assumption of a natural human propensity to 'truck' and 'barter' is false. They argue that there is little evidence of any society, ever, anywhere, conducting its material affairs on the basis of the comprehensive or even widespread barter assumed by economists as arising from the propensity to truck and barter, and so of necessity no evidence that money arose from such exchanges. Humans, according to anthropologists, are driven rather by social impulses, and the origins of money are to be found in the 'reciprocity and redistribution' described by Karl Polanyi, through which the material interests of earlier people were realised on the basis of social relationships. People gave gifts to one another to secure social relationships. These gifts at the same time provided people with material necessities. In addition, a central authority assembled contributions from its people and redistributed such goods, thus securing social harmony and material welfare across the community. Anthropologists maintain that money originated in societies of reciprocity and redistribution in the Eastern Mediterranean and Middle East. Money originated not in exchange, but by decree of rulers of states. States ordained what was to be money in the areas of their jurisdiction, so that money, far from being a creation of private initiative, originated in the authority of states.

Anthropologists argue also that money is not a 'common commodity' but a 'credit,' implying also a 'debt.' A theory of money as credit was introduced as early as 1913 by A. Mitchell Innes, writing in the *Banking Law Journal*.[12] It was largely dismissed or ignored by economists, but has gained prominence in recent years. Innes argued that all the evidence showed that the weight of 'precious metal' in a coin varied so much as to be incompatible with a theory of money that conceived precious metal as a commodity that functioned as money. Rather it was the 'promise' implied by the issue of such coins that gave them value.[13] For example, under the Frankish kings (AD 457–751):

> There can be no doubt that all the coins were tokens and that the weight and composition was not regarded as a matter of importance. What was important was the name or distinguishing mark of the issuer, which is never absent.[14]

Innes introduces the idea of credit as the determinant feature of money by reference to Adam Smith's account of transactions between a butcher, a baker and a brewer. According to Smith, if the butcher has a surplus of meat which he would like to barter, but has sufficient bread and beer, while a brewer and a baker want meat, but can only offer beer and bread, then there is no feasible transaction. Innes says all that is necessary is for the butcher to receive from the baker an acknowledgement that he has taken from the butcher so much meat. Then,

> all we have to assume is that the community would recognize the obligation of the baker and the brewer to redeem these acknowledgements in bread or beer, whenever they might be presented to them, and we at once have a good and sufficient currency.[15]

A sale, according to this theory, is not the exchange of a commodity for some intermediate commodity called the 'medium of exchange,' but the exchange of a commodity for a credit. What has to be accepted is not 'so clumsy a device as a medium of exchange,' but 'a general sense of the sanctity of an agreement.' Innes affirms on historical grounds that, 'The sanctity of an obligation is, indeed, the foundation of all societies not only in all times, but at all stages of civilization…'[16] Innes perhaps exaggerates the trust deriving from historical experience in order to persuade his readers of the feasibility of such a money. History is as much breaches of trust and the breaking of agreements. Relations between creditors and debtors have been universally and eternally acrimonious. Communal recognition of the probity of the baker and brewer is no small assumption. Without the communal trust, the credit notes from baker and brewer are just private IOUs which the butcher must hope will be honoured. But in principle Innes's account of money is sound. Money depends for its function as a bargaining counter on 'dependable debtors.' The theme recurs in this book and is recapitulated in the Conclusion (Chapter 12) in the context of the issue of modern 'bank money.'

Nigel Dodd, in his book on *The Social Life of Money*, records that 'Georg Simmel once described money as a "claim upon society" [Simmel 2004, 177[17]].'[18] In a review of Dodd's book, Heiner Ganssmann notes that the concept:

> is not Simmel's own, but stems from the mercantilist tradition. Simmel refers to it as the 'core of truth' in these old theories. In the mercantilist tradition, money was seen as a sort of certificate, a pledge, a token. That somebody holds money is proof that he has provided a service or a good and now holds a general claim to receive an equivalent. By accepting money instead of a commodity in exchange, he has turned into a 'creditor of society.'[19]

Gannsmann notes further that Simmel:

> describes a monetary economy as one in which the relation between two agents engaged in barter is replaced by a relation of the pair, of moneyholder and seller, to the collectivity [*Gesamtheit*, Simmel 1907: 163[20]] or the "social circle" of the users of the same money. [21]

Simmel himself elaborates on the 'claim upon society' as follows:

> When barter is replaced by money transactions a third factor is introduced between the two parties: the community as a whole which provides a real value corresponding to money. The pivotal point in the interaction of the two parties recedes from the direct line of contact between them, and moves to the relationship which each of them, through his interest in money, has with the economic community that accepts the money, and demonstrates this fact by having money minted by its highest representative. This is the core of truth in the theory that money is only a claim upon society.[22]

The redemption of the 'claim upon society' is explained by Simmel:

> The obligation that arises from a service in kind can be removed in only two ways: either by providing an equivalent service, or by creating a claim for an equivalent service. The owner of money possesses such a claim and, by transferring it to whoever performed the service, he directs him to an anonymous producer who, on the basis of his membership of the community, offers the required service in exchange for the money.[23]

In this way, the community redeems the credit. But the obligation to redeem simply on account of membership of the community seems insufficient motivation. Subsequent writers on money as a 'social credit' have recognized that the redemption is made through the provision of goods and services from economic providers in return for money. This is portrayed here, following Innes's account of the function of money, as a requirement for 'dependable debtors.' While the seller acts as a 'dependable debtor' in respect of the social credit, he or she does not experience any of the sensations of indebtedness. Rather, he or she will be motivated to sell what is produced and become himself or herself a creditor of society.

Ingham challenges the understanding of money that he imputes to economists. According to Ingham, if a private person providing two ducks in exchange for a pig accepts an IOU instead of immediate provision of the pig, which IOU he can later present to receive the pig, the IOU would constitute money in 'orthodox economic theory.'[24] But orthodox economists would require that the IOU had acceptance in the community before they would regard it as fulfilling the function of money, and hence being money. Nevertheless, Innes conforms with the orthodox economic account of the functioning of money; his credit money involves communal acceptance. The community has to have confidence that the baker and brewer will honour their obligations before the credit becomes money.

The baker or brewer might decide that their advantage lay in not honouring the credit notes they provided to the butcher; or they might run into difficulties such that they were unable to repay the credit in bread or beer. The community would need to assess such risk before accepting the credit notes as money. Nevertheless, if people had full confidence that the baker and brewer would dependably meet the obligations taken on with their credit notes, the credit notes could function as money. In times of shortages of currency that were common in the early stages of the industrial revolution in Britain, companies sometimes paid their workers in vouchers that could be redeemed at the company shop.[25] The companies took on roles something like those of Innes's butcher and baker. Their tokens had value and could circulate in a community confident that the company shop would honour the vouchers. The company shop issued a 'company credit' and itself constituted a 'dependable debtor.' The baker and brewer have to be 'dependable debtors' if their credit notes are to be traded. The value of a money depends on a 'dependable debtor' as the ultimate guarantor of the value of a money in goods or services. The 'dependable debtor' is the guarantor of the purchasing power of money.

Mitchell Innes affirms that 'Credit is the purchasing power so often mentioned in economic works as being one of the principal attributes of money...'[26] Credit confers purchasing power by virtue of the purchasing power of the money in which it is denominated. The borrower gets the immediate purchasing power of the money he borrows. The creditor depends on an unchanged purchasing power of the money he lends to get back an equivalent purchasing power when he is repaid; or the terms of the credit must reflect anticipated changes in the purchasing power of the money over the period of the credit.

The transaction between butcher and baker, or butcher and brewer, might also be completed through 'delayed' or 'deferred' barter. The butcher might provide meat to baker and brewer, trusting confidently that they would later provide whatever he needed in the way of bread or beer. In a small community, such commodity 'credit' is operable. If a provider is able to offer 'deferred return' for whatever he is proposing to provide, the provider potentially increases the range of potential customers, and hence strengthens his bargaining position, subject to trust, or suitable sanctions against default. Charles Goodhart notes that:

> Delayed barter could only exist generally in face to face communities in which every exchange partner has knowledge about others such that he can trust payments to be made for items given. But this is unlikely ever to be the case...[27]

Humphrey notes that 'Delayed barter, which often occurs with valuables, requires non-economic means of ensuring repayment.' Implying, it seems, some sort of social pressure, such as the withdrawal of support, on those who fail to honour their commitments. Humphrey notes further that, '"Delayed barter"...can only occur when there is a large amount of information about partners (or other social pressures for repayment).'[28] People have to know who can be trusted and who cannot be trusted. Localised social support-bargaining is limited in its capacity to enforce.

Deferred barter would not itself give rise to money, as might the credit notes of baker and brewer. It is readily conceivable, however, that deferred barter might lead to the introduction of credit notes, or IOUs, as tokens, or dependable records of who owes what to whom. Then in turn, if the issuers of the credit notes were deemed dependable, the notes might function as money. An established national money overcomes any lack of trust at the local level, originating in lack of information about trading partners. Transactions can be concluded without knowledge of the credit status of those involved. The sort of social support-bargaining that can enforce obligations to honour commitments at a local level is not so readily brought to bear at a national level. The will of a community at national level has to be enforced by governments, with authority, either accorded to them or assumed by them, to impose punishments for infraction of what is, or is taken to be, the communal interest. A government is needed to make people honour their commitment to a currency that represents a credit and a debt. The personalised social support-bargaining that can establish a local currency is reinforced in modern societies by the legislation of governments established through formal support-bargaining.

It was suggested in *The Evolution of Economies* that delayed barter, for example, a provision of garden produce to a fisherman being reciprocated at a later date after a good catch of fish, could be more conveniently carried on with tokens representing the value of the produce and fish provided. Instead of being in debt for the garden produce, the fisherman could pay with tokens. The debt then passes from an obligation of the fisherman to become an obligation of the community that recognises the significance of the tokens. Instead of an 'I Owe You,' there is established a 'Society Owes You.' Money then functions as a credit.[29] It is not, however, a credit of the normal IOU kind. As is apparent from Goodhart, money overcomes the lack of credit status in those undertaking transactions. The gardener does not have to have trust in the good faith of the fisherman if settlement is made in recognised money. Instead, the debt is taken on by an amorphous 'society.' A recipient of money can count on receiving goods or services in exchange for it at a later date from a wide variety of people. 'Society' becomes the 'dependable debtor' on which the value of a currency depends.

'Society' requires certain safeguards regarding the debt that it accepts through the use of money. 'Society' is given institutional representation in the form of the state, or a government, through formal support-bargaining. The state then ensures that the value of the money supported in a community is not eroded by circulation of counterfeit money or by excessive amounts of money, relative to the volume of transactions, being put into circulation. Personal debts can be translated into society-wide debt on a national scale through legislation conferring state recognition on a particular money and imposing penalties for actions likely to erode the purchasing power of the money.

As noted above, readiness to accept a variety of products in barter exchange for a commodity will potentially increase the bargaining position of the instigator of the barter. Readiness to accept deferred barter will further increase bargaining position. Readiness to accept an acknowledgement of receipt with local validity from the receiver of a commodity – that is, to grant credit to a buyer – will further increase the number of potential buyers, and hence further strengthen bargaining position. The bargaining position is strengthened still further if the instigator can accept a money payment from anyone that will be acceptable in exchange for goods and services across a whole national society. That gives someone with garden produce to dispose of not just a return in fish but a return in anything money can buy.

Commodity and Credit

Money has characteristics that make it easily understood as a 'commodity' like other commodities, even if distinguished from the general run of commodities by wide acceptance. But most money is distinguished from common commodities also by its lack of usefulness for practical purposes. Most money cannot be eaten or used for construction. It has no value by reference to a general situation. Its usefulness lies in exchange, or in relation to a budgetary situation.

This puts it more in the category of 'credit.' It is a claim to a certain volume of goods or services. A person holding money has a claim on goods or services just as if they had lent something to a friend and had a claim on the friend. Except that it is not an arrangement with a specific debtor agent. The debtor is the society that recognises the money as its trading currency. Those of the society who provide goods or services that the holder of the money wants will be ready to accept the money in exchange for his or her choice of goods or services. The sustained effectiveness of a money depends on confidence that the credit it represents will be reliably redeemed in goods or services as required by people of their society. There must be 'dependable debtors' to redeem the credit. Where there are 'dependable debtors,' money will have purchasing power. But equally, the presence of 'dependable debtors' becomes doubtful if there are doubts over the purchasing power of the money. To maintain purchasing power the volume of a money issued must have a stable relationship to the volume of goods and services being traded. If the supply of a money grows faster than the volume of goods and services offered for trade, the bargaining position of providers will seem to be strengthened. They will be able to obtain higher prices for their provision. Correspondingly, the bargaining position of the holders of money will deteriorate; the value of their money will decline. Money maintains support in a society when it maintains its purchasing power.

The importance of sustained support for a currency has meant that people and authorities are ready to give it whatever categorisation is most conducive to the maintenance of support for it. Thus gold provided a 'commodity' anchorage for support for currencies for centuries. If the community fixedly held the idea that gold was valuable, then gold was a suitable reference for the money the community chose to use. Even if it was not actually possible to get gold for paper money or tokens that were supposedly 'backed' by gold holdings in central banks, people still drew confidence from the idea that the currency was backed by gold. So for centuries confidence was maintained in currencies through cultivation of the notion that they were actually gold, or made largely from gold, or 'stood in' for gold, or 'represented' gold.

With well-established currencies in stable states, the features of money as 'credit' are more prominent. Provision of credit by banks is the major means by which money is put into circulation. People are confident that they will get 'value' for their money, in terms of goods and services, just as if they were owed that 'value' from a good and reliable person indebted to them. But 'money' remains what people support as money; what they have confidence in using as money. The metal content of many coins fell away as their value as credit tokens was increasingly recognised. The recoinage crisis in England in the late-seventeenth century caught John Locke and the authorities out of step with changing popular opinion with regard to precious metal value and token value.[30] Innes cites the deficient metal content of coins relative to their face value as confirmation that money is credit. But still, the fact that the coins contained precious metal meant that they still had value as commodities amongst those who understood money in that way.

This status of different commodities as 'money' and the conception of money as 'credit' are aspects of our use of frames of reference and the selections they impose on the information we accept and follow (Chapters 4, 6). 'Money' tends to be understood as a 'commodity' in a common frame of reference. People generally find it easier to understand money in terms of a commodity such as gold or silver. Gold and silver have firm basis in perceptual information. The sense of their value seems to have arisen spontaneously amongst ordinary people, rather than from those having an obvious direct interest in their value, or from imposition by authorities keen to establish them as valuable for enhancement of their rule. People in many cultures have instinctively regarded gold and silver as valuable, without any need for persuasion. The value of such 'sparkling metals' has been attributed to their pleasing appearance, their attraction as ornaments, and, at least in the case of gold, their freedom from tarnishing. There is then a romantic element to the valuation. If he or she likes it, it is valuable. Gold has also been associated with the sun, and hence with an object of worship in many societies. While there are difficulties in explaining in analytical terms the value set on commodity moneys like gold and silver, it is at the same time simple, being instinctive and spontaneous.

Money as credit is more a matter of analysis and more difficult to grasp. The idea of money as credit is used more by those concerned with the supply and administration of money or in conjecture regarding its nature. It derives more from a 'sophisticated' frame of reference, perhaps a banker's frame of reference. Even now, the 'credit' is often taken to be the credit of a bank loan. Private banks are understood as creating money through their provision of credit. David Graeber, for example, states that 'Money is credit, it can be brought into being by private contractual agreements (loans, for instance). The state merely enforces the agreement and dictates the legal terms.'[31] Hyman Minsky similarly remarks that, 'Money is unique in that it is created in the act of financing by a bank and is destroyed as the commitments on debt instruments owned by banks are fulfilled.'[32] Ingham accords it major importance: 'Capitalism is founded on the social mechanism whereby private debts are "monetized" in the banking system. Here the act of lending creates deposits of money.'[33] But credit becomes money only when a community ensures it can dependably be exchanged for goods or services; when people can obtain food, drink, clothing, accommodation, etc. with it; or when people will accept it in payment for their work. The acceptances of the brewer and baker can only become money if there is confidence in the community that the debtors are dependable, so that the whole community will use the IOU as money.

When the 'credit' in question is bank credit, there seems no 'dependable debtor' to assure people that their money has real value. The bank is the creditor and the borrower is the debtor. The solvency of banks depends on the faithful repayment of loans by their borrowers. Neither borrower nor bank has any part in the function of the loan as a national money. A bank will not give anything but money in exchange for money. Under a gold standard, private banks do not provide gold for money; only a central bank will do that, and then only under restricting conditions. Besides, a gold standard implies that credit is only dependable as money because it represents a commodity that has 'real' value.

The provision of bank credit has been used by governments, acting for their people, to put the national money into circulation. The practice of banks issuing their own money, in the form of paper inscribed with their name and promise to redeem, proved unsuccessful. Too often, the banks could not sustain the purchasing power of their money. Such issue has almost universally been made illegal. Instead, banks provide credit denominated in their national money, and hence put that money into circulation. The national money commonly has the name of the national central bank that issues it prominently inscribed on it. The money is withdrawn from circulation as the lending is repaid. Credit becomes money when there are 'dependable debtors' to provide value across a society in the form of goods and services. In the case of money put into circulation as bank credit, the 'dependable debtors' are everyone in the society that sells goods or services for money. People know their money is worth something because there are numerous people or companies who will provide goods and services in exchange for the money. The best sentence in Ingham's *The Nature of Money* is that quoted in Chapter 6 (Note 62): 'In the most basic sense, the possessor of money is owed goods.'[34] To ensure that people retain confidence in their money, central banks have to protect the purchasing power of the money they put into circulation by controlling its supply. Central banks are given authority over issue of credit by private banks so that they can control the supply of money. Measures adopted for putting money into circulation are considered further in Chapter 12. Ingham's 'best sentence' stands out as wise, but it stands out also as anomalous in a thesis that the value of money is determined by its acceptance in payment of taxes, independently of any exchange. The same is true of Ingham's later remark in a sociological context:

> It is true to say that no particular individual possessor of money is owed goods by any particular individual. But in general if possessors of goods cease to offer them for sale at a money price then the monetary system has in effect ceased to exist…'[35]

Without dependable debtors, the bargaining counter has no purchasing power and there is no money-bargaining system. The value of money is its purchasing power, not its acceptability in payment of taxes.

With this view of money as credit with dependable debtors, it can be seen that a commodity money can be understood as credit. A commodity such as gold can function as money because people will be ready to receive gold as a credit for their provision of goods or services, rather than immediately receiving goods in return. They know there are dependable debtors ready to provide goods in exchange for their gold. Everyone in a society that recognises gold, or any other commodity, as their money becomes a dependable debtor with regard to credits issued in the form of that commodity.

Whether commodity or credit, the use of money means that a transaction does not have the self-sufficient finality of a simple barter transaction. A transaction involving money payment is complete in the sense that there is no need for any follow-up between buyer and seller. But the seller has a money credit that is of value only when he or she has subsequent need for goods or services. There is a time gap between the earning of the money and the realisation of its value in goods or services. Money-bargaining creates chains or networks of economic activity. It is thus an important stimulus to economic expansion. Coin-money is of such convenience as to be particularly effective in stimulating the growth of money-bargaining chains.

Complement and Conflict in Support-Bargaining and Money-Bargaining

The anthropological objection to the economic account of money as originating in barter has a specific original target in the work of Adam Smith, who referred to the human propensity to 'truck, barter and exchange one thing for another' as the characteristic that gave rise by a very slow and gradual process to the division of labour, 'from which so many advantages are derived.'[36] Economic anthropologists, led by Malinowski (Chapter 2), regard humans as primarily social in their behaviour, maintaining a process of reciprocity and redistribution for the realisation of material needs. It was seen in Chapter 5 (Note 31) that Polanyi regards the propensity to barter, truck and exchange as almost entirely apocryphal.

The contrasting positions are best understood in terms of support-bargaining and money-bargaining. The social and political affairs of humans are ordered through support-bargaining, with violence determining issues that cannot be decided by support-bargaining (Chapter 2). More specifically material concerns are ordered through money-bargaining. Support-bargaining and money-bargaining interact very closely, sometimes reinforcing one another, sometimes the one weakening the motivational pull of the other. Often it is unclear which is the operative, or dominant, dynamic. The ambiguities of 'reciprocity' – to what extent it is social, and to what extent it is material – are apparent in Malinowski's account of the Kula round in the Trobriand Islands. The associations of support with violence make support-bargaining generally the dominant process in determining the evolution of societies. Those adept in support-bargaining, or concerned to establish positions of ascendancy in their society, will engage in support-bargaining, and are likely to welcome only such money-bargaining as they see as complementary to their cause. Yet the material necessities and material comforts of life are most effectively provided through money-bargaining, so that people readily respond to the requirements of those who will pay them. In pre-coinage times the scope for material trade would be more limited, but nevertheless propensities to 'truck, barter and exchange' would still be exercised to gain the material necessities of life, and material comforts. Monetary and material motivations can in some circumstances outweigh concerns for support, so that behaviour dictated by considerations related to support-bargaining can be curtailed in favour of behaviour that will bring monetary or material returns. The money-bargaining counter diverts activity away from support-bargaining and the use of support as bargaining counter.

The threat posed by money-bargaining is apparent in social support-bargaining as well as political support-bargaining. Money-bargaining, or at least too prominent a concern for the acquisition of money, is looked on with disapproval in social support-bargaining. The threat is that concern for the acquisition of money will divert people from their social obligations. People tend to emphasise their commitment to communal welfare and accepted social virtue, and condemn behaviour that advances individual interest. People gain support in this way, establishing their security in their community. They may even proclaim social motivations as cover for material and selfish motivations. Thus the view that humans are essentially socially oriented is true enough; humans seek support as a first priority, being essential to their sense of security. But individuals also aspire to the material necessities and comforts of life, and the options afforded by truck, barter and exchange, or money-bargaining, to acquire them. Dismissal of the motivations of truck, barter and exchange suggests a desire to protect support-bargaining from depredations of money-bargaining. Those who see their interests as lying with the ascendancy of the group are likely to favour dismissal, whilst those more concerned with individual freedom are likely to favour acceptance. The former are likely to present as benign the governments and rulers that dominate support-bargaining systems, whilst the latter are likely to view them more with suspicion and apprehension. The two interest groups will compete to shape their societies to their liking and to their interests. Different societies display different tolerances of the extent of money-bargaining in them.

The strength of the motivations to truck, barter and exchange is apparent in the energy that is devoted to money-bargaining. Given the freedom to do so, people organise, produce, provide, work and employ, so that societies become full of products and services that make life easy, both for individuals and for communities. In many societies around the world this impact is welcomed, and the systems by which it is accomplished have large measures of popular support. Popular comment tends to favour communal virtues, but popular behaviour suggests appreciation also of the benefits of individual initiative and energy.

Popular support is reflected in the efforts of governments to cultivate the development of private money-bargaining. Governments provide extensive infrastructure and services necessary to the conduct of money-bargaining. Instead of fearing the consequences of the erosion of their ascendancy from the insurgence of the moneyed, governments recognise that their ascendancy depends on the prosperity that derives from money-bargaining, and do their best to ensure its growth. The expansion of money-bargaining is usually complementary to the maintenance of support for a government in a support-bargaining system.

Whilst governments dependent on the support of people for their continuance in office are inclined as support-bargaining agencies to cultivate processes that sustain their support, authoritarian governments may see money-bargaining as potentially eroding or even displacing their support. Money-bargaining gives individuals the opportunity to advance their material interests to the point of becoming rich. Such riches can be used potentially to assemble and organise support against a political regime. Money can be used to organise violence for the overthrow of a government. Hence authoritarian states maintain surveillance of wealthy people and the emergence of well-funded organisations that could potentially pose a threat to their power. The ownership of key companies in a money-bargaining system under authoritarian rule is likely to be arranged so that owners are supporters of the government. Such attitudes and arrangements have been apparent in Russia in recent decades, the more prominent because there were earlier signs that Russia might move towards a more democratic and free society after the demise of the Soviet Union. It is difficult for a society to change attitudes established by long experience of autocracy and authoritarian rule.

Elsewhere such arrangements have been similarly embedded. In ancient societies of the Middle East rulers would of necessity be concerned that any material wealth was held by people supportive of their rule. Money-bargaining could be tolerated only in so far as it posed no threat to the regime. The anthropological arguments regarding the almost exclusive pre-eminence of social relationships and the dominance of political regimes in ancient societies, the rejection of material motivations and the portrayal of money-bargaining as a destructive force, can be seen as modern expressions of historic aversion to money-bargaining in a form relevant to modern political support-bargaining.

Barter and the Origins of Money

The anthropological argument that barter was never widespread as a means of accommodating material interests rests substantially on what is understood by 'barter.' George Dalton acknowledges that it is a 'treacherous term.'[37] He affirms that, 'To avoid ambiguity it is essential to confine the meaning of barter to moneyless market exchanges.' By 'market exchanges' he means exchanges in which each side seeks to get the best deal for itself, with the terms of trade determined by supply and demand. This has the effect of excluding all transactions of the 'gift-giving' type, or 'reciprocity.' Dalton notes that modern gift-giving in Western societies is of sociological interest, denoting kinship and friendship rather than any material interest. Such transactions are matters of 'reciprocity':

> Anthropologists now use the term *reciprocity* in a technical sense to characterize such gift-giving and to separate it as a distinct mode of transaction,

> different from market exchange: Reciprocity is obligatory gift-giving induced by a social relationship.[38]

Defined in this way, the scope for designating societies as 'barter societies,' or 'predominantly barter societies,' is much reduced. Dalton challenges the notion developed by economists of widespread barter giving way to monetary exchange, arguing that societies of widespread barter never actually existed.[39] He is able to conclude:

> Barter, in the strict sense of moneyless market exchange, has never been a quantitatively important or dominant model of transaction in any past or present economic system about which we have hard information.[40]

It becomes easier to establish that barter societies did not exist with a restrictive notion of barter. But the definition is provided on the basis of an understanding or preconception that societies function on the basis of reciprocity and redistribution. In such societies, barter can hardly exist, and the definition gives barter an appropriately limited role. If societies that accord with the definition of barter societies are not found, it merely reflects the preconception, not that barter societies, on a wider and more generally acceptable definition, did not exist. It was seen in Chapter 5, at Note 36, that Malinowski emphasises the ambiguities of gift-giving and barter exchange. It is not possible to 'avoid ambiguity' by defining away what is ambiguous in life. Dalton is 'drawing lines' contrary to 'sound method.' His conclusion is the echo of his preconception. Even the ritual gift-giving of armlets and necklaces of the Kula round are rated by Malinowski in the sixth category of a spectrum of provision ranging from 'Pure gift' to 'Trade, pure and simple,' with the 'Trade, pure and simple' constituting the seventh category. The 'spectrum' can be interpreted as a spectrum in which 'gifts' that are expressions of support in a support-bargaining system become associated with payments specifically concerned with material trade or money-bargaining.

Marshall Sahlins presents this spectrum with two extremes and a mid-category. 'Generalized reciprocity' is 'reputedly altruistic,' something like Malinowski's 'pure gift.' 'Balanced reciprocity' involves rough equality of value in whatever is exchanged, whether ostensibly as 'gift' or as trade. This category has less personal content and is, according to Sahlins, 'more economic,' with the material side at least as important as the social. 'Negative reciprocity' is the attempt to get something for nothing with impunity by appropriation or other means. Sahlins writes that, 'Indicative ethnographic terms include "haggling" or "barter," "gambling," "chicanery," "theft," and other varieties of seizure.' It is the 'most economic' and the 'unsociable extreme.' Sahlins thus recognises economic transactions as matters of 'balanced reciprocity,' but also associates them with 'appropriation' and 'seizure.'[41] Both Malinowski and Sahlins recognise a 'fine line' between gift giving and economic exchange. In the idea of support-bargaining and money bargaining the separation is made only on the basis of which frame of reference is in use by those involved, including those actually engaged in the transactions, as well as observers. It is a matter of how you look at it, what interpretation you put on it. It is a matter of the degree of social compulsion that is felt.

Dalton suggests that the great variety of objects used in 'primitive money' fall into two types. One type is a 'money-stuff' that fulfils the functions of money roughly in the way that francs or dollars do. The other he calls 'primitive valuables,' 'because they are peculiarly social and political rather than economic.'[42] For Dalton, these have import similar to trophies and wedding rings in modern Western societies. They can be understood in the idea of support-bargaining as tangible representations of support for persons or performance.

Dalton argues that barter is typically used in preference to known alternatives because of special circumstances. He describes Malinowski's account of the barter trade of some of the islanders, clearly referring to Malinowski's account of the barter trade of the Amphlett Islanders, as 'especially revealing.' He argues that barter was used by the Amphlett Islanders because they were socially despised. Those who exchanged yams for their wooden bowls 'despised both the wooden utensil craftsmen and their barter mode of transacting.'[43] The barter transactions 'are so clearly contrasted with non-barter alternatives (transactions of reciprocity).' Dalton implies that the Amphlett Islanders were kept out of 'reciprocal' relationships with other Trobriand Islanders because of their commitment to barter and their low status. But Malinowski makes clear that barter was common throughout the Trobriand Islands. There was an 'economic undertow' to all the transactions of Trobriand Islanders, even those that were apparently reciprocal. Malinowski describes the demeanour and behaviour of the Amphlett Islanders in very prejudicial terms, interpreted in Chapter 5 as a consequence of Malinowski's own aversion to trade unalloyed by concerns for social integration. The barter trade of the Amphlett Islanders suggests that they did not share Malinowski's aversion. But there is no contrast between the barter of the Amphlett Islanders and the reciprocity practiced by other Trobriand Islanders. All were engaged in barter. According to Malinowski, the focus on barter by the Amphlett Islanders was a consequence of the sparse resources on the rocky island.

Yet the Amphlett Islanders did themselves no favours. If they were as grim as Malinowski portrays them, they were not getting the best returns for their wooden bowls. A little 'sweet talk' and a few 'free gifts' would surely have boosted their returns. A sense of shared communal interest, however slight, makes material exchange, whether barter or money-bargaining, easier to transact. Support-bargaining and money-bargaining can be effectively interlinked.

Richard Seaford refers to a 'creation-myth' of money from barter, based on Dalton's article:

> It is easy to be misled by the creation-myth of money (out of barter) into believing that premonetary society was based on barter. In fact it has been concluded that barter, in the strict sense of moneyless market exchange, has never been a quantitatively important or dominant model or

> transaction in any past or present economic system about which we have hard information.[44]

Seaford implicitly accepts Dalton's definition of barter and the limitations it imposes on the extent of what can be called 'barter societies.' But Seaford's account of the customs of Homeric gift-giving or reciprocity confirm the imprecision of boundaries between expressions of friendship and esteem and desire for material benefit.

The 'myth of barter' is a common theme of economic anthropological analysis. Ingham refers to the 'mythical barter of the "real" economy.'[45] Humphrey has the 'myth' applying to the propensity to truck and barter. Her aims include escaping, 'the notion of "truck" or "barter" as natural human propensity which still appears as myth of our subject.'[46] It is not clear whether Humphrey wishes to discard the notion of truck and barter as a natural human propensity, or whether she wishes to discard the notion that the notion of truck and barter as a natural human propensity is a myth. In an anthropological frame of reference the former interpretation is likely. Anthropologists are keen to establish that Smith's idea of the origins of money in barter is a myth so as to clear the way for their own explanations of its origins. But 'bargaining,' or 'truck,' whether for support or money, is naturally essential to ideas of support-bargaining and money-bargaining. So in that frame of reference the latter interpretation seems apposite. The propensity to truck and barter is no myth. The ambiguity may have crept in on the back of authorial unease over the anthropological position.

Deferred Barter

Dalton defines barter with an explicit exclusion of 'reciprocity.' He excludes 'deferred barter' or 'delayed barter,' without mentioning them. For Dalton, deferred barter would fall into the category of 'reciprocity' and consequently would not be 'barter.' Specifically excluding 'reciprocity' implicitly excludes 'deferred' or 'delayed' barter. Deferred barter, however, is likely to be a very common form of barter. Deferred barter provides for a barter system the accommodating time shifts that credit provides for those operating with money budgets, as described in Chapter 2. It serves to bring outlays into balance with receipts over time. As noted above, gardeners might readily give surplus produce to fishermen, as a gift, but in the knowledge that the fishermen would be likely to give fish in return at a later date. The produce will go bad if not consumed quickly.[47] The understanding in terms of 'gifts' is maintained as a matter of communal expedience; it creates good feelings in the community, a sense of unity. There is no need to recognise competition or any suggestion of divisive interest. In the common frame of reference of the village, the transactions are gifts. The 'mutual aid' system described by Peter Kropotkin in 1902 is concerned with 'gift-giving' within villages as a way of life superior to that of more competitive societies.[48] The security of the villagers, physical and psychological, may depend on the maintenance of such mutual support. But obligations to commensurate return may still be present. A rough balance of provision has to be maintained. People who do not achieve the necessary balance will be deemed 'mean' or 'ungenerous' in the community. They will learn through oral and behavioural expression denoting withdrawal of support that receipt has to be roughly matched with provision. They have to 'play their part.' The transactions of support-bargaining merge imperceptibly with bargaining over matters of material interest. As was seen in Chapter 2, Glaucus and Diomedes exchanged gifts of armour, but Homer suggests that Glaucus was a mutt to give a gift worth 100 cattle when he received a gift worth only 9 cattle.

Deferred barter accommodates time disparities and is accordingly readily associated with the use of money as a form of credit for the accommodation of time disparities. A balance of exchange can be achieved through the use of the 'Society Owes You' credit of money, referred to above. As was seen earlier, deferred barter would achieve the desired outcomes for butcher, brewer and baker in the transactions described by Innes, though it would not generate the money that might derive from the acknowledgements. Excluding deferred barter from the understanding of a barter society excludes important considerations regarding the origins of money.

The rejection of any element of barter in reciprocity and the exclusion of deferred barter from the understanding of barter removes from consideration in the idea of barter all transactions that involve time delays. All barter transactions in Dalton's understanding are completed immediately, so there are no ongoing relationships. The emergence of money as 'credit,' in the way described by Innes, could not happen. The butcher, baker and brewer would all settle immediately, or their 'reciprocity' – 'delayed barter' – would fall outside the definition of barter. There is no requirement for credit or debt to cover time disparities. Credit and debt can then be portrayed as introduced for the subordination of one social group to another. But human relationships and material well-being both involve time disparities in provision and receipt, so that credit and debt are integral to both human relationships and material exchange. They have to be accommodated, whether in barter or in money-bargaining.

Einzig, in his book *Primitive Money*, first published in 1949, makes reference to disputes over the origin of money in barter and to problems of definition. On the former he remarks:

> It has often been suggested, not only by economists and economic historians, but even by some anthropologists, who ought to know better, that communities without some rudimentary forms of money have never yet been found. This assertion is in striking conflict with factual evidence relating to some past and present-day primitive communities.[49]

On problems with definition, he writes:

> The great use of definition, according to Shield Nicholson, is 'to lay bare the meanings of the terms employed, to clear up the ideas for which they stand and thus to get rid of all ambiguities.'[50] The great danger is that one is

> liable to impose unwarranted limitations to the scope of one's enquiry, and to prejudice one's conclusions.[51]

On this basis, Dalton could only discredit the derivation of money from barter by adopting a definition of barter that that made it unlikely that 'barter societies' could be found. But by using definition to discredit the barter theory, Dalton imposes 'unwarranted limitations.' Historical evidence, on a broader definition, suggests they were not uncommon.

'Primitive Money' and National Money

Dalton recognises that the first type of 'primitive money' functions 'as a crude proxy for francs or dollars.'[52] Salt, cowrie shells, tea and a host of other commodities have been used in this way. The usage occurred, as Dalton points out, in stateless societies. The implication is that they were sustained by the assent or support of the people in particular localities. They functioned as money because people in particular localities came to use them in that way. It was for them an 'institutional fact' that the commodity was money, in the sense that their support for the money made it money. It functioned as a local bargaining counter.

Newlyn cites 'general acceptability' as the criterion for something fulfilling the function of money. 'General acceptability,' according to Newlyn, 'falls within that perplexing but fascinating group of phenomena which is affected by self-justifying beliefs. If the members of a community think that money will be generally acceptable, then it will be; otherwise not.'[53] It can be seen that support-bargaining lies behind this phenomenon of self-justifying belief. It gives communal support to the notions that individuals share with others. It cements in place communal ideas. It makes possible social affirmation that is recognised and acted on in a society. Individuals can hold the most bizarre beliefs with the utmost conviction if their whole society is committed to the same beliefs. How people see and interpret what is around them and their experience of it is dictated by their communal frame of reference. Since money is so useful, support for it is relatively easy to maintain, so long as it retains the attributes necessary to fulfilment of its function, principally the attribute of purchasing power.

As was seen above, such money, such a bargaining counter, potentially suffers from instability of purchasing power due to lack of control over its supply. If commodity money is difficult to obtain, its value as money is likely to rise. On the other hand, if it is easily available, then prices denominated in the money are likely to rise, and the purchasing power of the money will diminish. If people can 'mint' money cheaply for their own use, they are likely to do so. The supply of money will increase. If there is no corresponding increase in the volume of goods traded, prices will rise. The necessary control over the supply of a currency or bargaining counter used in a large community has normally to be exercised by the government of that community. To control supply states establish monopolies for themselves in the minting of coins and the provision of currency notes, control the ways money is put into circulation, impose punishments for counterfeiters and regulate use of the currency. A 'primitive' or communally instituted currency becomes a 'national currency' when placed under the control of the state. Francs and dollars are national currencies; the commodities adopted as communal currencies are a 'crude proxy'[54] for the national currencies because they lack the state controls over their supply that are necessary to establish a stable currency. In small communities, as was seen above, some control of the currency may be possible through social support-bargaining, such that social exclusion, or withdrawal of support, shapes people's behaviour and protects the adopted currency. But in a nation such intimate sanctions cannot be applied. Political support-bargaining is required to establish legislation regarding administrative arrangements and punishments for contravening the rules necessary to sustain a currency.

The implication is that what Ingham refers to as 'moneyness' can be established as 'institutional fact' at a communal level. Similarly the quality of 'valuedness' can be established in a community. But the communal support is contingent on the purchasing power of the money, and the maintenance of its purchasing power. A currency with dependable stability across a large population requires governance to control its supply and safeguard its purchasing power. The involvement of the state is then necessary to the administration of a currency. State legislation can be seen as confirming the status as national currency of a currency that is acceptable to its people. Imposition of a currency that does not meet the requirements of the people of a nation, particularly with regard to purchasing power, is likely to lose its status as national currency.

There is thus an important distinction to be made, corresponding to the existing distinction between 'primitive money' and 'money proper,' between money established and used in a community on the basis of a shared popular recognition of its value – what might be called 'popular money' – and money that is regulated by some communal authority so as to fulfil the function of money more widely and more effectively – what might be called 'regulated' or 'managed' money.

The Purchasing Power of Money

Ingham is at pains to break any link between money supply and inflation, and hence the link between money supply and the purchasing power of money. As noted in Chapter 6, his conclusion on the attempt to use monetary policy in the 1970s and 1980s to control inflation is that 'it failed.' Monetarism failed, according to Ingham, because economists were unable to identify with necessary precision what constituted 'money.' The creation of capitalist 'credit-money' continuously confused measures of money supply. Ingham reviews at length various theories regarding money supply and the control exercised by the state through central banks. He notes an increasing dissociation of measures of money supply with rates of inflation and concludes that, 'the relationship between the orthodox conception of money in economic analysis and practical monetary policy is now tenuous to the point of incoherence.'[55] It was not possible to 'fine-tune' economic growth and rates of inflation through control of the money supply, as monetarist economists had thought might be possible.

But the link between money supply and inflation, and hence between money supply and the purchasing power of money, is still sufficiently well established to warrant states charging their central banks to control the supply of money, mainly through adjustment of base rates of interest and regulation of bank lending, to maintain inflation within acceptable limits. The orthodox macroeconomic conception of money is very much apparent in practical policy. The Reserve Bank of New Zealand was the first to adopt an inflation target, with legislation passed in 1989. The Bank of England, the US Federal Reserve and the European Central Bank all aim to keep inflation below 2 per cent. *Central Bank News* published a list of the target inflation rates of central banks in seventy-one countries in 2019.[56] The importance of controlling inflation lies not only in the inconvenience of high rates of inflation but in the difficulties that arise in the conclusion of monetary transactions when the purchasing power of the money is eroding. In particular, the negotiation of wage agreements is difficult when the purchasing power of money is eroding, and it is known that any wage settlement will itself affect the rate of inflation in the community, and hence the future purchasing power of the money. Modest rates of inflation can spiral to high rates as wage earners try to protect their real incomes. Inflation has been low in most Western nations in recent decades, but inflation rates are still closely monitored, for fear of a return to the high rates of inflation that prevailed at times in the latter half of the twentieth century. Rates well above the common target of 2 per cent have recently emerged in developed nations. Turkey is currently experiencing high rates of inflation associated with the conviction of President Erdogan that high rates of interest generate inflation. High rates of government borrowing in response to the covid pandemic have added to fears of high rates of inflation across the world. There have, of course, been spectacular examples of hyperinflation arising from failure to control money supplies, the hyperinflation in Germany in the 1920s being the most prominent. More recently Zimbabwe and Venezuela have experienced hyperinflation. Attempts by the government of Zimbabwe to introduce new currencies have been hampered by popular suspicion of their stability.

Barter in Modern Times

Dalton concludes that, under his definition of barter, it has never been an important mode of transaction (Note 39). But even on that definition the conclusion seems open to question. Malinowski emphasises the extensive barter carried on in the Trobriand Islands. Kula exchange of necklaces and bracelets might dominate people's perceptions of their trade. Support-bargaining is always dominant in people's minds, because their security depends on it. But as regards material returns, barter would apparently have a claim to dominance.

That is only more true if 'barter' is understood as something more extensive that Dalton's definition would have it. Malinowski records that barter is immediate exchange in the Trobriand Islands – 'the barterers directly require the other article.'[57] Hence he concludes that the islanders would have no use for money.[58] But he also records use of deferred barter, as part of ceremonial barter.[59] If gift-giving is recognised as having elements of material exchange, then barter is yet more dominant.

Humphrey agrees with Dalton's conclusion regarding the origin of money in barter 'pure and simple,' but over questions of the 'importance' or 'dominance' of barter in societies there is some conflict. She writes:

> No example of a barter economy, pure and simple, has ever been described, let alone the emergence from it of money; all available ethnography suggests that there never has been such a thing. But there are economies today that are nevertheless *dominated* by barter, and here anthropology can both learn from and add to the ancient debate.[60]

'A barter economy, pure and simple,' suggests Dalton's definition. But on a wider definition, the existence of barter economies is plain. Humphrey's comments are based on her study of the Lhomi people of north-eastern Nepal. What she observes is inconsistent in important respects with the preconceptions that gave rise to Dalton's definition of barter. She describes anthropologists as regarding barter as dominated by 'more socially embedded' transactions and itself generally despised: 'barter is found in a corner of the economy, and one that is despised by the people and anthropologists alike.'[61] The comment echoes Malinowski's description of the status of the Amphlett Islanders and his own attitude towards them. Sahlin's description of the relationship between barter and trade is similarly conditioned by his aversion to trade. Humphrey notes Sahlins's classification of barter as 'negative reciprocity, the unsociable extreme.'

As part of the Nepalese nation, the Lhomi would be expected to use the Nepalese currency, the Nepalese Rupee. However, the currency is used sparingly, for purchases such as lamps and oil that can only be acquired from outside Lhomi territory. The great majority of their trade is conducted by barter. It is, for the Lhomi, a preferred form of trade. Humphrey concludes that, 'If we take barter to be the more or less simultaneous exchange of one good for another with the possibility of bargaining, anthropologists have no right to classify barter as "negative reciprocity."' Barter is a complementary exchange, advantageous to both parties.

Humphrey records that, 'Among the Lhomi there is a continuum from petty money transactions or direct barter, through regular and then delayed trade by barter, to the occasional "big business"':[62]

> For the Lhomi, the pinnacle of barter is the occasional 'big business' deal. This is normally conducted between 'known people,' often distant kin, or

> 'ritual friends,' or kinsmen of ritual friends. A deal is often preceded by the giving of minor solicitory gifts and a ritual scarf.[63]

There is thus a variety of barter transactions, often involving tokens of goodwill analogous to those of Kula custom. Delayed barter features in a continuum of barter transactions. Humphrey concludes that the choice of barter in preference to monetary exchange is linked to Lhomi concern for their independence as a community: 'Barter is a response to increasing poverty on the part of people who wish nevertheless to maintain their autonomy.'[64] Cultural independence from the rest of Nepal is maintained at the cost of greater poverty than they might otherwise suffer. Barter is a means of keeping their community together.

The 'choice' is nevertheless in part a matter of necessity. Money is commonly in short supply. Humphrey, drawing on Thomas Crump, notes: 'A peripheral self-contained sub-economy must maintain a positive balance of payments in its external trade with the national economy if it is to import enough money to maintain its own monetary system.'[65] Lhomi exports to the rest of Nepal are not sufficient to ensure inflows of Nepalese rupees into their area to generate extensive chains of monetary transactions. Attitudes to credit may also restrict inflows of money. Humphrey records that many 'pending' transactions cannot be completed because of a lack of wealth. The consciousness of the lack of wealth 'is one factor among many that makes Lhomi refuse to give one another loans, and to prefer, whenever possible, the simultaneous transaction.'[66] Similar concerns over creditworthiness may inhibit the acquisition of credit from outside the region.

While barter dominates trade amongst the Lhomi, it conforms in some degree to Dalton's contention that barter is only maintained in special circumstances, when the alternatives are for some reason not attractive. Dalton's examples are rather far from Lhomi territory and not impressive as matters to be reckoned with in the overall conduct of economic affairs: baby-sitting cooperatives in the United States, in localities where cash incomes are low; an 'ethically flexible' dentist who works on teeth in exchange for carpentry, to avoid tax.[67] But still, the Lhomi seem intent on barter, if only because the mindset or frame of reference of their community rules out alternatives that are apparent to others.

Humphrey repeats the economic anthropologists' 'myth of barter' contention: 'As far as the economists' argument is concerned, we know from the accumulated evidence of enthnography that barter was indeed very rare as a system dominating primitive economies.'[68] The 'myth of barter' rests on Dalton's highly restrictive definition of barter, and in particular the exclusion of deferred barter. Humphrey appears to accept Dalton's definition, with such comments as, 'Barter...entails no further transactions. It is, in principle, a one-off affair, because the objects exchanged are mainly objects for use.'[69] But she also adds what is apparently the idea of time separation, consistent with her recognition of deferred barter:

> This implies the disentangling of two concepts of barter: (a) the notion of simple exchange without money and without specifying the mode of the

> non-monetary transaction, and (b) the process of barter in time as a practice which involves bargaining.[70]

Dalton's definition has already disentangled the two concepts. But deferred barter certainly needs to be reinstated. Humphrey proposes an 'alternative theory' that depends on the 'deferred barter' that Dalton omits from his account of barter. She follows Goodhart in distinguishing the deferred barter from immediate barter by reference to a distinction between 'exchange' and 'payment.' Immediate barter combines exchange and payment, while deferred barter distinguishes between the exchange and a later payment. Goodhart notes, as in the quotation earlier (Note 27) that deferred barter is risky because of the amount of information required about participants in such transactions. Some more secure means of payment is required, and money fits the bill. It is Innes's idea of the 'acknowledgement' that the brewer or baker gives to the butcher when he receives meat. The economists' idea of the emergence of money from barter is not discredited. Rather the definition of 'barter' which is the basis of the supposed discredit is shown to be mistaken.

The Emergence of Money from Barter

Humphrey presents the economic idea of the emergence of money from barter, originating with Adam Smith, on the basis of its restatement by R.W. Clower,[71] himself following William Jevons.[72] She writes that the high transaction costs of barter:

> would lead people at first to barter at fairgrounds, then to establish trading posts for particular goods, then to make use of one of the most common items as a means of exchange at all the posts and, finally, to establish this commodity also as a standard of value, means of payment and store of wealth, in other words, as money.[73]

Thomas Crump argued convincingly, according to Humphrey, that Clower was wrong, because a usable money requires control over its supply, and so it is unlikely that any 'good' emerging from frequent use in barter could 'turn into' money.[74]

In the conjecture based on bargaining theory described earlier, barter is seen as so inconvenient and constraining that 'favoured commodities' would be likely to emerge quite easily as bargaining counters, or forms of money, in primitive societies, and subsequently a singular 'favoured commodity' could emerge. And on that basis, the use of non-commodity money, such as cowrie shells, could gain acceptance. Primitive economies would generate bargaining counters for their conduct of exchange. When states form from primitive societies, the bargaining counters in popular use are adopted as state currencies, with controls over their supply.

No money has emerged from Lhomi barter, nor are they able to make much use of the Nepalese rupee. Social and political support-bargaining within the community seems to have determined that the use of money is threatening to their culture. The poverty of the community is apparently preferable to the adoption of alien ways of trade. The title of Humphrey's article suggests the disintegration of their community, but even that threat seems insufficient to induce a shift in the thinking of the community. Beliefs, traditions, customs, culture, theories, frames of reference can be so fixed in the minds of people that they are unable to conceive of life without such mental boundaries. People do not commonly change their minds over the frames of reference that dominate their lives; only succeeding generations can adopt something different.

Support-bargaining within Lhomi society determines that barter is preferred. The society fears that its cohesion will be lost if an alternative bargaining counter is accepted into regular use. Even though the society is under threat from the consequences of its commitment to barter, the outcomes of its support-bargaining still maintain its insistence on the exclusion of money. Attachment of the kind apparent in Lhomi society to established ways of life that would be lost through the introduction of money might have inhibited earlier societies from the bigger task of inventing money.

Durable currencies, currencies that can be used widely amongst strangers, require overall control of money supply. This can normally be provided only by strong central rule, the sort of arrangement that has come to be regarded as a 'state.' So national currencies, or currencies accepted across the jurisdiction of particular rulers, will only be possible where the rulers see no threat to their interests from the introduction of an alternative bargaining counter, or more demandingly, where they see positive advantages in opening up possibilities for their subjects to become rich. A dominant group in a state, largely insulated from popular opinion by a preponderant capacity for violence, might find it expedient to limit the acquisition of wealth to its own loyal members. The 'way of life' that the Lhomi fear to lose may elsewhere be the 'established rule' that is at risk for rulers. Nevertheless, even if central rulers oppose the availability of a national currency for use by ordinary people, communities might still find it useful to develop their own commodity-like bargaining counters for local convenience.

Barter in Congo and New Guinea

Crump acknowledges that, while it is easy to conceive of money emerging from barter, it has been difficult to identify barter economies from which money might conceivably have emerged. He nevertheless identifies three societies that have some of the appropriate characteristics[75]: pre-colonial Mexico,[76] the Congo basin,[77] the northern coast of New Guinea and the adjacent islands.[78]

While the economic transactions in these societies are not exclusively confined to barter, each has important sectors that can be analysed in terms of barter. In all three societies barter is used characteristically in long distance trade between populations culturally distinct and independent from each other. Crump notes that this accords with Georg Simmel's contention that barter would be likely to prevail in circumstances in which social ties were difficult to maintain. 'Self-liquidating transactions,' or transactions that involved no extended ties, could be expected to predominate.[79] Crump's examples thus appear consistent with the anthropological understanding that barter takes place largely between strangers. But in all three cases commodities have emerged as bargaining counters for internal trade.[80] Cocoa-beans are accepted in pre-colonial Mexico[81]; cloth is accepted in the Congo basin[82]; pigs are accepted in the Siassi islands off the north coast of New Guinea.[83]

In the Congo basin other commodities, besides cloth, also function as money. Cloth itself is distinguished as local or imported cloth. Vansina notes that, by 1880, alternatives include brass rods, shells and possibly also lead ingots. By 1881, the *mitako*, the brass rod, had entirely taken over. Vansina records that, 'Payments could be made in these currencies or objects might be bartered directly once their value had been assessed in terms of currency.'[84] In the Siassi Islands shillings, a national currency, were in use alongside pigs.[85] Hogbin also notes that shillings were in use, alongside pigs, in the New Guinea village he studied.[86] Crump remarks that a system of local money 'readily adapts to the use of an established exogenous money, a process that van Leynseele has described for the Congo basin.'[87] It seems that, if inflows of an exogenous money can be earned, the money is used in local exchange. The Lhomi could not bring in significant quantities of Nepalese rupees.

The practices described by the researchers suggest a 'makeshift' mixture of commodity moneys and national currencies all functioning together to perform the function of money, the usage in any particular situation dependent presumably on the convenience, the supply and the acceptability of the different moneys to the transactors. In so far as there is any recognisable 'system,' it is that of replacing the inconvenience of barter with bargaining counters that facilitate exchange. They facilitate specific exchanges and also generate chains of transactions using a common bargaining counter. The *mitako*, or brass rod, seems to have emerged as a single favoured commodity in the Congo.

Pigs were established as money in New Guinea, though they do not well fulfil requirements for portability and durability, nor is their supply likely to be well-regulated. They retain substantial 'fall-back' value, or 'value in use,' as food. If they are not needed in a budgetary situation, they can resolve a food situation. This presumably offset some of the disadvantages of using pigs as money.

Crump expresses misgivings about the strength of anthropological studies as evidence one way or the other for the emergence of money from barter. He comments:

> Scientifically, the greatest problem consists in finding adequate empirical support for the transition from potential into actual money objects.

> Anthropologists, who are the only scientists concerned with populations where such a transition is likely to occur, are not well equipped to observe what is essentially a historical process.[88]

A transition from 'potential' to 'actual' money as the transition from barter to the use of money presents the transition as being from one type of money to another. The transition is, however, interpreting the empirical evidence assembled by Crump by reference to the idea of money-bargaining, a transition from a host of commodities exchanged by reference to their inherent usefulness to the selection of a few commodities of such wide interest as to function as useful bargaining counters, and then to the emergence of one such commodity as the most widely accepted of all in a budgetary reference. If 'potential money' is the range of commodities that might be used as money, then adoption as 'actual money,' in the sense of 'popular money,' depends on what is best suited to immediate circumstances. The obvious 'makeshift' in the adoption of bargaining counters confuses analysis.

The quest for the pure 'barter' society that might blossom into monetary usage is misguided when money is recognised as a bargaining counter. It is apparent that barter is so very inconvenient that communities will move away from it as rapidly as possible, and there are plenty of commodities or materials that will serve at least as temporary popular bargaining counters. The Lhomi experience suggests that barter systems are operable up to a point, but the Lhomi protect their culture at the expense of economic disintegration.

Makeshift and Money

Efforts to circumvent the problems with barter result in the 'makeshift' of bargaining counters apparent in the anthropological studies covered by Crump, perhaps particularly the account of trade in the Congo by Vansina. There is a hint of 'makeshift' in Humphrey's concept of barter as innovative and accommodative, as in the quotation at Note 5. Lhomi society, distinctly a barter society, has a continuum of barter arrangements, involving direct barter, regular barter, delayed barter and 'big business.' An observer unconcerned with categorisation might see 'makeshift' in the conduct of barter amongst the Lhomi. It is the business of analysts to identify patterns and form coherent explanatory theories, and 'makeshift' suggests abandonment of that function. But it is a systematic reaction of sorts to the circumstances in which people find themselves.

In making shift, people adapt what they offer to what they may receive in return; what they will accept to what is realistically likely to be available. They can accept a range of commodities in a 'standard' barter deal; they can accept a promise to provide a commodity later in a 'delayed barter' deal; they can accept something that is in wide demand, so they will be able to exchange it later for something they need; they can accept a mixture of various returns, some now, some later; or they may even use the accredited currencies of the nation states of which their locality forms part, if anyone has that currency to offer. If they lack money tokens, they may conclude barter deals involving a variety of products, balancing the value of the transaction by reference to valuations of the items involved in terms of a recognised money. When people want to make an exchange, they make it in the best way possible, in the light of circumstances. Any perceived marginal imbalances can potentially be smoothed over with communal sentiment – consoling support can be offered to compensate for any perceived concessions that might be disappointing. Where exchanges with distinct social implications are involved, such as bride prices or dowries, social custom regarding what constitutes appropriate forms of payment will constrain options far more than in transactions recognised as being of purely material account.

'Makeshift' is apparent in the transactions of the ancient world. David Schaps describes transactions in ancient Egypt that are simple barter. One wooden stela is exchanged for a chest; two coffins are exchanged for a bed.[89] 'Private deals were sometimes simply swaps, with no clear statement of value.'[90] But then also 'Credit might be extended, though we generally know about it only in cases where there were difficulties with collection.'[91] A scribe allegedly took a coffin, saying he would later give a calf for it, but the calf has not been provided. The coffin was taken in a delayed barter transaction. When a complaint was lodged, the creditor who demanded the calf was asked to give a bed in addition to the coffin, and the debtor would then both provide and raise a calf, providing it to his creditor when grown. The bed was given, but no grown calf was provided.[92] Schaps remarks, 'This is the sort of barter that Mill envisaged, although the possibility of credit has made it more practical than he realized.'[93] Mill did not envisage delayed barter, perhaps because the economic model that formed his frame of reference was concerned with immediate and self-sufficient transactions. Guarantees against default may be agreed. A workman gave a pot of fat to a chief, who undertook to pay for it in barley, to be provided by his brother. After failing to pay, the chief undertakes to pay within a certain period, and to suffer a hundred blows of stick, and pay double, if he does not fulfil the undertaking. No quantity of barley is stated in the complaint, suggesting that the relevant amount would be well-known.[94]

The use of reference money values in ancient Egypt is illustrated by the attribution of values in silver to the various items of Upper Egyptian cloth that a lady offered for a slave: one shroud at 5 kite of silver; one blanket at 3 1/3 kite; one djayt-garment at 4 kite; three sdy-garments at 5 kite; one dress at 5 kite. She provided also various items taken from friends and neighbours to make up the total price of four deben and one kite: bronze vessels, beaten copper, a jar of honey, and shirts. Schaps comments: 'Here we have elements that we had not seen previously: a merchant, a price calculated in silver…and a list of commodities every one of which has a recognized price.[95] People put together what was possible to make up a package of the required value, making reference to valuations in silver, copper or barley. Schaps notes that at the period of this purchase Egyptian Pharaoh's were at the height of their 'redistibutive' powers. He remarks:

> For all that, we are still in the world of barter. To get the price she had offered to pay, Erënofre threw together anything on which she could lay her hands…A purse full of coins or even a household store of silver…had no place in Erënofre's mental universe.[96]

Egypt had no silver mines, as Athens had from the early fifth century BCE. It had to acquire silver by foreign trade, so silver could be in short supply. As the Lhomi preference for barter was influenced by their lack of capacity to acquire Nepalese Rupees, Egyptian practices might also have been influenced by difficulties in obtaining silver. The 'money supply' problem relates to the putting of money into circulation, as well as controlling against excessive supply (Chapter 12). The use of a 'reference money' involved no inconveniences of weighing and testing for fineness.

The 'makeshift' makes clear that the presentation of 'barter' as requiring any sort of 'double coincidence of wants' in the simple sense conceived by Newlyn and Mill, or the confinement of the idea of a barter society to Dalton's definition of barter, is no help in the understanding of pre-coinage trade. Trade was carried on using any means that were effective in the local circumstances. The obvious inconveniences of simple barter were overcome rapidly by various innovations, including the use of commodities as bargaining counters. The extreme variety of things that have been seen as fulfilling the function of money is a consequence of the instinct for making shift with whatever is available. The cigarettes used as currency in German prisoner of war camps in the Second World War are a more recent example of the ability to make shift. Where hyperinflation extinguishes the purchasing power of money, people make shift as best they can to procure the necessities of life.

Money and Coin-Money

The appearance of something so unsystematic as 'makeshift' in the societies described by Crump and Humphrey arises partly from our familiarity with modern monetary practice. We are accustomed to a more orderly arrangement of currencies, with each society having its own distinctive individual currency. Societies in which there are many bargaining counters in use at the same time challenge our analytical capacities. The hotchpotch of currencies observed is discordant to our accustomed frame of reference.

It is apparent, however, that the makeshift was gradually replaced by more orderly and durable arrangements involving metallic moneys. Much of the usage of these moneys seems to have been restricted to specialist traders, who could handle the necessary weighing and assay, with ordinary people still resorting of necessity to makeshift. But even for ordinary people, the metallic moneys provided a reference for the values of whatever they wanted to exchange, even if they did not actually hold the metallic money. Schaps notes that in the first half of the first millennium BCE copper and then silver were used as standards in the Near East, though payments were normally in kind.[97] Later, in Babylon of the seventh and sixth centuries BCE, the situation is different, with payments specifying the kind of silver to be provided.[98] There are questions as to whether, 'a substance mentioned should be considered a currency or merely a commodity, but there is no doubt that silver, barley, and sometimes other items performed monetary functions in Mesopotamia.'[99] In a more limited professional group in ancient Kanesh Schaps notes precious metals functioning as money:

> Their use of precious metals was certainly chiefly commercial, and this particular colony in this particular era was surely using silver in a way that we would call monetary and, in fact, downright capitalistic...[100]

The evidence is found strong enough to support a more sweeping statement regarding the use of silver and precious metals in the ancient world:

> In a sense, then – in almost every sense – Mesopotamia used money and had been using money for a millennium before the Greeks discovered it. Silver, or its alternatives, was a universally recognised standard of value; it was a potential and, in many circumstances (in particular long-distance trade), a real medium of trade...[101]

Schaps nevertheless maintains that the introduction of coins marked a critical watershed in economic and social history. In his Appendix 2, on 'Pre-Greek Coinage,' Schaps evaluates various claims to the status of 'coin' before the advent of Greek coinage. He defines a coin as: 'an object, usually but not necessarily of metal, which circulates as a medium of trade, and whose value is guaranteed by the stamp of the issuing authority.' In a note, Schaps indicates that the 'value' guaranteed is normally the weight and fineness of the metal, but making that part of the definition would exclude coins whose value, like those of today, is not related to their metal content. That reflects the transition from 'commodity money' to money as 'credit.'

On this basis, he concludes:

> We may thus ignore without further discussions such items as spits, rings, and sealed bags of silver, which although they served many of the purposes that coins later served were not by themselves coins at all. They belong to the history of 'primitive money.'[102]

Schaps evaluates a range of items and references, including 'Mesopotamian sealed silver,' the Egyptian 'piece' and Cappadocian lead disks for characteristics that might justify their acceptance as coins. He concludes that no items qualify. The adoption of coinage in Greek city states was a radical innovation that changed Greek society.

Morris Silver adopts an economist's frame of reference and comes to a different conclusion. He maintains that there is little distinction to be made between the usage of silver as money and the later use of coin-money. He suggests that Schaps underestimates the extent of the use of silver as money in the ancient world and underestimates the arrangements that were made to provide qualities in silver bullion close to those of coins. Weighing and testing complicated the use of silver, metals in general, and other commodities, but there were ways round the complications. Silver cites the use of silver ingots in the Ancient Near East (ANE) in ways that suggest they were of standard weight and purity: 'The evidence is reasonably clear that the ANE went a good part of the way toward coinage by circulating ingots of guaranteed quality.'[103] He cites also the use of sealed bags of silver that could be exchanged with confidence that their weight and purity were dependable.

Silver concludes that: 'In my view, sealed bags provide evidence for widespread use of "coinage" in the ANE.'[104] Silver also questions Schaps's claim that the Egyptian *shaty* (or *Š'ty*) was not used in exchange, but was rather a unit of weight or value.[105] Silver claims instead: 'In fact, there is evidence for the circulation of *shaty's* in texts of the Ramesside era (second half of the second millennium).'[106]

Nor was the use of silver bullion as money necessarily limited to a few specialist traders. Morris Silver suggests that innovations making silver function more like coins made it possible for precious metals to be used quite widely. In Syria silver was used to purchase ordinary goods, such as clothing, grain, wine and semi-precious stones. In Mesopotamia in the middle of the second half of the third millennium BCE street vendors were using silver to pay rents and purchase dates, oil, barley, animals, slaves and real estate. Silver was also widely used in personal loans.[107] The extent of such usages is not easily determined, but it seems that, especially amongst traders, support assembled in the ANE for certain forms of precious metal that fulfilled the functions of money in a way analogous to coins.

Silver does not contest Schaps's definition of a coin. He argues, however, that whatever the form they took, the transfer of value in the course of trade, the most essential part of the Schaps definition, was commonly fulfilled by certain items before the advent of coins. The 'stamp' of official guarantee might even be present in some instances. And consequently, the introduction of coins should not be accorded the revolutionary importance that Schaps gives it.

The different frames of reference of Schaps and Morris Silver cause them to select for emphasis different features of ancient society and make different interpretations. Schaps, the historian, sees extensive social change arising from the introduction of coinage, so great as to warrant use of the term 'revolution.' In support of his argument, he cites the differences between coins and their usage and the difficulties of using silver bullion in trade. Silver bullion was effective, but lacked the convenience of coins. In consequence, silver bullion was limited in the extent of its usage. He remarks, in his main text, 'Convenience, however, can be destiny.'[108] Morris Silver, the economist, reckons that the adaptations of silver bullion for use in trade were so effective as to make it almost indistinguishable from coinage. They fulfilled the role of medium of exchange, store of value and unit of account almost as well as coins, so that there is no need to view the introduction of coins as a watershed, and certainly no justification for claiming 'revolution.' Arrangements close to coinage were already effective before the introduction of coins; Hellenic economic performance was not so influenced by coinage; there was no new concept of money introduced with coinage. Schaps notes that economists have so little interest in the introduction of coin-money that economic histories pay little or no attention to the subject, or even to the period in which it was introduced. Their focus is on European economies, beginning around 600 AD, or even later.[109]

Nevertheless, Greek coinage was clearly more distinctive in its physical form and stamps than anything precedent, except perhaps the Lydian coinage, and the Greek embrace of coins from about 600 BCE was plainly more widespread and influential in their society than anything that had occurred earlier in the Eastern Mediterranean or Near East. Greek coins were available in small denominations, so could be used for small transactions. The advent of coinage is sometimes understood as the advent of money. In the frame of reference of money-bargaining, the adoption of coinage is the crucial event that establishes a well-defined and versatile new bargaining counter, unleashing the potential of money-bargaining as never before. It dispels the 'makeshift' formerly characteristic of much trading, spreading networks of money-bargaining between ordinary people. It greatly reduces, if it does not entirely eliminate, the necessity for equipment and procedures associated with non-coin metal money that tend to limit money-bargaining both in relation to those engaged and the sort of transactions that are concluded. It is the dawn of the sort of economic practices with which we are now familiar. It provides new opportunities for the interlinking of support-bargaining and money-bargaining. For Schaps, it gives rise to a new concept in social intercourse. The economic frame of reference does not give prominence to issues of convenience, and consequently misses much of the attraction, and much of the impact, of coinage. Nor does it make prominent the importance of communal ideas and communal concepts of social intercourse, both of which were important in the revolutionary changes brought about by coinage.

French Institutionalist Theories of Money

Ingham makes reference to the work of French scholars concerning the nature of money but does not pursue their theories.[110] An English translation of a selection of this work has recently become available as *Institutionalist Theories of Money*.[111] The theories portray money as a comprehensive focus for whole societies, the 'total social fact.'[112] The single-discipline approach of economics is seen as inadequate to the explanation of such a complex phenomenon: 'Money is an institution, a higher order social relation whose complexity cannot be fully captured by a single-disciplinary approach.' *La Monnaie Souveraine* (1998) constitutes a central text for the research group, developing the 'debt-sovereignty-trust triptych.'[113] The movement challenges the economic understanding of human societies. In the Introduction to *La Monnaie Souveraine* leading theorists of the movement affirm that institutionalist theory:

> grasps the unity of the phenomenon of money in its special relationship with the social whole: money expresses and reinforces the overall values of the society in question. This is the central hypothesis defended in this book. While it will hardly surprise anthropologists or historians...it is a tremendous intellectual challenge for economists, as it is so very much opposed to the mainstream of their discipline which gives precedence to an instrumental conception of money as a medium of exchange.
>
> For the current authors, it is over-simplistic to see money as a purely economic object. Modern money remains an expression of society in its totality. It maintains its standing as an operator of social belonging. This is why we have placed the concept of legitimacy or sovereignty of money at the centre of our analytical approach.[114]

Debt is recognised as a central factor in the relationship between individuals and their societies:

> The instrumental conception of money, namely money as an intermediary facilitating transactions, is an avatar of this general view of social relations. But the effects of this change can also be measured by the reversal it induces in the relationship of indebtedness between the individual and society. This relationship, which this book makes the fundamental concept for understanding the social bond, is nowadays thought of as society's indebtedness to the individual and no longer as the debt each member of society owes to the whole.[115]

The movement refers extensively to the 'barter myth' as a critical part of their objection to economic theory and the economic theory of the origin of money. It affirms that money can be created in the 'non-market' circumstances of ancient societies. Being a 'total social fact' of societies, it is ubiquitous. Bernard Courbis, Eric Froment and Jean-Michel Servet maintain that the exchanges of ancient societies were infinitely more complex than is possible to recognise through the stunted idea of barter. They argue that products were transported over great distances, and were not exclusively goods necessary to physical survival; rather they served as social differentials between men and women, seniors and juniors, family groups and so on. The travellers constituted a distinct group of 'exchange intermediaries.' Furthermore, it can be observed that

> each 'primitive' society produced a *privileged* good (stone axes for some, salt slabs, bark capes for others, etc.) with a deliberate view to trading it and that became the means of payment for the output of each of the other groups.[116]

These writers conclude that

> In terms of theory, it is noteworthy that, while there were no market based monetary instruments with the essential and specific function of acting as an 'exchange intermediary,' commodities were nonetheless reciprocally means of payment for each other in these relations. These hard truths that we have outlined are a million miles from the illusions about the birth of money through barter and its confusions.[117]

It may be that the concept of 'money' discerned by economic anthropologists in the work of economists, involving the presence of 'markets,' makes it difficult to associate the sort of exchanges depicted as having any connection with barter. But certainly with the idea of money as a bargaining counter it seems instantly apparent that the exchangers identify bargaining counters, the commonly traded commodities, and in that sense *privileged* goods, and use them to trade. For long-distance trade silver was used extensively in the ancient world as a bargaining counter.[118] Rather than being 'a million miles away' from barter, makeshift money as a convenient escape from the difficulties of barter seems precisely what is described. Without the connection of money to barter, and the establishment of money as an instrument of exchange, it is easier to argue for money as a 'money of account.'

As a general concept, the French institutionalist theory of money does no more that attribute all the evils and adequacies of societies, connected and unconnected with debt, to money itself. It makes of money a mysterious encapsulation of the complexity of societies. It imputes to money all the characteristics that are involved in support-bargaining – violence, competition, tension, trust, cooperation, class distinction, snobbery, social ascendancy, etc. It imputes abstract complexity to simple material circumstances. The French 'institutions' are, like the 'institutions' of customs, habit and rules developed in English language institutionalism, outcomes of support-bargaining.[119] Support-bargaining provides the 'general model of the social bond' that Michel Aglietta and Jean Cartelier doubt can be constructed.[120] The support-bargaining relationship between individuals and their societies is the basis of social functioning and evolution. Understood as a bargaining counter, money has a simple and clear function. The complexities of society arise from the support-bargaining that is carried on to direct society, and to accommodate money. The 'total social fact' is created by support-bargaining and is multifarious, not singular. Money emerges from barter as an alternative and supplementary bargaining counter to support, functioning not in accordance with neoclassical economic understanding, but with the dynamic of money-bargaining. In this role it inevitably impacts support-bargaining. Societies are changed to accommodate the alternative bargaining counter. Since most societies have been very prominently communities of faith, money has had to be accommodated, or resisted, by religious organisations. Since these organisations, by virtue of the support accorded to them, are influential, sometimes dominant, elements in the governance of societies, money has a radical influence on the organisational structures by which societies are governed.

Bob Jessop, of the University of Lancaster, in his Foreword to *Institutionalist Theories of Money*, identifies the main inspirations behind the theories as Durkheim, Marx, Keynes, Polanyi and Simmel. He implies also that they have become a foundation for Modern Monetary Theory.[121] If money is understood as 'total social fact,' there is some danger that such understanding will be allowed to override other facts of stronger provenance.

Notes

1 Menger, Karl, 1892, 'On the Origin of Money', *The Economic Journal*, Vol. 2, No. 6, pp. 239–55. See also Spread, Patrick, 2016a, *The Evolution of Economies: Money-Bargaining, Economic Change and Industrial Revolution*, London: Routledge, pp. 14–5.
2 Mill, John Stuart, 1885, *Principles of Political Economy*, New York: D. Appleton and Company, p. 334.
3 Mill, 1885, L. 7078–85.
4 Samuelson, Paul, 1973, *Economics*, 9th Edition, New York: McGraw-Hill, p. 55.
5 Humphrey, Caroline, 1985, 'Barter and Economic Disintegration', *Man*, New Series, Vol. 20, No. 1, pp. 48–72, p. 50.
6 Newlyn, Walter T., 1971, *Theory of Money*, 2nd Edition, Oxford: Oxford University Press, p. 1.
7 Davies, Glyn, 1994, *A History of Money from Ancient Times to the Present Day*, Cardiff: University of Wales Press, p. 27.
8 Einzig, Paul, 1966, *Primitive Money*, 2nd Edition, Oxford: Pergamon Press. First published 1949.
9 Smith, Adam, 2008/1776, *An Enquiry into the Nature and Causes of the Wealth of Nations*, Selected Edition, Introduction by Kathryn Sutherland, Oxford: Oxford University Press, p. 32. Smith, Adam, 2009/1976, *An Inquiry into the Nature and Causes of the Wealth of Nations*, Project Gutenberg eBook, Adobe Digital Editions, p. 20.
10 Schaps, David, 2004, *The Invention of Coinage and the Monetization of Ancient Greece*, Ann Arbor: University of Michigan Press, Kindle Edition, L2243–59.
11 Hudson, Michael, 2004, 'The Archaeology of Money: Debt versus Barter Theories of Money's Origins', in L. Randall Wray (Ed.), 2004, *Credit and State Theories of Money: The Contribution of A. Mitchell Innes*, Cheltenham: Edward Elgar, p. 100.
12 Innes, Alfred Mitchell, 1913, 'What Is Money?' *Banking Law Journal*, May, pp. 377–408. Reprinted in Wray, 2004, pp. 50–78.
13 Innes, 1913, pp. 381–2.
14 Innes, 1913, p. 382.
15 Innes, 1913, p. 391.
16 Innes, 1913, p. 391.
17 Simmel, G., 1907/2004, The Philosophy of Money, 3rd Enlarged Edition, London: Routledge, p. 177. First published 1907.
18 Dodd, Nigel, 2016, *The Social Life of Money*, Princeton: Princeton University Press, p. 4.
19 Wagner, V. F., 1936, *Geschichte der Kredittheorien*, Wien: Springer, p. 83.
20 Simmel, G., 1907, *Philosophie des Geldes*, 2nd Edition, Leipzig: Duncker & Humblot, p. 163.

21 Ganssmann, Heiner, 2015, 'Money Does Not Live', *European Journal of Sociology*, Vol. 56, No. 3, p. 464.
22 Simmel, G., 1907/2011, *The Philosophy of Money*, London: Routledge, pp. 189–90.
23 Simmel, 1907/2011, p. 190.
24 Ingham, Geoffrey, 2004, *The Nature of Money*, Cambridge: Polity Press, p. 12.
25 Mathias, Peter, 2001, *The First Industrial Nation: The Economic History of Britain 1700–1914*, 2nd Edition, Abingdon: Routledge, pp. 139–40.
26 Innes, 1913, p. 392.
27 Goodhart, C. A. E., 1975, *Money, Information and Uncertainty*, London: Macmillan, pp. 7–8. Quoted by Humphrey, 1985, p. 51.
28 Humphrey, 1985, pp. 48, 52.
29 Spread, 2016a, p. 203.
30 Backhouse, Roger E., 1993, *Economics and the Economy: The Evolution of Economic Ideas*, New Brunswick and London: Transaction Publications, pp. 114–7.
31 Graeber, David, 2011, *Debt: The First 5000 Years*, Brooklyn and London: Melville House, p. 54.
32 Minsky, Hyman, 1986, *Stabilizing an Unstable Economy*, New Haven: Yale University Press.
33 Ingham, Geoffrey, 2004b, 'The Nature of Money', *Economic Sociology: European Electronic Newsletter*, Vol. 5, No. 2, pp. 18–28, p. 26.
34 Ingham, 2004, p. 12.
35 Ingham, Geoffrey, 2012, 'Revisiting the Credit Theory of Money and Trust', in Jocelyn Pixley (Ed.), *New Perspectives on Emotions in Finance: The Sociology of Confidence, Fear and Betrayal*, London: Routledge, 121–39. Quoted by Wray, L. Randall, 2014, 'From the State Theory of Money to Modern Money Theory: An Alternative to Economic Orthodoxy', *Working Paper No. 792*, Levy Economics Institute of Bard College, p. 27.
36 Smith, Adam, 1986/1776, *The Wealth of Nations*, Books I–III, London: Penguin Classics, p. 117. First published 1976. Smith, Adam, 2009, p. 13.
37 Dalton, George, 1982, 'Barter', *Journal of Economic Issues*, Vol. 16, No. 1, pp. 181–90, p. 181.
38 Dalton, 1982, p. 182.
39 Dalton, 1982, p. 183.
40 Dalton, 1982, p. 185.
41 Sahlins, Marshall, 2004/1972, *Stone Age Economics*, London: Routledge. First published 1972, pp. 193–5.
42 Dalton, 1982, p. 184.
43 Dalton, 1982, p. 187.
44 Seaford, Richard, 2004, *Money and the Early Greek Mind*, Cambridge: Cambridge University Press, p. 292, fn. 1. Seaford's reference: Dalton 1982, p. 185.
45 Ingham, 2004, p, 201.
46 Humphrey, 1985, p. 49–50.
47 See, for example, Hogben, H. I., 1951, *Transformation Scene. The Changing Culture of a New Guinea Village*, London: Routledge and Kegan Paul, p. 121.
48 Kropotkin, Peter, 2003/1902, Mutual Aid: A Factor of Evolution, Project Gutenberg Etext, Adobe Digital Editions. First published 1902, London: Heinemann. For comment, see Spread, Patrick, 2012, *Support-Bargaining, Economics and Society: A Social Species*, London and New York: Routledge, pp. 141–3, 204.
49 Einzig, 1966, p. 332.

50 Einzig's referemce: Nicholson, J. Shield, 1895, A Treatise on Money and Essays on Monetary Problems, 3rd Edition, London, p. 13.
51 Einzig, 1966, p. 309.
52 Dalton, 1982, p. 184.
53 Newlyn, 1971, pp. 2–3.
54 Dalton, 1982, p. 184.
55 Ingham, 2004, p. 9.
56 www.centralbanknews.info/p/inflation-targets.html. Accessed 25 November 2019.
57 Malinowski, Bronislaw, 1921, 'The Primitive Economics of the Trobriand Islanders', *The Economic Journal*, Vol. 31, No. 121, p. 14.
58 Malinowski, 1921, p. 13.
59 Malinowski, Bronislaw, 2002/1922, *Argonauts of the Western Pacific: An Account of Native Enterprise and Adventure in the Archipelagoes of Melanesian New Guinea*, London: Routledge, p. 187. First published 1922.
60 Humphrey, 1985, p. 48. Original emphasis.
61 Humphrey, 1985, p. 49.
62 Humphrey, 1985, p. 64.
63 Humphrey, 1985, p. 65.
64 Humphrey, 1985, p. 67–8.
65 Humphrey, 1985, p. 52. Humphrey's reference: Crump, Thomas, 1981, *The Phenomenon of Money*, London: Routledge & Kegan Paul, p. 212.
66 Humphrey, 1985, p. 66.
67 Dalton, 1982, p. 186–7.
68 Humphrey, 1985, p. 49.
69 Humphrey, 1985, p. 51.
70 Humphrey, 1985, p. 50.
71 Clower, R.W. (Ed.), 1969, 'Introduction', *Monetary Theory*, Harmondsworth: Penguin.
72 Jevons, William S., 1910, *Money and the Mechanism of Exchange*, London: Kegan Paul.
73 Humphrey, 1985, pp. 50–1.
74 Humphrey, 1985, p. 51.
75 Crump, 1981, p. 58.
76 Crump's reference: Katz, F., 1956, 'Die social ökonomischen Vehältnissen bei den Azteken im 15. und 16. Jahrhundert', *Ethnogrpahisch-Archa ologische Forschungen*, Vol. 3, No. 2, pp. 10–166.
77 Crump's reference: Vansina, Jan, 1973, *The Tio Kingdom of the Middle Congo 1880–1892*, Oxford: Oxford University Press, Chapters X and XI.
78 Crump's references: Hogbin, 1951; Harding, Thomas G., 1967, *Voyagers of the Vitiaz Strait: A Study of a New Guinea Trade System*, Seattle: University of Washington Press, for the American Ethnological Society.
79 Crump, 1981, p. 54. Crump's reference: Simmel, 1978/1907, *The Philosophy of Money*, London: Routledge, p. 225. Simmel uses a subheading 'Money's congruence with those who are marginal,' pp. 221–7.
80 Crump, 1981, p. 58.
81 Crump's reference: Katz, F., 1956, p. 58.
82 Crump's reference: Vansina, 1973, p. 297.
83 Crump's reference: Harding, 1967, p. 35.
84 Vansina, 1973, p. 282.
85 Harding, 1967, pp. 35, 41.
86 Hogbin, 1951, pp. 121, 124.

87 Crump, 1981, p. 58. Crump's reference: Van Leynseele, P., 1979, *Les Libinza de la Ngiri, l'anthropologie d'un people des marais du confluent Congo-Ubangi*, Leiden: Academisch Proefschrift, pp. 80f.
88 Crump, 1981, p. 57.
89 Schaps, 2004, L1047.
90 Schaps, 2004, L1047.
91 Schaps, 2004, L1048–53.
92 Schaps, 2004, L1048–55.
93 Schaps, 2004, L1056–65.
94 Schaps, 2004, L1056–74.
95 Schaps, 2004, L1074–89.
96 Schaps, 2004, L1098–105.
97 Schaps, 2004, L1194.
98 Schaps, 2004, L1194–203.
99 Schaps, 2004, L1203.
100 Schaps, 2004, L1211.
101 Schaps, 2004, L1273–9.
102 Schaps, 2004, L5703–11. Quoted by Silver, Morris, 2004, 'Review of Schaps, David M. 2004, *The Invention of Coinage and the Monetization of Ancient Greece*, Ann Arbor: University of Michigan Press', EH.net, p. 8.
103 Silver, 2004, p. 6.
104 Silver, 2004, p. 8.
105 Schaps, 2004, L5719–36.
106 Silver, 2004, p. 7.
107 Silver, 2004, p. 5.
108 Schaps, 2004, L2743.
109 Schaps, 2004, L5604–18.
110 Ingham, 2004, pp. 90, 214 N. 4.
111 Alary, Pierre, Blanc, Jérôme, Desmedt, Ludovic, and Théret, Bruno (Eds.), 2020, *Institutionalist Theories of Money: An Anthology of the French School*, Cham (Switzerland): Palgrave Macmillan.
112 Alary, Pierre, Blanc, Jérôme, and Desmedt, Ludovic, 2020, 'Introduction to the English Edition: Birth and Development of an Institutionalist Theory of Money', in Pierre Alary et al (Eds.), 2020, *Institutionalist Theories of Money: An Anthology of the French School*, Cham (Switzerland): Palgrave Macmillan, pp. 8, 14. Théret, Bruno, 2020, 'An Interdisciplinary Approach to Money as Cultural Capital and Total Social Fact', Chapter 7 in Alary et al. Eds., 2020.
113 Aglietta, Michel and Orléan, André (Eds.), 1998, *La Monnaie Souveraine*, Paris: Odile Jacob.
114 Aglietta, Michel, Andreau, Jean, Anspach, Mark, Birouste, Jacques, Cartelier, Jean, de Coppet, Daniel, Malamoud, Charles, Orléan, André, Servet, Jean-Michel, Théret, Bruno, and Thiveaud, Jean-Marie, 'Collective Introduction to *La Monnaie Souveraine*', Chapter 4 in Alary et al. (Eds.), 2020, p. 99.
115 Aglietta et al., 2020, p. 100.
116 Courbis, Bernard, Froment, Eric, and Servet, Jean-Michel, 2020, 'Enhancing the Political Economy of Money Through History', Chapter 3 in Alary et al. (Eds.), 2020, p. 71. First published 1991 as 'Enrichir l'économie politique de la monnaie par l'histoire', *Revue Economique*, Vol. 42, No. 2, pp. 315–38.
117 Courbis et al., 2020, p. 71.
118 Schaps, 2004, L. 1264.

119 On English language institutionalism, see Spread, 2016a, esp. Chapter 4, 'Evolutionary Economics.'

120 Aglietta, Michel and Cartelier, Jean, 2020, 'The Monetary Order of Market Economies', in Alary et al. (Eds.), 2020, p. 124. First published in Aglietta and Orléan (Eds.), 1998, pp. 129–57.

121 Jessop, Bob, 2020, 'Foreword' to Alary et al. (Eds.), 2020, pp. v, vi.

References

Aglietta, Michel and Cartelier, Jean, 2020, 'The Monetary Order of Market Economies', in Alary et al. (Eds.), 2020, p. 124. First published in Aglietta and Orléan (Eds.), 1998.

Aglietta, Michel and Orléan, André (Eds.), 1998, *La Monnaie Souveraine*, Paris: Odile Jacob.

Aglietta, Michel, Andreau, Jean, Anspach, Mark, Birouste, Jacques, Cartelier, Jean, de Coppet, Daniel, Malamoud, Charles, Orléan, André, Servet, Jean-Michel, Théret, Bruno, and Thiveaud, Jean-Marie, 2020, 'Collective Introduction to *La Monnaie Souveraine*', in Pierre Alary et al. (Eds.), 2020, *Institutionalist Theories of Money: An Anthology of the French School*, Cham (Switzerland): Palgrave Macmillan.

Alary, Pierre, Blanc, Jérôme, and Desmedt, Ludovic, 2020, 'Introduction to the English Edition: Birth and Development of an Institutionalist Theory of Money', in Pierre Alary et al. (Eds.), 2020, *Institutionalist Theories of Money: An Anthology of the French School*, Cham (Switzerland): Palgrave Macmillan.

Alary, Pierre, Blanc, Jérôme, Desmedt, Ludovic, and Théret, Bruno (Eds.), 2020, *Institutionalist Theories of Money: An Anthology of the French School*, Cham (Switzerland): Palgrave Macmillan.

Backhouse, Roger E., 1993, *Economists and the Economy: The Evolution of Economic Ideas*, New Brunswick and London: Transaction Publishers.

Central Bank News, www.centralbanknews.info/p/inflation-targets.html. Accessed 25 November 2019.

Clower, R. W., (Ed.), 1969, 'Introduction', *Monetary Theory*, Harmondsworth: Penguin.

Courbis, Bernard, Froment, Eric, and Servet, Jean-Michel, 2020, 'Enhancing the Political Economy of Money Through History', Chapter 3 in Alary et al. (Eds.), 2020, p. 71. First published 1991 as 'Enrichir l'économie politique de la monnaie par l'histoire', *Revue Economique*, Vol. 42, No. 2, pp. 315–38.

Crump, Thomas, 1981, *The Phenomenon of Money*, London: Routledge & Kegan Paul.

Dalton, George, 1982, 'Barter', *Journal of Economic Issues*, Vol. 16, No. 1, pp. 181–90.

Davies, Glyn, 1994, *A History of Money from Ancient Times to the Present Day*, Cardiff: University of Wales Press.

Dodd, Nigel, 2016, *The Social Life of Money*, Princeton: Princeton University Press.

Einzig, Paul, 1966, *Primitive Money*, 2nd Edition, Oxford: Pergamon Press. First published 1949.

Ganssmann, Heiner, 2015, 'Money Does Not Live', *European Journal of Sociology*, Vol. 56, No. 3, pp. 462–473.

Goodhart, C. A. E., 1975, *Money, Information and Uncertainty*, London: Macmillan.

Graeber, David, 2011, *Debt: The First 5000 Years*, Brooklyn and London: Melville House.

Harding, Thomas G., 1967, *Voyagers of the Vitiaz Strait: A Study of a New Guinea Trade System*, Seattle: University of Washington Press, for the American Ethnological Society.

Hogbin, H. I., 1951, *Transformation Scene. The Changing Culture of a New Guinea Village*, London: Routledge & Kegan Paul.

Hudson, Michael, 2004, 'The Archaeology of Money: Debt versus Barter Theories of Money's Origins', in L. Randall Wray (Ed.), *Credit and State Theories of Money: The Contribution of A. Mitchell Innes*, Cheltenham: Edward Elgar 2004.

Humphrey, Caroline, 1985, 'Barter and Economic Disintegration', *Man*, New Series, Vol. 20, No. 1, pp. 48–72.

Ingham, Geoffrey, 2004, *The Nature of Money*, Cambridge: Polity Press.

Ingham, Geoffrey, 2004b, 'The Nature of Money', *Economic Sociology: European Electronic Newsletter*, Vol. 5, No. 2, pp. 18–28.

Ingham, Geoffrey, 2013, 'Revisiting the Credit Theory of Money and Trust', in Jocelyn Pixley (Ed.), *New Perspectives on Emotions in Finance: The Sociology of Confidence, Fear and Betrayal*, London and New York: Routledge.

Innes, Alfred Mitchell, 1913, 'What Is Money?' *Banking Law Journal*, May, pp. 377–408.

Jessop, Bob, 2020, 'Foreword', to Pierre Alary et al. (Eds.), 2020 *Institutionalist Theories of Money: An Anthology of the French School*, Cham (Switzerland): Palgrave Macmillan.

Jevons, William S., 1910, *Money and the Mechanism of Exchange*, London: Kegan Paul.

Katz, F., 1956, 'Die social ökonomischen Vehältnissen bei den Azteken im 15. und 16. Jahrhundert', *Ethnogrpahisch-Archa ologische Forschungen*, Vol. 3, No. 2, pp. 10–166.

Kropotkin, Peter, 2003/1902, *Mutual Aid: A Factor of Evolution*, Project Gutenberg Etext, Adobe Digital Editions, London: Heinemann. First published 1902.

Malinowski, Bronislaw, 1921, 'The Primitive Economics of the Trobriand Islanders', *The Economic Journal*, Vol. 31, No. 121, p. 14.

Malinowski, Bronislaw, 2002/1922, *Argonauts of the Western Pacific: An Account of Native Enterprise and Adventure in the Archipelagoes of Melanesian New Guinea*, London: Routledge. First published 1922.

Mathias, Peter, 2001, *The First Industrial Nation: The Economic History of Britain 1700–1914*, 2nd Edition, Abingdon: Routledge.

Menger, Karl, 1892, 'On the Origin of Money', *The Economic Journal*, Vol. 2, No. 6, pp. 239–55.

Mill, John Stuart, *Principles of Political Economy*, Abridged, Public Domain, Kindle Edition.

Minsky, Hyman, 1986, *Stabilizing an Unstable Economy*, New Haven: Yale University Press.

Newlyn, Walter T., 1971, *Theory of Money*, 2nd Edition, Oxford: Oxford University Press.

Nicholson, J. Shield, 1895, *A Treatise on Money and Essays on Monetary Problems*, 3rd Edition, London: Adam & Charles Black.

Pixley, Jocelyn. (Ed), 2012, *New Perspectives on Emotions in Finance: The Sociology of Confidence, Fear and Betrayal*, London and New York: Routledge.

Sahlins, Marshall, 2004/1972, *Stone Age Economics*, London: Routledge. First published 1972.

Samuelson, Paul, 1973, *Economics*, 9th Edition, New York: McGraw-Hill.

Schaps, David, 2004, *The Invention of Coinage and the Monetization of Ancient Greece*, Ann Arbor: University of Michigan Press, Kindle Edition.

Seaford, Richard, 2004, *Money and the Early Greek Mind*, Cambridge: Cambridge University Press.

Silver, Morris, 2004, 'Review of Schaps, David M. 2004, *The Invention of Coinage and the Monetization of Ancient Greece*, Ann Arbor: University of Michigan Press', EH.net.

Simmel, G., 1978/1907, *The Philosophy of Money*, London: Routledge.

Simmel, G., 1907/2004, *The Philosophy of Money*, 3rd Enlarged Edition, London: Routledge, p. 177.

Simmel, G., 1907/2011, *The Philosophy of Money*, London: Routledge.

Simmel, G., 1907, *Philosophie des Geldes*, 2nd Edition, Leipzig: Duncker & Humblot.

Smith, Adam, 1986/1776, *The Wealth of Nations*, Books I–III, Introduction by Andrew Skinner, London: Penguin Classics. First published 1776.

Smith, Adam, 2008/1776, *An Enquiry into the Nature and Causes of the Wealth of Nations*, Selected Edition, Introduction by Kathryn Sutherland, Oxford: Oxford University Press. First published 1776.

Smith, Adam, 2009/1776, *An Inquiry into the Nature and Causes of the Wealth of Nations*, Project Gutenberg eBook, Adobe Digital Editions. First published 1776.

Spread, Patrick, 2012, *Support-Bargaining, Economics and Society: A Social Species*, London and New York: Routledge.

Spread, Patrick, 2016a, *The Evolution of Economies: Money-Bargaining, Economic Change and Industrial Revolution*, London and New York: Routledge.

Théret, Bruno, 1920, 'An Interdisciplinary Approach to Money as Cultural Capital and Total Social Fact', in Pierre Alary et al. (Eds.), *Institutionalist Theories of Money: An Anthology of the French School*, Cham (Switzerland): Palgrave Macmillan.

Van Leynseele, P., 1979, *Les Libinza de la Ngiri. L'anthropologie d'un people des marais du confluent Congo-Ubangi*, Leiden: Academisch Proefschrift.

Vansina, Jan, 1973, *The Tio Kingdom of the Middle Congo 1880–1892*, Oxford: Oxford University Press.

Wagner, V. F., 1936, *Geschichte der Kredittheorien*, Wien: Springer.

Wray, L. Randall (Ed.), 2004, *Credit and State Theories of Money: The Contribution of A. Mitchell Innes*, Cheltenham: Edward Elgar.

Wray, L. Randall, 2014, 'From the State Theory of Money to Modern Money Theory: An Alternative to Economic Orthodoxy', *Working Paper No. 792,* Levy Economics Institute of Bard College.

8 Graeber, Smith and Capitalism

David Graeber was one of the most outspoken writers on debt, with a strong anti-capitalist commitment.[1] He was the extreme exponent of the 'anti-capitalist' sentiment often apparent in varying degrees in the work of economic anthropologists. The 'money of account' idea of the origin of money is part of a wider search for an alternative to capitalism, inspired initially by Polanyi. Graeber held academic posts in anthropology at leading universities in the United States and United Kingdom. He was a leading participant in the Occupy Wall Street movement in 2011. His book on *Debt* is rated an 'international bestseller.' The book is polemical and abusive and no doubt partly for that reason has not received the fullest academic attention. Its assertive and often muddled arguments are difficult to untangle in narrow academic frames of reference. It is covered here because its range across politics, morality, violence, human relationships, finance and economics can potentially be untangled in the wide frame of support-bargaining and money-bargaining; also because its popularity suggests many are misled by it.

Graeber focuses initially on the economic theory of Adam Smith regarding the origin of money. He renews the assault on 'The Myth of Barter' in an early chapter with that title. Smith's account of the origin of money in barter is presented as the foundation of all the misconceptions of economists regarding the origins of money and the nature of economic behaviour.[2]

Graeber takes up the basic objection of economic anthropologists to Smith's account of the origin of money: there is no historical evidence for such a transition.[3] Graeber supports his case by reference to the work of Caroline Humphrey. He affirms that 'The definitive anthropological work on barter, by Caroline Humphrey, of Cambridge, could not be more definitive in its conclusions,'[4] and quotes the first sentence of the quotation from Humphrey in the previous chapter: 'No example of a barter economy, pure and simple, has ever been described, let alone the emergence from it of money; all available ethnography suggests that there never has been such a thing.'

Humphrey's comment is concerned with barter 'pure and simple.' The original assault on 'the myth of barter' depended on Dalton's restricted definition of barter, assigning all exchange other than the most simple barter exchange to the category of 'reciprocity.' Graeber makes no mention of this restricted

DOI: 10.4324/9781003313472-10

understanding. He ignores Humphrey's second sentence: 'But there are economies today that are nevertheless *dominated* by barter, and here anthropology can both learn from and add to the ancient debate.'[5] Humphrey suggests that these modern societies dominated by barter are instructive with regard to likely practices in earlier times.

The implication is that barter exchange would have been used in earlier times. But barter with any density of transactions would be so cumbersome as to give rise to a search for an alternative. Commodities that could fulfil the function of bargaining counters would be easy enough to adopt into use, even if in makeshift fashion. Barter is unlikely to be a durable practice, because of the inconvenience of barter, and the ease with which useful bargaining counters can emerge. 'Pure' barter societies in Dalton's sense would be vanishingly rare. Smith notes that 'a prudent man' would keep to hand a commodity that he expected to be generally acceptable. He notes the use in 'the rude ages' of various commodities, such as cattle, salt and shells, in common exchange.[6] The main impediment to the emergence of a more settled commodity money would most likely be the establishment of other communal objectives through support-bargaining, such as the ascendancy of a certain group or way of life, that would be threatened by the introduction of an alternative bargaining counter. The Lhomi people regarded barter as the only means of preserving their cultural identity, and were prepared to suffer the material privations it involved. Money as an alternative bargaining counter erodes the value of support as a bargaining counter.

Graeber seems to recognise that on any common understanding of barter it was no myth, and probably extensive in the ancient world. He rapidly retracts his initial condemnation of Smith's account with an acknowledgement that barter was perhaps not uncommon. Instead he argues that barter was mainly practiced not within communities but with strangers. He writes, 'this hardly means barter does not exist…It just means it's almost never employed, as Smith imagined, between fellow villagers. Ordinarily it takes place between strangers, even enemies.'[7] Graeber cites examples of barter transactions from anthropological literature demonstrating that barter is carried on between strangers with strong overtones of violence, sometimes erupting into actual violence.[8] They thus confirm Graeber's association, described in Chapter 6, of material exchange with violence. Material interests are identified as the source of violence in societies.

Confinement of barter to exchange between strangers means also that the wider argument regarding the origins of money – that it did not originate in barter – is sustained, even if it has to be accepted that there was barter. Money is recognised as dependent for its functioning on acceptance in a community, so that it would not emerge in the course of barter between strangers.

Graeber is not much concerned with 'reciprocity' as an account of internal social relationships. He notes Marshall Sahlins's account of 'generalized reciprocity,' but tends to discount the usefulness of the concept of 'reciprocity' on the grounds that a sufficiently broad definition of the term can make it necessarily true.[9] He also refers to Peter Kropotkin's[10] concept of 'mutual aid.'[11] Instead of these earlier accounts of social relationships that preclude barter, Graeber prefers his own concept of 'everyday communism,' or 'baseline communism' in which people share on the basis of neighbourly accommodation.[12] He conceives such arrangements as the 'human economies' that are destroyed by capitalism. The internal peace of such societies contrasts with the stress and violence of barter with strangers.

Humphrey, Graeber's acknowledged authority, is clear that barter takes place within the Lhomi community, rather than with strangers. She provides a very practical explanation:

> Barter tends to take place between people who know one another, because it is only by the establishment of customary times and places for exchange that the costs of search for partners, waiting etc. are avoided. [13]

It is not, of course, barter 'pure and simple,' in the Dalton sense. It is barter ranging from simple exchange through deferred barter to 'big business.' The 'big business' of the Lhomi was conducted between 'known people' by arrangement (Chapter 7, at Note 51). The Lhomi were arranging the confluences of people which provide the best opportunities for barter, as well as for money-bargaining. Such confluences of people promote the density of transactions that is most likely to see the emergence of bargaining counters. Whilst the Lhomi arranged their confluences through established social support-bargaining within their communities, confluences for barter can be arranged between strangers. The broader and stronger connections of an established community are not essential to the arrangement of meetings for purposes of barter. Graeber's examples of barter between strangers involve agreement on times and places. 'Community' is a matter of degree. People can come together to arrange matters of mutual interest without developing the loyalties and range of support-bargaining that is characteristic of a 'community' in the fuller sense. Modern trade treaties provide a basis for trade between strangers, without creating integrated communities. Traders build trading relationships that are sufficient for the conduct of trade.

Malinowski's study of the *Kula* custom in the Trobriand Islands (Chapter 2) similarly makes it plain that barter is conducted within communities. The *Kula* society, as described by Malinowski (Chapter 2), involved barter both within island communities and between islands whose people might have been antagonistic to one another if the *Kula* exchange of gifts had not established friendly relations. The *Kula* exchanges were sufficient to establish the degree of communal harmony necessary for the conduct of barter exchanges. They established ground rules of exchange and a degree of trust between people from different island communities.

In Chapter 7 it was seen also that barter of a makeshift nature, involving exchange of 'packages' of goods, delayed barter and barter mixed with the use of bargaining counters, was used in ancient Egypt, and in the Congo in the nineteenth century. The emergence of money, or money-bargaining counters, can be discerned amidst the makeshift. With regard to Mesopotamia and ancient Egypt, Seaford notes, 'There is also considerable agreement on the importance of barter in local exchange.'[14] In Homer, barter generally requires 'knowledge of co-transactors and personal trust.'[15]

Humphrey attributes to Karl Marx the origin of the idea amongst economic anthropologists that barter is largely confined to transactions with strangers. She refers to Marx's 'well known proposition that the origin of commodity exchange is the barter of products *between* communities.'[16] She continues:

> Only in dealing with the outside world, Marx wrote, are individuals freed from the social obligations ('property rights') which render their goods inalienable inside their own communities. Commodity exchange, i.e. transaction of alienable commodities, has therefore to take place with outsiders. This idea has taken root in anthropology and been elaborated in many influential theories (Sahlins, 1972; Servet, 1981–2; Gregory, 1980).[17]

For Marx, social obligations preclude the exchange within communities of alienable commodities. But an exchange of yams for coconuts, or fish for cassava, seems dialectically innocuous. The products will rot if surpluses are not traded. The exchanges may be construed as exchange of gifts, or they may be construed as barter. If the fisherman, seeing that no one else has caught fish that day, asks for an extra measure of cassava, then the ambiguity veers towards barter. Marx, like Graeber, is concerned to establish that material exchange is unsociable and associated with violence. It was seen in Chapter 7 that Sahlins, who supervised Graeber's doctoral studies, classifies economic exchange as 'negative reciprocity' and 'the unsociable extreme.' Within a community, people engage with what Graeber calls 'baseline communism.' Only with outsiders can they engage in the contested exchange of barter.

The contention over whether barter has been conducted within a community or only with strangers is, like the contention over the place of money in societies, related to the basic conflict of support-bargaining between individuals and the group. The group will see any erosion of the value of support as detrimental to its interest, and hence to be opposed. Individuals will want freedom to act in furtherance of their individual interests. Barter, like the use of money, tends to advance individual material interests beyond the purview of the group. In some societies, groups successfully resist pressures from individualists for freedom to trade. Societies have existed that exemplify Graeber's, and Marx's, contention that barter is conducted with strangers, though that does not rule out 'neighbourly relations' within communities. The ambiguities of 'gift-giving' for the cultivation of social relations and exchanges based explicitly on material considerations mean that the same exchanges can be interpreted differently, according to social expedience and the frame of reference adopted. 'Neighbourly relations' and 'mutual aid' can be interpreted as barter, with socially acceptable interpretations placed upon them. But whilst groups may successfully suppress individual freedom to trade in some societies, there are also societies in which individuals have gained the freedom to pursue barter transactions within their societies. For the most part the freedom to barter results in the emergence of bargaining counters, initially as temporary expedients but gaining over time established status. Their status may change from 'popular money' to 'regulated money.' The Lhomi people, fearful for their culture if money were permitted to intrude too extensively into their society, remained in the limbo of barter – accepting of the individualism of barter but eschewing the intensified individualism of money.

The Marxist view sees the 'group,' or society, as the centre of harmony and peace, with strangers the potentially violent contact. It was seen in Chapter 2 that ruling groups often cultivate external 'enemies' as a means of developing internal cohesion. The home society is portrayed as harmonious and united. But the intensity of group support that creates internal cohesion also diminishes individual freedom. Individual freedom to barter is likely to be constrained, with emphasis on cohesive bonds of support. Barter with outsiders becomes perilous missions into enemy territory.

As was seen also in Chapter 2, support-bargaining is necessary to money-bargaining. Support-bargaining is also necessary to barter. For barter exchange, some assurance of security is necessary before anyone goes unarmed into material transactions that have the potential to degenerate into acrimony and violence. Security will be enhanced by agreement on certain basic rules and regulations regarding aspects of barter that are most likely to generate acrimony: agreements have to be kept; items have to be in fair condition; produce has to be fairly presented; deferred barter agreements have to be honoured. A support-bargaining process has to be maintained amongst the agents to ensure that material exchange, whether barter or money-bargaining, proceeds smoothly. Support is associated with violence, so that support-bargaining tends to determine the extent of barter, as well as money-bargaining.

The case for barter trade, or for money-bargaining, and the associated case for freedom of individual initiative, will gain support the more apparent it is that there are material advantages to be derived from trade. Complementarity of provision, whereby one agent can provide what another wants, and that other can provide what the first agent wants, is conducive to trade. Similarity of provision, in which agents can only provide similar items or commodities, is not conducive to trade. Gardeners and fishermen can trade advantageously. Inland people can trade with coastal people. Country people can trade with town people. Mountain people can trade with people of the plains. This complementarity of provision is likely to bring about trade if not inhibited by security risks. Once the complementarity of positions is apparent, there are incentives for all to engage in support-bargaining to establish ground rules under which they can trade. Trade with strangers under the impulse of complementarity of provision is likely to give rise to arrangements through support-bargaining that minimise security risks to those involved. If there is potential advantage in material exchange, then support-bargaining can be initiated to make it happen.

Barter, Credit and Politics

Graeber mistakenly condemns Smith's propagation of a 'myth' that money originated in barter. But he more justifiably holds Smith accountable as the origin of the neglect in economic theory of the role of credit in economic affairs. Smith's concept of barter accords more with the confining definition of Dalton than with any broader understanding of barter. In particular, it takes no account of delayed or deferred barter. Barter is a matter of immediate exchange, and money emerges to facilitate immediate exchange, seemingly giving it the character of 'commodity' rather than 'credit.' This is the basis of the commodity theory of money generally adopted by economists. It removes from economic contemplation all the time disparities that are integral to economic processes. It removes from contemplation also the credit and debt that is necessary to accommodate time disparities. In removing credit and debt, it removes economic theory from the political measures that are a necessary part of the use of credit and debt. Credit requires non-economic arrangements for enforcement, whilst commodity money seems self-sufficient. With commodity money, economic exchange can be presented as independent of political processes. Graeber notes that the idea of money as a commodity emerging from barter is the basis of the separation of an 'economic system' from moral and political life.[18]

Graeber affirms strongly in the opening to his chapter 'The Myth of Barter' the importance of credit in the conduct of economic affairs and its neglect by economists: 'When economists speak of the origins of money, for example, debt is always something of an afterthought. First comes barter, then money; credit only develops later.'[19] He cites several economic textbooks whose authors 'imagine' barter to the exclusion of credit.[20] Smith's argument regarding the origins of money in barter is held to be the 'founding myth of the discipline of economics,' and whilst it is not, as argued here, mythological in identifying the origins of money, it has certainly caused economists to neglect the role of credit.

Smith's account of money, accepted by successive generations of economists, thus removes from economic contemplation the concerns of economic anthropologists regarding the social relations that derive from the use of credit and debt. As Michael Hudson remarks: 'The analysis of economic relations in terms of barter unrealistically separates monetary from debt analysis. Yet most monetary discussion assumes that trade always has needed to be financed by full immediate payment, either in bartered goods or in money.'[21] 'Full and immediate payment' can easily be portrayed as independent of social relations; credit and debt require social arrangements.

Anthropologists have nevertheless made their own contribution to this division between immediate settlement and credit transactions. Dalton's definition of barter, extensively taken up by economic anthropologists, confines barter to immediate settlement. 'Credit' and 'debt' are absorbed in the social relationships of 'reciprocity and redistribution.' They become matters of political or social concern, rather than matters of economic concern. As 'reciprocity' delayed barter is necessarily a part of social relations, with only incidental economic content. Instead of requirement for a 'non-economic' means of regulating the credit and debt implied by deferred barter, the deferred barter is assigned to the category of reciprocity, which is a matter of social relations. The notion of 'debt' can then be seen as an imposition of 'capitalists' that displaces the harmonious social relations of normal societies. Economists drive economics apart from political concerns by neglecting credit, whilst economic anthropologists drive economics into politics by a narrow definition of what is to be called barter and the categorisation of credit as political.

Graeber chooses to interpret debt in this way. He identifies the importance of credit and debt, and their neglect in Smith's account of the emergence of money. But he assumes they are important because they have provided the means by which capitalists have subordinated others to their material interests. With that interpretation, he misses the importance of the time disparities that are part of all social and economic transactions, and which require credit and debt for their resolution. His 'anti-capitalist' frame of reference imposes that interpretation on him, and filters out the positive role of credit and debt in making possible the accommodation of time disparities and hence the conduct of economic affairs.

Mainstream microeconomic theory has been similarly diverted. Smith's account of the emergence of money from barter and the focus on money as a commodity has diverted the mainstream of economic thinking away from time disparities and the use of credit and debt. The neoclassical model developed in the late-nineteenth century and into the twentieth century assumes immediate transactions. The Arrow-Debreu model of 1959 assumes that all transactions take place at the same time.[22] Without such diversion, economists might recognise more easily the gaps in their understanding of economic exchange that have given rise to anthropological theories of money and debt. The microeconomic frame of reference makes it difficult for its users to take account of the objections raised by economic anthropologists and anti-capitalists.

Not Ending Capitalism

Graeber understands debt and the enforcement of obligations to repay debts as the basis of capitalism. He notes that, 'nobody seems to know exactly what debt is,' and holds that this uncertainty about debt gives debt its power.[23] The power of debt is the fundamental of capitalism. In keeping with the obscurity surrounding the nature of debt, there is no consensus on what capitalism is. He remarks, 'The word was originated by socialists, who saw capitalism as that system whereby those who own capital command the labour of those who do not. Proponents, in contrast, tend to see capitalism as the freedom of the marketplace.'[24] The nature and role of 'markets' is a further obscurity of the capitalist system.[25] Graeber rejects the economic idea of free markets, insisting that states have always had a major role in the creation of money and with it the creation of markets.[26] Markets do not, however, for Graeber, originate with states; they originate in theft. According to Graeber there is a 'great embarrassing fact...that historically, impersonal, commercial markets originate in theft.' Thieves, burglars, marauding soldiers and debt collectors would have been the first to assess a house full of objects in terms of what the objects might raise on the market, and hence markets originate in theft.[27] If that was the way burglars assessed their targets, then markets must already have existed. More likely is that markets were found preferable to theft. Markets could operate when sufficient support-bargaining was operative to minimize the risk of marauders and establish rules for the conduct of trade. Confluences of people provided opportunities for the conduct of money-bargaining.

The uncertainties surrounding debt, capitalism and markets leave scope for imputation to them of all sorts of injustice and abuse. Graeber's own understanding of debt is that it is founded on violence; that violent relationships are made to seem moral by reframing them in the language of debt. The International Monetary Fund is regarded as the 'world's debt enforcers' – 'the high finance equivalent of the guys who come to break your legs.'[28] Violence is used to enforce debt in much the same way as gangsters extort money.[29] He implicates 'markets' in the more general infamy of capitalist behaviour when he affirms that the sale of children emerged as a common practice 'right around the time when we also start to see evidence of money, markets and interest bearing loans.'[30]

Graeber conceives debt in a social as well as economic context. People have social obligations that are given precision when conceived as debt: 'morality consists largely of fulfilling our obligations to others, and we have a stubborn tendency to imagine those obligations as debts.'[31] Moral obligations are reduced to debt. Debt can be precisely quantified, so that 'the crucial factor...is money's capacity to turn morality into a matter of impersonal arithmetic.'[32] The precision of debt is seen as having destructive effects on communal obligations and morality. For Graeber violence and quantification are intimately linked.[33] Those with a capacity for violence and calculation use credit and debt to destroy the moral integrity and mutual aid of peaceful communities. Creditors versus debtors is a matter of rich versus poor and the exercise of violence by the rich, including 'debt peonage' and the selling of debtors' children into slavery, to extract what they think is due to them from the poor.[34]

It was seen in Chapter 1 that ideas of social obligation and social debt are readily understood in the context of support-bargaining. It is partly because efficacy of support as a bargaining counter is a matter of psychological reactions, and hence imprecise, that it is so readily utilized in maintenance of the sense of psychological obligations to a society. By analogy, the idea of social debt becomes associated with obligations to repay material debts. In this context, the precision of money gives it positive advantage, since it deals with material things that are readily quantifiable. Social obligations are sometimes morally enforced, in that the enforcement is consistent with the codes of behaviour developed in the society through social support-bargaining, but may also be immorally enforced, by means that are not part of the accepted codes, such as violence and intimidation. The same is true of material debts.

Graeber tries to establish that the 'human economies' of early societies were changed by capitalists using debt and the enforcement of debt, in alliance with those who controlled armed forces, to establish systems of violence and oppression. The 'human economies' are conducted on the basis of neighbourly accommodation, what Graeber calls 'baseline communism.'[35] Communism is redefined as something with homely appeal rather than one of the two most destructive, manipulative and ruthless ideologies of the twentieth century. Such redefinition will presumably offend not only those who see communism in that way, but also those who still see communism in its Marxist revolutionary form as the only sure path to social justice.

Graeber describes capitalism as the means of enslaving people. He remarks that, 'There is, and has always been, a curious affinity between wage labor and slavery.'[36] Wage labour is akin to slavery because in slavery people sell their freedom and in wage labour they rent their freedom. In both cases freedom, a natural right, is disposed of.[37] Surely, slavery is the result not of people selling their freedom but having it taken from them by force, and is consequently well removed from wage labour. Graeber dates the dawn of capitalism to 1700 and the establishment of a gigantic financial apparatus of credit and debt 'to pump more and more labour out of just about everyone…'[38] The European conquest of the Americas exemplifies the propensity of capitalism to enslave and subsequently subject people to debt peonage or 'indentured service,' conceived as little better.[39] Graeber seeks to establish that the violence engendered by money and debt, and the emergence of markets related to military action, gave rise to the emergence of a 'military-coinage-slavery complex.'[40] His favoured connections are those which associate money, debt and markets with murder, massacre, rape, enslavement, imprisonment, prostitution, sale of children, cruelty and other abominations.

It is convenient to Graeber that 'debt' should be obscure, so that such other attributes can be associated with it. But in a common frame of reference debt is straightforward. If someone buys a washing machine and undertakes to pay for it at a later date, they incur a debt. They incur an obligation to pay for the washing machine in a prescribed period. The idea is easily grasped. It may be that it is easily grasped because we have a similar idea regarding social obligations. If someone gives us a lift in their car, or provides us with a meal when we are hungry, or helps to teach our children, we recognise that we 'owe' something to them in return. It is a case of keeping a balance of services.

Graeber's account of debt as 'obscure' reflects his own inability to recognise the origin of debt. As noted above, Graeber does not recognise the time disparities that are inseparable from the conduct of human affairs. Whether in social life or in economic relations, there are time disparities between what is received and what is paid out. Credit and debt are the essential means of overcoming these time disparities. In money-bargaining the reconciliation of time disparities is conducted with precision through budgets. In social relations we have a sense of balancing the services we give with those we receive. We do not like to be seen as 'spongers,' 'taking everything and giving nothing,' or unable to meet our social 'obligations.' Without this fundamental concept of time disparities in human affairs, as described in the Introduction and Chapter 1, there is no sense to credit and debt, either monetary or social. To make sense of it, Graeber sets up the conflict between debtors and creditors, the rich and poor, the human and the inhuman. He thinks it 'paradoxical' that the 'super-structure' of capitalism, the financial services agencies and financial securities, existed before the rise of factories and wage labour.[41] But there is no paradox. Time disparities have always been part of money-bargaining, and agencies to provide financial services have developed to accommodate them. Without the idea of support-bargaining and money-bargaining, and the time disparities involved with both, Graeber is unable to provide a coherent explanation of credit and debt.

Instead of providing a coherent explanation, Graeber tries to assemble support for the ending of the 'capitalism' to which he imputes all the evils that beset human societies. Money, credit and debt are the means by which capitalism advances its evil. But money, credit and debt are means of accommodating time disparities. They are used for purposes that are beneficial to human societies, as well as for damaging purposes. It is the business of ideological entrepreneurs, as described in Chapter 5, to assemble support for the notion that their cause is 'good' in some absolute moral sense. The assembly of intellectual and moral support is potentially transferrable to political support-bargaining, so that the interests of those opposed to the existing order are given political expression and put into practice. Graeber sees money, credit and debt as undermining the 'human economies,' the neighbourly relations, that are all he can present as an alternative to capitalism. But money, and with it credit and debt have also presented alternatives to regimes based on violence and the suppression of human freedom. Authoritarian regimes have generally looked on money and wealth as threats to their continued ascendancy, at least when they operate outside their own direct control. Money and free markets have been seen more often as threatening to oppressive rule than as themselves instruments of oppressive rule. Graeber's ideology derives from simple failure to explain some basic features of human society.

The extent of his failure is apparent from the retraction he makes late on in *Debt*. Drawing on the work of Craig Muldew,[42] he recognises that 'markets' using money, credit and debt can be seen as extensions of the 'mutual aid,' Graeber's 'human economies,' prevailing in pre-monetary communities, whereby neighbours helped each other. He comments:

> The reason that this upends our assumptions is that we're used to blaming the rise of capitalism on something vaguely called 'the market' – the breakup of older systems of mutual aid and solidarity, and the creation of a world of cold calculation, where everything had its price. Really English villages appear to have seen no contradiction between the two.[43]

In the villages, lending, provided it took place within the context of established communal relationships, was acceptable. It was recognised, for example, that widows might respectably lend money as a means of securing income. Trust in the community extended to trust in financial transactions between members of the community, including the provision of credit.

Balked by the evidence of Muldew, Graeber switches his attack: credit and debt become virtuous; the new villain is 'cash.' Graeber distinguishes money-credit from 'cold cash,' involving immediate payment, which was used between strangers, and with landlords, bailiffs, priests and above all in dealings with governments.[44] Governments used gold and silver to purchase arms and pay soldiers. Coins were thus associated with authority and the promulgation of violence. Even 'cash' is not the ultimate villain. That status is accorded to the state:

> The story of the origins of capitalism, then, is not the story of the gradual destruction of traditional communities by the impersonal power of the market. It is, rather, the story of how an economy of credit was converted into an economy of interest; of the gradual transformation of moral networks by the intrusion of the impersonal – and often vindictive – power of the state.'[45]

The 'market' is not previously presented as impersonal, but as the tool of vindictive capitalists out to enslave a populace, and even subsequently presented as originating in theft. An economy of credit is necessarily an economy of interest – the interest of both creditors and debtors in accommodating time disparities. The villagers, on Graeber's account, happily use credit that they see as falling within the moral compass of their society. The origin of the trouble is the 'impersonal – and often vindictive – power of the state' and not 'the alliance of warriors and financiers on which capitalism itself was originally founded.'[46] 'The state,' in the shape of war-lords, monarchs, sheriffs, dictators and preening presidents, is hardly impersonal; it can be very personal and very personally vindictive. Graeber covers more than 300 pages attributing every conceivable social evil to money, debt, markets and calculation, before finally acknowledging a very different interpretation of the historical record.

The doubts of Graeber about his own thesis become further apparent in his conclusion. In spite of the evidence of Muldew, he claims that the associations he makes between money and the use of debt with violence and cruelty are increasingly clear, and point to the imminent demise of capitalism.[47] It should then be easy to provide guidance on how capitalist societies might be set on a happier course. The analysis suggests an end to military spending, government borrowing (since the money is used for war), the use of money (since it engenders a calculating approach to human relationships, is inseparable from debt and is used to pay mercenary soldiers), teaching theories of Adam Smith, wage labour (since it is tantamount to slavery) and calculation (or perhaps just restriction of calculation to authorised material, to be identified by moral authorities). Yet Graeber avoids any such conclusions. He claims to do no more than 'throw open perspectives, enlarge our sense of possibilities.'[48] But perspectives so heedless of inconsistencies do not enlarge possibilities. Besides, his purpose is plainly to rally support for the anti-capitalist movement by giving it some semblance of scholarly justification. He seems to have no faith in the conclusions that would be drawn from his analysis. That should have told him that his analysis is most likely flawed. If nothing else, it selects from 5,000 years of human history whatever contributes to its thesis of the iniquity and the impending doom of capitalism, whilst omitting all that is detrimental to that thesis. The omissions would to a large extent explain why the above measures are unlikely to command wide support.

Graeber does nevertheless make one specific concluding proposal, though it is not altogether consistent with his analysis. His concluding paragraphs propose the cancellation of all debt, because, 'A debt is just the perversion of a promise. It is a promise corrupted by both maths and violence.'[49] Whilst the proposal may be seen as deriving from that part of the analysis concerned with morality, maths and violence, it is notably inconsistent with his account of social relations as 'laced with debt and sin.' He concludes that, 'The only way out is to annihilate debt,' but since social relations are so laced with debt there is the prospect that 'social relations vanish too.'[50] The proposal to end debt is then a proposal to end social relations. It is also, of course, an end to the accommodation of time disparities.

Graeber makes one comment, in the context of his discussion of economic models, that might have alerted him to an aspect of his analysis that is of fundamental importance. In the context of his discussion of theoretical 'models,' in particular the economic model, he remarks: 'Actually, I think a fair case can be made that we cannot think without them.'[51] Such a remark seems disingenuous from an academic anthropologist. It merely touches on the idea of the use of paradigms or frames of reference. Such concepts are, or should be, standard components of the analytical tool-box of anthropologists, given the different societies and different cultures they encounter. As was seen in Chapter 4, Malinowski recognised that every human culture gives its members a distinctive vision of the world. Frames of reference are assembled through intellectual support-bargaining to focus attention on phenomena that are of interest to the theory groups that create them and ensure that the phenomena are interpreted in ways that will assemble support for the theory group. Adopting such an idea into his work would mean that Graeber lost the force of his arguments. Anti-capitalists would find insipid anything less than assertive. The idea of frames of reference is inconvenient for ideological entrepreneurs, since it implies they are advancing their own particular interests, rather than affirming universal moral certainties.

Graeber reverts in his conclusions to a common frame of reference, and finds that the observations assembled and interpreted in the anti-capitalist frame of reference are highly discordant in the common frame of reference. He cannot recommend the apparently clear courses of action suggested by his analysis. He acknowledges that his treatment of 'communism' will seem 'provocative.'[52] But that acknowledges only the smallest part of what is clearly a work of comprehensive provocation. It is best to start *Debt* at the end, where the status of the text is made apparent. A text is less provoking when there is clear intention to provoke.

Notes

1 Graeber, David, 2012, *Debt: The First Five Thousand Years*, Brooklyn: Melville House.
2 Graeber, 2012, p. 25.
3 Graeber, 2012, p. 28.
4 Graeber, 2012, p. 29.
5 Humphrey, Caroline, 1985, 'Barter and Economic Disintegration', *Man*, New Series, Vol. 20, No. 1, pp. 48–72, p. 48. Original emphasis.
6 Smith, Adam, 1986/1776, *The Wealth of Nations*, Books I–III, London: Penguin, p. 127. Smith, Adam, 2009/1776, *An Enquiry into the Nature and Causes of the Wealth of Nations*, Project Gutenberg eBook, Adobe Digital Editions, p. 27. First published 1776.
7 Graeber, 2012, p. 29.
8 Graeber, 2012, pp. 29–34.
9 Graeber, 2012, p. 100, p. 405, Note 21.
10 Kropotkin, Peter, 2003/1902, *Mutual Aid: A Factor of Evolution*, Project Gutenberg eBook, Adobe Digital Editions. First published 1902, London: Heinemann. For comment, see Spread, Patrick, 2012, *Support-Bargaining, Economics and Society: A Social Species*, London and New York: Routledge, pp. 141–3, 204.
11 Graeber, 2012, p. 404 Note 9.
12 Graeber, 2012, pp. 97–102.
13 Humphrey, 1985, p. 48.
14 Seaford, Richard, 2004, *Money and the Early Greek Mind: Homer, Philosophy, Tragedy*, Cambridge: Cambridge University Press, p. 334.
15 Seaford, 2004, p. 155.
16 Humphrey, 1985, p. 68. Humphrey's reference: Marx, Karl, 1887/1854, *Capital*, Volume 1, (1887 Edition), London: Lawrence and Wishart, pp. 91–2.
17 Humphrey, 1985, p.68, Note 7. Humphrey's references: Sahlins, Marshall, 1972, *Stone Age Economics*, London: Tavistock; Servet, J-M., 1981–2, 'Primitive Order and Archaic Trade', *Economy and Society*, Vol. 10, pp, 451–66, Vol. 11, pp. 22–59; Gregory, C., 1980, 'Gifts to Men and Gifts to God: Gift Exchange and Capital Accumulation in Contemporary Papua', *Man*, New Series, Vol. 15.
18 Graeber, 2012, pp. 27–8.
19 Graeber, 2012, p. 21.
20 Graeber, 2012, pp. 22–4.
21 Hudson, Michael, 2004, 'The Archaeology of Money: Debt versus Barter Theories of Money's Origins', in R. Wray (Ed.), *Credit and State Theories of Money: The Contribution of A. Mitchell Innes*, Cheltenham: Edward Elgar, p. 117.
22 Geanakoplos, John, 2004, 'The Arrow–Debreu Model of General Equilibrium', *Cowles Foundation Paper No. 1090*, Cowles Foundation for Research in Economics at Yale University, p. 116. For comment see Spread, Patrick, 2016, *The Evolution of Economies: Money-Bargaining, Economic Change and Industrial Revolution*, London and New York: Routledge, pp. 49–55.

23 Graeber, 2012, p. 5.
24 Graeber, 2012, p. 345.
25 Graeber, 2012, pp. 114–5.
26 Graeber, 2012, pp. 47–52.
27 Graeber, 2012, p. 386.
28 Graeber, 2012, p. 4.
29 Graeber, 2012, p. 7.
30 Graeber, 2012, p. 129.
31 Graeber, 2012, p. 13.
32 Graeber, 2012, p. 14.
33 Graeber, 2012, p. 14.
34 Graeber, 2012, p. 8.
35 Graeber, 2012, pp. 97–102.
36 Graeber, 2012, p. 353.
37 Graeber, 2012, p. 206.
38 Graeber, 2012, p. 346.
39 Graeber, 2012, p. 350.
40 Graeber, 2012, p. 248.
41 Graeber, 2012, p. 345.
42 Muldew, Craig, 1998, *The Economy of Obligations: The Culture of Credit and Social Relations in Early Modern England*, New York: Palgrave; Muldew, Craig, 2001, '"Hard Food for Midas": Cash and its Social Value in Early Modern England', *Past and Present*, Vol. 170, pp. 78–120. See also further references in Graeber's bibliography to *Debt*.
43 Graeber, 2012, p. 327.
44 Graeber, 2012, p. 329.
45 Graeber, 2012, p. 332.
46 Graeber, 2012, p. 367.
47 Graeber, 2012, p. 381.
48 Graeber, 2012, p. 383.
49 Graeber, 2012, p. 391.
50 Graeber, 2012, p. 266.
51 Graeber, 2012, p.354.
52 Graeber, 2012, p. 386.

References

Geanakoplos, John, 2004, 'The Arrow–Debreu Model of General Equilibrium', *Cowles Foundation Paper No. 1090*, Cowles Foundation for Research in Economics at Yale University.

Graeber, David, 2012, *Debt: The First Five Thousand Years*, Brooklyn: Melville House.

Gregory, C., 1980, 'Gifts to Men and Gifts to God: Gift Exchange and Capital Accumulation in Contemporary Papua', *Man*, New Series, Vol. 15.

Hudson, Michael, 2004, 'The Archaeology of Money: Debt versus Barter Theories of Money's Origins', in R. Wray (Ed.), *Credit and State Theories of Money: The Contribution of A. Mitchell Innes*, Cheltenham: Edward Elgar.

Humphrey, Caroline, 1985, 'Barter and Economic Disintegration', *Man*, New Series, Vol. 20, No. 1, pp. 48–72.

Kropotkin, Peter, 2003/1902, *Mutual Aid: A Factor of Evolution*, Project Gutenberg eBook, Adobe Digital Editions. First published 1902, London: Heinemann.

Marx, Karl, 1887/1854, *Capital*, Volume 1, London: Lawrence and Wishart.

Muldew, Craig, 1998, *The Economy of Obligations: The Culture of Credit and Social Relations in Early Modern England*, New York: Palgrave.

Muldew, Craig, 2001, '"Hard Food for Midas": Cash and its Social Value in Early Modern England', *Past and Present*, Vol. 170, pp. 78–120.

Sahlins, Marshall, 1972, *Stone Age Economics*, London: Tavistock.

Seaford, Richard, 2004, *Money and the Early Greek Mind: Homer, Philosophy, Tragedy*, Cambridge: Cambridge University Press.

Servet, J-M., 1981–2, 'Primitive Order and Archaic Trade', *Economy and Society*, Vol. 10, pp, 451–66, Vol. 11, pp. 22–59.

Smith, Adam, 1986/1776, *The Wealth of Nations,* Books I–III, London: Penguin.

Smith, Adam, 2009/1776, *An Enquiry into the Nature and Causes of the Wealth of Nations*, Project Gutenberg eBook, Adobe Digital Editions. First published 1776.

Spread, Patrick, 2012, *Support-Bargaining, Economics and Society: A Social Species*, London and New York: Routledge.

Spread, Patrick, 2016, *The Evolution of Economies: Money-Bargaining, Economic Change and Industrial Revolution*, London and New York: Routledge.

Wray, R., (Ed.), 2004, *Credit and State Theories of Money: The Contribution of A. Mitchell Innes*, Cheltenham: Edward Elgar.

9 State Money and Corporate Budgets

Anthropological followers of Polanyi argue that money did not emerge from private barter exchange of material goods but from the designation of a 'money of account' by state agencies in ancient societies. State authorities, in the form of temple and palace organisations, determined what constituted money. A unit designated for internal accounting convenience became 'money' by virtue of its acceptance in payment of taxes and other obligations to the state. Private material needs were met through 'reciprocity,' a process of gift-giving aimed principally at the maintenance of social relationships. Reciprocity gave societies cohesion. The prices established in the accounting of the central agencies were adopted for private exchange. Since markets did not exist in the ancient world, money values could not be determined in markets. The temples primarily served the deities, with the priesthood as intermediary between the gods and their people. They derived revenue as offerings from adherents, ostensibly voluntary but often in reality more or less compulsory, and akin to taxation. They also farmed extensive landholdings and traded their produce. Palace revenues included levies, rental income, fees, fines and confiscations. A part of these resources was redistributed in support of the security and well-being of the people.

This understanding of the origins of money is sharply at variance with the idea of money as a bargaining counter. As a bargaining counter, money is bound up with the use of money in exchange; it has value as a result of the goods and services that can be acquired with it. The supposed absence of 'markets' in the ancient world relates to 'markets' in the neoclassical sense, as understood by Polanyi. 'Money-bargaining' remains a matter of exchange, but it has a different dynamic to that envisaged in mainstream economic theory. As was seen in Chapter 5, prices are formed in money-bargaining by reference to the unit cost of their provision. The unit cost establishes a minimum price necessary to the viability of an agent's money-bargaining. Viability will be achieved if a sufficient volume of sales at the minimum price can be achieved. 'Markets' in the understanding of money-bargaining are the confluences of people in which an agent is most likely to achieve the necessary volume of sales, and buyers are most likely to find the goods or services that will accommodate their situations, including their budgetary situations. The minimum

DOI: 10.4324/9781003313472-11

price can be adjusted by reference to the demand encountered in markets. No great assembly of sellers and buyers is necessary to this process. Small farmers can sell small volumes of produce. They will set base prices by reference to their unit costs of production, and adjust those prices in accordance with the demand from buyers and the alternative sources of the produce they offer. All agents involved, sellers and buyers, will experience disparities in time between what they need to expend and what they are able to receive as revenues. All will operate budgets by which they can accommodate the time disparities. They will set aside savings to meet anticipated future expenditures. Where necessary and possible, they will use credit to make expenditures that must necessarily be made in advance of revenues. Thus money-bargaining involves the pursuit of viability by agents providing goods and services, pricing by reference to unit cost of provision, bargaining strength developed through organisation, locations selected by reference to enhancement of bargaining position, buyout of competitors to enhance bargaining position, buyers choosing by reference to their situations, manipulation of information to enhance bargaining position, confluences of people offering the best opportunities for achievement of the necessary level of sales and the operation of budgets by all agents to deal with time disparities. These elements, in their essentials, can be present across the ages.

The state is engaged in the accommodation of communal interest, whether defined in a whole community or by a sub-set of a community. States require that their revenues have purchasing power, so that they can deliver the necessary services. Rather than accepting payments in an arbitrarily determined 'money of account,' they will require that payments of tax and other obligations are made in a money that has purchasing power. They will accommodate time disparities between expenditures and revenues, like all other agents, through the operation of budgets. In order that the revenues and expenditures recorded and forecast in these budgets shall correspond to actual values in the transactions of their community, they will adopt as the unit of budgeting the money that is used for common trading. The 'money of account' is a 'money of budgeting.' Only in that way can the state ensure that its budgetary provisions relate to the actual provisions it must make to deliver on its commitments. A 'money of account' detached from values established in money-bargaining cannot fulfil this function. The value of a money depends not on its acceptance in payment of taxes, but on acceptance in payment for goods and services. Geoffrey Ingham, the prominent proponent, after Mitchell Innes, of the idea of valuation by taxation, accepts the point in his 'best sentence,' as quoted in Chapter 7, at Note 34. The money of budgeting has to be the money of common exchange whether the 'money' in use is coin-money or the various moneys that were used prior to the introduction of coinage, so that money is always a 'money of exchange' and does not, as suggested by Ingham, metamorphose from a 'money of account' to a 'money of exchange' on the introduction of coinage (Chapter 6, Note 63). The efforts of economic anthropologists to establish their frame of reference as consistent with what is known of behaviour in the ancient world has given rise to what is arguably significant misinterpretation of evidence concerning such behaviour.

Michael Hudson worked with the International Scholars' Conference on Ancient Near Eastern Economies (ISCANEE), a group of philologists, archaeologists and economists, to study the economic history of civilisation prior to the classical era.[1] Hudson identifies the practices of the temples and palaces of Sumer (Southern Mesopotamia) in the third millennium BC as the basic evidence for the origin of money as a unit of account. Of these institutions he writes:

> Their large scale and specialisation of economic functions required an integrated system of weights, measures and price equivalencies to track the crops, wool and other raw materials distributed to their dependent labour force, and to schedule and calculate the flow of rents, debts and interest owed to them. The most important such debts were those owed for consigning handicrafts to merchants for long-distance trade, and land, workshops, ale houses and professional tools of trade to 'entrepreneurs' acting as sub-contractors.
>
> Accounting prices were assigned to the resources of these large institutions, expressed in silver weight-equivalency, as were public fees and obligations. Setting the value of a unit of silver as equal to the monthly barley ration and land-unit crop yield enabled it to become the standard measure of value and means of payment, although barley and a few other essentials could be used as proxies as their proportions were fixed. Under normal conditions these official proportions were reflected in transactions with the rest of the economy.[2]

This description has much in common with budgetary processes, but one characteristic means that it is not a matter of budgeting. The prices used in internal accounting do not derive from prices established in private transactions. Rather, prices in private transactions tend to follow the prices adopted for accounting purposes:

> Mesopotamia's temples and palaces were redistributive institutions. Their internal accounting and transfer prices were not market prices set by private barter exchange, although under normal conditions these public prices tended to provide a model for prices in the economy at large.'[3]

The requirements of internal accounting established a 'money' and 'prices,' which were then used in private exchange. Hudson refers to the temples and palaces as 'the largest economic institutions of their day and the prototype for modern corporations.'[4] They operated in 'mixed public-private' economies, 'alongside the family-based rural economy, endowed with their own land, herds of cattle and dependent labour rather than taxing the community's families for their means of support.'[5]

Deriving from the studies by Bernard Laum[6] of guild organisations of a religious character, Hudson associates the revenues of the Mesopotamian temples with the contributions made to later religious organisations. The contributions acquired connotations of fixed obligatory payments, becoming taxation when they were levied on conquered cities. Citizens gained status by contributing to temples, but lost status when forced to pay tax that was effectively tribute.[7]

The 'money of account' was apparently not entirely a matter of administrative convenience. Silver gained value from its role in long-distance trade:

> ...the public sector gave value to silver, and initially the public sector supplied it to the community at large via its external trade ventures. Assyriologists are not yet entirely clear as to just how this occurred, but evidently it involved long-distance trade in which the temples and palaces supplied textiles and other handicrafts to export for foreign raw materials, including silver. The public institutions seem to have spent this silver and provided other metals to the population in exchange for crops.[8]

The unit of account, expressed in 'silver weight equivalencies,' was then linked to the value of silver as it emerged from long distance trade transactions. This in addition to setting its value as equal to the monthly barley ration and land-unit crop yield. Accounts were kept 'interchangeably in silver and barley.'[9] The monthly barley ration functioned as a commodity money, used for payment of labour, and a unit of account. It was not a matter of arbitrary administrative convenience. But Hudson still affirms that:

> Silver's use in exchange derived from its role as a unit of account...these public institutions were the ultimate guarantors of the value of silver, by accepting it in payment of obligations owed to them.[10]

In the opening paragraph of his conclusion, he states:

> Rather than originating with private individuals trucking and bartering, money was created as a medium to denominate and pay obligations to the large public institutions.[11]

Hudson relates ancient state designation of the value of silver by acceptance of it in fulfilment of obligations to modern state acceptance of paper money and the broader authority of the state over money described by Georg Fredrich Knapp in his 1924/1905 presentation of *The State Theory of Money*.[12] He concludes with a strong endorsement of the principle of state acceptance of a money as the determinant of its role as money: '*What is true for today's paper money thus was true of silver. Its value was established by public institutions accepting it as payment*.'[13]

Hudson notes that the conduct of exchange in Bronze Age Mesopotamia (4400–1200 BC) through the use of debt balances, with periodic settlements at harvest time, the return of a ship from a trading voyage, or similar occasions of economic significance, is similar to that found by anthropologists in many parts of the world in later periods. The debts owed to tribal chiefs are analogous to those owed to the Mesopotamian temple and palace authorities. The phenomena found in tribal chiefdoms 'were hyperdeveloped in Mesopotamia's large institutions.'[14] The phenomena encountered in Malinowski's study in the Trobriand Islands can thus be associated with practices in the temples and palaces of Bronze Age Mesopotamia.

Hudson's affirmation that the value of money depends on its acceptance by public institutions places Hudson firmly in the 'state money' camp, but his descriptions of the money of account, related to the value of silver and the monthly ration of barley, at least associate him with the money-bargaining camp that sees the value of money as deriving from private exchange usage. The private trading usage of silver and the monthly barley ration provide private measures of value that are adopted for state budgeting. The state unit of account incorporates values derived from private long-distance trade and local private trade. Hudson's broader picture of Mesopotamian society and economy is consistent with the understanding of money-bargaining. He describes a mixed economy, with public and private sectors in symbiosis. Referring to Polanyi's three modes of exchange – gift exchange and mutual aid; redistribution with prices administered by large institutions; price making markets responding to shifts in supply and demand – he writes:

> All three types of exchange and pricing have tended to coexist in any given epoch. Most palace-dominated economies had room for private transactions (Edzard, 1996)
>
> ...Most economies throughout history have been 'mixed economies' in which public and private sectors have coexisted in a symbiosis. Gift exchange still applies to many interpersonal transactions, even as market exchange in one form or another is found in archaic Mesopotamia.'[15]

The primacy of private or popular valuation of money is apparent also in the value accorded to silver. Hudson insists that the value of silver rests on its acceptability to public institutions in payment of debts. But he still asks, 'Why were individuals willing to accept silver in exchange?'[16] His answer is speculative: 'No doubt silver jewellery had a symbolism that gave it value in conspicuous consumption in the form of prestigious ceremonial gifts...' Because of this, 'people were led to accept it as a general means of settlement at the point where temples and palaces accepted it in payment for public fees.'[17] The implication is that the acceptance of silver in payment by public institutions did not itself give silver value. It was because silver had popular recognition as valuable independent of any state endorsement that made it acceptable in payment of obligations to the state. The popular recognition of the value of silver gave silver purchasing power, and hence made it acceptable in payments to the state. The instinctive acceptance of 'sparkling metals,' particularly gold and silver, as valuable has enhanced their acceptability as money and the idea of money as 'commodity' (Chapter 7).

Private valuation impinges on the unit of account, as described by Hudson, in a more subtle way. It is linked to the unit cost structure of private exchange through the monthly barley ration and the 'land-unit crop yield.' The basic determinant of the price of a product in a money-bargaining system, as described in Chapter 5 in the context of the company viability condition (sales × price > unit cost of provision × volume of provision), is the unit cost of provision of the product. If the product sells well, the price may be raised. If it does not sell, the 'mark-up' on unit costs may be temporarily reduced, but if the product still does not sell, it will no longer be provided. Unit cost of provision gives the minimum price for a product if it is to remain in provision, that is, if it is to be exchanged for money. The monthly barley ration, and also a measure of dates, are the cost of a month of labour.[18] The yield of crops from land is the second major determinant of the unit cost of provision of an agricultural product. The higher the yield of a certain crop, the lower the unit cost of provision. Taken together, the barley ration and the yields give a measure of the unit cost of provision of products involving the use of labour and land. They are thus proxy for values prevailing in private trading. Through these links, the accounting price is linked to the unit cost of private provision. No 'markets' in the neoclassical sense, the sense adopted by Polanyi, are necessary to the use of a money based on private valuations in the budgets of ancient temples and palaces.

In The Economist's account of the 'Big Mac' index of currency values, the value of a currency is related to the cost of a 'Big Mac' hamburger (Chapter 6). The indexation is based on the assumption that the ingredients and work that go into production of 'Big Mac' hamburgers is uniform across nations, and hence the unit cost of a 'Big Mac' is an acceptable, or fairly acceptable, proxy for the unit costs of products in any nation. Similarly, the ancient authorities took the monthly barley ration, in combination with the yield of land, as an approximation to the unit costs of provision in their territory, and hence a good indicator of the value of their currency. It is the value of the currency that would be arrived at through formatting and pricing by 'companies' in the ancient world, as described in Chapter 5. The ideas are similar: unit costs determine prices, hence the purchasing power of a currency, and hence the value of a currency; and relative unit costs determine the relative values of currencies. But the ancients were more 'techie' than The Economist. They were also better observers and theorists than modern economists. They had the money-bargaining understanding of markets and market prices, based on unit costs.

Anthropologists have been misled into thinking that private exchange has to be excluded from explanations of the origins of money because of the supposed rarity of the barter systems from which money would develop, and because there were no 'markets' of the neoclassical type, involving many buyers and sellers, in which prices might be established. The neoclassical concept implies a conceptual divorce of economic processes from political processes, which is fairly challenged by economic anthropologists. But price formation and exchange are very common, with no necessity for 'markets' in the neoclassical understanding. Exchange takes place when a sufficient number of people find themselves in situations where they want a product on offer, and have the budget necessary to afford the asking price, or something close. Money-bargaining is 'trial and error' by providers to establish which goods and services, in which specifications, fit to consumer situations, rather than marginal adjustments amongst many assembled buyers and sellers. Exchange in this understanding of money-bargaining is widespread in all eras, ancient and modern. The neoclassical concept of a market leads Ingham, following other writers, to conclude that such markets need a money before they can create prices, so that a money of account is 'logically anterior' to the operation of markets.[19] But a bargaining process involving material goods is likely to create its own bargaining counters.

It was seen in Chapter 5 that large scale of provision of a product tends to be accomplished with the lowest unit costs. In consequence, large companies tend to gain dominant positions in the 'markets' for many products. Such companies may reach such a size that many livelihoods and economic ventures depend on them. 'Company towns,' in which a single company provides the bulk of employment and recreational amenities are common in modern times. Local small businesses depend on supplying the company and on the purchases made by its employees. Hudson describes the temples and palaces of ancient Mesopotamia as large scale in their operations and largely self-sufficient.[20] They would provide employment and amenities. They also sold goods of their own production. Within their vicinity they would be the dominant organisations. Their mixed sources of revenue would make it unnecessary for them consistently to relate prices to costs, so that they could influence prices for products in their communities as they saw fit. Employment of slaves would affect their costs of provision, as compared to the cost involved with free wage labour. If they chose to relate prices to costs, their large scale would make them providers with low unit costs, and hence potentially low prices. They would thus influence the prices of commodities traded in their vicinity. Fritz Heichelheim records that, 'According to certain Cuneiform archives the temples and state institutions sold at a cheaper rate than the private merchants of the same period.'[21] Whilst money derives its value from purchasing power in exchange, a dominant trading organisation, private or public, can influence the value of a money through its influence on prices. Hudson recognises that the range of influence of the temples and palaces of ancient Mesopotamia was limited: 'Trade outside the large institutions was less regulated. In times of scarcity, prices for commodities might rise for sales by individuals.'[22]

Hudson and Heichelheim

Hudson sees his account of ancient economies as correcting the misrepresentations of Heichelheim in his *Ancient Economic History*, first published in 1938 and expanded in an English translation in 1958.[23] Hudson insists that Heichelheim's preconceptions caused him to ignore anything positive about public institutions and reconstruct ancient history on an individualistic basis.[24]

Hudson records that 'Heichelheim (1958: pp. 111, 184) cited barley, copper, wool, sesame oil, and about a dozen other commodities as examples of how "in the earliest city cultures every form of exchangeable goods could be used as money."'[25] Hudson does not deny that such commodity moneys were used. Rather he applies his own frame of reference to their interpretation. He argues that Heichelheim, 'failed to recognize that the commodities he cited as "exchangeable goods" were produced in the large public institutions and hence fell under their administered pricing.'[26]

Heichelheim sees the use of capital as the critical factor in the emergence of town cultures in the ancient world. 'Capital' is understood firstly as building construction, with major construction programmes, such as that of Uruk in Southern Mesopotamia, suddenly transforming villages into towns. Heichelheim comments:

> Therefore I think it most probable, if not certain, from the evidence we have excavated that the revolutionary change from townless to town civilization was mainly produced by the factor capital, and that there was a sudden change-over in the fourth millennium BC...[27]

'Capital' is equally presented as credit, or the adoption of usury. This aspect of capital constituted a second revolutionary change.[28] The transition from rural village life to the life of the town was accomplished through the use of credit. Credit was used in rural life, but only to a very limited extent. A changeover to 'practically unlimited usury' made possible the transition to something like modern economic life and the life of towns:

> Capital was used as money in all its forms and to its fullest extent, that is that all capital was used as a technical means of valuation and exchange, with a definite rate of exchange. This practice was a complete antithesis to the barter systems of the townless cultures...[29]

The development of credit had an impact on what was used as money:

> Ancient Oriental money, then, had a particular and characteristic economic use in the earliest period of town civilization. Metals like gold, silver, lead, bronze, and copper, which had religious significance too, were used for this novel form of usury.[30]

Older forms of money were still used in the provision of credit, such as seeds of cereals, dates, figs and similar fruits.[31] Some forms of money proved less suitable to credit provision:

> ...other 'exchangeable goods' were found which were scarcely used any longer as money in the subsequent Iron Age civilizations [roughly 1,300 to

> 550 B.C.], materials like honey, sesame, reeds, garlic, oil, wine, beer, brandy, yeast for intoxicating drinks, sun dried bricks, rolls of papyrus, sticks, wood, grass, bones, leather, kawri shells, clothing materials, and arms.[32]

The preferred characteristics of the moneys adopted were that they could be easily measured out, or weighed.[33] Durability was desirable, but not essential.[34] The provision of credit in the new monetary forms involved the charging of interest. 'Money' was conceived as living organisms that could bring forth progeny, as livestock brought forth progeny. The progeny of money was interest.[35] Heichelheim conceives credit as a critical feature of urbanisation in the ancient world, bringing with it preferences for certain forms of money.

Palaces were the main usurers.[36] Heichelheim notes, however, that the practice did not extend to what he calls 'finance capitalism' – the provision of money for great undertakings. He remarks:

> There were not yet sufficient people in existence who possessed financial wealth to produce and maintain finance capitalism...In the ancient orient we find practically never phenomena resembling a modern capitalist pattern in the fields of finance.[37]

The system nevertheless favoured the rich and hence threatened social disruption. Heichelheim describes the response of the state as measures to stabilise the rates of exchange between exchangeable goods. 'In that way, for long periods, the prices, wages and the cost of living for all classes of the population were fixed as far as possible, a principle which not always succeeded.'[38] State supervision of money extended further:

> 'Exchangeable' materials received money status in the way that their quality was checked more or less officially according to traditional standards, and that they were weighed or measured out under official or semi-official control. There are frequent references found in the preserved documents to the effect that the measure of a certain town or some particular temple was to be used in paying out grain, or that the weight of a certain city or temple was to be adopted for certain metal payments.[39]

The dominance of the Ancient Oriental state economy was so great that Heichelheim, contrary to Hudson's characterisation of his work, describes it as exerting 'almost totalitarian influence on the production in the state territories.'[40] The state was one of the main producers, consumers and distributors of the economy:

> The state domains did not mainly produce for the courts, but for a market in agriculture, trade and craftsmanship and, as far as we are able to judge, in free competition with individual owners and temple estates.[41]

He concludes: 'For the Ancient Oriental economy was, as we have seen already, by no means free, but perhaps controlled by the state up to 90% of its potential.'[42]

Heichelheim notes the importance of planning in the ancient world and affinities of planned city life in ancient Mesopotamia, Asia Minor and Egypt with twentieth-century regimes enforcing control at the expense of personal liberty.[43] Just as the twentieth-century regimes brought private money-bargaining under strict control, or suppressed it entirely, so the ancient regimes, concerned for their survival, might have looked upon free money-bargaining as threatening their ascendancy.

Whilst Heichelheim notes this major role of the state in all affairs of ancient oriental societies, there is little evidence in his work for the anthropological concept of ancient states operating on a basis of reciprocity and redistribution, or even significant scope for re-interpretation of his evidence to show reciprocity and redistribution as the dominant character of such societies. He notes the importance of gift-giving within village communities in the earliest times, often as a matter of ritual or customary procedure.[44] Gift-giving was also important as part of recognised obligations of hospitality involved in external trade.[45] Gift-giving is, however, portrayed more as a sociable accompaniment to trade than as in itself a means of satisfying material needs or even as a means of maintaining social cohesion. He sees ancient societies as more like a European feudal system:

> the characteristic pattern of work for the Ancient Orient was one of more or less feudal labour. Men gave service to the state or for temples and landowners in the forms of villeinage, hired labour, tenant labour, fief, or slavery.

These patterns of employment arose from 'the introduction of a rational monetary system' and 'the appearance of the institution of the planning kingdom.' The first of these gave rise to hired and tenant labour, and the latter to villeinage, fief tenure, and slavery.'[46]

Heichelheim notes that palace revenue from its own production and sales, and its income from taxation, meant that, 'A very large part of the economic surplus of society consequently went to the crown…'[47] He refers to 'the distributing of the surplus production of society by the king and the palace.'[48] The revenues are expended on advisers, temples, sacrifices, servants, slaves, staff, provisions, construction and maintenance, and naval and military services.[49] The revenues are 'redistributed' from private persons to advance the interests of the state, as assessed by kings and leading people. The interest of the state was largely the interests of its leading people, but whether as a matter of principle or of expedient government, it included assistance for the poor. Heichelheim describes kings as being demi-gods with a responsibility, based on religious teaching, to protect the poorer people against the exploitation of priests, clans and overlords.[50] 'The Sumerian king Urukagina, slightly before 2300 B.C., promulgated laws protecting farmers, shepherds, fishermen, sailors, widows and orphans from economic oppression by priests, nobles and officials.'[51] There was also regular cancellation of debt.[52]

Heichelheim also records 'a very effective state collectivism' in Sumerian city states in the early third millennium established by a priest king.[53] This is the location and the beginning of the period studied by Hudson. What Heichelheim describes as 'collectivisation' might be what is interpreted by economic anthropologists as a state of 'reciprocity and redistribution.' Heichelheim remarks that certain questions of interpretation have still to be resolved, due to the fragmentary nature of the available texts and the difficulties of accurate translation.

Heichelheim recognises the significance of the financial administration of temples and palaces. Noting the treasure houses and strong rooms maintained by temples and palaces across the ancient world,[54] he remarks: 'Under these circumstances it is not surprising that now for the first time in history, the beginnings of drawing up a definite state budget appeared as a forerunner of our own systems.'[55] The corporate giants of the time maintained control of their financial affairs through budgets.

Heichelheim recognises the influence exercised by ancient palaces and temples as 'almost totalitarian,' with the authority extending to authority over money. He distinguishes between 'exchangeable materials' and 'money status' by reference to state endorsement of the quality and weight of the money. This is consistent with the process portrayed in Chapter 7 whereby a 'popular money' becomes a national money, or 'regulated money,' through state engagement. All 'exchangeable' goods could be used as money.[56] Money was not established as a 'money of account,' without reference to exchange processes. The state nevertheless had an essential role in ensuring that money in use was of proper purity and that weights were accurate and consistently used. Metals such as gold, silver, lead, bronze and copper were favoured as particularly suited to credit provision, but people used many different commodities as money. So the state established equivalent values of the commodities in the metallic money that predominated. Insecure commodity moneys were thus invested with sufficient stability to maintain confidence in their use. They could have 'dependable debtors' in the communities that used them (Chapter 7). With the proclaimed values of the different moneys, relating their weight to certain weights of metal, being maintained for decades or even centuries,[57] it would be easy to conclude that the state determined what was money and how it was valued. But from Heichelheim's account, the money adopted by the state originated in the establishment of its purchasing power in popular usage. Money originating as a bargaining counter in private money-bargaining needs the support of states to give it wide acceptance, but money adopted and regulated by states has to retain the confidence of private traders using it as a bargaining counter.

Heichelheim implies, in the quotation at Note 38 above, that the state valuations would not necessarily hold. Private traders would not necessarily follow the regulated prices of the state. Modern experience of currency trading is that if official exchange rates do not represent the values derived from trade that are consistent with purchasing power, 'black market' exchange rates emerge for the actual conduct of exchange. Further, state proclamations of value would apply only within the jurisdiction of the state, and within the scope of government inspection. Hudson, as was seen above (Note 22), acknowledges that the influence of the administrative prices had limited range.

Heichelheim records that Mesopotamians made use of bills of exchange as money, though their circulation was very limited. Their value depended on confidence that a debtor could be located, with a risk of 'debtors vanishing in the nameless mass of the Ancient Orient population.'[58] In this case, 'dependable debtors' appear to have been elusive.

Heichelheim suggests that metallic forms of currency were favoured because of their suitability for use in credit provision. This attribute is perhaps related to their durability, and to the ease of weighing them, which would in any case be good reasons for favouring them. They became available in many different forms: 'flat cakes, rings, spirals, wire, grains, tile shaped bars, lumps of gold and silver, copper or lead, heads of animals, animal tongues, axes, and so on.'[59] Heichelheim's stress on the role of credit in the transformation of ancient societies suggests the importance of time disparities in the conduct of economic affairs. He attributes great importance to usury as a factor in the growth of towns. In the money-bargaining frame of reference, confluences of people provide the best opportunities for viable business ventures.

Hudson recognises that ancient economies were mixed economies, involving both public and private initiatives. He describes the relationship as 'in a symbiosis' (Note 15). Heichelheim sees the various commodity moneys, both organic and metallic, as originating as money in private transactions and subsequently regulated and controlled by the state. Hudson maintains that, 'the commodities he cited as "exchangeable goods" were produced in the large public institutions and hence fell under their administered pricing' (Note 26). But Heichelheim's 'exchangeable goods' were not all produced in the large public institutions, and those that were produced there were not necessarily exclusively produced there, and their use in exchange did not necessarily originate in administrative fiat. Most of them are items of common husbandry and usage. Their use as bargaining counters would very likely arise from common money-bargaining, whilst their designation as 'money of account,' even in some cases their official valuation in terms of a 'money of account,' would seem unlikely. They suggest 'makeshift' arrangements for exchange, governed by the convenience of time and place and the people involved. Ordinary people would not be distinctively dependable as debtors, but in sufficient numbers they would potentially provide sufficient reassurance to sustain the use, within a limited community, even of apparently makeshift money like honey, sesame, reeds and garlic. They might be sufficient to sustain confidence in the purchasing power of a money at least to a degree that made it preferable to barter. The 'money of account' identified by economic anthropologists as the origin of money is clearly used for budgetary purposes in the temples and palaces, and must consequently, to fulfil its budgetary function, have the same purchasing power over goods and services as the money used in private transactions. Silver, the monthly barley ration and the yield of land are all connected with pricing in private transactions. The 'symbiotic' relation of private and public economic engagement most likely requires recognition of the private purchasing power of a money rather than state designation of a money, with the state endorsing the private selection and facilitating its function by regulation against fraudulent trading, counterfeiting and debasement.

Organisations and Budgeting

In support-bargaining and money-bargaining, as described in Chapters 2 and 3, organisations play a major role as the strongest bargaining agencies in both support-bargaining – political, social and intellectual – and money-bargaining. They achieve their bargaining strength through the use of hierarchies to focus the activities of groups of people on objectives established by those at the head of the hierarchy, and the use of money to provide material incentives for group members to accept an organisational hierarchy and work intensively for the advance of organisational interests. Use of money is planned, tracked and controlled through budgets. Budgets are used to reconcile time disparities between expenditures and receipts, and to allocate financial resources to best advance organisational interests.

Anthropologists, as would be expected, derive much of their 'economics' from accredited economists. The absence of any understanding in neoclassical economic theory of the central importance of budgets for reconciliation of time disparities and the management of money has meant that economic anthropologists have no ready explanation of the nature of the monetary management they find in the ancient organisations of Mesopotamia. They have been left free to speculate for themselves on the nature of the accounts. They have mistakenly identified the 'money of account' used in temple and palace budgeting as the origin of money.

The temples and palaces of ancient Mesopotamia can be seen as the dominant organisations of their time, operating as political-religious support-bargaining agencies, but operating also as money-bargaining agencies and maintaining budgets for the financial control of their operations. The 'money of account' is the money used for purposes of budgetary control. For effective budgetary control, as described in Chapter 6, it is necessary that the money in which budgets are maintained is the money whose values are established in trade external to the organisations.

Organisations running temples would be focussed on the fulfilment of religious obligations, as defined by successive generations of those at the head of the organisations. The revenues of such organisations are primarily the donations of adherents to the faith, made as a matter of religious observance. Such offerings, whilst not legally enforced, might be enforced by a strong personal sense of guilt if they are not made; the personal sense of guilt reinforced by expressions of rejection by organisational leaders. These offerings, becoming obligatory under the pressures of organisational support and religious conviction, are naturally conflated with tax payments. They are payments imposed on people by a recognised communal authority.

Ingham understands taxation as originating in these offerings driven by religious commitment. It was seen in Chapter 6 (Notes 20, 21) that gold, silver and clay tokens are interpreted by Ingham as tokens of debt symbolic of the sovereign and priestly power. Obligations to the priesthood, a kind of taxation, linked sacred to material practices: 'The basic link between society and the sacred was mediated by obligation and taxation (debt) and controlled by the temple priesthood.'[60] Taxes are payments of debt by virtue of the obligations imposed on people by the priesthood. And since money is understood as a means of settling debts, taxation is associated with the 'money of account':

> Money is not a medium that emerges from exchange. It is rather a means of accounting for and settling *debts*, the most important of which are tax debts. The value of debts is expressed in money of account…[61]

The contributions of temple adherents are thus associated with taxation and the origin of money. The mediaeval linguistic associations of taxation with sin and guilt described in Chapter 6, drawing on Ingham's work, imply also religious impulses behind the raising of taxes.[62]

The palaces would be focussed on governance, involving both support-bargaining and the use of armed force. In many cases the revenues of palaces depended on the exercise of violence. Conquest by violence was a common means by which states gained territory and wealth in the ancient world. Conquest brought plunder, property, tribute, slaves and rent. The sub-categories of 'Branches of Human Labour' discussed by Heichelheim in Chapter V of *Ancient Economies* include 'Robbery and War' and in Chapter VI 'War, Piracy and Robbery.' Some states were particularly involved in the acquisition of wealth by this means:

> Another irregular, but important source of profit for an ancient oriental state was warfare. The New Kingdom in Egypt, the Hittite and especially the Assyrian kingdoms were true robber states, and gained a large proportion of their wealth from wars and conquests.[63]

War is notoriously costly (Chapter 2), so that a large part of the money raised by a state is commonly spent on military affairs, whether defensive or offensive. Defence is invariably recognised as the first obligation of any ruler. With such an obligation goes some right to raise revenues for the maintenance of a defence force. So the obligation to defence provides an alternative rationale for the raising of taxes. When William Pitt the Younger introduced the first British income tax in 1798, he justified it on the basis of financing the war against Napoleon. The rationale can be extended to cover a host of other obligations and duties that a ruler might take on in the interests of his people, and his own interests in cultivating support.

Organisational Debt and the Origin of Money

The temples and palaces of ancient Mesopotamia, being strong organisations, especially in cooperation with one another, would potentially be in a position to establish a money, themselves playing the role of 'dependable debtors' by which the purchasing power of their money was assured. They could issue tokens for work done by their employees, redeemable with goods of their own provision. The temples were, according to Hudson, in addition to their religious role, producers and sellers of diverse items of common consumption. According to Heichelheim, palaces engaged similarly in trade. The arrangements are in principle those of the company that issues tokens for work done by its labour force, which are accepted for goods in the company store. When received and spent by the same person, the tokens constitute private acknowledgements of debt, but if the tokens are used for trade in the community, they constitute a local bargaining counter, or a local money. It is conceivable that such a system could have been introduced by the temples and palaces of ancient Mesopotamia. People could be expected to recognise the issuer as a 'dependable debtor' and hence have confidence that the tokens could be redeemed for goods at the temple shops. The tokens could then be used for private trading outside the temples.

As was seen above, Ingham notes that ancient temples issued clay tokens. The tokens, along with gold and silver, are understood as tokens of debt to the priesthood, symbolising sovereign and priestly power. As tokens of debt, they are associated with taxation and with money. It seems possible, however, that, along with gold and silver, they could have been used for the acquisition of goods and services from the temple that issued them, fulfilling a function like that of the tokens issued by companies, redeemable at the company store. They might have had the same function as the 'acknowledgements' issued by brewer and baker on receipt of meat from the butcher in Innes's illustration of the potential origin of money.

It is conceivable that money could have originated through issue of organisational debt in this way, with the issuing organisation performing itself the function of 'dependable debtor,' thereby assuring the purchasing power of the money. The large organisations of a state seem the most likely origins of money of this kind. But it seems no organisation made such innovation. Temple tokens were apparently not used in this way. It was instead the informal debt of irregular but communally recognised bargaining counters that fulfilled the functions of money, evolving into more abstract tokens of value. With adoption by the state, these various bargaining counters, or a dominant bargaining counter among them, were given status as 'national' or 'regulated' money and made more regular in supply. Heichelheim's account indicates that the bargaining counters in use had their origins in private exchange, subsequently regulated by the state, and used as units of account in state budgeting. The products listed by Heichelheim seem just the sort of items that are commonly produced and traded in a rural setting, as part of farming and village life. Hudson describes the economies of ancient Mesopotamia as involving mixed private and state engagement (Note 5).

The use of the homely commodities listed by Heichelheim as money would clearly have disadvantages. Silver seems to have emerged as money, providing both intrinsic attraction as a 'sparkling metal,' and practical qualities in favour of its use as money. It provided sufficient attraction to significant numbers, perhaps mostly professional traders, as opposed to casual household traders or small farmers, to function as money. In Hudson's account, Mesopotamian temples used a certain weight of silver as its unit of account, whose value, or purchasing power, was dictated by its purchasing power in long distance trade (Notes 2 and 8). Its value was linked also to a monthly barley ration (Note 2), thus linking it to a prominent commodity related to value in consumption and value in terms of labour time. Silver and the monthly barley ration could be used interchangeably for budgeting (Note 9). Silver was linked also to the 'land-unit crop yield.' The link to labour time and to the yield of land in crops meant that the silver weight had also a connection to the underlying determinants of unit costs in private provision, and hence to prices and purchasing power in private exchange.

Money seems to have emerged on the basis of communal acceptance, rather than the debt of ruling organisations, as a matter of expedience. People used money that emerged from their communal trading; no state saw fit to issue tokens for which it stood itself as 'dependable debtor' in terms of goods and services. An organisation issuing such tokens controls both the issue of tokens and the volume of items it provides in settlement of the debts implied by the tokens. They are likely to exercise that control in their own interests. Companies issuing tokens in the modern era have been seen as unsatisfactory in their provision, to the extent of being 'exploitative.' They were only able to operate in confined circumstances, for example, when national money was in short supply, or when they were in isolated locations. The strong bargaining positions established by confining circumstances enabled them to establish to their own advantage the purchasing power of their tokens. The Soviet Union is a modern example of a giant organisation providing the goods and services that maintained the purchasing power of the state money. It maintained its role only through the exclusion of alternatives by coercion. People were not free to choose how they would exercise the purchasing power given to them with the rouble. The state organisation fell notably short of the standards of provision available elsewhere. State organisations were not regarded as dependable debtors, in the sense of providing full and fair value for the debt, or were less dependable in that sense than the debtors who assumed that role elsewhere. Private 'dependable debtors' operated as such through their assent to a communal bargaining counter, but with more potent incentive deriving from the prospect of accumulating money, making them large creditors. A 'multiple debtors' solution, having the collective effect of 'dependable debtors' who gave 'good value,' was preferred to the 'single debtor' option for the maintenance of the purchasing power of money. Many people offering goods and services in exchange for a money has been more efficacious in providing dependable purchasing power of a money than money designated by a state, whose purchasing power depends on what the state chooses to provide.

The function of state organisations as creators of money in this way may also have been inhibited by the common ethos of state organisations. Those employed in palaces would be required to focus on state purposes, principally the maintenance of domestic order and defence against external assault. The elite of state service are inclined to regard 'trade' as degrading. The way to wealth would be through conquest.

In the temples also the priests and their attendants would be committed to serving the deity as their focal purpose. The priesthood seems to have dominated its people by virtue of its recognised responsibility for interpretation of the will of deities, and through charitable provision, particularly at festivals. They were also, however, as attested by Hudson, engaged in other activities, including agriculture and associated trade. Mediaeval monasteries in Europe were similarly engaged in agriculture and trade. The extent of lands donated to religious organisations, and the availability of labour, seems almost to impose on them diversification into trade. Being producers of material wealth, such organisations might have issued tokens redeemable in their own 'shops.' Such practice would, however, have changed their relationship with their people.

In both palaces and temples, token systems might have been seen as threatening to elite control. Rulers need to sustain support, and they do so by patronage as well as threat. The leaders of hierarchies need to sustain support at all levels. Tokens, at least in extensive use, would constitute alternative bargaining counters to support, and a threat to the ascendant. As was suggested in Chapter 7, in the context of the Lhomi people of Nepal protecting their culture, an alternative bargaining counter can be seen as threatening to a dominant group. Payment in kind for any services, with food rations and accommodation, maintains dependent status very effectively. Providing negotiable tokens would give choice and a degree of independence. With much of the labour force in ancient societies having the status of slaves, provided only with food and shelter, the use of tokens might have been regarded as risky. Money is too much like freedom. The interest in a bargaining counter is likely to be felt most strongly by those obliged to make their living by trading. A popular bargaining counter would be more likely to emerge through private exchange than as the debt of a state organisation. The popular acceptance of silver was perhaps an important factor in determining that money became established through exchange rather than as a token valued as organisational debt.

Money Valued in Taxation

Organisational debt seems the most plausible theoretical basis for a state origin of money. The economic anthropologists inspired by Polanyi have, however, argued that money originated as a 'money of account' in temples and palaces to facilitate maintenance of accounts, independent of private exchange, and was validated by acceptance in settlement of obligations to the state, the chief of which were tax debts. The 'money of account' was not indicative of any organisational debt. Rather, as was seen in Chapter 6, the valuation by reference to taxation implied the imposition of a debt on those accepting payment in the money of account. The state pronounced itself creditor, not debtor. The state coerced its people into paying tax with money earned from their provision of services to the state. It is exaction of tribute, or extortion. It is as if the company issuing tokens to its workers turns round and tells the workers that they must return all their tokens to the company for nothing.

Innes, in his 1914 credit theory of money, possibly the first account of valuation of money by taxation, relates money very directly to taxation in this way. State issue of money establishes the state as debtor to the community. But everyone is taken to have a share in the debt of the state, so everyone is required to pay tax to redeem their share of the debt. By this means, money gains value:

> The holder of a coin or certificate has the absolute right to pay any debt due to the government by tendering that coin or certificate, and it is this right and nothing else which gives them their value...
>
> Whenever a tax is imposed, each taxpayer becomes responsible for the redemption of a small part of the debt which the government has contracted by its issues of money...He has to redeem or cancel that portion of this debt...
>
> This, then – the redemption of government debt by taxation – is the basic law of coinage and of any issue of government 'money' in whatever form...
>
> The fact, however, is that the more government money there is in circulation, the poorer we are.[64]
>
> From what I have said in these two articles follows the important principle that a government issue of money must be met by a corresponding tax. It is the tax that imparts to the obligation its 'value.' A dollar of money is a dollar, not because of the material of which it is made, but because of the dollar of tax which is imposed to redeem it.[65]

Innes maintains that the United State is issuing currency without imposing any corresponding taxes, with consequent expansion of debt, without provision for its repayment, and with consequent depreciation of the currency.[66]

Rather than gaining a credit by receipt of money, as is the case in the idea of corporate debt, people are made debtors.

Ingham endorses Innes's account of the valuation of money by quoting the last sentence (abbreviated) in the quotation at Note 65 above.[67] But he does not take it further. Anthropologists are less specific than Innes in their account of the way in which the value of money arises from taxation. Innes's idea of 'sharing of debt' is tacitly dropped, presumably because even to economic anthropologists, who have an interest in some such rationale, it is implausible. Anthropologists specify less clearly the connection between the value of money and taxation. Yet even if not specified, the implication is still present, that if people become indebted to the state when they receive the state's money, they are sharing the state's debt.

Ingham's sociological approach to money was considered in Chapter 6. He stresses the importance of tax obligations as the factor that renders a money of account valuable in a community. He conceives money as a 'claim' or 'credit' constituted by social relations independently of the production and exchange of commodities. His explanation of the valuation of money by reference to taxation is intricate. As described above, he establishes people's indebtedness on the basis of their obligations to temples, the obligations fusing into tax-like impositions. The 'debts' that people must redeem through tax payments are then not debts imposed by the state, but debts assumed by people themselves as part of their religious practice.

Ingham also distinguishes between 'valuableness' and 'value.' His dual valuation of money is based on Georg Simmel's theory of value by which things have primary value by virtue of their usefulness, but a further value which is a matter of *pure abstraction*. Simmel's notion of *pure abstraction* is ambiguous. In the context of his contention that changes in money supply would not have uniform effects on prices, because things are valued other than by monetary exchange, he writes:

> The argument may be summarised as follows. Money performs its services best when it is not simply money, that is when it does not merely represent the value of things in pure abstraction. Precious metals are also valuable as jewellery or for technical purposes, but this has to be conceptually distinguished as a primary fact from the secondary fact that they are valuable on account of it; whereas it is the first and only quality of money to be valuable. [68]

The comparison suggests that Simmel has possibly in mind merely the distinction between 'value in use' and 'value in exchange,' the latter constituting the abstraction. But it might also be that Simmel has in mind the distinction between values formed in monetary exchange and values formed through social intercourse, that is, values formed by money-bargaining and values formed by support-bargaining, as described in Chapter 6. Neither provides a clear explanation of why people would accept an obligation to pay tax when they might reasonably expect a credit for the services provided in acquiring their money. Simmel may have contemplated an abstraction so pure as to be abstracted from nothing and nowhere.

Ingham expounds more strongly than Hudson the pure idea of money originating as a unit of account without reference to exchange, deriving its value from its acceptability in payment of tax debts to the state. Hudson is more concerned with the empirical circumstances of ancient Mesopotamia. Hudson describes the temples of ancient Mesopotamia as largely self-supporting, and not dependent on taxation. Hence he attributes the validation of units of account more to their acceptability in general payments to the state, rather than specifically taxation. As was seen in Chapter 6, Hudson regards 'taxation' as a bridging concept linking contributions to ancient religious institutions to modern money, on the basis of etymological connections between 'gold' and taxation. Ingham is more concerned to develop a sociological theory of money. He acknowledges Hudson as the source of his account of Mesopotamian practices.[69] He is nevertheless in accord with Hudson, and both are in accord with Knapp, in arguing that acceptance by the state is the determinant of what constitutes money.

Randall Wray ridicules the economic understanding of the origin of money in barter.[70] He regards an origin of money in the compensation payments of *wergeld* as unlikely, assigning the origin of money to the use of a unit of account for the levy of taxes:

> All the evidence points to the common origins of money, debts and writing, in the tax levies of the palaces...Money, then, originated not as a cost minimizing medium of exchange, but as the unit of account in which debts to the palace (tax liabilities) were measured.[71]

This understanding of money forms the basis for Wray's formulation of a modern theory of money, drawing extensively on the views of Georg Friedrich Knapp in *The State Theory of Money*[72] and John Maynard Keynes in *A Thesis on Money*.[73] The work of these two authors is considered in Chapter 10. Wray's modern theory of money is considered further in Chapter 12.

It was seen in Chapter 7 that whilst money is a form of credit, it is not of the kind that has a creditor agent and a debtor agent. A state money is a communal or social debt owed by 'society' to whoever holds money. It is a 'Society Owes You' ('SOU'), rather than an IOU. The holder of money is a creditor, but there is no specific debtor agent. The expectation, on which depends the effectiveness of a bargaining counter as money, is that the social debt will be repaid to the holder of the money in any goods or services that they care to claim from anyone who is part of the society that accepts the bargaining counter as their communal money and is offering for sale the goods or services required. So long as people receive satisfactory repayment of the credit represented by the bargaining counter, all members of a society will happily play their part in accepting the bargaining counter in exchange transactions and fulfilling the 'SOU' obligation. A tax 'debt' is an obligation imposed by coercion, only becoming an accepted obligation through support-bargaining systems. It is not a debt of the kind commonly recognised as debt, nor of a kind that can give value to money. The role of private banks in putting money into circulation and of central banks in controlling the overall supply of the money provided by banks as credit is described in Chapter 12.

As was seen above, Hudson recognises that the value of silver did not depend solely on acceptance by the state. It was popularly recognised as valuable, independent of any state acceptance. Ingham's emphasis on a money of account validated through taxation makes the popular and independent valuation of gold and silver problematic. It means at least that taxation is not the sole basis of the valuation of money. Ingham gives gold and silver a 'statist' complexion by affirming that their value is a facet of state power: 'It is of the utmost importance to note that the value of precious metals derives, in the first place, from their use as symbols of power and prestige.'[74] But they functioned as symbols of power and prestige only because they were popularly regarded as valuable. Other societies have valued birds' feathers and furs, and their leaders have adorned themselves in such valued items. The popular recognition of the value of precious metals, particularly gold and silver, also gave them purchasing power in terms of goods and services. Their effectiveness as units of account in budgeting, their use in borrowing and the provision of credit, and their value to government in the form of taxation, derived from their purchasing power.

Attitudes to Taxation

Innes suggests that money is a burden and taxation a blessing:

> We are accustomed to consider the issue of money as a precious blessing, and taxation as a burden which is apt to become well nigh intolerable. But this is the reverse of the truth. It is the issue of money which is the burden and taxation which is the blessing.[75]

This is perhaps a further reason why economic anthropologists have not followed Innes's theory closely. But still, the implication of the economic anthropologists' arguments for valuation of money by taxation is that taxation is a joyous thing. If it is not, it has to be imposed by coercion. The value of money and the use of money do not appear as compatible with the interests of private individuals, so if money is to be valued and used, it must be a matter of coercion.

In modern societies, with highly developed support-bargaining systems for the identification and fulfilment of communal interests, there is general acceptance of taxation. Coercion is a threat, but very much in the background. In the ancient times in which money emerged, attitudes to taxation were different. Taxation was effectively plunder, tribute, extortion from the conquered. It is scarcely conceivable as a basis for valuation of a money in the way suggested by economic anthropologists.

Hudson records the progression from voluntary contributions to religious organisations that raised the social standing of the givers to the loss of status accorded to those obliged to pay taxes: 'As taxes were coercive levies, their payers lost status by submitting to a tributary position.'[76] He notes the difference between modern concepts of taxation and those of the ancient world: 'The modern fiscal mode is to leave profit-making activities to the private sector and then tax its income, but antiquity viewed such taxation as a form of tribute reflecting a subjugated and hence unfree status.'[77] The associations of the word 'taxation' were different in the ancient world to the associations it carries today.

David Graeber records that free citizens did not pay taxes; rather taxes were levied on conquered populations. Ancient Mesopotamians did not pay taxes, and neither did Athenians. Ancient Greeks looked on taxes as tyrannical. Persians did not pay taxes; they levied taxes on their conquered provinces. Roman citizens did not pay taxes for a long period, and had the right to the proceeds of taxation levied on others, in the form of imperial provision of bread.[78] There was certainly no impulse to pay taxes comparable to the impulse to truck, barter and exchange. Taxation was extortion of wealth from conquered peoples. Tax payments had more the nature of 'protection money' than communally accepted contributions to accepted authority. States receiving tax revenues in these circumstances would clearly be looking for real revenues, or purchasing power. Their exactions would hardly confer value on any commodity or item in which they might be denominated. If silver had purchasing power, they would demand silver. Their acceptance of silver would not confer value on the silver.

Taxes were not entirely unacceptable in the ancient world. It was presumably recognised by many that the upkeep of law and order and defence of a realm required funds. But acceptable taxes were those levied not directly on people but on functions, or best of all on foreigners. Darel Engen writes of Athenian taxes: 'Most taxes were indirect: market taxes, port taxes, import-export taxes, and taxes on foreigners who took up long-term residence in Athens.'[79] This pattern is reproduced in later European tax regimes. Taxes were levied as far as possible on 'foreigners.' In Europe customs duties formed a substantial proportion of states' revenues for many years, because they could be presented as taxes on foreigners.

Subsequently, as state budgets became more open to scrutiny, taxes were found more acceptable if levied as a proportion of earnings or expenditures. People work voluntarily for money, and come at least to tolerate a part of their revenues from such work being paid to the state, on the understanding that the state would use the money to provide communal services. Similarly, it is found tolerable that a proportion of private expenditures is taken in taxation. Taxes, such as head taxes, that are not associated with voluntary earnings or expenditures, are forms of taxation most likely to be challenged.

As Wray and Graeber note, such taxes have been imposed as a conscious strategy to make people work for money.[80] The idea of promoting monetary trade in countries where barter or various makeshift forms of trade are the normal mode of material exchange has led some rulers to impose taxes with the express purpose of making people use money in their trading. Graeber notes the perceived injustice of this imposition of the use of a currency by imposition of tax obligations. He remarks of the imposition of a head tax in modern Madagascar:

> Not only was this tax quite high, it was also only payable in newly issued Malagasy Francs. In other words, Gallieni did indeed print money and

then demand that everyone in the country give some of that money back to him.[81]

A money imposed on a people by a state requirement that such money be provided to the state in taxation on pain of punishment is unlikely to be taken up with enthusiasm. The coercion necessary to make people work simply to pay taxes arouses powerful resentments. People are not happy to lay in valuables so they have something for thieves to take when they call. States are generally inclined to avoid measures that are likely to incite people to mount demonstrations or otherwise disturb the peace.

Ingham records that Wray's analysis 'points to the more fundamental role of coercion. Flogging, imprisonment and branding with red hot coins were the penalties for not paying taxes in the money issued and accepted by the state.'[82] Ingham interprets this as 'a refreshing counter to the increasing emphasis on the role of "trust" as the basis for the use of money.' Ingham seems to accept that money, being valued by reference to tax payments, necessarily involves violence and repression. But alternatively, the necessity for violence suggests that valuation by taxation is not feasible. It involves a money based on coercion rather than, as with a money based on dependable debtors and purchasing power, voluntarism and trust. Money as a bargaining counter depends on the trust of a community that its money will maintain purchasing power through the role of citizens as dependable debtors. The dependable debtors have, moreover, a primary motivation in gaining money incomes for themselves. Ingham effectively concedes the case against money valued by taxation – it involves high levels of coercion rather than voluntarism, trust and motivation. It clearly does not mean that taxation is a blessing. It was seen in Chapter 7 (Note 35) that Ingham plainly recognises the necessity of dependable debtors.

Taxation as a means of financing government seems to derive more directly from payments of tribute or, more pacifically, impositions on foreigners, rather than voluntary contributions, becoming what are in effect compulsory contributions, to religious organisations. The function of government was and is closely associated with armed force, so that the funding of government may also be linked to armed force. In bargaining societies, the effects of armed force can be replicated through formal support-bargaining, at least with regard to the raising of revenues. Taxes can be imposed on citizens with at least the consent of majority support. Even ancient societies, Athens for example, recognised a justification for exacting levies necessary to fund the costs of government. Accepting the need for governance meant acceptance also of the cost of governance and a means of meeting it. Contributions to religious organisations arise from the support-bargaining by which such organisations are created, and which establish their notions of appropriate behaviour. So the acceptance of such contributions is rooted in similar procedures as those by which taxation comes to be accepted. Nevertheless, the roots of the religious contributions seem to flower today more in contributions to charities, religious and secular, with still the potent fertiliser of guilt cultivated by the beneficiary organisations amongst those hesitant in their contributions.

Mercenaries and the Origin of Money

It was noted above, particular with reference to the evidence of Heichelheim, that violence perpetrated both by states and private people was prominent in the ancient world as a means of obtaining wealth. It was not only commonplace, but to a large extent acceptable:

> The historian Thucydides certainly considered piracy to be quite legal also, and declared it to be the oldest general means of acquisition on the part of Greek and barbarian coastal dwellers throughout the Mediterranean.[83]

Heichelheim notes that, 'In Homer, Odysseus, Menelaus, the Phoenicians, Taphians, and others are pirates and robbers par excellence.'[84] Achilles's dispute with Agamemnon concerns the distribution of plunder (Chapter 2). Heichelheim records what was effectively cost–benefit analysis of engagement in war in the Classical age (Chapter 2, Note 13). Support for war was overtly assembled on the basis of just causes and noble endeavour, but less conspicuously with an eye to material profit and loss. An 'economy,' in the sense of a system for provision of material needs, included in the ancient world a large element of acquisition by violence. The 'mixed economy' was very mixed.

Money cannot be other than deeply implicated. Graeber's work on *Debt*, as was seen in Chapter 8, accords money the leading role in the instigation of violence and atrocities. Other economic anthropologists pursue a similar theme. It is suggested that the origin of coinage lies in the necessity for a convenient means of paying mercenary soldiers. The idea was first put forward by Robert Cook in a 1958 article, 'Speculations on the Origins of Coinage.'[85] Ingham takes up the idea:

> The critical step in the integration of value by weight – as in the shekel weight of silver – with countability and portability came with the world's first large-scale wage labour – mercenary soldiers (Cook, 1958; Kraay, 1964).[86]

The use of coins for payment of mercenary soldiers leads Ingham to conclude that: 'It would be no exaggeration to refer to a "military-coinage complex" in the second half of the first millennium BC.'[87] Graeber suggests that it was more accurately a 'military-coinage-slavery' complex.[88]

Wray links the use of coins to the payment of mercenaries and also to the origins of money in acceptance by the state in taxation:

> According to Cook (1958), coins were probably invented to pay mercenaries. It was probably recognized from the very beginning that the purpose

> of the coin was to give the population a convenient means for paying taxes. Use of these early coins as a medium of exchange was probably an 'accidental consequence of the coinage,' and not the reason for it.[89]

Wray is suggesting that coins were invented to pay mercenaries in a way that facilitated payment of taxes. Both Wray and Cook see the use of coins as medium of exchange as incidental to their use in payments to mercenaries and payments of tax. But it is in this context that Ingham affirms a transition from money as a 'money of account' to money as 'medium of exchange,' referred to in Chapter 6. Where Wray sees coinage as reinforcing the concept of the money of account valued by taxation, and along with Cook sees only an incidental use in exchange, Ingham finds himself obliged to recognise that the introduction of coins made the use of money in exchange so prominent as to constitute a transition away from the idea of a money of account.

Recruitment of mercenaries would not have been easy if the sergeants could assure their potential recruits only that their pay would give them the means of paying their taxes. It was seen above that Wray's analysis points to a 'fundamental role of coercion' (Note 82) in getting people to accept money so that they could pay taxes. In the case of mercenaries, the potential coercers have to be coerced. Mercenaries would want to know that they would have something worthwhile to send home, or take home, or something that would at least afford them a good night out on the town. Seaford, speculating on the origins of coinage, makes the point:

> Again, even if we knew that coinage had been introduced for a specific purpose, say paying Greek mercenaries, it is difficult to see how payments with small pieces of precious metal...would be generally acceptable unless those pieces also had fairly general exchange value in a wide area.[90]

Money has to have purchasing power before it will be acceptable to mercenary soldiers.

Cook's 'speculations' on the origin of coinage in payments to mercenary soldiers hardly justify the prominence given to them in anthropological accounts of the origins of money. He suggests that coins did not originate in commercial practices. For larger transactions bullion would have been more trustworthy than stamped tokens. For small everyday transactions small denominations of coin would be required, but the most common coin in the earliest issue of electrum coins was the 'third,' which as a best estimate, based on other ancient valuations, was worth more than ten sheep. With no reason to believe that coinage was introduced for commercial purposes, Cook suggests that it arose from some Lydian paymaster preparing electrum 'dumps' of the correct weight ready for payment to mercenaries, like a pay-packet. These 'dumps' were then given a mark, which made them coins.

Martin Price questions Cook's analysis on the grounds that any such coins could only have value (or purchasing power) in the locality of their issue, and would hence be unattractive to mercenaries, and that their face value would have to be higher than their 'intrinsic' value, or value as bullion. Price concludes:

> If the above observations are correct, it is clear that the theory proposed by R. M. Cook, and now widely accepted, that coinage was to provide payments for mercenaries, does not fit the facts as we know them. Not only is it clear that the localised circulation would require that such mercenaries settled in local communities, but it is also doubtful whether mercenaries would happily have accepted overvalued lumps of electrum as payment.[91]

Later research has shown that smaller denominations suitable for retail trade were available. The issue is considered further in Chapter 11, under the heading 'Retail Trade and the Denominations of Coins,' in the context of assessment of the impact of the introduction of coinage in ancient Greece.

If coins really did originate in payments to mercenary soldiers, it would be expected, given the widespread use of mercenaries, that there would be other references in the records of the time, either explicit or associative, to the link of coins with mercenaries. As it is, the Greek coins 'obol' and 'drachme' are, as was seen in Chapter 6, associated by name with the spits used in Greek sacrificial feasts. Seaford makes a good case for an origin of coinage associated with religious feasts. There are no similar associations relating coinage to mercenary soldiers. The introduction of coinage in Greece is associated with the egalitarian ethos of Greek sacrificial feasting and the poleis, rather than militaristic and authoritarian government. Corroborative evidence is lacking for Cooke's speculation.

The uptake and emphasis accorded to Cook's theory of the mercenary origin of coinage in the work of some economic anthropologists seem to arise from its admirable 'fit' to a frame of reference identifying the state as the origin of money. Within a theory group an idea can gain ground and assemble support on account of its accord with the frame of reference. The idea of an origin of money in payments to mercenaries fits also very nicely into an anti-capitalist frame of reference. It is endorsed by Graeber in a roundabout way. Graeber remarks in his text that, 'one theory is that the very first Lydian coins were invented explicitly to pay mercenaries.'[92] He suggests that such an origin would help to explain why the Greeks, who supplied most of the mercenaries, took up the use of coins so readily. Then in an endnote he records that Cook's theory has lost favour, citing several sources (Price, 1983; Kraay, 1964; Wallace, 1987; Schaps, 2004, pp. 96–101), on the grounds that paying soldiers with coins implies that there are markets where they can be spent.[93] This is the argument used by Seaford, in the quotation above. Graeber dismisses the argument on the grounds that a government could make the coins acceptable currency by 'insisting that they were the only acceptable means of payment for obligations to the state itself.' This assumes that mercenaries will be anxious to pay their taxes. Or it is a way of saying that mercenaries must accept whatever the government says is money. That is what mercenaries will not do. It is hard to force mercenaries to accept payment in a form they are not ready to accept. It is just the forced monetisation that Graeber so hotly opposes in his account, mentioned above, of the imposition of taxes by colonial powers in Madagascar. Faced with such imposition, mercenary recruits, and the recruiting sergeant too, are likely to look elsewhere for an employer who can pay with money that has purchasing power. Or for other means of recompense – David Schaps notes that war provides plenty of opportunities for enrichment other than salary.[94]

Notes

1 Hudson, Michael, 2004, 'The Archaeology of Money: Debt versus Barter Theories of Money's Origins', in L. R. Wray (Ed.), 2004, *Credit and State Theories of Money: The Contribution of A. Mitchell Innes*, Cheltenham: Edward Elgar, p. 121.
2 Hudson, 2004, pp. 99–100.
3 Hudson, 2004, p. 101.
4 Hudson, 2004, p. 101.
5 Hudson, 2004, p. 104.
6 Laum, Bernard, 1924, *Heiliges Geld*, Tübingen: Mohr.
7 Hudson, 2004, p. 104.
8 Hudson, 2004, p. 107.
9 Hudson, 2004, p. 112.
10 Hudson, 2004, p. 115.
11 Hudson, 2004, p. 122.
12 Knapp, Georg Friedrich, 1924, *The State Theory of Money*, 4th Edition, Trans. H. M. Lucas and James Bonar, New York: Macmillan. First published in German, 1905.
13 Hudson, 2004, p. 107.
14 Hudson, 2004, p. 102.
15 Hudson, 2004, p. 110. Hudson's reference: Edzard, Dietz Otto, 1996, 'Private Land Ownership and Its Relation to "God" and the "State" in Sumer and Akkad', in Hudson, M. and Levine, B. (Eds.), 2004, *Privatization in the Ancient Near East and Classical World*, Cambridge: *Peabody Museum Bulletin No. 5*, Harvard University, pp. 109–28.
16 Hudson, 2004, p. 123.
17 Hudson, 2004, pp. 123–4.
18 Hudson, 2004, p. 112.
19 Ingham, Geoffrey, 2004, *The Nature of Money*, Cambridge: Polity Press, p. 34.
20 Hudson, 2004, pp. 99, 110–11.
21 Heichelheim, Fritz, 1958, 1964, 1970, *An Ancient Economic History, from the Palaeolithic Age to the Migrations of the Germanic, Slavic and Arabic Nations*, Trans. Joyce Stevens, Leiden: A. W. Sijthoff; Vol. 1, 1958; Vol. 2, 1964; Vol. 3, 1970, quotation 1958, p. 185. First published 1938.
22 Hudson, 2004, p. 117.
23 Heichelheim, 1958, 1964, 1970.
24 Hudson, 2004, p. 116.
25 Hudson, 2004, p. 116.
26 Hudson, 2004, p. 116.
27 Heichelheim, 1958, p. 103.
28 Heichelheim, 1958, p. 105.

29 Heichelheim, 1958, p. 106.
30 Heichelheim, 1958, p. 106.
31 Heichelheim, 1958, p. 106.
32 Heichelheim, 1958, p. 106.
33 Heichelheim, 1958, p. 107.
34 Heichelheim, 1958, pp. 106–7.
35 Heichelheim, 1958, pp. 104–5. For further comment and source material on interest, see Heichelheim, 1958, p. 432, Note 16.
36 Heichelheim, 1958, p. 173.
37 Heichelheim, 1958, p. 189.
38 Heichelheim, 1958, p. 111.
39 Heichelheim, 1958, p. 110.
40 Heichelheim, 1958, p. 179.
41 Heichelheim, 1958, pp. 179–80.
42 Heichelheim, 1958, p. 184.
43 Heichelheim, 1958, p. 99.
44 Heichelheim, 1958, p. 88.
45 Heichelheim, 1958, p. 93.
46 Heichelheim, 1958, p. 114.
47 Heichelheim, 1958, p. 179.
48 Heichelheim, 1958, p. 180.
49 Heichelheim, 1958, p. 180.
50 Heichelheim, 1958, pp. 166, 171.
51 Heichelheim, 1958, p. 184.
52 Heichelheim, 1958, p. 184.
53 Heichelheim, 1958, pp. 186–7.
54 Heichelheim, 1958, p. 178.
55 Heichelheim, 1958, p. 179.
56 Heichelheim, 1958, p. 111.
57 Heichelheim, 1958, p. 185.
58 Heichelheim, 1958, p. 112.
59 Heichelheim, 1958, p. 107.
60 Ingham, 2004, p. 93.
61 Ingham, 2004, p. 47.
62 Ingham, 2004, p. 90.
63 Heichelheim, 1958, p. 178.
64 Innes, Alfred Mitchell, 1914, 'The Credit Theory of Money', *The Banking Law Journal*,Vol. 31, pp. 151-168, p. 161.]
65 Innes, 1914, p. 163.
66 Innes, 1914, p. 163.
67 Ingham, 2004, p. 84.
68 Simmel, G., 1978/1907, *The Philosophy of Money*, London: Routledge, p. 165.
69 Ingham, 2004, pp. 93, 215, Note 10.
70 Wray, L. Randall, 2000, 'Modern Money', in John Smithin (Ed.), *What Is Money?* London: Routledge, p. 42.
71 Wray, 2000, p. 43.
72 Knapp, 1924.
73 Keynes, John Maynard, 1930, *A Treatise on Money*, London: Macmillan. First published 1930.

74 Ingham, 2004, p. 94.
75 Innes, 1914, p. 160.
76 Hudson, 2004, p. 104.
77 Hudson, 2004, p. 110–1.
78 Graeber, David, 2012, *Debt: The First Five Thousand Years*, Brooklyn NY: Melville House, p. 63.
79 Engen, Darel Tai, 2004, 'The Economy of Ancient Greece', EH.Net Encyclopedia, p. 15. http://eh.net/encyclopedia/the-economy-of-ancient-greece/ (Page numbers refer to article displayed in MS Word.)
80 Wray, R., 1998, *Understanding Modern Money*, Cheltenham: Edward Elgar, pp. 37, 54–5, 60–1, 155–6, 162. Referred to in Ingham, 2004, p. 55. Graeber, 2012, pp. 50–1.
81 Graeber, 2012, p. 50.
82 Ingham, 2004, p. 55.
83 Heichelheim, 1958, p. 260.
84 Heichelheim, 1958, p. 260.
85 Cook, R., 1958, 'Speculations on the Origins of Coinage', *Historia*, Vol. 7, pp. 257–62.
86 Ingham, 2004, p. 99. Ingham's references: Cook, 1958; Kraay, C., 1964, 'Hoards, Small Change and the Origin of Coinage', *Journal of Hellenic Studies*, Vol. 84, pp. 76–91.
87 Ingham, 2004, p. 99.
88 Graeber, 2012, p. 129.
89 Wray, 2000, p. 46. Wray's reference: Cook, 1958.
90 Seaford, Richard, 2004, *Money and the Early Greek Mind*, Cambridge: Cambridge University Press, p. 134.
91 Price, Martin J., 1983, 'Thoughts on the beginnings of coinage,' in C. N. L. Brooke, et al. (Eds.), *Studies in Numismatic Method Presented to Philip Grierson*, Cambridge: Cambridge University Press, pp. 1–10, quotation p. 6.
92 Graeber, 2012, p. 227.
93 Graeber, 2012, p. 426, Note 11. Graeber's references: Price, 1983; Kraay, 1964; Wallace, Robert B., 1987, 'The Origin of Electrum Coinage', *American Journal of Archaeology*, Vol. 91, pp. 385–97; Schaps, David, 2004, *The Invention of Coinage and the Monetization of Ancient Greece*, Ann Arbor: University of Michigan Press, pp. 96–101.
94 Schaps, 2004, L3727–34.

References

Brooke, C. N. L. et al., (Eds.), 1983, *Studies in Numismatic Method Presented to Philip Grierson*, Cambridge: Cambridge University Press.

Cook, R., 1958, 'Speculations on the Origins of Coinage', *Historia*, Vol. 7, pp. 257–62.

Edzard, Dietz Otto, 1996, 'Private land ownership and its relation to "God" and the "State" in Sumer and Akkad', in M. Hudson and B. Levine (Eds.), 2004, *Privatization in the Ancient Near East and Classical World*, Cambridge: *Peabody Museum Bulletin No. 5*, Harvard University, pp. 109–28.

Engen, Darel Tai, 2004, 'The Economy of Ancient Greece', EH.Net Encyclopedia. http://eh.net/encyclopedia/the-economy-of-ancient-greece/

Graeber, David, 2012, *Debt: The First Five Thousand Years*, Brooklyn, NY: Melville House.

Heichelheim, Fritz, 1958, 1964, 1970, *An Ancient Economic History, from the Palaeolithic Age to the Migrations of the Germanic, Slavic and Arabic Nations*, Trans. Joyce Stevens, Leiden: A. W. Sijthoff; Vol. 1, 1958; Vol. 2, 1964; Vol. 3, 1970. First published 1938.

Hudson, Michael, 2004, 'The Archaeology of Money: Debt versus Barter Theories of Money's Origins', in L. Randall Wray (Ed.), *Credit and State Theories of Money: The Contribution of A. Mitchell Innes*, Cheltenham: Edward Elgar.

Hudson, M. and Levine, B. (Eds.), 1996, 'Privatization in the Ancient Near East and Classical World', Cambridge: *Peabody Museum Bulletin No. 5*, Harvard University, pp. 109–28

Ingham, Geoffrey, 2004, *The Nature of Money*, Cambridge: Polity Press, p. 34.

Innes, Alfred Mitchell, 1914, 'The Credit Theory of Money', *The Banking Law Journal*, Vol. 31, pp. 151–168.

Keynes, John Maynard, 1930, *A Treatise on Money*, London: Macmillan. First published 1930.

Knapp, Georg Friedrich, 1924, *The State Theory of Money*, 4th Edition, Trans. H. M. Lucas and James Bonar, London: Macmillan. First published in German, 1905.

Kraay, C., 1964, 'Hoards, Small Change and the Origin of Coinage', *Journal of Hellenic Studies*, Vol. 84, pp. 76–91.

Laum, Bernard, 1924, *Heiliges Geld*, Tübingen: Mohr.

Price, Martin J., 1983, 'Thoughts on the Beginnings of Coinage,' in C. N. L. Brooke, et al., (Eds.), *Studies in Numismatic Method Presented to Philip Grierson*, Cambridge: Cambridge University Press.

Schaps, David, 2004, *The Invention of Coinage and the Monetization of Ancient Greece*, Ann Arbor: University of Michigan Press, Kindle Edition.

Seaford, Richard, 2004, *Money and the Early Greek Mind*, Cambridge: Cambridge University Press.

Simmel, G., 1978/1907, *The Philosophy of Money*, London: Routledge.

Smithin, John, (Ed.), 2000, *What Is Money?* London: Routledge.

Wallace, Robert B., 1987, 'The Origin of Electrum Coinage', *American Journal of Archaeology*, Vol. 91, pp. 385–97.

Wray, L. Randall, 1998, *Understanding Modern Money*, Cheltenham: Edward Elgar.

Wray, L. Randall, 2000, 'Modern Money', in John Smithin (Ed.), *What Is Money?* London: Routledge.

Wray, L. Randall, (Ed.), 2004, *Credit and State Theories of Money: The Contribution of A. Mitchell Innes*, Cheltenham: Edward Elgar.

10 Knapp, Keynes and the State Theory of Money

Anthropological and sociological accounts of money invariably mention Georg Friedrich Knapp and John Maynard Keynes, the first as the originator of *The State Theory of Money* in his book with that title and the second as a leading economist endorsing Knapp's theory in his *Treatise on Money*.[1]

Geoffrey Ingham, for example, follows Knapp in affirming that acceptance by the state is decisive to the 'moneyness' of money.[2] Money is money when it is adopted by the state as its unit of account, is issued by the state and is accepted by the state in payment of obligations to the state. Ingham comments:

> Knapp considered it absurd to attempt to understand money 'without the idea of the state' (Knapp, 1973, '1924', vii–viii). Money is not a medium that emerges from exchange. It is rather a means of accounting for and settling *debts*, the most important of which are tax debts.[3]

Michael Hudson, as was seen in Chapter 9, draws on Knapp to establish his theory of the state origins of money. He makes an analogy between the acceptance in modern states of their paper money in settlement of obligations to the state and the acceptance of silver by ancient states in settlement of obligations to them as the determinant of the value of silver (Chapter 9, Note 13).

It was noted in Chapter 9 that Randall Wray makes numerous references to the work of Knapp and Keynes in his account of 'Modern Money.'[4]

This chapter considers, in turn, the theories of Knapp and Keynes on the origins of money in the context of the theory of money based on support-bargaining and money-bargaining.

Knapp's State Theory of Money

Knapp's book opens with an unequivocal statement of the legal basis of money: 'Money is a creature of law. A theory of money must therefore deal with legal history.'[5] On the following page he reaffirms this legal foundation, contrasting it with a material understanding of money: 'The soul of currency is not in the material of the pieces, but in the legal ordinances which regulate

DOI: 10.4324/9781003313472-12

their use.'[6] Knapp describes the establishment of money on the basis of law as 'chartal':

> Perhaps the Latin word 'Charta' can bear the sense of ticket or token, and we can form a new but intelligible adjective – 'Chartal.' Our means of payment have this token, or Chartal, form.[7]

This legal foundation of money contrasts with the conventional foundation of money, espoused by most economists, in materials, especially metals. Knapp's opponents are 'metallists.' Metallists understand the value of a piece of metal as dependent on its material and its weight. The contrast between the two ideas of value is thus on the one hand a matter of tokens given value by legal documentation and on the other a matter of the weight of a material. Knapp affirms that 'Chartality and pensatory practice are mutually exclusive, like morphism and amorphism.'[8]

Knapp's theory is about the role of the state in establishing money as a matter of legal provision, state proclamation or state acceptance, whether metallic or token, and the rejection of the idea of any intrinsic value attaching to metals that permits their use as money. His theory is developed mainly in the context of monetary practice in Germany and Austria in the late-nineteenth century and early-twentieth century. *The State Theory of Money* was published in German in 1905. An English translation of the major parts of it appeared in 1924, in the midst of debate in Britain about a return to the gold standard at pre-war parity. Britain returned to the gold standard in 1925. Questions regarding the origins of money are peripheral in Knapp's book, though they are, of course, of central interest to economic anthropologists.

In Knapp's understanding, the value of money is determined historically. Any 'new' money has value by virtue of its proclaimed exchange rate with the money it legally replaces. The 'original money,' the start of the chain, seems nevertheless to lie in some material standard of value. Knapp describes the transition from valuation in terms of relative values of commodities to chartal valuations as involving nominal values, but reaches only the conclusion that 'Now, however, all we can say is that the first judgments of value came about in that way.'[9] At some time in the past value was judged by relative values of commodities. This is further affirmed when he writes, 'In former times the unit of value had to be "really" defined, i. e. in some material.'[10] Knapp argues that debt provides the link between the material unit of value and monetary means of payment: 'Debts in units of value arose from this [the "real" or material definition of value], and the means of payment were the result of the definition of the unit of value.'[11] Then he concludes that, 'by reason of these debts the present unit is defined no longer "really" but historically.'[12] Debt is conceived as a link across time, a historical link, of current money with previous money, and in some distant past, an historic material valuation. A debt incurred in the past in a certain money has a 'nominal value' which may be expressed later in a different means of payment. The value of the new money is linked historically to the old.

Knapp conceives the 'nominal value' of a debt as something existing independently of monetary valuations, so that, 'Each alteration of the means of payment implies that the unit of value, at least at the moment of transition, should be regarded as "nominal."'[13] The idea of 'nominal' debt distinguishes the existence of a debt from any units in which it might be settled.

This reference back to an original material unit of value suggests 'commodity money' or primitive money. Knapp suggests the establishment of commodity money as a convenience of exchange through social intercourse, and the subsequent adoption of such money by the state: 'The general exchange-commodity is, accordingly, an institution of social intercourse; it is a commodity which has obtained a special use in society, first by custom, then by law.' Knapp later mentions primitive money, and undertakes to trace it, but it is not covered further in the 1924 English version of his work. His comments on primitive money are:

> We shall assume a knowledge of primitive forms of money, and investigate how the monetary system of a State at a given time grows out of these primitive forms; for they can occur side by side. It may be that an actual monetary system exhibits side by side kinds of money of fundamentally different origin. In particular hylogenic and autogenic money may very well occur in combination. But for our purpose all that matters is that, in some way or another, the State has made the rules...[14]

State money grows out of primitive money. The state determines what is money, and primitive money lies outside that determination. There are passages referring to material means of payment that might be inferred as describing a transition from primitive money to modern money. Knapp writes: 'So long as a given material is *per* se a means of payment, money has not yet come into being.'[15] He then suggests that non-material money might be a development from material money:

> The question is now whether the means of payment can reach a still higher stage of development; whether a state of things is conceivable in which the means of payment is something other than a material elected for this purpose.[16]

The involvement of the state does not establish money where none existed previously, but lifts a previous functional money, referred to as a 'means of payment,' to a higher state of development. Or the state money 'grows out of these primitive forms.' Or the state money is the legal establishment of a money established by custom.

Knapp's theory of money is thus kin to the process described in Chapter 7 in which a commodity money becomes a national money, or a token money deriving from the use of commodity money becomes a national money, or in the terms suggested in Chapter 6, 'popular money' becomes 'regulated money' or 'managed money.' Knapp recognises the origin of money in some material or commodity form of money, so that whatever the modern role of the state, money did not, on Knapp's account, originate with the state. Knapp is then not relevant to the concerns of economic anthropologists building the case for a state origin of money. It is only that, in the course of his arguments for state ascendancy over metallism, he makes statements that in isolation can be presented as affirming a state origin of money. The idea of an origin of money in designation of a 'money-of-account' is readily associated with a 'chartal' money, a money, as it were, 'chartered' or engineered by the state, or designated by the state.

Categories and Chartalism

'Hylogenic' money is material money, whether metallic or of some other material. Gold is hylogenic money. 'Autogenic' money is money that is not related to a material regarded as having value. Paper money is autogenic money; the paper being of no value in itself. Hylogenic money can be proclaimed as money by the state, and is then chartal money. Autogenic money is necessarily chartal; it is created by proclamation. The answer to the question 'What is money?' is, according to Knapp, 'Money always signifies a Chartal means of payment. Every Chartal means of payment we call money. The definition of money is therefore a Chartal means of payment.'[17] The 'State theory of money' is thus that 'Money is what is designated chartally,' and only the state can designate what is chartal, so only money designated by the state can be money. 'In modern monetary systems proclamation is always supreme.'[18] There is 'money' and there is a further category 'money proper': 'Money proper' is money, hylogenic or autogenic, that is chartal.[19] Commodity money is not money proper unless it is made chartal by proclamation. The tautological nature of the definition is difficult to miss, even when enveloped in an unfamiliar vocabulary of classification. The definition establishes a frame of reference which requires that commodity money, unless made chartal, is understood as non-money. The tautologies establish consistency within the frame of reference, but not necessarily consistency with observations deriving from alternative frames of reference and alternative definitions.

Knapp presents a theoretical classification of money with a very extensive and complex, mostly Greek- and Latin-derived, vocabulary to describe the different character of various theoretically distinct aspects of money. Eighty-nine terms are listed in Knapp's Index of Technical Terms. Few writers on Knapp's theory have welcomed his categorisations.[20] They do not make for easy reading or instant illumination. In places the text reads like a parody of pedantic obfuscation. For example, Knapp comments on a supposed inconvertibility of gold metal into gold coins in Bremen before 1871:

> gold would then not be a hylic metal and in spite of the platic use of gold, there would have been no hylodromy. For the hyloleptic branch of the

> lytric administration was missing, even though the hylophantic branch was nearly complete, in the rules limiting the abrasion allowed in those foreign gold coins.[21]

Knapp recognises his classification is likely to cause difficulty: 'I have renounced the advantages of a pleasing style to obtain the greater advantage of scientific treatment.'[22] But the words impose Knapp's preconceptions on what is observed, rather than classifying in accordance with what might be more widely accepted. He is, moreover, notably unscientific in his treatment of other writers. 'Metallists' are treated as an undifferentiated, amorphous group, sometimes with an element of ridicule:

> Similarly he [the metallist] cannot with all his heart recognise that valuta money is occasionally notal. Notal money, because he hates it, seems to him to be unworthy and even incapable of such a pre-eminent position, and he talks of 'anomalous developments.'[23]

'Metallism' has a long history, including a notable dispute between proponents of a gold peg and mercantilists in England in the early-seventeenth century, and another between 'bullionists' and 'anti-bullionists,' proponents of inconvertible bank notes, at the Bank of England in the early-nineteenth century. A link to a metal was seen as giving automatic checks on the supply of money, and hence a check on inflation and erosion of the purchasing power of the money. There was, furthermore, the advantage of popular recognition, for whatever reason, of value in 'sparkling' metals. The non-metallists, the anti-bullionists, have emphasised the necessity of maintaining supplies of money consistent with the requirements of trade. There is then advantage in the issue of paper money based on trust, whether trust that it can be exchanged on demand for metallic money, or trust that it will retain purchasing power.

Knapp sees metallism not in terms of this distinction on the basis of economic effectiveness or practicality, but more as a commitment to the intrinsic value of precious metals and a refusal to accept the possibility of other forms of money. His theory is concerned with the way non-metallic forms of money, established by state proclamation, can fulfil the function of money. He is concerned with the state management of a money that has already become established, way back in history, as money, and linked to a present money by chartal linkage of exchange rates. Knapp's theory is widely cited in support of a state origin of money, but it does no more than affirm state responsibility for management of money. The state can manage both commodity money and token money, since it can accord both chartal status.

Chartalism and Politics

Knapp makes central to his concept of money the idea of legal status and legal ordinance. The word 'chartal' has an appropriate 'legal' tone. The concept is amplified at length. Nevertheless, shortly after introducing it, Knapp changes it substantially, making it more a political concept than a matter of legal fixity. He writes:

> If we have already declared in the beginning that money is a creation of law, this is not to be interpreted in the narrower sense that it is a creation of jurisprudence, but in the larger sense that it is a creation of the legislative activity of the State, a creation of legislative policy.

'Money' is a creation of law, but law is a creation of politics, so that 'chartal' money is a creation of politics. The different emphasis gives money a more flexible and contestable nature than is apparent from the chartal-legal understanding. It loses the fixity of the chartal-legal concept. The change necessitates a change of classifications to take account of the actual functioning of money, as opposed to his theoretical construct. The change of classifications, which involves change in definitions, is at the same time a change in frame of reference.

It would have been better, from a student's point of view, if Knapp had adopted from the outset the functional frame of reference and identified in that frame the political foundations of money. Many of the inconsistencies encountered by Knapp as a result of his continued use of the chartal-legal frame would have been eliminated. But such revision might have forced him to abandon, certainly to modify, his state theory of money. The bold and seemingly more conclusive declaration of legal status is preferred, and has been substantially adopted by theorists of the state origin of money. A 'money-of-account' seems better established with the fixity of law than through the vagaries of politics.

Knapp sees nothing strange in his theoretical classification having no application in the practical context. He writes: 'The functional classification of money, especially the most important one into valuta and accessory, is totally independent of the genetic classification…'[24] And on the next page: 'So long as we are only describing, we take it as an axiom, that money can be regarded genetically or functionally; in this way we are led to classifications which are independent of each other.'[25] Having established a frame of reference which seemingly requires everyone to understand money as whatever is proclaimed by the state to be money, he himself dispenses with that understanding. He creates a new framework of definitions and vocabulary to accommodate what is observed, or at least, to accommodate more of what is observed.

In this new frame of reference Knapp recognises money as an outcome of 'politics' rather than a matter of law. Money is adapted to the demands made on it through the political system. The 'politics' is not confined to the formal political processes by which laws are made. That aspect of politics tends to be less prominent than the informal politics of the administration of financial services. The law can be ignored, given the authority of state administration. Knapp is notably unhappy with the politics he observes in Germany. On 'valuta money,' the money in ordinary usage under Knapp's functional classification, distinct from 'accessory money,' or money valued by acceptance,[26] he writes:

> The concept of valuta money cannot be arrived at merely from Acts of Parliament; but it can be found without difficulty from the point of view of the administration. That is the only explanation which fits the facts. It is of no use to ask censoriously whether the State itself is observing the law or not. The State is not, in fact, bound by its laws, which it only maintains for its subjects: from time to time it of itself creates new rights and obligations to meet the facts administratively, and perhaps afterwards changes the law to make it correspond. We neither commend nor defend this proceeding, but only call attention to it as a fact of political experience.[27]

The chartal-legal account of money is thus rejected. Money is designated as money by political and administrative practice, despite what the law may say. Laws may or may not be enacted later to establish in law what has come about by administrative practice. But:

> Regulations are not based merely on law, but on human powers and political situations... This, of course, is not jurisprudence, bound to adhere to a given regulation; but it is politics, and money matters are in the domain of politics.[28]

The difficulties of changing classifications are apparent when Knapp, retaining the chartal-legal account of money, tries to explain the existence of different forms of money that, while clearly to be accounted money in common theory, are ruled out as money with the definitions of the chartal-legal frame of reference. Bank notes are private money issued by private banks or other financial institutions that are accepted by banks in settlement of obligations to them. Private bank notes are the money commonly used in private trading in the financial systems that are the focus of Knapp's attention. Bank notes carry what is ostensibly a promise that they can be redeemed in valuta money, as currently recognised by the state.[29] But Knapp argues that such a promise is of no significance. A bank note is rather, 'a chartal means of payment issued privately; it is a private till-warrant available for payments to the bank (*epitrapezic* payments).'[30] 'Chartal' money is redefined, so that it can be non-state money, as well as state money. In using such bank notes, 'These customers and the bank form, so to speak, a private pay community; the public pay community is the State.'[31]

Knapp spends several pages reconciling the private nature of bank notes with their extensive role in trade and commerce. They seem to be 'money' in any common usage of the term, but are privately issued, so they are not obviously state money. They are of the nature of the tokens issued by companies which can be redeemed at the company store, though they can be redeemed only for 'valuta,' and even then perhaps only nominally. Knapp describes them as 'chartal,' which under his theoretical definition means they must be state money. Knapp concludes that they become state money when they are endorsed by the state, or when the state accepts them in payments. The state and its law create both public and private means of payment.

Besides, according to Knapp, the private banks that issue their own notes can do so because that right is accorded to them by the state. Knapp holds that, 'It is a great favour to the banking world that the State permits the issue of notes.'[32] Other businesses are not permitted to issue notes, so that:

> The State is giving to the holders of bank shares a means of increasing their profits which it absolutely denies to other businesses. 'Capitalism' is thus not indeed begotten but certainly brought up by the State. [33]

The state not only creates money, but also nurtures 'capitalism.' The laws that establish how money is to be regulated and managed are also the laws that provide opportunities for the provision of credit and the emergence of a group of people who provide credit. But the favour of the state to private banks can be understood as accorded in response to communal requirements for sound management of a national money. The state uses banks to get money into circulation in accordance with the requirements of trade and credit. When the right to issue money is confined to a central bank, which issues a national money, the central bank uses private banks to put the national money into circulation (Chapters 7, 12).

The question of whether, following acceptance by the state, bank notes are to be classified as 'valuta' or 'accessory' money remains a difficulty for Knapp. He opts to suspend judgement on the matter, resting content with the recognition that bank money can at least become state money: 'It is therefore necessary to lay emphasis on the fact, that if bank notes become recognised even as accessory money of the State, they have made their appearance as State money.'[34] Even the new 'functional' frame of reference does not satisfactorily explain observed practices. It would, again, have been preferable, from the student's point of view, if Knapp had revised his exposition, starting with a frame of reference that provided consistent explanation of what was observed. Pursuing a frame of reference that is demonstrably inconsistent with observations is indicative of a desire to assemble support for partisan political or factional interests at the expense of any concern for assembly of support for consistent explanations.

Knapp's new functional frame of reference brings with it a new definition of money, in terms of what is to be regarded as part of the state monetary system, displacing the theoretical chartal-legal definition. 'Money' is part of the state monetary system when it is accepted by the state at state pay offices. Knapp asks rhetorically, 'What forms part of the monetary system of the State and what does not?'[35] He cautions that:

> The criterion cannot be that the money is issued by the State, for that would exclude kinds of money which are of the highest importance; I refer

> to bank-notes: they are not issued by the State, but they form a part of its monetary system.[36]

The conclusion then is:

> We keep most closely to the facts if we take as our test, that the money is accepted in payments made to the State's offices. Then all means by which a payment can be made to the State form part of the monetary system. On this basis it is not the issue, but the acceptation, as we call it, which is decisive. State acceptation delimits the monetary system.[37]

'Money' is no longer a matter of proclamation and legal documentation, but a matter of state acceptance. Acceptance by the state determines what is money, whatever the law may say.

Support-Bargaining, Acceptance and Purchasing Power

Knapp's difficulties arise from his own initial presentation of a theoretical frame of reference in which money is established by legal proclamation of the state and his subsequent presentation of an alternative frame of reference taking account of the phenomena of actual monetary administration. In his second frame of reference money is a matter of politics, and what is money is determined by state acceptance in payment of obligations to the state. An initial chartal-legal account of money is reformulated as a chartal-political account of money. Knapp's inclination to assess private bank money as state money is entirely acceptable, in that it is possible only within a framework of state law. It is a necessary part of the state management of money. His difficulties arise only because in his theoretical frame of reference he has defined money in such a way that private bank money is not state money.

Knapp's adoption of the criterion of 'acceptability' to the state as determinant of what constitutes money suggests again the idea of the tokens issued by companies constituting money on the basis of their acceptance at the company store. Knapp illustrates and commends his idea of state money with a similar illustration. When someone deposits their coat in a cloakroom at a theatre, they are given a tin disc bearing a sign or perhaps a number. The disc entitles them to return of the cloak they have deposited.[38] The disk acknowledges a debt. Presentation of the disk by a holder, whoever that may be, results in provision of the cloak. The company tokens and the disk both gain value by their acceptability, but their status as money to the holders depends on their receipt of goods in exchange for the tokens or disk. It is the dependable conversion of the tokens or disks into goods or services that sustains their value as money. A national money has to be acceptable not just to the state in payments to the state, but to its people, in exchange for whatever goods and services they are ready to provide. The value of a bargaining counter depends on its purchasing power, or confidence in the existence of dependable debtors in the society who will provide goods or services in exchange for the bargaining counter.

Acceptance by the state will itself depend on its recognition of the purchasing power of the money. The state itself has to buy goods and services, and the money it receives must be such as will make that possible. R. G. Hawtrey remarks of Knapp, in his review of *The State Theory of Money*, that, 'He will not admit the relevance of the quantity theory or indeed of anything to do with the purchasing power of the currency unit.'[39] That, perhaps, is the weakest part of Knapp's state theory of money, and the weakest part of the anthropological theories based on it regarding the origins of money.

It was seen above that Knapp regards the 'promise to pay' on bank notes as of no significance. It may, for example, only be valid on the date it is written – subsequent legislation may relieve banks of the obligation to honour their pledge. Holders of Austrian bank notes frequently experienced such a situation.[40] Knapp concludes that bank notes are wrongly defined. Their pledge has to be seen as a ruse to inspire confidence. Their value resides in their acceptance by banks in settlement of obligations to the banks. That constitutes a chartal payment, even if it is a private chartal payment.[41] Hence Knapp's insistence on the 'chartal' nature of the value of money is vindicated.

In Britain such promises to pay have mostly been understood as promises to provide gold in exchange for notes. But gold has not been available on demand from private banks, and has been available from the Central Bank only on very restrictive conditions. The promises are rather designed to maintain confidence in the notes issued. If people have confidence in gold as money, for whatever reason, then it is appropriate to link the value of the notes to the value of gold, even if it is impossible, in practical terms, to provide gold to the value of notes issued. The 'gold standard' was ostensibly the foundation of the strength of the pound sterling in the nineteenth century, and hence the foundation of international trade. But Peter Mathias describes sterling as highly vulnerable, because of the large and volatile short-term capital that was attracted into London financial markets. Gold reserves fell far short of the value of such capital.[42] Sterling was vulnerable to any concerted demand for gold. Sterling held confidence rather because the productivity of the British economy was such that people around the world were assured that its purchasing power would be maintained. There were 'dependable debtors' in Britain and around the world who would ensure that sterling could be reliably exchanged for goods and services. Mathias describes international trade in the nineteenth century as operating more on a 'sterling standard' than a 'gold standard'.[43] Confidence in sterling was maintained with the assurance that it was backed by gold reserves, because many people regarded gold as the basis of value. But its value was underpinned more fundamentally by the strength of the British economy that assured the purchasing power of sterling. The arrangement is more accurately described as a 'dependable sterling debtor standard.' The 'promise to redeem' provided with bank notes might not be fulfilled in gold, but people could redeem their money in goods and services from the numerous agents ready to provide goods and services in exchange for sterling. It would function as an 'SOU' within that community.

The 'bullionist' view of money gives precious metals an international role, providing supposedly automatic adjustments of levels of economic activity in different countries through inflows and outflows of precious metals. Knapp's understanding of metallism and money established by state proclamation does not accommodate the international use of money. Knapp acknowledges the deficiency:

> The Chartal form can never be effective internationally, or, rather, it can never be effective from State to State, as long as States are totally independent of one another. This is a striking limitation of it, compared with autometallism.[44]

This is another show-stopping admission which might be better aired 'up front.' If the chartal form of money is not compatible with an international role, then the state theory of money has to be rejected as a theory of money, since money is plainly used for international trade. Ancient Mesopotamian states certainly engaged in long-distance trade, and used silver as their bargaining counter. Hudson's comment linking silver to modern paper money, at Note 13 in Chapter 9 and mentioned earlier, is not an accurate representation of the role of silver in the ancient world. Knapp's perception of the incapacity of a state money to accommodate international trade seems to rest on his theory rather than any understanding of likely practice. Disparities between theory and practice in economics have been remarked on earlier – neoclassical theory has no need for money at all, but still money is used; and microeconomic theory is incompatible with macroeconomic theory. Knapp's perceived incapacity of chartal money to accommodate international trade arises because it is formulated without regard to the primary characteristic of money as a bargaining counter – its purchasing power. A chartal money, even if practically valued by acceptance in payments to the state, would necessarily be used in private exchange, and would acquire purchasing power in that context. Its value in relation to other currencies would be established by relative purchasing power. The 'Big Mac' illustration was used in Chapter 6. If prices rose in one country faster than in another, implying a faster depreciation of the money of the one country than of the other, exchange rates would change, and the exports and imports of the two countries would adjust. This exchange value would almost inevitably become the most widely accepted value. The 'official' value, used in payments to government, would, even if it could be sustained, be seen as anomalous. The problem is not simply that a chartal money as defined cannot accommodate international trade, but that a chartal money does not take account of purchasing power, and consequently is liable to displacement when established alongside a money with purchasing power.

Knapp's state theory of money is superficially plausible because of the very apparent necessity for state management to maintain the effectiveness of a national currency. Money, in whatever form, has to be channelled into circulation and its supply controlled in accordance with the requirements of trade. Bank notes constitute an effective form of money. The complexity of currency management and debates over currency management give the government role with regard to currencies great prominence.

Economic anthropologists seeking to establish an alternative theory of money compatible with their antipathy to 'markets' and capitalist enterprise have taken Knapp's chartal theory as affirming a state origin of money. Knapp's idea of state endorsement of money as legal or 'chartal' money has been presented as supportive of their idea that money originated in proclamations of a state. Knapp's idea of acceptance in state payments as the critical valuator of money has also been taken up, with incorporation of Mitchell Innes's idea of acceptance in payment of taxes as the critical acceptance. But 'acceptance' by the state is no part of Knapp's chartal-legal theory of money, but rather a matter of observed and deprecated administrative practice. More fundamentally, Knapp's theory relates to a dispute over metallism and token-money in the fairly recent past. 'Chartalism' is the alternative to 'metallism' in the administration of money, not an alternative origin of money. Knapp makes no claim for either chartal-legal or chartal-political money as the origin of money. He argues only that a national money needs endorsement by the state, and with endorsement it can be bank money or metallic. Knapp acknowledges a far-back origin of money in primitive money and 'custom.' The use of Knapp's work by those arguing a state origin of money misrepresents evidence to advance a cause. Knapp's account of the origin of money, brief though it is, is consistent with an origin of money as bargaining counter in private exchange.

Keynes and the State Theory of Money

John Maynard Keynes endorses Knapp's chartalist theory that money is the creation of a state. The first sentence of his *Treatise on Money* establishes his position: 'Money-of-Account, namely that in which Debts and Prices and the General Purchasing Power are *expressed*, is the primary concept of a Theory of Money.'[45]

He continues in his third paragraph:

> Money itself, namely that by delivery of which debt-contracts and price contracts are *discharged*, and in the shape of which a store of General Purchasing Power is *held*, derives its character from its relationship to the Money-of-Account, since the debts and prices must first have been expressed in terms of the latter.[46]

Keynes makes a distinction between the mode in which debts, prices and purchasing power are expressed, which is the money-of-account, and the mode in which debts and prices are discharged, and the way purchasing power is held, which is 'money itself.' 'Money itself' depends on, or 'derives its character,' from the money-of-account. It is close to being a distinction between the records of money transactions and the physical money that changes hands, with the records regarded as the reference by which the physical money is valued. But such terminology undermines the argument. Money-of-account is the primary concern; it provides the means of expressing debt and prices.

Keynes then adds a further category of 'convenient medium of exchange,' which might be money itself, but preferably is not. He continues immediately from the last quotation above:

> Something which is merely used as a convenient medium of exchange on the spot may approach to being Money, inasmuch as it may represent a means of holding General Purchasing Power. But if this is all, we have scarcely emerged from the stage of Barter. Money-Proper in the full sense of the term can only exist in relation to a Money-of-Account.'

Keynes covers the accepted basic concepts of money: the medium of exchange; the store of value; the unit of account. He nevertheless wishes to establish the 'unit of account' as ascendant, and consequently is at pains to discredit the 'medium of exchange' idea as primitive. Its significance as holder of purchasing power means that it may approach to being money, but only approach. He introduces a further category, 'Money-Proper,' to imply that money as medium of exchange is 'improper' money. 'Money itself' becomes 'Money-Proper,' only by connection to the money-of-account.

The status of the 'money-of-account' rests apparently on the authority of a government to say 'this shall be the "money-of-account."' The classification assumes that the state creates money. As well as the 'chartalist' view of money, Keynes takes from Knapp the idea of the 'grand proclamation' by which the nature of things is settled. 'Money as unit of exchange' is not supported by proclamation, and is no more than primitive. It is an outcome of popular dealing. Civilised and sophisticated modern people should not accept as money a 'money of exchange' that is not legitimised by state proclamation. It might be argued on the basis of functional performance, as opposed to theoretical construction, that what functions as money is money. This means generally, as a necessary condition, that what is money depends on what holds purchasing power. The medium of exchange, in common understanding, appears very much like what would be understood as 'money,' without needing any reference to a money-of-account.

Keynes creates the notion of a 'money-of-account' in accordance with the idea of the state as originator of money, derived as an interpretation of Knapp's theory, though Knapp, as was seen above, did not see the state as originating money. Keynes uses neoclassical economic theory as his basic frame of reference, and that frame has no notion of budgeting. Hence Keynes cannot recognise that a 'money-of-account' is a unit of budgetary accounting, and as such is dependent on values established in exchange transactions. Far from having an ascendant position, the use of money for accounting purposes depends on values already established in exchange. Budget values have to be synchronised with the prices operative in the exchange transactions with which the budgeting agency is involved. The money-of-account derives from the money of exchange, not the other way round. This, as was seen in Chapter 9, is one of the misapprehensions passed on by economists to economic anthropologists. With regard to budgeting, Keynes is as blind as economic anthropologists.

Keynes likens his distinction between money-of-account and money for discharge of debts or holding of value to the distinction between the idea of a 'King of England' and King George. 'King George' fulfils the notion of the idea of a 'king.' Keynes argues, 'It is for the State to declare, when the time comes, who the King of England is.'[47] Or it is like the state claiming the right to re-edit the dictionary that determines what thing answers to the name 'money-of-account.'[48] According to Keynes:

> This right is claimed by all modern States and has been so claimed for some four thousand years at least. It is when this stage in the evolution of Money has been reached that Knapp's Chartalism – the doctrine that money is peculiarly a creation of the state is fully realised. Thus the Age of Money had succeeded to the Age of Barter as soon as men had adopted a money-of-account.[49]

The jump from barter to money occurs when a state pronounces what shall be the money-of-account and determines what shall be used in the discharge of debts expressed in the money-of-account. The 'money-of-account' becomes a kind of 'holding' concept, a 'placeholder' that can be filled with a money.

But the relationship between institution and incumbent, 'King of England' and 'King George,' is mistaken. The idea of kingship is abstracted from actual experience of the behaviour and nature of kings. People understand the role of 'King' by observing the behaviour of different kings. The 'money-of-account' derives from the experience of using money in exchange. Because it is used in exchange, it is used as a unit of budgetary account. Similarly the notion of a dictionary derives from the use of words. A 'dictionary' cannot exist independently of the use of words. Words go into a dictionary when they become established in common usage. Keynes wants theory to be precedent over practice, but theory is abstracted from practice. The theory is abstracted purposefully from the practice. As was seen in Chapter 4, theories are formed for the advance of interests and their content is selected and shaped to assemble support for the interest of their makers. Theories of kingship include both the benign and the brutal. Keynes's theory of a money-of-account is formulated to advance the idea of the state origin of money.

Even if the 'King of England' and 'King George' relationship was as Keynes assumes, it would not be a close analogy for the relationship between the money-of-account and money itself. It would not be consistent with the money-of-account as defined by Keynes. The money-of-account expresses debts and prices. Such debts and prices can then be discharged with money itself – i.e. with pieces of metal or some other designated commodity or token. But to express debts and prices, there must be a unit of value in which the debts are incurred and the prices settled. The 'records' must have a unit of value. The money-of-account has to be determined as money itself. That is perhaps why Keynes gives no examples of a money-of-account separate from money itself. All that is offered is 'King of England' and 'King George,' or a dictionary and words in a dictionary. Money-of-account as defined seems a redundant concept, gaining credence only because people are accustomed to a money of budgetary account. Knapp did not conceive a chartalist money-of-account in the Keynesian definition, but a chartalist money that would function as an alternative to the prevailing metallism of his time.

Keynes was heavily involved in the intellectual support-bargaining relating to the resumption of a sterling peg to gold in the 1920s. He opposed any return to the gold standard. He described the gold standard as a 'barbarous relic.'[50] He helped to bring about the publication in English of Knapp's *The State Theory of Money* through the Royal Economic Society as a contribution to the debate over return to the gold standard. His use of Knapp was thus initially consistent with the actual content of Knapp's theory, promoting 'chartalism' over 'metallism.' However, Keynes subsequently interprets Knapp as advancing chartalism as the origin of money. Keynes employs debating techniques – the 'put down,' ridicule and alienation – to assemble support for his cause. He implies that money as a means of exchange is a primitive and uncivilised usage of what in all civilised countries is now a matter of state. The implication is that his opponents are similarly primitive and uncivilised in their intellectual capacities. Keynes exploits the associations of words (Chapter 6). But if money is conceived and used in that way, then primitive or not, it is the true nature of money.

The prominence of states in the administration of money has led some governments to believe that they can define what shall be money and what value it shall have, even against the indications of its value provided by exchange transactions. Recent examples include the governments of Argentina, Lebanon and Zimbabwe. Innes records the experience of French monarchs in the Middle Ages trying to establish desired valuations of their coinage.[51] He also records the similar difficulties of European and United States governments in the nineteenth century and earlier.[52] Even the United Kingdom could not sustain its definition of the value of sterling relative to other European currencies in the European Exchange Rate Mechanism in the early 1990s. The state's choice of what is 'money' has to accord with what functions as a bargaining counter in exchange transactions. As with kings and words, support on the street is needed if a money is to be sustained with conviction. A money will be sustained on the street if there are dependable debtors ready to earn it, thereby giving it purchasing power.

The state nevertheless has an essential function with regard to money. The state is needed to take money to what Knapp calls 'a higher stage of development.' Money as a convenient medium of exchange may become a national money if the community that uses it institutes communal means of controlling its supply and providing other necessary protections to its purchasing power. With that done, those using the convenient means of exchange will find it expedient to use it as a unit of account in their budgets. It will keep their finances in synchrony with the prices ruling amongst other agents of the money-bargaining system. It will prevent the presentation of a false situation in their budget accounts resulting from disparities between the prices of goods and services assumed in the budget and actual prices that prevail in the money-bargaining system. The state becomes involved not through designation of a money-of-account, but in providing the necessary management of a money so that it can be used with confidence across a broad society.

Definitions and Frames of Reference

Keynes also follows Knapp in creating careful definitions for the concepts that sustain his theory of the state origins of money, though happily Keynes's technical vocabulary is not as extensive or quite as obscure as that of Knapp. Nevertheless, it serves a similar purpose. It creates a frame of reference for the selection and interpretation of monetary phenomena. The definitions create specific intellectual anchorages, playing a comparable role to the psychological anchorages described in Chapter 4 in the context of Sherif's account of anchorages and frames of reference. They also provide a vocabulary which can, as was seen in Chapter 6, become distinctively associated with a frame of reference. In Keynes's vocabulary the term 'Money-Proper' is introduced to confine money to that which is designated by the state. The state theory of money is then a state theory of 'Money-Proper' – the money that is designated by the state. All other money is not 'Money-Proper' because it does not have the imprimatur of the state. The definitions establish a frame of reference in which money is tautologically state money. If a money is not proclaimed as such by a state money, it is not money. Money used in exchange may be convenient, but it is primitive. And not being designated by the state, it is not 'Money-Proper' and only to be deemed an approach to money by the indulgence of monetary authorities. Keynes insists that 'To-day all civilised money is, beyond the possibility of dispute, chartalist.'[53] But that is only because he has defined money is such a way that it is indisputably chartalist. There is no reason why money that functions as a medium of exchange should not be proper money. It may be an early stage of development; it may be 'uncivilised'; but these characteristics are hardly good reason for denying it the status of money. Functionally it is money. In the money-bargaining frame of reference, it is a bargaining counter. Keynes is imprisoned by his own definitions, so that he cannot comprehend a process by which common commodities emerge as bargaining counters, subsequently evolving into tokens of value, all fairly described as money, since they fulfil the functions of money. According to Keynes's definitions, the 'age of money' succeeds the 'age of barter' when a state proclaims a chartalist form of money.

The weakness of Keynes's frame of reference established by definitions is apparent when he seeks to establish the continuity of a money-of-account. This may or may not be coincident with a change in the money 'which answers to it'[54] – i.e. the 'money itself' which discharges debts. Keynes holds merely that the new unit of account must have a defined relationship to the old. If there is no state decree to define the relationship, then he observes that 'the market cannot help establishing for itself a parity between the two.' Thus a new money will be related in value to an old money by 'the market,' or by equivalence of purchasing power. And if the money-of-account is not changed by decree of the state, a new money will establish a new money-of-account through its relationship to the old money. The transition is akin to that described by Ingham when he notes a transition from 'money-of-account' to 'money of exchange' on the introduction of coinage (Chapter 6, Note 63). Keynes's 'money-of-account' becomes a 'money of exchange' by default, if the state fails to decree a new 'money of account.' The 'money-of-account' becomes the same as what is adopted as 'money itself'; or the 'money of exchange.' The 'money of exchange' is used as the money-of-account in budgeting. Records of transactions are maintained; transactions are not adjusted to proclamations about records. Keynes seems to accept that values in a transition from one money to another are determined by 'the market,' or by exchange, and that his concept of a money-of-account is redundant.

Keynes's account of continuity derives directly from Knapp's account of what happens when a state changes its recognition of what shall constitute money. As was seen above, Knapp conceives debt as having a 'nominal value' underlying any stated value in terms of units of money. If a state changes its recognition of what constitutes money from copper to silver, then at the moment of transition the debts of the state are conceived as being in the 'nominal' state.[55] They are conceived as disconnected from any valuation in terms of units of money. Keynes recognises, however, that 'primitive' exchange will give money a value, and that value will be adopted into a 'money-of-account'; that is, the money used for exchange will be used as a budgetary unit of account. In effect, the 'market' value of Keynes gives what Knapp conceives as the 'nominal value.'

Keynes identifies a category 'Bank-Money' that consists of deposits denominated in the 'money-of-account' held in a bank. The distinction is between 'Bank-Money' and 'cash,' physical money and cheques, the latter being 'state money.' This Bank-Money derives from cash or cheques deposited with a bank by private citizens, or from loans made by a bank to customers, or from purchase of assets by a bank, with payment in the form of a deposit at the bank in the name of the seller.[56] Bank-money does not constitute 'Money-Proper:' 'When acknowledgements of debt are used in this way, we may call them Bank-Money – not forgetting, however, that they are not Money-Proper.'[57] 'Bank-Money' includes Bills of Exchange and letters of credit.[58] Keynes's difficulties with 'Bank-Money' are similar to those of Knapp: it is accepted as money to such a degree that a realistic state theory of money must make it state money; but since it is of private creation, it cannot be state money. The definitions of Keynes's frame of reference imply that what is not state money is not money. Keynes allows, following Knapp,[59] that Bank-Money may cease to be private debt and become a State debt. It then becomes 'Money-Proper,' or at least a species of 'Money-Proper': 'A particular kind of Bank-Money is then transformed into Money-Proper – a species of Money-Proper which we may call Representative Money.'[60] This 'Representative Money,' however, still does not have quite the full status of 'Money-Proper,' since, 'To regard Representative Money, even when it conforms to an objective standard, as being still a debt will suggest false analogies.'[61] But if it is not a debt, it would appear that it has not become the state debt that makes it 'Money-Proper.' 'Representative Money' seems to need a further classification as 'Nearly-Money-Proper.' To deny the status of Representative Money as debt because it suggests 'false analogies' seems again to condemn those who might object to the analysis as people too lacking in judgement for their support to be of any account. Keynes's definitions force him into inconsistencies that suggest that the frame of reference established by the definitions is inadequate to deal with the phenomena encountered. Instead of illuminating the origin, use and nature of money, the definitions of both Keynes and Knapp deepen the obscurity. The further definitions intended to resolve the obscurities only make matters worse, because the anomalies arise from the fundamental misconceptions of the original definitions.

In the theory of support-bargaining and money-bargaining, money is a bargaining counter used in a way analogous to the way 'support' is used in support-bargaining. It brings to exchange transactions qualities that cannot be provided, or are difficult to provide, through the use of support. It offers the precision of counting or weighing. For the most part, it is understood in material form, so that it can be understood perceptually, though transfers between electronic accounts with financial institutions facilitate its usage. It gives rise to the use of money budgets in support-bargaining organisations, such as political parties. It also gives rise to the formation of specialist money-bargaining agencies for which a money budget provides a reckoning of their success in their central purpose of making money. The unit of account used in these budgets is the unit of account used in the money-bargaining in which they are engaged. Thus the money-of-account derives from the valuations reached through exchange transactions, rather than being established by state pronouncement.

The difficulties of both Knapp and Keynes with 'state money' and its definition result from their attempts to identify a 'state money.' They define 'state money' easily enough in theory, either as 'chartal' or 'money-of-account.' But when they try to apply the theory to the practice, they find that what is called 'money' does not correspond to their definition of 'state money.' Both invent classifications that make private money a form of state money, or make it possible for state money to be private. The distinction they miss is that described in Chapter 7 between the credit provided by private banks, as part of the profitable conduct of bank business, for which the bank is creditor and the borrower the debtor, and the use made of that same provision of credit to put into circulation a national money, the holder of which is creditor and for which the debtor is 'society,' or the dependable debtors operating in the society. The same credit is both provider of bank credit and issuer of social credit in the form of a national money. The issue of national money has to be regulated by a central bank, acting for the state, in accordance with levels of trade. Over-issue will result in inflation, which is erosion of the purchasing power of the money. Money does not originate in proclamations by a state, but the state has a central role in administration and management of a national money.

The Sparkle of Precious Metals

Like Hudson and Ingham (Chapter 9), Keynes also runs up against the peculiar, apparently spontaneous, acceptance by people that silver and gold are valuable. He refers to an 'objective standard,' mainly understood as the gold standard.[62] Keynes resorts to further classification. He identifies three forms of State-Money: 'Commodity Money,' 'Fiat Money' and 'Managed Money,' the last two being sub-species of Representative Money. Of Managed Money he remarks that it:

> may be considered to degenerate into Commodity Money on the one side when the managing authority holds against it a hundred per cent of the objective standard, so that it is in effect a warehouse warrant, and into Fiat Money on the other side when it loses its objective standard.[63]

The implication is that the 'objective standard' exists independently of any designated money-of-account. It is rather a standard upon which a state money-of-account can be based, with the state fully backing its own money with the 'objective standard' money. So that state money is dependent fundamentally on popular valuations. Knapp, as was seen, recognises that state money may be metallic, or 'hylogenic,' as well as 'autogenic.' But he stresses that the value of the material money arises from state proclamation rather than any intrinsic property of the material. Randall Wray similarly does not see the 'objective standard' as negating the state-origin status of money: 'Even if it chooses a strict commodity system, the *value* of the commodity does not derive from the commodity accepted as money…'[64] Money only gets value when it is designated as money by the state. Wray quotes Keynes:

> Money is the measure of value, but to regard it as having value itself is a relic of the view that the value of money is regulated by the value of the substance of which it is made, and is like confusing a theatre ticket with the performance.[65]

The idea that gold is valuable is old-fashioned, so not to be entertained. But nevertheless, people generally ascribe value to gold, and the managers of a currency cannot overlook that fact, and have not been inclined to do so, since they can make use of it to foster support for their currency. It is because gold is seen as valuable amongst ordinary people that a currency based on it gains support as a bargaining counter. Many commodities have had localised support as currencies, but none has had, like gold, the enduring and global support that has made it possible to establish a global gold standard, with many currencies linked explicitly to weights of gold. It is popular support that makes possible state designation of a currency as a national currency. That means popular confidence in its purchasing power, whether by virtue of confidence in the value of a commodity or by virtue of their confidence in the enduring acceptance of the currency in exchange for goods and services. Gold may have value in itself, because of its 'sparkle' and malleability for the production of attractive adornments, but its value lies also in the purchasing power that arises from this perception of its having value in itself. As regards the theatre ticket, its significance lies in what it can be exchanged for – its purchasing power.

Further evidence for the redundancy of the concept of a 'money-of-account' comes from Keynes's early retreat from it. In presenting his three types of money – commodity, fiat and managed – and the potential degeneration of managed money either into commodity money or fiat money, he notes that, 'the best typical modern Moneys…approximate more and more to the form of Managed Money.' He adopts for his further analysis the concept of managed money: 'For these reasons the theory which will be developed in the following chapters is expressed with primary reference to a Managed Money.'[66] 'Managed Money' becomes the primary focus of analysis. Keynes's idea of a managed money is not precisely the same as that of money managed by the state, whilst deriving from usage in exchange in a community, as described in Chapter 7, but it at least incorporates the idea of the state administering rather than creating money. Keynes joins Ingham and Knapp in backtracking on his primary theory.

This shift of focus, and the necessity for it, is apparent in his following chapter on Bank-Money. 'Money,' because it is mainly Bank-Money, is created largely by banks, but then comes under state management. He records that in the United States roughly nine-tenths of the aggregate of Current Money (Bank-Money plus cash) is Bank-Money, and the trend is 'towards State Money occupying a definitely subsidiary position.'[67] In Britain he estimates state money to be about one-fifth of Current Money.[68] He then comments:

> Thus in Great Britain and the United States…the use of Bank-Money is now so dominant that much less confusion will be caused by treating this as typical and the use of other kinds of currency as secondary, than by treating State-Money as typical and bringing in Bank-Money as a subsequent complication. The latter practice…leads to insufficient emphasis being placed on some of the most typical features of modern money, and to its essential characteristics being treated as anomalous or exceptional.[69]

The 'typical features' and 'essential characteristics' of money might be seen as more private than state. Considering his own precept against confusion, Keynes might have revised his first chapter. But in doing so, he might have found himself forced to abandon Knapp and a state origin of money. He might also have found it necessary to recognise that the state was managing a money that was money by virtue of its acceptance and use in a trading community.

The need to revise the first chapter is reinforced by the admission at the opening of Book II of Keynes's Treatise, titled 'The Value of Money,' that:

> A man does not hold money for its own sake, but for its Purchasing Power – that is to say, for what it will buy. Therefore his demand is not for units of money as such, but for units of purchasing power. [70]

His demand is not for a 'money-of-account,' but for a 'money itself' that has dependable purchasing power, without reference to a money-of-account. The transactional value of a money is of primary importance, not its designation by the state as money-of-account or even as 'money.' The concept of a 'money-of-account' again seems redundant. The role of the state lies in the establishment of regulations and management that ensure a currency holds popular confidence by maintaining its purchasing power. This means, amongst other measures, control of its supply through control of bank credit. Once a currency is established as having dependable purchasing power, it is used by all agents to control their transactions and protect their solvency through budgeting. They use the dependable money as their money-of-account. Chapter 8 of Book II is 'The Theory of Comparisons of Purchasing Power.' The classifications provided in Book I on 'The Nature of Money' are in effect displaced in Book II on 'The Value of Money' by an entirely different emphasis. Like Knapp, Keynes changes his frame of reference and his classifications when he moves from a theoretical context to a practical context.

The support of so prominent an economist as Keynes for the state theory of money has been seen as valuable to the advance of the idea of economic anthropologists that money has its origin in state proclamations. Keynes's observations on the subject are widely quoted by economic anthropologists. But it is not all approbation. Ingham notes that state and credit theories of money remove money from its anchorages in commodities and the 'real' economy, and consequently require a decisive break with neoclassical economic theory. He notes that Keynes and other established economists are unable to make the break: 'By the 1930s, they had reverted – or perhaps one should say regressed – towards the orthodox economics of the "real" and had abandoned the radical conception of money.'[71] Graeber recognises the importance of Keynes's acceptance of credit and state theories of money, and the recognition that provision of credit by private banks created money, but follows Ingham in concluding also that Keynes in the end reverted to the orthodox neoclassical position.[72]

Definitions and the Significance of Coinage

The frame of reference established in the *Thesis* through theoretical definitions gives rise to an interpretation of the significance of coinage that is at variance with much historical assessment, though not with the assessment of other economists. Keynes maintains that:

> Coined money, which the state alone can mint and which may have a value superior to that of the commodity of which it is composed, is at the most a first step in the direction of Representative Money. Thus coinage is not one of the three vital innovations in the evolution of money…[73]

The 'three vital innovations' are apparently the Chartalist designation of 'the objective standard which shall correspond to the money-of-account'; the introduction of Representative Money, which 'begins when money is no longer composed of its objective standard'; and Fiat Money, which 'only appears when the State goes a step further and abandons the objective standard.' Coinage merely 'made easier the subsequent transition to Representative Money and Fiat Money.' The ambiguities noted above over the nature of 'chartalism,' the 'objective standard' and 'Representative Money' make the status of these innovations questionable. Keynes recognises that coinage has been regarded as an important innovation, even to the extent of being regarded as the first money in any full sense. 'Money' is coins in the pocket. His response is: 'But I do not think that the act of coinage effected so significant a change as is commonly attributed to it.' For economists more widely money is commonly conceived as a veil over transactions that conform basically to the patterns of barter, represented mathematically in the economic model, so that the introduction of coins may be also for them of little importance. But with money-bargaining as frame of reference, coins are portable, divisible and convenient bargaining counters, acceptable amongst large populations, and setting up chains of transactions that transfer credit between agents. Coins are the essential facilitators of economic exchange and because of their potency have come to be regarded as 'money' in origin and common understanding. Convenience is a practical matter, so that it does not gain prominence in a theoretical frame of reference such as that of microeconomics. Successive innovations, such as paper money, card payments and electronic transfers, have enhanced the convenience of money, but coinage was the original convenience money. One measure of the significance of coinage, arising from its functionality, is apparent in that it was not adopted until an entirely new system of government was introduced that could tolerate the individual opportunity that arose with the use of coin-money. The use of coins meant that ordinary people could become rich and threaten the ascendancy of those who ruled them. Rulers under previous systems preferred to keep money-bargaining under their own close control. Economists have separated economics from politics, so that in their frame of reference, as well as missing convenience, they cannot comprehend such political influences. The introduction of coin-money is considered further in Chapter 11.

Definition and Redefinition in the *Thesis* and *General Theory*

Keynes uses theoretical definitions to place the origin of money with states, rather than identifying forms and functions of money to establish its nature on an empirical basis, and deriving from that its likely origins. He employs a similar technique in his 1936 *General Theory of Money, Interest and Employment.*[74] He provides theoretical definitions of certain central variables or concepts which then lead to the conclusions he wishes to arrive at. For example, he defines 'involuntary unemployment' in a way that such unemployment cannot possibly be identified in an economy.[75] But the definition also means that workers cannot negotiate their way out of unemployment, as is at least possible in a common frame of reference. On the basis of the definition, an economy can reach equilibrium at high levels of unemployment. William Beveridge noted early on Keynes's preference for concepts of his own formulation over facts that were discernible to everyone else.[76]

In the *Treatise on Money* 'savings' are defined in the following terms:

> We shall mean by Savings the sum of the differences between the money-incomes of individuals and their money-expenditures on current consumption. Thus profits, not being part of the income of the community, are not part of its savings either – even when they are not spent on consumption.[77]

Keynes specifically discounts the idea that the amount of investment is equal to the amount of saving. He affirms that, 'Saving…consists in the negative act of refraining from spending the whole of his current income on consumption.'[78] He continues:

> It might be supposed – and has frequently been supposed – that the amount of investment is necessarily equal to the amount of saving. But reflection will show that this is not the case, if we exclude from income and from saving – as we must for reasons already given – the windfall profits and losses of entrepreneurs.[79]

In the *General Theory* saving is defined arithmetically in terms of income and consumption: 'the excess of income over consumption.' Current investment is the:

> current addition to the value of the capital equipment which has resulted from the productive activity of the period. This is, clearly, equal to what we have just defined as saving. For it is that part of the income of the period which has not passed into consumption.[80]

Keynes thus arrives at the fundamental theoretical foundation of the *General Theory* that savings must be equal to investment. The identity rests, however, on the definition of 'savings' rather than on any empirical investigation of the nature of saving. It involves the discard of the variable 'profits' from consideration as a factor in movement towards equilibrium.

'Profits' in the Treatise are the difference between the Value of Output and the Cost of Production. This in turn is equal to the difference between Investment and Savings.[81] Entrepreneurs make profits when investment exceeds savings, and a loss when they are less than savings. In equilibrium, profits will be zero and Investment will be equal to Savings, as defined in the Treatise. In terms of the format of companies described in Chapter 5, 'profits' are the excess of revenues over costs which determines a company's success in meeting the viability condition. There is thus in the Treatise what can be seen as a budgetary concept that is missing from the *General Theory*. In the *General* Theory, 'profits' are subsumed into aggregate income; savings are defined as the excess of income over consumption; and profits, potentially the most volatile element, are given no role. An element of budgetary surplus or deficit in companies is not conceivable in the frame of reference established by definitions in the *General Theory*.

Working from theoretical definitions always involves the risk that the definers will adjust the definitions to ensure that analysis will confirm what they have already concluded. Definitions are not, as often assumed in academic analysis, a neutral preliminary to analysis, in order to avoid lengthy disputes over 'meaning.' Definitions are always made from a particular frame of reference and serve to establish that frame of reference as operative in further analysis.[82] Where the relevant frame is not contested, as for example when working within a particular theory group, the definitions are likely to be generally agreed, and welcomed as performing a useful role. But where appropriate frames of reference are contested, as when different theory groups are involved, the definitions are themselves likely to be part of the contention. While in Keynes's *Thesis* the initial theoretical definitions are implicitly modified as the narrative progresses to a more practical context, in the *General Theory* he retains his initial theoretical definitions as depictions of the actual functioning of economies and on that basis prescribes remedies for improvement.[83]

There is a more deep-seated problem with Keynes's analysis in the *General Theory*. It was seen in Chapter 5 that neoclassical microeconomic theory is incompatible with macroeconomic theory. Macroeconomic theory was presented as focused on analysis of the actual performance of economies, typically represented by statistical series, while microeconomic theory was concerned with ideas of marginal adjustments towards equilibrium expressed in mathematical terms. The incompatibility suggests that the two have to be treated as entirely separate. Money-bargaining provides a microeconomic theory, as well as macroeconomic theory. But many economists find it acceptable to approach macroeconomic analysis on the basis of neoclassical microeconomic theory. There has been extensive research into macroeconomic equilibrium on the understanding that macroeconomies function in accordance with neoclassical microeconomic theory. A lecture by Paul Romer, delivered in 2016, gives an indication of the serious difficulties encountered with this research.[84] The influence of neoclassical theory extends more broadly into macroeconomic management, since economists are invariably taught neoclassical theory in their university courses. One of the contributory factors to the financial crisis that took hold in 2008 was the avowed faith in the self-adjusting effectiveness of free markets of some of those with leading responsibilities in financial management.

Keynes made major contributions to the development of macroeconomic theory, but he retained the neoclassical idea of equilibrium. He was concerned to demonstrate the continued validity of the neoclassical model, modified only by his supplementary definitions, creating a new frame of reference in which a kind of neoclassical equilibrium could occur without clearance of the labour market. On Keynes's definitions, in an otherwise neoclassical context, labour could be unemployed without the possibility of negotiating their employment. Such recourse was designed to save economics and economists from lasting discredit.[85]

The deep-seated problem with Keynes is that economies evolve; they do not move towards equilibrium positions. Macroeconomists implicitly accept that economies evolve in accordance with changing social policies, changing technologies, the impact of events and other factors. People's decisions on savings are not just a matter of 'not consuming.' Budgets are used to accommodate time disparities. In a support-bargaining and money-bargaining system, people judge their interests by reference to their situations, and act accordingly. There is an inbuilt evolutionary process from situation, to accommodation of related interests, to a new situation, and new interests. Companies formatting to meet the viability condition will make constant innovations in technology and organisation to reduce their unit costs. Some will fail; some will make very substantial profits. In the course of time economies evolve from agricultural predominance, to manufacturing, to service industries, to information technology. While the neoclassical assumption of tendencies to equilibrium suggests stability and permanence, the idea of money-bargaining makes plain that there are many decisions and events that can throw an economy, local, national or global, off its most beneficial course for years, or even decades. 'Involuntary unemployment' in that context is when people, try as they may, cannot find employment because of the dislocation to company formats and the budgets of many agents. The remedies depend on the causes of such dislocations. With an evolving macroeconomy, subject to disruptive political and economic events, the analysis of the *General Theory*, based on the neoclassical frame of reference, is not a useful guide.[86]

The Influence of the Frame of Reference

The idea of support-bargaining and money-bargaining provides a more comprehensive frame of reference than any other. In particular, the idea suggests that the construction of frames of reference and their associated theory groups are fundamental to the intellectual support-bargaining by which interests are advanced (Chapter 4). We can never penetrate beyond what is in our minds, and being so confined, we build consistencies in our minds, sharing them with others and bolstering our security with their support. We assemble theory groups to advance interests implied by the theories. If a theory can be made to appear logical, rational and reasonable, then support will accrue from those who value such characteristics. If it can be shown to accord with information derived from empirical observation and experience, it will accrue support from people who demand empirical evidence. If it advances the interests of significant numbers of people, it will accrue support from those people. Multiple frames of reference are created in the course of support-bargaining and money-bargaining. Multiple frames of reference dampen the echoes of any particular frame. They make it more difficult for people to become entrapped in single frames of reference. The particular feature of both Knapp's and Keynes's use of frames of reference is that, while it is desirable that definitions and assumptions are readily acceptable in common theory, those of Knapp and Keynes are very distinctly related to the theories they wish to advance, and require some suspension of common understanding to accept. They create their own 'reality.' They lead to the conclusions their authors are trying to establish. If a rabbit is put into a hat, it is easy to draw a rabbit out of the hat.

Notes

1 Knapp, Georg Friedrich, 1924, *The State Theory of Money*, Trans. H. M. Lucas and James Bonar, London: Macmillan. First published 1905. Keynes, John Maynard, 1930, *A Treatise on Money*, London: Macmillan.
2 Ingham, Geoffrey, 2004, *The Nature of Money*, Cambridge: Polity Press, p. 48.
3 Ingham, 2004, p. 47.
4 Wray, L. Randall, 2000, 'Modern Money', in John Smithin (Ed.), *What Is Money?* London: Routledge.
5 Knapp, 1924, p. 1.
6 Knapp, 1924, p. 2.
7 Knapp, 1924, p. 32.
8 Knapp, 1924, p. 34.
9 Knapp, 1924, p. 17.
10 Knapp, 1924, p. 55.
11 Knapp, 1924, p. 54.
12 Knapp, 1924, p. 55.
13 Knapp, 1924, p. 19.
14 Knapp, 1924, pp. 93–4.
15 Knapp, 1924, pp. 25–6.
16 Knapp, 1924, p. 26.
17 Knapp, 1924, p. 38.
18 Knapp, 1924, p. 31.
19 Knapp, 1924, p. 44.
20 For example, Hawtrey, R. G., 1925, 'Review: *The State Theory of Money* by Georg Friedrich Knapp', *The Economic Journal*, Vol. 35, No. 138, pp. 251–5; Wray, L. Randall,

2014, 'From the State Theory of Money to Modern Money Theory: An Alternative to Economic Orthodoxy,' *Working Paper No. 792*, Levy Economics Institute of Bard College, p. 4.
21 Knapp, 1924, pp. 85–6. Quoted by: L, 1926, 'Review: *The State Theory of Money*', *Journal of Political Economy*, Vol. 34, No. 3, pp. 404–6, p. 405.
22 Knapp, 1924, p. ix.
23 Knapp, 1924, pp. 112–3.
24 Knapp, 1924, p. 112.
25 Knapp, 1924, p. 113.
26 Knapp, 1924, pp. 43, 105–6, 112–4, 194.
27 Knapp, 1924, p. 107.
28 Knapp, 1924, p. 109.
29 Knapp, 1924, pp. 131–2.
30 Knapp, 1924, p. 134.
31 Knapp, 1924, p. 134.
32 Knapp, 1924, p. 136.
33 Knapp, 1924, p. 137.
34 Knapp, 1924, p. 138.
35 Knapp, 1924, p. 95.
36 Knapp, 1924, p. 95.
37 Knapp, 1924, p. 95.
38 Knapp, 1924, pp. 31–2. Quoted in Wray, 2000, p. 50.
39 Hawtrey, 1925, p. 254.
40 Knapp, 1924, pp. 132–3.
41 Knapp, 1924, p. 134.
42 Mathias, Peter, 2001, *The First Industrial Nation: The Economic History of Britain 1700–1914*, Abingdon: Routledge, p. 329.
43 Mathias, 2001, p. 329.
44 Knapp, 1924, p. 41.
45 Keynes, 1930, p. 3. Original emphasis and capitalisation.
46 Keynes, 1930, pp. 4–5.
47 Keynes, 1930, p. 4.
48 Keynes, 1930, p. 4.
49 Keynes, 1930, pp. 4–5.
50 Keynes, John Maynard, 1923, *A Tract on Monetary Reform*, London: Macmillan.
51 Innes, A. Mitchell, 1913, 'What Is Money?', *The Banking Law Journal*, Vol. 30, No. 5, pp. 377–408, pp. 395–7.
52 Innes, A. Mitchell, 1914, 'The Credit Theory of Money', *The Banking Law Journal*, Vol. 31, No. 2, pp. 151–68, pp. 153–5.
53 Keynes, 1930, p. 5.
54 Keynes, 1930, p. 7.
55 Knapp, 1924, pp. 13–5.
56 Keynes, 1930, p. 24.
57 Keynes, 1930, pp. 5–6.
58 Keynes, 1930, p. 15.
59 Knapp, 1924, p. 135.
60 Keynes, 1930, p. 6.
61 Keynes, 1930, p. 6.
62 Cf. Keynes, 1930, pp. 18, 21–2.

63 Keynes, 1930, p. 8.
64 Wray, 2000, p. 56.
65 Wray, 2000, p. 56, quoting Keynes, John Maynard, 1983, 'Economic Articles and Correspondence, Academic', in D. E. Moggridge (Ed.), *The Collected Writings of John Maynard Keynes*, Vol. XI, London: Macmillan, p. 402.
66 Keynes, 1930, p. 8.
67 Keynes, 1930, p. 31.
68 Keynes, 1930, p. 32.
69 Keynes, 1930, pp. 32–3.
70 Keynes, 1930, p. 53.
71 Ingham, Geoffrey, 2004, *The Nature of Money*, Cambridge: Polity Press, p. 50.
72 Graeber, David, 2012, *Debt: The First Five Thousand Years*, Brooklyn NY: Melville House, p. 54.
73 Keynes, 1930, p. 11.
74 Keynes, John Maynard, 1961, *The General Theory of Employment, Interest and Money*, London: Macmillan, New York: St Martin's Press. First published 1936.
75 Keynes, 1961, p. 15.
76 Beveridge, William, 1937, 'The Place of the Social Sciences in Human Knowledge', *Politica*, Vol. 2, No. 9, September, pp. 459–79, p. 464; Farewell Address as Director of the London School of Economics and Political Science, 24 June 1937. See Spread, Patrick, 2019a, *Economics for an Information Age: Money-Bargaining, Support-Bargaining and the Information Interface*, London and New York: Routledge, pp. 16–8.
77 Keynes, 1930, p. 126.
78 Keynes, 1930, p. 172.
79 Keynes, 1930, p. 172.
80 Keynes, 1930, p. 62.
81 Keynes, 1930, p. 151.
82 Spread, Patrick, 2016, *The Evolution of Economies: Money-Bargaining, Economic Change and Industrial Revolution*, London and New York: Routledge, pp. 79–82.
83 Spread, 2016, pp. 220–43.
84 Romer, Paul, 2016, 'The Trouble with Macroeconomics', lecture, delivered 5 January 2016 as the Commons Memorial Lecture of the Omicron Delta Epsilon Society. https://paulromer.net/wp-content/uploads/2016/09/WP-Trouble.pdf. Accessed 27 April 2017. See also Spread, 2019a, pp. 52–4; and Spread, 2016, pp. 44–6.
85 Keynes, 1961, p. vi.
86 Spread, 2016, pp. 220–43.

References

Beveridge, William, 1937, 'The Place of the Social Sciences in Human Knowledge', *Politica*, Vol. 2, No. 9, September, pp. 459–79. Farewell Address as Director of the London School of Economics and Political Science, 24 June 1937.

Graeber, David, 2012, *Debt: The First Five Thousand Years*, Brooklyn NY: Melville House.

Hawtrey, R. G., 1925, 'Review: *The State Theory of Money* by Georg Friedrich Knapp', *The Economic Journal*, Vol. 35, No. 138, pp. 251–255.

Ingham, Geoffrey, 2004, *The Nature of Money*, Cambridge: Polity Press.

Innes, A Mitchell, 1913, 'What Is Money?', *The Banking Law Journal*, Vol. 30, No. 5, pp. 377–408.

Innes, A. Mitchell, 1914, 'The Credit Theory of Money', *The Banking Law Journal*, Vol. 31, No. 2, pp. 151–168.

Keynes, John Maynard, 1923, *A Tract on Monetary Reform*, London: Macmillan.

Keynes, John Maynard, 1930, *A Treatise on Money*, London: Macmillan. First published 1930.

Keynes, John Maynard, 1961, *The General Theory of Employment, Interest and Money*, London: Macmillan, New York: St Martin's Press. First published 1936.

Keynes, John Maynard, 1983 'Economic Articles and Correspondence, Academic', D. E. Moggridge (Ed.), *The Collected Writings of John Maynard Keynes*, Vol. XI, London: Macmillan.

Knapp, Georg Friedrich, 1924, *The State Theory of Money*, Trans. H. M. Lucas and James Bonar, London: Macmillan. First published 1905.

Knapp, Georg Friedrich, 1973/1924, *The State Theory of Money*, New York: Augustus M. Kelley.

L, 1926, 'Review: *The State Theory of Money*', *Journal of Political Economy*, Vol. 34, No. 3, pp. 404–6.

Mathias, Peter, 2001, *The First Industrial Nation: The Economic History of Britain 1700–1914*, Abingdon: Routledge.

Moggridge, D. E. (Ed.), *The Collected Writings of John Maynard Keynes*, Vol. XI, London: Macmillan.

Romer, Paul, 2016, 'The Trouble with Macroeconomics', lecture, delivered 5 January 2016 as the Commons Memorial Lecture of the Omicron Delta Epsilon Society. https://paulromer.net/wp-content/uploads/2016/09/WP-Trouble.pdf. Accessed 27 April 2017.

Smithin, John, (Ed.), 2000, *What Is Money?* London: Routledge.

Spread, Patrick, 2016, *The Evolution of Economies: Money-Bargaining, Economic Change and Industrial Revolution*, London and New York: Routledge

Spread, Patrick, 2019a, *Economics for an Information Age: Money-Bargaining, Support-Bargaining and the Information Interface*, London and New York: Routledge.

Wray, L. Randall, 2000, 'Modern Money', in John Smithin (Ed.), *What Is Money?* London: Routledge.

Wray, L. Randall, 2014, 'From the State Theory of Money to Modern Money Theory: An Alternative to Economic Orthodoxy,' *Working Paper No. 792*, Levy Economics Institute of Bard College.

11 Coins and Greek Feasts

Even today, the transfer of rule from one political faction to another is frequently a matter of armed force rather than democratic procedure. Throughout history, the rulers of states have been those displaying superior capacity for violence. There is a finality about violence that has made it so often the decisive factor in struggles for power. Echoes of this fundamental reality were heard even in the United States when in January 2021 an armed force, urged on by President Donald Trump, occupied the legislature to assert the President's unsubstantiated claim that the democratic election by which he had been displaced was illegitimate. If the outcomes of formal support-bargaining are not accepted as determinant, the fallback is violence.

Before democracy, the main modification to this rule of violence was the idea of a hereditary right to rule. A son might succeed his father as ruler of a state. The idea was held in a context of belief in divinities. Monarchs were understood as divinely appointed, so that defiance of a monarch or a legitimate heir would be defiance of the divinity. As was seen in Chapter 3, faith is a major focus of support, so that defiance of the divinities of any particular faith is likely to arouse strong reactions. With such support, monarchic systems sometimes achieved peaceful transfers of power. Monarchs were, nevertheless, obliged to retain soldiers on call.

Rulers ascendant by the exercise of armed force hardly need instruction in the threats to their rule. They are all aware that many of those around them covet their position. They provide patronage to retain the loyalty of the loyal and imprison those whose behaviour suggests any possibility of disaffection. They disrupt, in particular, any attempts at organisation outside the established structures of government and faith. Organisation is necessary to the exercise of military force (Chapter 2), so attempts to organise are seen as precursors to insurrection. Organisation requires money budgets, so anyone who can potentially fund a budget is viewed as potentially disruptive of established rule. Wealth can be tolerated only in those of demonstrated loyalty to the ruler, preferably being formally or informally in the service of the ruler and contributing to the upkeep of the established regime.

Hence the argument here that the advent of coinage was delayed long after the technical capacity to mint coins was available. Coins offer convenience in

DOI: 10.4324/9781003313472-13

exchange and opportunities for large numbers to become rich. A great swathe of social life seems likely to move beyond the control of a ruler. Such a threat to their rule would have been so unacceptable to rulers that they would not have contemplated such an innovation, even if someone had had the temerity and insight to suggest it. It would have seemed like an invitation to insurrection. The innovation was possible only when a political order became established that gave people sufficient role in governance as to obviate any threat from coinage.

The violent threat arising from coinage is a consequence of the effectiveness of coins as bargaining counters. People will provide services in return for material rewards, including payments in non–coin-money. While money is cumbersome and inconvenient, any threat from such payments is limited, and can for the most part be controlled. But the convenience of coin-money raises the real possibility of extensive diversion of effort from the pursuit of support to the pursuit of money. While non–coin-money is so cumbersome as to be confined to the use of a few specialist traders, coin-money can potentially be used by large numbers. Threats become apparent on all sides.

Money constitutes an alternative bargaining counter. Rulers engage in support-bargaining to sustain the loyalty of their people, using patronage to maintain their support. Society is held together around a ruler by cultivation of support, diminishing and in some cases largely obviating the necessity for the actual exercise of violence. The value of support is diminished by the use of money. Those apparently loyal to the ruler may determine that there is more to be gained by pursuit of money, and the pursuit is made easier and more readily covert by the use of coin-money. Rulers would at least find their bargaining positions weaker, and be obliged to increase the value and extent of their patronage. Coin-money threatens to divert loyalties forged in support-bargaining.

Coinage would constitute a threat of such magnitude as to be beyond the contemplation of ruling factions for millennia. Material prosperity would be desirable up to a point – desperation may drive starving people to insurrection. But a people of independent wealth would not be subordinate. A step change such as that represented by coinage would open up opportunities for greatly enhanced prosperity of a populace and a much lesser dependence on the benevolence of a ruler. Coin-money could be and was only adopted when support-bargaining took a form that made acceptable the opportunities that would arise from it.

The reaction of the King of Tonga in the early-nineteenth century, as recorded by William Mariner, to the idea of the introduction of coin-money from Australia into his Kingdom, exemplifies such concerns.[1] King Finow objects that coin-money will be stored instead of shared, and chiefs ought to share out produce; people will become selfish. But it is apparent that he is concerned at the potential erosion of the importance of his own distribution of produce to his people, on which his support depends.

Fear of insurrection explains the belated introduction of coin-money. Similar fears are apparent in the conduct of modern rulers towards the wealthy.

President Putin of Russia, for example, is seen as having contracted with his 'cronies' that they can make themselves as rich as they like provided they keep out of politics. To make clear the arrangement, Mikhail Khodorkovsky, a very wealthy oligarch, who criticised President Putin, was given a ten-year prison sentence. Maintaining authoritarian political ascendancy involves control of the kind of money-bargaining agencies that could potentially launch political insurrection.

Such analysis sets 'reciprocity and redistribution' in a different context and implies a different interpretation. An ascendant group will wish to keep material reward 'embedded' in the political sphere, not from any concerns over the well-being of its people, but to protect its own ascendancy. People who can earn and enrich themselves outside the control of the ruling group are potentially destructive of the ruling group. The patronage accorded close associates of a ruler is extended to ordinary people through 'redistribution.' The state alleviates some of the hardships of poor people to gain support for itself and the existing social order. The redistribution can be presented as disinterested benevolence, in accordance with moral principles developed by the religious organisations often associated with rulers. Expenditure is also more directly aimed at maintaining the means by which ascendancy is enforced. Military expenditure protects the state from external attack, but also protects the ruling group against domestic insurrection. It is apparent that the behaviour of chiefs described by Malinowski in the Trobriand Islands was as much a matter of authoritarian imposition as benign redistribution, albeit sanctioned by 'tradition' or 'custom.' In ancient Mesopotamia also the temples and palaces maintained authoritarian rule, tempered differently at different times and in different places by measures designed to sustain support; such measures shaped by ideas of morality and appropriate rule created by the educated personnel of the temples and palaces themselves. Both types of rulers were at pains to ensure that they sustained a necessary level of support amongst their people for their rule, involving their exercise of control over the distribution of material wealth across their societies.

Greek Flux and Mesopotamian Stability

It was seen in Chapter 2 that Homeric society, as presented by Richard Seaford, was disrupted by conflicts over traditional concepts of honour and the exchange of gifts, interpreted here as material expressions of social support, and aspirations to material reward in proportion to contributions made to the society, as depicted in Achilles's demands that distinction should be made in the distribution of booty between those who had been most prominent and effective in the fighting and those who had played a lesser part. Achilles is fully imbued with the values of his warrior society; he seeks honour through prowess in battle. But at the same time he is concerned that his material rewards should be commensurate with his contribution to the success of his faction. Not that Achilles gives any support to notions of the importance of trade; his concerns are over the distribution of booty. The particular ideological frame of reference of the *Iliad*, commensurate with the frames of reference of the people who are prominent in it, is that of a support-bargaining community rather than a money-bargaining community. Trade is marginal in the Homeric epics. But Seaford remarks that it was probably an important part of the world in which the narratives were set.[2] There is a question then of the adequacy of the support-bargaining system, the honorific system, of Homeric society to meet material aspirations, suggesting also a threat to the maintenance of such a society. Seaford notes that Greek society as portrayed by Homer is unstable, compared with the societies of the ancient Near East.[3]

Seaford also investigates how it was possible for coinage to take such a hold on Greek society in the sixth century BCE. As described in Chapter 2, he contrasts the regimes of ancient Mesopotamian temples and palaces with the society of Archaic Greece. Ancient Mesopotamia has an authoritarian character:

> In the elaborate state systems of Mesopotamia the centralisation has reached an extreme point: redistribution has become the enforced collection of goods and services at a central building (notably temple or palace), where they are used for the upkeep of the central institution, for redistribution among the population, and for communal functions such as storage against famine, the administration of justice, and irrigation.[4]

Feeding the deity is the prominent concern; feeding of the numerous personnel of the temple is a more practical concern.[5] In Archaic Greece, by contrast, the emphasis is on egalitarian distribution amongst the people. The chieftain exchanges largesse for the loyalty, or support, of his people. 'However...the emphasis is on consumption and on the inclusiveness of the consuming group.'[6] There are to be equal shares for all.

Homer does not mention any institutional infrastructure, such as temples or palaces, in which Greek feasting might have been organised, but from the eighth century BCE onwards, when Greece established such structures, the tradition of egalitarian inclusiveness persists. In contrast to Mesopotamian arrangements, 'the Greek sanctuary combines the storage of wealth with the *communal* distribution of sacrificed meat.'[7] There is a contrast of ethos and attitudes between authoritarian elite administration in the name of service to deities, and communal control for communal edification.

Greek Feasts and the Adoption of Coinage

The apparent gaps in Greek administrative capacity, both human and material, lead Seaford to ask:

> How – in the absence of a large-scale redistributive economy, of a deity and his household demanding to be fed, of temple ownership and control of herds – was it possible for the Greek community to organise the communal feasts on which its solidarity depended?[8]

Seaford's first answer is very practical: that they did so through the use of precious metals. Receipt of donations in the form of precious metal, rather than in the form of commodities, made it possible to coordinate all that was necessary to feasting. Traditional offerings of food gave way to durable goods and precious metals. This solution is the basis of Seaford's claim, a prominent thesis of his book, that, 'Sacrifice is an early agent of monetisation.'[9] The monetisation of Greece developed in response to the exigencies of communal organisation of feasts. The sanctuaries around which feasting was centred became also centres for economic transactions: 'At least as early as the classical period some Greek sanctuaries functioned as banks or as places (during festivals) for tax-free trading.'[10] The organisation of communal feasts required budgetary control and receipt of revenues in the durable and standardised forms of durable goods and precious metals.

Seaford's second answer concerns Greek social organisation: 'But the provision of sacrifice was a matter not just for the sanctuaries but also for the polis.'[11] Seaford notes that the relationship between polis and sanctuaries is 'hard to disentangle,' but he suggests a degree of control by the polis over the storage of precious metal in sanctuaries. Public precious metal was generally stored in sanctuaries. He notes further (Chapter 2, Note 40) that the polis performed various social functions that had been performed in ancient Mesopotamia by the temples, and financed public sacrifice for communal feasting, rather than for an elite. The polis was the emerging influence in Greek society.

David Schaps describes the polis as a new development, though with trace origins in earlier city-state organisations.[12] The Greek polis originated as groups of villages, but as populations grew, they became urban centres managing their affairs with a degree of independence.[13] A polis may refer either to an urban centre ('poleis' being the plural) or to the people living in an urban centre. They are 'city states' in both material and human senses. Their growth, according to Schaps, gave rise to requirements that could not be met through the earlier and simpler arrangements of gift-giving, plunder and communal feasting.[14]

Schaps sees the requirements of poleis as the basis for extensive adoption of coinage:

> It was Greece that was searching for new forms of government and administration to manage the new complexity of the poleis and new ways of organization to maintain its people, and coins made that administration and that organization simpler and more manageable than spits and cauldrons could have done.[15]

Like Seaford, Schaps emphasises considerations of organisational convenience surrounding the introduction of coins, but the organisation is part of the 'new forms of government' that are necessary to accommodate the new interests of the poleis. Seaford has it 'almost certain' that spits were used as money in Attic Greece.[16] He states that it is, 'extremely likely that iron spits did at some time, somewhere, perform one or more of the functions of money…even if never a *general* means of payment and exchange.'[17] Schaps gives the use of spits, along with tripods and cauldrons, and other utensils, similar credence as being used as money: 'Iron spits have been found in contexts that strongly suggest a use as currency.'[18] Coin took over from iron spits and other makeshift currencies as more convenient in exchange and in the budgeting necessary to the organisation of feasts.

'Cauldrons' seem almost impossibly cumbersome to use as money, but Schaps records that cauldrons seem to have actually been used for payments in Gortyn (Crete); the actual cauldron, not just a cauldron full of something useful.[19] Seaford also refers to Cretan experience. An inscription specifies payment in staters, in triobols, and in *lebētes* (cauldrons), which he takes to be coins named after sacrificial cauldrons.[20] Morris Silver dismisses any suggestion that actual cauldrons were used as money as 'preposterous,' and suggests that 'cauldron' might have been a name given to an ingot, perhaps stamped with the image of a cauldron.[21] But 'preposterous' has never been an insuperable barrier to human acceptance of an idea or practice.

As part of the 'makeshift' of pre-coinage exchange, these objects are feasible as performing in some instances the functions of money. The attribution to them of the function of money can be seen in part as a reflection of the fine line between provision of objects as gifts to secure support and provision of objects as 'money' in payment in material exchange. It is the fine line between the 'Ceremonial Barter' of the *kula*, Malinowski's sixth gradation of exchange, and 'Trade, pure and simple,' the seventh gradation (Chapter 5). 'Twenty cauldrons' are listed as amongst the gifts that Agamemnon offers to Achilles, but they are also part of the 'price' that Agamemnon will pay for Achilles's return to battle.[22] Cauldrons were favoured as 'gifts,' which makes it conceivable that they also made shift on occasions as money.

Such ambiguity is understandable as a matter of how the cauldrons are interpreted by their givers and receivers: some understand them as gifts, albeit in recognition of some service rendered, or requiring some gift in return at a suitable later date; some understand them as payments for provision of specific services or goods. People will interpret mostly in accordance with traditional ways of conducting relationships, the ways in which they were brought up, the 'common theory.' The emerging influence of the poleis would mean changes in the common theory. Modern interpretations of ancient behaviour are inevitably derived from frames of reference developed for the assembly of support in modern times. But people today still have some of the ancient ways of looking at transactions, in that there are occasions when a person will not be sure if he or she has received a present as expression of regard, or a payment, or a present in anticipation of a reciprocal present, or a present that presages demand for some future service. Unsolicited gifts can make people uncomfortable with regard to their implications.

The ambiguity over 'gifts' and 'trade' is also an ambiguity over the two bargaining systems, support-bargaining and money-bargaining. A material transfer may constitute an expression of support, an overture for acceptance of the giver into the group represented by the receiver. Or it may represent a monetary payment for a service rendered or anticipated. Presenting a cauldron is likely to be an expression of support, but it could also be a payment. People are sometimes upset when a person for whom they have performed a service, conceived by the performer as a free expression of support or neighbourly friendship, tries to make payment for the service. It relocates the service from support-bargaining to money-bargaining. It represents rejection of an overture of friendship, an indication that the more impersonal relationship of money-bargaining is preferred.

Spits, tripods and cauldrons are all associated with feasts. Seaford's thesis of the origins of coin-money in communal feasting seems borne out by this usage. As was seen in Chapter 6, the smallest silver coins of the classical period were called *oboloi*, 'spits,' and six of them made a *drachme*, or handful. Receptacles have been found designed to hold six spits.[23] Even if spits were not used with the specific concept of monetary exchange, the use of the words *oboloi* and *drachme* indicates the associations that the Greeks wanted their coins to have. Public support for the coins would be promoted through such associations. Coins were a communal innovation for material advantage, as the feasts were a communal expression of fellowship.

The communal adoption of coins and the communal expression in feasting both derived from the thinking of the poleis. The poleis supported the feasts as an egalitarian celebration of their communal identity. A polis was, in its human form, a self-forming group, as described in Chapter 1. A polis would have something of the self-assurance and convictions that arise from a sense of independent being and thought, and the knowledge that its thinking had communal support. The poleis were masters of their own destinies. Coins might threaten the ascendancy of a ruling group, but it could not threaten the ascendancy of a people who were themselves in charge.

While Greek adoption of coinage seems to derive from the Greek arrangements for communal feasting, Seaford's thesis that coins originated with that connection is inconsistent with the accepted origin of coins in Lydia. The Greeks adopted money for extensive use, but they recognised its origin in Lydia.[24] Seaford acknowledges the inconsistency but suggests that Lydia was under extensive Greek influence. Greeks provided the idea of coinage while the Lydians provided the metal.[25] Lydian coins were made from electrum, or white gold, an alloy of gold and silver, panned from the River Pactolus that flowed past the Lydian capital Sardis.[26] While the Lydians invented coins, the Greeks were able to take advantage of their potential for wide scale usage in exchange. Henry Kim observes that, 'Even though the initial idea may have 'non-Greek' (Lydian) origins, it is within the Greek world and with silver that coinage becomes a widespread phenomenon.'[27] Coins fitted into Greek culture, otherwise expressed in its feasting, so that coins in small denominations could be minted and used in several of the poleis. The use of silver coins developed early in Thrace and Macedon, which also exported silver.[28] Athens was obliged to import silver until it became available in sufficient quantity from the Laurion mines in the early-fifth century BCE. Athenian coins came to dominate the eastern Mediterranean.[29] Use of coinage spread rapidly during the last quarter of the sixth century BCE and the first quarter of the fifth. By about 480 BCE around 100 mints were producing coins in Greece and surrounding areas.[30] King Croesus of Lydia abandoned electrum in favour of gold and silver coinage. The Lydian engagement with coinage came to an end in 546 BCE when the Lydian state was expunged by Cyrus the Great of Persia.[31] The rapid spread of Greek silver coinage thus occurred after the demise of the Lydian state.

Schaps describes coinage as defining and reinforcing the existing social order in Greece.[32] He remarks, 'To meet one's needs, reward one's friends and dependents, and establish one's own independence and power by means of exchange was behavior congenial to the archaic Greek.'[33] Coins were a means of breaking down traditional social barriers: 'In a world where class conflicts were sharply felt and the moral authority of the wellborn was not taken for granted, coins offered a basis for evaluating worth and behaviour at every level of society.'[34] Coinage was seen as 'subversive of traditional distinctions, denying by its very universality the inherited structure of the society into which it was introduced.'[35] The sense of community and equal right that is visible in the arrangements for Greek feasting is apparent also in the adoption of coinage. While coinage clearly did not originate in Greek feasting, its wide adoption in Greece was facilitated by the same communal dispositions that gave Greek feasts their particular character.

Opponents of Coinage

Whilst Schaps presents coinage as consistent with the general dispositions of Greek society of the time, Leslie Kurke suggests that its introduction was strongly disputed, along precisely the lines suggested here as the reason why coinage was not introduced earlier.[36] Traditional landowners continued to play a major role in politics, and opposed the growing use of money. Sitta von Reden argues that the introduction of coinage involved recognition of the polis as controlling the justice that had been understood as part of a divine order.[37] Kurke acknowledges von Reden's identification of the rise of the polis as foundational, but suggests that von Reden 'has ignored or elided crucial elements of conflict.'[38] Kurke suggests that von Reden's emphasis on religious and metaphysical aspects of the introduction of coinage causes her to miss the political motivations. Aristocratic Greeks opposed the introduction of coinage. They did so in defence of their ascendancy in Greek society: 'elite opposition to money is not so much economic as political – it is part of a larger project of aristocratic resistance to the encroaching authority of the polis.'[39] The polis constituted a threat to the established ascendancy, and coinage was part of the threat. So the established ascendancy opposed the introduction of money. Kurke depends on literary sources rather than historical for her evidence, and the strength of her evidence has been questioned by some writers.[40] There is inevitable inclination to look kindly on evidence when it fits so well the present frame of reference.

Another literary source, Homer, provides the evidence for the state of Archaic Greek society. Kurke herself acknowledges that she cannot deal with 'reality'; it is the text and images of the literary sources that constitute the 'facts.'[41] The opposition described by Kurke to 'new money' is echoed by the disdain of landowning nobility in later ages for the 'nouveau riches' who challenge their ascendancy.

Darel Engen also recognises the continued exercise of substantial authority by landowners. The rising classes did not have the esteem accorded to those in traditional landed occupations: 'Since the bulk of economic wealth was produced from the land and *banausic* [manufacturing, business, trade] occupations were not esteemed, the elite of ancient Greek society were landowners who consequently dominated politics, even in democratic *poleis* like Athens.'[42] Only male citizens had anything like democratic rights in Greek poleis. In Athens in 431 BCE the best estimate is that they numbered about 40,000 in a population of 305,000. About 40,00 females and 80,000 children were also citizens. There were about 25,000 free resident foreigners (*metics*) and about 120,000 slaves.[43]

The contrasts made between Archaic Greek society and the societies of Ancient Mesopotamia and Mycenaean civilisation, the latter failing around 1100 BCE, involve substantial disparities in time and, in the case of Ancient Mesopotamia, of space. 'Other factors' may be present that make attribution of different outcomes to a single factor potentially misleading. But in the case of Greek adoption of coinage there is a contemporary contrast that provides further evidence for the aversion of authoritarian states to coinage. Sparta lived in fear of an uprising of the helots, a numerically superior but conquered people forced to work as serfs on land they had previously owned. They were periodically subjected to violent attacks as a matter of state policy. Schaps writes:

> There was one Greek state that did maintain an economy based on the brutal exploitation of dependents by a small and hereditary class of fighting but nonproducing citizens. That state was Sparta, and for centuries, Sparta refused, apparently on principle, to adopt a silver currency.[44]

The principle apparently applied only to internal usage of silver coins, since Sparta employed foreign mercenaries in military engagements, presumably paying them in foreign coin.[45] The vulnerability of Spartan rulers and the scope for tight cohesive grouping are apparent from its population. Male Spartan citizens were never more than 9,000, and for most of its history not even that.[46]

Jeremy Trevett also notes the Spartan aversion to coin: 'One prominent feature of Spartan society was the failure to issue coins, indeed the virtual absence of coined money.'[47] Trevett cites Spartans as employing iron spits as a 'deliberately cumbersome form of token money.'[48] Earlier rulers may similarly have preferred cumbersome money. For the rulers of Sparta, the prospect of coins in the hands of helots would have been seen as an invitation to rebellion. Coins were minted by the state in Athens and extensively used for state payments. Trevett suggests democracy could hardly have existed without coined money.[49]

He concludes his article: 'The anti-democratic ideal was of a world without coinage. Conversely, the democratic polis, and Athens in particular, was a world of coins.'[50]

Pre-Coinage Money in the Near East

Seaford pursues further the question of the use of money in the Near East in his concluding Chapter 15, presented as an Appendix: 'was money used in the early Near East?' His response is based on assessment of whether the candidate moneys conform to seven characteristics established in his earlier definition of money, which may be abbreviated as: (1) something not valued in use but for its *power to meet social obligations*; (2) money tends to be *quantified*; (3) money provides a *measure of value*, other commodities being valued in terms of the money; (4) the performance of one of the functions does not mean that it necessarily performs any of the others; (5) *exclusive acceptability* is not necessary; (6) there must be *fiduciarity*, a collective trust in future value; (7) the state may be involved.[51]

He notes the scattered evidence for the marking of metal pieces for purposes other than decoration, including copper ingots of around 1330 BCE and the Egyptian *shaty*.[52] He is notably critical of Morris Silver's 1985 account of the use of money in the ancient Near East, in which Silver argues for recognition that the arrangements in the ancient Near East constituted use of money (Chapter 7).[53] His conclusion is that none of the candidate moneys meet the definition of money, so that there is no good reason to claim that money existed before the invention of coinage.[54]

He reaches the same conclusion by reference to the question, 'What distinguished a coin from a marked, standardised piece of metal that is not a coin?' His response is that a mark on a coin 'endows it with a general acceptability in payment without being weighed or tested.'[55] In Near Eastern usage it seems that metal used in payment was always weighed rather than counted. So that on this criterion also, there was no money in the ancient Near East. It is acknowledged, however, that commodities performed the functions of money. 'Silver is a commodity (quantified by weight) that, like other commodities, may be used to perform money functions.'[56]

The negative conclusion is implicit in Seaford's definition of money. The Greek introduction of coinage would appear the more momentous if it were also the introduction of money. The full functions of money were only provided with coinage, so 'money' that meets the definition of 'money' did not exist before the introduction of coinage. But if 'money' is something that fulfils essential functions of money, then such things existed in the ancient Near East, and the ancient Near East had money. Money as a bargaining counter existed before the use of coin-money. Other commodities, besides silver, such as grain and copper, seem to have functioned as bargaining counters, fulfilling the functions of money.[57] An element of 'makeshift' is apparent in the way 'money' was used in transactions, and what 'money' was used. It no doubt complicated the transactions of the time, and clearly complicates the analysis of modern commentators accustomed to a single distinct 'money' with extensive administrative trappings. Conceived as a bargaining counter, something to be called 'money' need only be observed in operation as a bargaining counter. Money, in this conception, existed in many forms prior to the introduction of coinage. The earlier forms were, however, cumbersome and constrained the type and number of transactions that could be undertaken. That inconvenience and constraint suited authoritarian governments seeking to maintain their monopoly of power. The Greek adoption of coinage was momentous because the convenience of coin gave it application in a much wider range of transactions and amongst a much wider range of people. Only the social order of the poleis found it possible to risk such usage. Seaford remarks that, 'the Mesopotamians did not invent coinage – because they did not feel the need for it.'[58] But it is more than that: those in charge would not have thought of anything so subversive of their rule.

Retail Trade and the Denominations of Coins

Schaps describes the impact of coin-money across Greek society, including its impact on politics, warfare, labour, farming and business. One major impact is on and through markets, in the sense of local markets for sale of livestock, food and other everyday consumer goods. Schaps notes an immediate monetisation of markets. It took only a few decades for coin to displace barter. The poleis already had centres for the confluence of people for political purposes – the '*agora*' is the 'meeting place.' The *agora* admirably provided a venue for trade. Coinage facilitated trade, and in so doing provided alternative ways in which ordinary people could make a living; alternative, for example, to the '*thetes*' system under which free men contracted to provide labour in exchange for their maintenance, an arrangement little better than slavery. Coinage facilitated day labour.[59] The new bargaining counter – coin-money – diminished the importance of the established bargaining counter – support – and the social order that had been built on the importance of support. Schaps notes: '… even a peasant or a shopkeeper could amass enough money to buy the most prestigious of goods.'[60] The consequence was: '…the opening up of new and individual roads to wealth broke the circle of dependency that reinforced the distinction between rich and poor.'[61] These changes in retail trade were at the root of other developments, not least because the growth of the *agora* gave impetus to the growth of cities.[62]

Retail trade such as that of a Greek *agora* requires not only the convenience of coinage but coins of small denomination. The absence of coins, and more specifically the absence of coins of suitable denominations, seems to have kept retail trade to a minimum before its Greek development.[63] It was seen in Chapter 9 that Robert Cook's 1958 theory that money originated in payments to mercenary soldiers was based on the absence of appropriate denominations of coins for commercial usage. Colin Kraay, in a paper published in 1964, questioned whether coinage had in fact brought about expansion in retail trade. His conclusions were based on the content of hoards of coins found in the Eastern Mediterranean and Asia Minor. The small number of low denomination coins found in the hoards suggests that retailing was not the reason for the introduction of coins. Kraay rejected the argument that coins had been created for retailing, or that coins had a significant impact on retailing, on grounds that few Greek states provided a regular supply of low denomination coins; many places had no coinage; coinage originated not in Greece but in Lydia; and the electrum coins minted in Lydia were of such high denominations as to preclude their general use in retail trade. Kraay recognises that hoards, by their purpose, are likely to include high denomination coins in preference to low denominations, and hence the evidence is not conclusive with regard to the extent of the minting of low denomination coins.[64]

Kim cited new evidence in an article in 2001 indicating that low denominations suitable for retail trade were extensively minted in Greece.[65] Many of the mints identified by Kraay as producing no small change or insufficient quantities for widespread use in small transactions have been shown to have had significant levels of production of low-denomination coins.[66] Kim comments on the new evidence: 'It represents a fundamental change in our understanding of how early coins could be used.'[67] Darel Engen in 2004 cites Kim in arguing that the minting of large quantities of small denomination coinage in Greece demonstrates the concern of the state to promote use of coinage by common people in everyday exchanges.[68] Schaps remarks in 2004:

> But rather more of the first Attic coins occur in small denominations than in large, and numismatists have also noted that small coins are more likely to have disappeared through wear or to have been ignored by archaeologists and by treasure hunters – and are, for that matter, less likely to have been hoarded and buried in the first place. In the Athenian agora, where coins recovered are mostly coins dropped by their owners, the small denominations predominate.[69]

It appears that the more recent evidence sustains the idea that coins of low denominations were minted in sufficient quantity to bring about a significant expansion of retail trade and the invigoration of the *agora* as a place of trade.

Schaps also remarks on the wider impact of coinage: 'Coins, too, though superficially only a convenience, made the behaviours that they enhanced – trading, paying, evaluating, and hoarding – a much larger part of Greek life than they had ever been.'[70] Coins took the 'makeshift' out of material exchange. This is what makes the introduction of coinage momentous rather than just notable. People at last had a distinct and universally acceptable (within their community, and such other communities as chose to avail themselves of it) 'money.' Money as a bargaining counter extends money-bargaining across the people who accept the bargaining counter. More than non–coin-money, coin-money was a supplementary bargaining counter, as much as an alternative bargaining counter. Coin-money proved to have extensive acceptance. Coinage changed the nature of societies – their everyday affairs and their mental horizons. People travelled extensively before the introduction of motor vehicles, but when they came, motor vehicles did not just substitute a new mode of travel for the old; they changed the habits of their societies, the physical appearance of their societies and the way people thought of distance and their association with others. The changes associated with the introduction of coins appear to have been of a comparable order of social importance.

Coinage and the State

Karl Polanyi's idea of embedding supposes a benign state looking after its people in a system of 'reciprocity and redistribution.' The comment of the opening section to this chapter suggests rather a controlling state governed by a ruling group concerned primarily with its own continued ascendancy. In that context, 'embeddedness' is a matter of controlling material provision to protect the ascendant. It was suggested that the introduction of coinage to widespread use became possible only with the increasing exercise of authority by *poleis*, as early forms of democracy. Ascendancy, or at least substantial authority, passed to the common people, who had no need to regard coinage as a threat to their ascendancy – it helped them to assert themselves. The introduction of coinage was thus made possible by a radical change in the nature of 'the state,' from controlling faction towards control by something like popular opinion. The changes wrought by the introduction of coins as bargaining counters are thus entwined with a radical change in the arrangements governing the use of the existing bargaining counter, support. The support of a whole populace, sadly excepting slaves and females, mattered in the conduct of the affairs of the state.

'Embedding' thus takes on different meaning. It is no longer a vague idea of an autocratic state 'looking after' the material needs of its people, but a people negotiating amongst themselves to direct the affairs of their state, through support-bargaining, and accommodating the use of money in a money-bargaining system to facilitate material exchange in the society. The use of coins, compared with use of earlier 'makeshift' bargaining counters, certainly gives material exchange a more distinct identity and wider scope. But the money-bargaining system is still 'embedded' in the support-bargaining system, since the two forms of bargaining and the two bargaining counters are interlinked. Support-bargaining is necessary to the use of coins as bargaining counters.

The extension of political support-bargaining to take account of the support of common people enhanced the importance of individuals in their societies. But the support-bargaining process also makes possible the identification of communal interests and provision for the transfer of funds from private agents to a communal budget for expenditure on the communal interest (Chapter 5, under the heading 'Transformation by Companies'). It was done in ancient Athens. Schaps writes:

> the lower classes succeeded in harnessing the state machinery to give them the power to mobilize and to employ the power of money – to make the demos wealthy as a class even though its members remained impoverished as individuals. The maintenance and proper functioning of the fiscal structure became and is today an indispensable part of the maintenance of democracy.[71]

This is the development dreaded by the ascendant of previous eras – the capture of the state machinery by ordinary people, threatening the ousting of existing rulers and appropriation of their wealth. It is, however, clear that the takeover in Athens was incomplete. The Greek landowning nobility, as Kurke attests, maintained extensive influence over the affairs of state – enough to prevent the appropriation of their land by the poleis.

Kurke endorses Polanyi's idea of the 'embedded' economy, but follows: 'To say that an economy is embedded, however, is not to say that its participants are unable to think and act in terms of economic advantage…'[72] Kurke notes that both aristocrats and polis sought to establish themselves as true custodians of the communal spirit:

> Both the aristocracy and the polis lay claim to the good, 'embedded' economy for themselves, and both vilify the other side by representing it not as an alternate order, but as disorder – socially ruinous disembedding perpetrated by selfish economic interests. [73]

The aristocrats present a greedy polis disembedding material interest from the traditional social order; the *polis* presents aristocratic gift-exchange as grotesque betrayal of the community for individualistic profit.

Landowners were not alone in their resistance to the new order. Schaps notes that the introduction of coinage made possible the pursuit of money as an end in itself. A person could have enough of a particular commodity, but there was no end to how much money was desirable.[74] Aristotle saw the same thing and disapproved. He argued that the accumulation of money implies a confusion of money with wealth. When money is the goal of a transaction, rather than the means to some other objective, there is corruption of the nature of exchange.[75] Aristotle affirms that courage should produce daring; soldiering should produce victory; medicine should produce health. Yet people use these things to produce money.[76]

Schaps observes that the pursuit of money as an end in itself was an important consequence of the adoption of coinage. Coins did not merely expand trade because of their convenience, but opened up new concepts of trade. People could trade not just to acquire specific items or commodities but to accumulate money. Instead of selling chickens and buying shirts, an agent could raise chickens for the accumulation of money. Coinage thus makes prominent the idea of companies formatting to meet a viability condition (Chapter 5), though the 'company' would in ancient times typically be a family. 'Companies' in family form formatted for the provision of financial services.[77] The idea of accumulating money, in the form, for example, of gold and silver, as an end in itself, or as a matter of security, or for payment of dowries, or as the key to 'the good life,' was surely not novel. But coinage made the accumulation of money easier. Trading families would have found it easier to accumulate coin-money than any of the 'moneys' that had previously been used.

Aristotle has subsequently had the support of countless people, all of them condemning the pursuit of money as immoral, ungodly, selfish, degrading or in some other way antipathetic to human society. But people still pursue money, with varying degrees of commitment. And open support-bargaining systems invariably promote money-bargaining as conducive to the overall well-being of their societies.

Coinage and Individual Advantage

Seaford and other writers recognise that the use of money, and coin-money in particular, gives advantage to individuals. It makes individuals less dependent on the group.[78] Personal relationships can potentially be set aside as what is needed is acquired through the payment of money. The freedom that money brings to individuals is an aspect of the threat posed by money to rulers. Seaford suggests that we have 'internalised a metaphysics of money' by which we believe money to be *a thing* and believe, secondly, 'that we are primarily individual agents and only secondarily (if at all) members of a larger entity, whether defined by kinship, politics, religion or anything else.'[79]

This 'individualisation' is seen also as equalising. Every individual can advance his interests, without reference to social pressures, and in particular independently of the social pressures arising from the obligations and constraints imposed by a ruling class. Seaford remarks: 'To be sure, the astonishing new power of coinage is egalitarian, for it may be used by all citizens of the advanced polis and – as Aristotle points out – *equalises* the two parties to an exchange.'[80] Aristotle observes that currency creates commensurability in exchange and hence a community of equals.[81]

In terms of bargaining theory, the introduction of coin-money as an alternative bargaining counter immeasurably strengthens the position of the individual in relation to the group. Hence one major consequence of the introduction of coin-money is the release of the individual from the heaviest of social constraints. Writers such as Polanyi and Marx condemn the erosion of social relationships that arises from the introduction and spread of coin-money. Coin-money seems to 'disembed' material transactions from group relationships, and in so doing 'disembed' individuals from their societies. But where such societies are oppressive, the disembedding will be welcomed by the oppressed.

Coin-money strengthens the position of individuals, but individuals remain subject to the constraints of support-bargaining. Through the interlinking of money-bargaining and support-bargaining, the release of individuals from the sharper constraints of the group strengthens both individuals and group.

Individual versus group, the central contention in support-bargaining, appears as essentially a 'zero-sum' engagement – the loss of one is the gain of the other. But the individualism released through the introduction of coin-money lifts the group to a new level. The energies released in pursuit of money have been the salvation of human societies from short life-spans, ignorance and grinding poverty, making possible, in conjunction with support-bargaining systems, the immense growth of human population around the world and enabling many of them, especially those which have made space freely available in their societies for the pursuit of money, to lead prosperous and intellectually engaging lives. Bargaining societies are full of friction, but their material prosperity, used individually and communally, helps to alleviate insecurity and emotional pain. The well-being of the group depends on the freedom of individuals to act both for their own and for communal advantage. Support-bargaining identifies and realises the communal advantage.

Coinage is not then a matter of disembedding material transactions from social and political affairs, rather the embedding is of a different kind. The use of coin-money is dependent on the assent of the group. Coin-money derives its value from the readiness of many agents to provide goods and services in exchange for it. Such agents perform the role of dependable debtors, and hence give the money purchasing power. Coinage is not viable in the absence of a community that supports its usage and accords it value. Coin-money is a 'Society Owes You' by which a community undertakes to restore value to those who have accepted the communal money. For a money of wide usage across a community – a national money – state administration of supply of the bargaining counter is required.

Thus while transactions with coins appear to be disembedded from social and political affairs, the overall functioning of a money-bargaining system and the bargaining counters it employs remain embedded in support-bargaining. The group concedes significant liberty to the individual, but within a context of communal management. A socially supported bargaining counter replaces 'social transactions,' the former no less dependent on social acceptance than the latter. It was a particular quality of Greek society in the sixth century BCE that it felt secure enough to concede such individual freedom. It was 'a distinct social formation' that made possible the rapid and widespread diffusion of coinage in Greek lands.[82] Coinage disembedded specific economic transactions from the social context, but is itself embedded in social relations.

This collective aspect of the individualism of coin-money is apparent in Seaford as the 'paradox' by which the communal solidarity expressed in Greek feasting gave rise to a means of payment and exchange which must have greatly increased impersonality and personal autonomy.[83] Seaford sums up:

> The paradox of ignorant individualism dependent on invisible communality, inherited from the mysteries, expresses the paradox of the circulation of monetary value, which bestows autonomy on the individual only by uniting everybody into a single system.[84]

Individual autonomy bestowed by visible money depends on invisible support and support-bargaining, experienced as communality and communal management of the bargaining counter.

Similar 'paradox' is apparent when the requirements of support-bargaining make it necessary for those who favour individual autonomy to group together and form organisations for the advancement of the individual interest. 'Individualists' of the political right find it necessary to form 'parties' to advance individualist interests. The reverse paradox also arises, where supporters of the primacy of the group are obliged by the exigencies of effective organisation and support-bargaining to settle on an individual who can effectively lead an organisation that will advance the group interest.[85] 'Paradox' is fundamental, since the primary interest of every individual lies in the acquisition of support from others, so that the most ardent individualists will seek the support of other individualists, and an 'individualist group' will form. A community is necessary to sustain the individualist advantages of coinage. Individuals vie with their communities, but in so doing they also build them.

The Individualism of Credit

Seaford acknowledges that credit and borrowing may create lasting relationships and consequently reduce the individual advantages deriving from the use of money.[86] Credit provision requires external engagement to ensure that obligations are met when they do not necessarily accord with the individual interests of the agents concerned. Few people, without some social or political prompting, stick fastidiously to obligations to pay their debts. Before receiving credit, borrowers are contriving to get the money they need, and give the assurances and guarantees necessary to realisation of that objective. But once they have what they need, they may be inclined to contrive how they can avoid repayment, with as little damage to themselves as possible. The change in situation from not having money and wanting it, to having money and not wanting to be deprived of it, changes interests and induces new trains of thought. Bargaining positions change with the changes in situation.

External sanctions are necessary to make people pay their debts with the consistency necessary to widen the provision of credit beyond 'neighbours.' The appropriate sanctions are established through support-bargaining. The conflict between capitalists and anti-capitalists is launched. Both sides assemble support for their cause. Credit has for the most part fallen well short of what is needed to meet the time disparities of money-bargaining, because lenders find it difficult to collect repayments, and interest rates rise to reflect the risks involved. Lenders have historically confined their lending to those they trust, on the basis of kinship or social affiliations. In effect, they adopted the 'neighbourly' approach – you only lend to the sort of people you can trust, or whose communal membership implies sanctions on them if they fail to meet their obligations. Credit has only become more widely available with the introduction of legal measures to protect the interests of creditors, involving also the protection of the interests of debtors. Social and political support-bargaining has been essential to the use of credit.

These arrangements place money-bargaining more closely under the supervision of the state, and hence may be seen as diminishing the individual advantages deriving from the use of money. Yet time disparities are an integral part of money-bargaining. In the neoclassical frame of reference, without time or space, there are no time disparities, hence no need for credit, and no need for budgeting. In the understanding of money-bargaining, time disparities between receipts and expenditures are inseparable from trade. A money-bargaining system needs credit and budgets. Credit may therefore be recognised as part of the usage of money that gives opportunities for individuals to act at least more independently of the community than would otherwise be possible. It offers opportunities to individuals that they would not otherwise have. A bargaining counter has to be managed by a community to ensure its function in a money-bargaining system, but credit involves communal management also of transactional relationships.

The availability of credit might also be seen as promoting equality in a community. Availability of credit means that anyone can access means of overcoming the time disparities they face. If obligations to repay debt were universally and unfailingly fulfilled, credit provision might have this levelling effect. However, as noted earlier, creditors have historically found it necessary to limit their provision to those with whom they share some social affinities. Much less credit has been provided than would have been necessary to accommodate all those who could usefully and effectively use it. Credit provision has been in the hands of wealthier members of communities who have lent mostly to their own 'neighbours.' Credit provision has given scope for individuals to pursue their own interests independent of communal or state direction, but the risks associated with credit provision have confined its advantages to a limited group of individuals.

Seaford suggests in his footnote on credit that instruments of credit in ancient Greece were undeveloped and transactions of short duration, implying that the individualising effects of coinage were scarcely compromised.[87] But while credit provision was limited in ancient Greece, it was not negligible. Schaps notes that lending and borrowing had been common in Greece well before the introduction of coinage, often as a matter of neighbourly cooperation. Coinage gave impetus to the process:

> Loans of coin were extremely common in Athens by the late classical period, and like Darwin's finches, they had differentiated into various different forms of loan, each filling a particular need in the society and each providing a particular advantage to the borrower and to the lender.[88]

Lenders responded to the requirements of traders with credits ranging from small loans for market traders up to substantial sums for international trade ventures. The charging of interest was a central issue. Usury was widely condemned, but 'a competing ideology had arisen that considered interest perfectly legitimate.'[89] All suffered the inherent problems of credit and debt relationships. A framework of legal sanctions to make possible secure credit provision and borrowing was clearly emerging.

Schaps records that during the fifth century BCE family-based banks took deposits and hence were able to offer substantially larger loans than other providers of credit. While in terms of value of loans they were leading providers of credit in Athens, in terms of breadth of clientele, they were marginal.[90] Moses Finley describes banking as rudimentary.[91] There were few practitioners: 'Not thirty Athenians are known from the whole of the fourth century who are specifically identified as bankers, a reflection of the rarity of the occupation, not a defect of the available sources.'[92]

Finley, in a 1953 article, gives a varied picture of lending in ancient Athens. Cash transactions were the normal practice, but short-term person-to-person loans for consumption were common. Landowners secured credit on their land in order to maintain the expenditures necessary to their social status. Stone markers, or *horoi*, were put in place displaying details of encumbrances. This land-based indebtedness largely involved debtors and creditors of the same landowning class.[93] Then as subsequently, credit went with most confidence to 'neighbours.'

Exchange and Definitions in Finley's *Ancient Economy*

Polanyi conceives the 'embedding' of material provision within the framework of social relations. An independent 'disembedded' system of material exchange is regarded as impossible in ancient societies, since the conditions for 'markets' in the neoclassical economic understanding did not exist in ancient times (Chapter 5). Polanyi's theme is taken up by Finley in *The Ancient Economy*, which came to be accepted as the definitive account of economic affairs in ancient Greece and Rome. Finley notes early questioning of classical economic theory and follows: 'More recently the inapplicability to the ancient world of a market centred analysis was powerfully argued by Max Weber and by his most important disciple among ancient historians, James Hasebroek;[94] in our own day by Karl Polanyi.'[95] While his argument is for embedding, Finley's title suggests an 'ancient economy' can be distinguished from its society.

Finley follows the theme of Polanyi, but his treatment is substantially different. He provides a detailed historical account of the economies and societies of ancient Greece and Rome. He makes no use of the idea of 'reciprocity and redistribution' in *The Ancient Economy*, nor does he use the term 'embedded,' though his account of the ancient economies emphasises the predominance of state and social processes. But like Polanyi, he affirms the irrelevance of the economic idea of 'markets' to the ancient world. Dispensing with that idea, without replacement, means a shortfall in his analytical capacity.

Finley bases his idea of 'economics' on a definition by Eric Roll:

> If, then, we regard the economic system as an enormous conglomeration of interdependent markets, the central problem of economic enquiry becomes the explanation of the exchanging process, or, more particularly, the explanation of the formation of price.[96]

Finley also makes reference to the idea of a frame of reference influencing our thinking, as described in Chapter 4: 'The economic language and concepts we are all familiar with, even the laymen among us, the "principles," whether they are Alfred Marshall's or Paul Samuelson's, the models we employ, tend to draw us into a false account.'[97] A frame of reference can draw us into a 'false account,' but Finley seems confident that he is in a position to identify what is 'false,' rather than simply adopting another frame of reference. Karl Marx was similarly confident that he could identify 'false consciousness' in the minds of those whose opinions he opposed.

One consequence of Finley's identification and rejection of the Roll definition is that he skirts consideration of exchange in the ancient Greek economy. His explanations are focused on social 'orders' and the 'status' of people, the extensive role of the state and the use of political influence to gain economic advantage. He affirms that the authority of the state was total, whether city-states or autocracies.[98]

Finley deals with trade mainly in the context of relationships between town and country, so that the theoretical context is that of trade within socio-political groups, with no theory of the 'market' kind. The central concern, for Finley, is to explain how the town paid for what it needed from the country. There was extensive trade. Engen writes of the dispute amongst anthropologists over the understanding of that trade:

> Seeing extensive trade and use of money in Greece from the fifth century B.C. onward, the modernists extrapolated the existence of a market economy in Classical Greece. On the other hand, seeing traditional Greek social and political values that disdained the productive, impersonal, and industrial nature of modern market economies, the primitivists downplayed the existence of extensive trade and the use of money in the economy. Neither primitivists nor modernists could conceive of the existence of extensive trade and the use of money unless the ancient Greek economy was organized according to market principles.[99]

Finley was the leading advocate of what is classified in the above quotation as 'primitivist.' On the overall picture he writes, 'What is being claimed is the existence of powerful social and political attitudes, and of important economic consequences.' With regard to the motivations of people he affirms, 'the prevailing mentality was acquisitive but not productive.'[100] Trade of all kinds is conducted on the basis of socially imposed 'orders' and 'status.' At the top of the scale of status are a few large landowners, while at the bottom are the chattel slaves.

Finley gives no account of the dynamics of this trade; no account, for example, of how prices are determined. Sitta von Reden acknowledges the contribution made by Finley, but comments 'the criticism must be made that he seriously underestimated the relevance of exchange within the politics and society of the *polis*.'[101] Like the title of her book, *Exchange in Ancient Greece*, the comment refers to all types of exchange, including gift exchange and other social and political exchanges.

The nearest Finley approaches to an alternative theory of exchange to substitute for his rejection of the idea of economic 'markets' is an idea of 'empirical knowledge,' as in, 'There was of course enough empirical knowledge, without generalized concepts and theories, for *ad hoc* decisions in one or another situation.'[102] He notes that ancient states did not have budgets in the modern sense, but 'Greek and Roman statesmen had a fair empirical knowledge of annual revenues and expenditures.'[103] Or he uses the phrase 'in some concrete way,' as for example, a failure to set maximum interest rates, 'has to be explained in some concrete way, not by reference to rights or to private spheres beyond the reach of the state.'[104] These are incidental references rather than committed attempts to provide alternative theory. They do not explain as theory explains. The shortfall in analytical capacity is not made good.

Most importantly, in the present context, the neglect of exchange causes Finley to misjudge the significance of the adoption of coinage in Greek city-states. In *The Ancient Economy* he describes coinage in terms of state monopolies over minting of coins and the provision of coins by state payments, leading to chronic shortages of coin. The shortages were exacerbated by hoarding. The absence of any fiduciary issue of money further limited the supply of money.[105] Engen summarises Finley's understanding of coinage as follows:

> Finley's model, of course, holds that coinage had strictly political functions. Finley believed that coinage was merely a tool designed to reinforce and project a city-state's civic identity. States minted coins not to facilitate economic transactions among their citizens, but merely for state purposes so that, for example, it had a convenient medium through which to collect taxes or make state expenditures.[106]

Finley makes no attempt to evaluate the significance of the introduction of coinage and its impact on Greek society. In the context of exchange, and most especially in the context of the idea of money as a bargaining counter, the adoption of coinage was of immense significance. Nor was it simply a matter of a bargaining counter that facilitated material exchange. In accordance with Finley's theme, it arose from particular social and economic circumstances. It arose from one of the most momentous political developments in the history of mankind.

People asked for their understanding of economics might say, 'something to do with money,' or in more formal terms, 'economic matters are those matters that involve the use of money; and economic theory is the study of such usage.' For some, coins are money, and money is economics. In common theory, economics is concerned with money. Such an understanding, though it excludes barter, is not too wide of the mark set by reference to the idea of money-bargaining. Furthermore, the subsequent history of money in society suggests that the introduction of coin-money was a matter of importance. Finley's rejection of the Roll 'market' definition of economics, as giving a false account of economic processes, causes him, or allows him, to omit any evaluation of the significance of coinage. Finley wishes to minimise the importance of the 'market' sort of exchange, which is just the sort of exchange fostered by coins. Evading Roll is evading exchange and evading the impact of coinage. It also means Finely misses an essential element in his own contention regarding the omniscience of social and political control. Social and political innovation was crucial to the Greek adoption of coinage. The importance of coin-money to exchange and the ramifications of extended exchange through use of coin-money are sufficiently apparent as to cause Geoffrey Ingham, as noted in Chapter 9, under the heading 'Money valued in Taxation,' to abandon his primary theory of money as a unit of account in favour of a concept of money as a medium of exchange.

Alternative Definitions

Finley might have adopted a definition of economics that was nearer to his own understanding of ancient societies. He affirms, '"Satisfaction of material wants" is the key concept, not synonymous with the needs of the economy, of trade as such, or of a mercantile class.'[107] Alfred Marshall opens his *Principles of Economics* with the following definition:

> Political Economy or Economics is a study of mankind in the ordinary business of life; it examines that part of individual and social action which is most closely connected with the attainment and with the use of the material requisites of wellbeing.[108]

Marshall adds immediately:

> Thus it is on the one side a study of wealth; and on the other more important side a part of the study of man.

This definition connects economics with material wants, whether acquired by individual or social action. With this definition, Finley would have had the scope he clearly demands in an account of an economy. Users of Marshall's definition would surely be concerned with the impact of coin-money. They would also be able to take into account the role of Greek feasting in the conduct of the material affairs of ancient Greece and the adoption of coinage. Finley makes no mention of feasts. Either Finley has missed something important or Seaford exaggerates the significance of feasts. Seaford, of course, had access to a further thirty years of research. People's supernatural beliefs, and the organisation that goes with them, are commonly important to the conduct of state affairs. That Greek coins were called *oboloi* and *drachme* constitutes an obvious connection between money and feasts.

If Finley had wanted to follow in the footsteps of Polanyi, he might have adopted the definition of economics provided by Lionel Robbins:

> Economics is the science which studies human behaviour as a relationship between ends and scarce means which have alternative uses.[109]

Geoffrey Hodgson records that this definition was introduced by Robbins in 1932 to establish his economics faction at the London School of Economics in control of the discipline of 'economics,' at the expense of 'institutionalist' economists and 'historical' economists.[110] The definition opens up economics to mathematical codification, even requires a mathematical approach. The Robbins definition has dominated economics since the Second World War. Samuelson's textbooks teach resource allocation, with a strong mathematical content. 'Allocation of resources' is the principle on which mainstream economics is based. Robbins's definition is also, though not specifically referenced, the understanding of economics that Polanyi has in mind, since it has the distinctive 'self-regulating' quality emphasised by Polanyi. It is also very specifically limited to private agencies; state intervention would prevent the self-regulation that produces an optimal allocation of resources. Polanyi emphasises the requirement in economic theory for the state to keep out of economic affairs. That emphasis would not apply with Marshall's definition, or even with that of Roll. Finley is apparently familiar with the Robbins definition, since he refers to the element of 'scarce resources that is common in other formulations' in an endnote.[111] He argues that the resource-based definition would not affect his point, but the Robbins definition gives a different 'false account' and requires a different response. The Robbins definition, along with the formulation of neoclassical economic theory in the late-nineteenth century, has obscured for economists the nature of money and the significance of the introduction of coin-money. People engage in money-bargaining, not resource allocation. Resource utilisation and allocation are incidental outcomes of money-bargaining. Resources are more directly allocated through political and social processes; that is to say, through support-bargaining. Politics deals very specifically with 'who gets what?' Politics indirectly allocates resources through money-bargaining by choosing to accept extensive money-bargaining.

The economic model adopted into mainstream usage in accordance with the Robbins definition disembeds economics from society. It also disembeds theory from common observations of the reality of economic exchange. It was suggested in Chapter 5 that Polanyi mistakes economic theory for reality. That is in part the consequence of the detached character of the economic model. Reden notes that Polanyi fails to distinguish between economic principle and economic practice. His concept of market exchange is that of neoclassical theory, but he seeks the origin of it in market places and ports.[112] Polanyi's analysis founders partly because of the deficiencies of what he takes as economic theory. Finley denies himself any understanding of exchange through his treatment of economic theory.

What a pity that the Robbins definition of economics assembled the overwhelming support required to institutionalise it after the Second World War amongst professional academic economists, leaving definitions such as that of Marshall close to oblivion. Post-war students of economics were indoctrinated with neoclassical theory, so that microeconomic theory was constructed by reference not to economic behaviour but to the requirements of mathematical codification (Chapter 6). The takeover was surely connected to fears of communism and the Soviet Union in the aftermath of the War.[113]

Economics, Money-Bargaining and Slavery

Finley asks rhetorically, referring to the Roll definition of economics, 'But what if a society was not organized for the satisfaction of its material wants by "an enormous conglomeration of interdependent markets"?'[114] The implication, as Finley takes it, is that exchange and markets can be discounted as having relevance to ancient economies. But, of course, 'enormous conglomeration' is not necessary. Small confluences of people, as described in Chapter 5, under the heading 'Markets as Confluence,' can constitute functional markets for purposes of trade. Just two people can fix a price between them, though for the viability of anything like an ongoing business, some higher degree of confluence is normally necessary, so that sales are sufficient to meet the viability condition. Unit cost of provision is the primary consideration in the setting of prices. Towns and cities develop because they provide the conditions in which agents are most likely to format successfully. Dispersed populations trade in nearby cities, or failing that, arrange times and places where they will all assemble to trade. Money-bargaining is localised, not universal, like the market concept of mainstream economics, because situation, including locality, is the reference by which people assess their interests. This localism is accentuated by problems of transport, which do not arise in the neoclassical model. Someone wanting supper in the rural hinterland of ancient Athens would not be interested in a supper for sale in the middle of Athens. Cities are the confluences that incubated money-bargaining. Markets have evolved from small beginnings, only becoming 'enormous' in the era of railways, steam ships and globalisation in the nineteenth century.

The prominence of phenomena such as 'orders' and 'status,' and the pre-eminence of the state, are best understood in terms of social and political support-bargaining. Greek society, like every other society, moved in accordance with accumulations of support, both in a social context and a political context. Finley's account links status to occupations on the basis of moral concepts of what is 'right.' It reflects the same social attitudes as in nineteenth-century Britain, where the middle class disdained 'trade.' Military service, the church and a few professions were all the occupations in which a 'gentleman' could engage. It is a structure established by support-bargaining, but it required the reinforcement of money-bargaining. European societies in the nineteenth century were well stratified by 'status,' with each level made aware of what was expected of it, and not encouraged to neglect is assigned duties. India today still operates an informal caste system which assigns occupations on the basis of birth.

Engen acknowledges the wide acceptance of Finley's account of ancient economies, based on the subordination of economic activities to social and political considerations, and emphasising the well-being of the community over that of the individual.[115] He acknowledges also that the general picture presented by Finley has not been superceded.[116] But in spite of his general endorsement of Finley's account, Engen's own assessment of the ancient Greek economy has a markedly different emphasis:

> Throughout most of ancient Greek history before the Hellenistic period, a free enterprise economy with private property and limited government intervention predominated. This places Greece in sharp contrast to most other ancient civilizations, in which governmental or religious institutions tended to dominate the economy. The main economic concerns of the governments of the Greek city-states were to maintain harmony within the private economy (make laws, adjudicate disputes, and protect private property rights), make sure that food was available to their citizenries at reasonable prices, and obtain revenue from economic activities (through taxes) to pay for government expenses.[117]

Described in such terms, ancient Greek society and its economy seem comparable to modern European society. An 'economy' did exist, identifiably separate from social and political affairs. Yet Engen also accepts Finley's general account of how the 'free enterprise economy' worked: based on 'orders' and 'status,' which largely eliminated the freedom necessary to the market dynamic. Agricultural occupations were socially acceptable, while the *banausic* trades were for those of inferior status.[118] Chattel slaves constituted the lowest order of society. Wage labour was akin to slavery.[119] 'Market pressures' to improve productivity were not felt. Even so, Engen's account of trade suggests a fair degree of freedom to innovate and take advantage of opportunities.[120] The freedom to trade included the freedom to buy and sell slaves, thus denying a large section of the population its freedom. Engen's description of price setting suggests the dynamic of money-bargaining: 'For the most part in ancient Greece, prices were set in accordance with local conditions, personal relationships, and haggling.'[121]

Engen seems conflicted over the nature of the ancient Greek economy, perhaps because, as he remarks, 'Basically, given the quantity and the quality of the available evidence, our attempts to understand the ancient Greek economy are greatly affected by the perspective from which we approach it.'[122] Engen views both from Finley's point of view and from the point of view of modern macroeconomic theory. Finley's view derives, as he acknowledges, from Weber, Hasebroek and Polanyi. But it also derives more broadly from modern theory groups on the left.[123] Deficiencies of evidence leave great scope for analysts to fill in the gaps with whatever 'fits' their frame of reference. Analysts select, interpret and impute by reference to the modern frames of reference they have adopted. Assessments of ancient economies then owe as much to modern intellectual support-bargaining as to the facts of ancient societies.

The major distinction between ancient Greek society and societies of today may lie not so much in the presence or absence of markets as in the prominence of violent coercion by the state. Coercion was essential to the maintenance of slavery as a fundamental of ancient Greek society and economy. Engen writes:

> Slaves comprised an undeniably large part of the labor force of ancient Greece. In fact, it is fair to say, as Finley did, that ancient Greece was a 'slave dependent society.' There were so many slaves; they were so essential to the economy; and they became so thoroughly embedded into the every day life and values of the society that without slavery, ancient Greek civilization could not have existed in the manner it did.[124]

The Greek poleis were the beginning of democracy, but only the beginning. The support deployed in support-bargaining is proxy for violence, but actual violence was readily on call as an essential element in the maintenance of the social order. The harshness of slavery, and no doubt the threat from disgruntled slaves, was tempered by the scope for slaves to take on significant jobs and obtain freedom.

Engen is also conflicted over slavery. In spite of the above quotation, he writes, 'Slaves existed, but not in such large numbers as to make the economy and society dependent on them.'[125] But 120,000 slaves in Athens in a total population of 305,000 speak for themselves – Engen himself draws attention to the implications of such numbers.[126] Slavery on that scale would seriously weaken the bargaining positions of free people in pursuit of remunerative occupations. Wage labour creates diverse money-bargaining chains that sustain varied economic activity across a society; the maintenance of slaves by their owners constrains the emergence of such chains. Take away the slaves and the society and economy would be radically different.

It is understandable that Finley should reject modern mainstream economic theory as a basis for analysis of the ancient economy. But in citing Roll's definition of economics, and emphasising the 'enormous conglomerations,' he obscures for himself some important aspects of the ancient economy. Engen concludes with the comment that, 'As more research is done, it may even be necessary to replace the Finley model altogether in favor of one that fits the evidence better.'[127] The idea of money-bargaining provides a theoretical framework by which the functioning of ancient economies can be better understood. In particular, it provides a framework in which the significance of the adoption of coin-money can be appraised, not just in relation to its impact on society, but in relation also to the social and political conditions necessary to its adoption. Slavery is part of money-bargaining, in that slaves could be bought and sold. But the existence of such sales was made possible by violent coercion, and the labour of slaves was similarly exacted through violent coercion. Slavery exemplifies in extreme form the coercive character of societies, which over time increasingly used support-bargaining for the conduct of their affairs. The polis exemplifies the early emergence of support-bargaining in this role, albeit with limited scope. Over time, the labour of all, though not all labour, under the aegis of political support-bargaining, became a matter of money-bargaining.

Finley exemplifies the difficulties that anthropologists and historians have in interpreting economic aspects of ancient history. The available mainstream economic frame of reference is plainly inapplicable; inapplicable to any economy in any age, but perhaps particularly irrelevant to ancient economies. Yet it is hard to interpret an ancient economy without some theoretical reference dealing with material exchange. As was seen in Chapter 4, some frame of reference seems essential to our thinking.

Notes

1 Martin, John, 1991/1817, *Tonga Islands: William Mariner's Account*, Tonga: Vava'u Press, p. 154. First published London, 1817. See also Spread, Patrick, 2013, *Support-Bargaining, Economics and Society: A Social Species*, London: Routledge, pp. 200–6.
2 Seaford, Richard, 2004, *Money and the Early Greek Mind*, Cambridge: Cambridge University Press, p. 34.
3 See quotation from Seaford at Chapter 2, fn. 41; see also Seaford, 2004, p. 67.
4 Seaford, 2004, p. 69.
5 Seaford, 2004, p. 76.
6 Seaford, 2004, p. 76.
7 Seaford, 2004, p. 76. Original emphasis.
8 Seaford, 2004, p. 80.
9 Seaford, 2004, p. 81.
10 Seaford, 2004, p. 81.
11 Seaford, 2004, p. 81.
12 Schaps, David, 2004, *The Invention of Coinage and the Monetization of Ancient Greece*, Ann Arbor: University of Michigan Press, Kindle Edition, L2162.
13 Schaps, 2004, L2155.
14 Schaps, 2004, L2164.
15 Schaps, 2004, L2712–5, 2709.
16 Seaford, 2004, p. 103.
17 Seaford, 2004, p. 108.
18 Schaps, 2004, L2192.
19 Schaps, 2004, L2184.
20 Seaford, 2004, p. 78.

21 Silver, Morris, 2004, 'Review of Schaps, David M., 2004, *The Invention of Coinage and the Monetization of Ancient Greece*', Ann Arbor: University of Michigan Press, EH.net, p. 13. https://eh.net/?s=The+Invention+of+Coinage+and+the+Monetization+of+Ancient+Greece. Accessed 6 April 2021. (Page numbers refer to article displayed in MS Word.)
22 Seaford, 2004, pp. 36–7, 157–8.
23 Schaps, 2004, L2192–2201.
24 Seaford, 2004, p. 125.
25 Seaford, 2004, p. 127–8.
26 Schaps, 2004, L. 2469–75.
27 Kim, Henry S., 'Archaic Coinage as Evidence for the Use of Money', in Andrew Meadows and Kirsty Shipton, *Money and Its Uses in the Ancient World*, Oxford: Oxford University Press, p. 10.
28 Schaps, 2004, L2671.
29 Schaps, 2004, L2671–9.
30 Kim, 2001, p. 11.
31 Schaps, 2004, L2495–503.
32 Schaps, 2004, L2716–26.
33 Schaps, 2004, L2716–20.
34 Schaps, 2004, L2720.
35 Schaps, 2004, L2726.
36 Kurke, Leslie, 1999, *Coins, Bodies, Games and Gold: The Politics of Meaning in Archaic Greece*, Princeton: Princeton University Press.
37 Reden, Sitta von, 1995, *Exchange in Ancient Greece*, London: Duckworth, p. 175.
38 Kurke, 1999, p. 17.
39 Kurke, 1999, p. 18–9.
40 See, for example, Seaford, 2004, p. 15.
41 Kurke, 1999, p. 23.
42 Engen, Darel Tai, 2004, 'The Economy of Ancient Greece', *EH.Net*, p. 9. https://eh.net/?s=the+economy+of+ancient+greece. Accessed 6 April 2021. (Page numbers refer to article displayed in MS Word.)
43 Engen, 2004, p. 19.
44 Schaps, 2004, L3066.
45 Schaps, 2004, L3753–61.
46 Finley, Moses, 1973, *The Ancient Economy*, London: Chatto & Windus, p. 30.
47 Trevett, Jeremy, 2001, 'Coinage and Democracy at Athens', in Meadows and Shipton, 2001, p. 24; see also p. 33.
48 Trevett, 2001, p. 33.
49 Trevett, 2001, pp. 24–5.
50 Trevett, 2001, p. 33.
51 Seaford, 2004, pp. 7, 16–9. Original emphasis.
52 Seaford, 2004, p. 320.
53 Seaford, 2004, p. 319, Note 4; referring to Silver, Morris, 1985, *Economic Structures of the Ancient Near East*, London: Croom Helm.
54 Seaford, 2004, pp. 318, 333–7.
55 Seaford, 2004, p. 320.
56 Seaford, 2004, p. 323.
57 Seaford, 2004, pp. 323–5.
58 Seaford, 2004, p. 321.

59 Schaps, 2004, L3894–966.
60 Schaps, 2004, L2996.
61 Schaps, 2004, L3002.
62 Schaps, 2004, L2959.
63 Schaps, 2004, L2952–9.
64 Kraay, C., 1964, 'Hoards, Small Change and the Origin of Coinage', *Journal of Hellenic Studies*, Vol. 84, pp. 76–91, p. 85.
65 Kim, H. 2001. 'Archaic Coinage as Evidence for the Use of Money', in Meadows and Shipton, 2001.
66 Kim, 2001, p. 12–3.
67 Kim, 2001, p. 13.
68 Engen, 2004, p. 34.
69 Schaps, 2004, L2733.
70 Schaps, 2004, L2745–52.
71 Schaps, 2004, L5196.
72 Kurke, 1999, p. 5.
73 Kurke, 1999, p. 32.
74 Schaps, 2004, L4598–604. See also Seaford, 2004, pp. 157–62.
75 Schaps, 2004, L4624.
76 Schaps, 2004, L4624–34.
77 Schaps, 2004, L4770–81. Schaps's modern sources on Greek banking include: Bogaert, Raymond, 1966, *Les Origines Antique de la Banque de Dépôt*, Leiden: Sijthoff; Bogaert, Raymond, 1968, *Banques et Banquiers dans les Cités Grecques*, Leiden: Sijthoff; Cohen, Edward E., 1992, *Athenian Economy and Society: A Banking Perspective*, Princeton: Princeton University Press; Millet, Paul, 1991, *Lending and Borrowing in Ancient Athens*, Cambridge: Cambridge University Press.
78 Seaford, 2004, p. 293.
79 Seaford, 2004, p. 317.
80 Seaford, 2004, p. 15. Original emphasis.
81 Seaford, 2004, p. 292.
82 Seaford, 2004, p. 321.
83 Seaford, 2004, pp. 292–3, 298–301.
84 Seaford, 2004, p. 300.
85 Spread, 2013, pp. 256–7; Spread, Patrick, 2019, *Economics for an Information Age*, London: Routledge, p. 55.
86 Seaford, 2004, p. 295, fn. 8.
87 Seaford, 2004, p. 294–5, fn. 8.
88 Schaps, 2004, L4701–10.
89 Schaps, 2004, L4726.
90 Schaps, 2004, L4895–919.
91 Finley, M. I., 1981, *Economy and Society in Ancient Greece*, London: Chatto & Windus, p. 74.
92 Finley, 1981, p. 73.
93 Finley, M. I., 1981, 'Land, Debt and the Man of Property in Classical Athens', in Finley, M. I., 1981, *Economy and Society in Ancient Greece*, London: Chatto & Windus, pp. 64–76. Reprint of Finley M. I., 1953, 'Land, Debt and the Man of Property in Classical Athens', *Political Science Quarterly*, Vol. 68, pp. 249–68.

94 Hasebroek, J., 1933, *Trade and Politics in Ancient Greece*, Trans. L. M. Fraser and D. C. MacGregor, London: G. Bell. Original: Hasebroek, J., 1928, *Staat und Handel im alten Griechenland*, Tübingen: J.C.B. Mohr (P. Siebeck).
95 Finley, 1973, p. 26.
96 Roll, Eric, 1945, *A History of Economic Thought*, London: Faber and Faber, p. 373. Quoted by Finley, 1973, p. 22.
97 Finley, 1973, p. 23.
98 Finley, 1973, p. 154.
99 Engen, 2004, p. 5.
100 Finley, 1973, p. 144.
101 Reden, Sitta von, 1995, *Exchange in Ancient Greece*, London: Duckworth, p. 5.
102 Finley, 1973, p. 155.
103 Finley, 1973, p. 174.
104 Finley, 1973, p. 155.
105 Finley, 1973, pp. 141, 166–9.
106 Engen, 2004, p. 33.
107 Finley, 1973, p. 160.
108 Marshall, Alfred, 1920, *Principles of Economics*, 8th Edition, London: Macmillan, p. 1.
109 Robbins, Lionel, 1932, *An Essay on the Nature and Significance of Economic Science*, London: Macmillan, p. 15.
110 Hodgson, Geoffrey, 2001, *How Economics Forgot History: The Problem of Historical Specificity in Social Science*, London and New York: Routledge, p. 207.
111 Finley, 1973, p. 180, Note 16.
112 Reden, 1995, p. 105.
113 For further comment see Spread, Patrick, 2016, *The Evolution of Economies: Money-Bargaining, Economic Change and Industrial Revolution*, London and New York: Routledge; Spread, 2019a.
114 Finley, 1973, p. 22.
115 Engen, 2004, pp. 7–8.
116 Engen, 2004, p. 10.
117 Engen, 2004, p. 15.
118 Engen, 2004, p. 8.
119 Engen, 2004, p. 20.
120 Engen, 2004, pp. 24–32.
121 Engen, 2004, p. 28.
122 Engen, 2004, p. 11.
123 Shaw, Brent D. and Saller, Richard P., 1981, 'Introduction' to Finley, M. I., 1981, *Economy and Society in Ancient Greece*, London: Chatto & Windus, pp. ix–xiii.
124 Engen, 2004, p. 21.
125 Engen, 2004, p. 12.
126 Engen, 2004, p. 21.
127 Engen, 2004, p. 39.

References

Bogaert, Raymond, 1966, *Les Origines Antique de la Banque de Dépôt*, Leiden: Sijthoff.
Bogaert, Raymond, 1968, *Banques et Banquiers dans les Cités Grecques*, Leiden: Sijthoff.

Cohen, Edward E., 1992, *Athenian Economy and Society: A Banking Perspective*, Princeton: Princeton University Press;
Engen, Darel Tai, 2004, 'The Economy of Ancient Greece', EH.Net. https://eh.net/?s=the+economy+of+ancient+greece. Accessed 6 April 2021.
Finley M. I., 1953, 'Land, Debt and the Man of Property in Classical Athens', *Political Science Quarterly*, Vol. 68, pp. 249–68.
Finley, M. I., 1981, 'Land, Debt and the Man of Property in Classical Athens', in M. I. Finley (Ed.), *Economy and Society in Ancient Greece*, London: Chatto & Windus, pp. 64–76.
Finley, M. I., 1981, *Economy and Society in Ancient Greece*, London: Chatto & Windus.
Finley, Moses, 1973, *The Ancient Economy*, London: Chatto & Windus.
Hasebroek, J., 1928, *Staat und Handel im alten Griechenland*, Tübingen: J.C.B. Mohr (P. Siebeck).
Hasebroek, J., 1933, *Trade and Politics in Ancient Greece*, Trans. L. M. Fraser and D. C. MacGregor, London: G. Bell.
Hodgson, Geoffrey, 2001, *How Economics Forgot History: The Problem of Historical Specificity in Social Science*, London and New York: Routledge.
Kim, Henry S., 2001, 'Archaic Coinage as Evidence for the Use of Money', in Andrew Meadows and Kirsty Shipton (Eds.), *Money and Its Uses in the Ancient Greek World*, Oxford: Oxford University Press.
Kraay, C., 1964, 'Hoards, Small Change and the Origin of Coinage', *Journal of Hellenic Studies*, Vol. 84, pp. 76–91.
Kurke, Leslie, 1999, *Coins, Bodies, Games and Gold: The Politics of Meaning in Archaic Greece*, Princeton: Princeton University Press.
Marshall, Alfred, 1920, *Principles of Economics*, 8th Edition, London: Macmillan.
Martin, John, 1991/1817, *Tonga Islands: William Mariner's Account*, Tonga: Vava'u Press. First published London, 1817.
Meadows, Andrew and Shipton, Kirsty, 2001, *Money and Its Uses in the Ancient Greek World*, Oxford: Oxford University Press.
Millet, Paul, 1991, *Lending and Borrowing in Ancient Athens*, Cambridge: Cambridge University Press.
Reden, Sitta von, 1995, *Exchange in Ancient Greece*, London: Duckworth.
Robbins, Lionel, 1932, *An Essay on the Nature and Significance of Economic Science*, London: Macmillan.
Roll, Eric, 1945, *A History of Economic Thought*, London: Faber and Faber.
Schaps, David, 2004, *The Invention of Coinage and the Monetization of Ancient Greece*, Ann Arbor: University of Michigan Press, Kindle Edition.
Seaford, Richard, 2004, *Money and the Early Greek Mind*, Cambridge: Cambridge University Press.
Shaw, Brent D. and Saller, Richard P., 1981, 'Introduction' to Finley, M. I., 1981, *Economy and Society in Ancient Greece* , London: Chatto & Windus, pp. ix–xiii.
Silver, Morris, 1985, *Economic Structures of the Ancient Near East*, London: Croom Helm.
Silver, Morris, 2004, 'Review of Schaps, David M., 2004, *The Invention of Coinage and the Monetization of Ancient Greece*', Ann Arbor: University of Michigan Press, EH.net. https://eh.net/?s=The+Invention+of+Coinage+and+the+Monetization+of+Ancient+Greece. Accessed 6 April 2021.
Spread, Patrick, 2013, *Support-Bargaining, Economics and Society: A Social Species*, London: Routledge.

Spread, Patrick, 2016, *The Evolution of Economies: Money-Bargaining, Economic Change and Industrial Revolution*, London and New York: Routledge.

Spread, Patrick, 2019a, *Economics for an Information Age*, London: Routledge.

Trevett, Jeremy, 2001, 'Coinage and Democracy at Athens', in Andrew Meadows and Kirsty Shipton (Eds.), *Money and Its Uses in the Ancient Greek World*, Oxford: Oxford University Press.

12 Conclusion

Money as a Bargaining Counter

It must be familiarity that makes money seem so simple, for its complexity has brought confusion to both economists and economic anthropologists. The concept of money as a bargaining counter maintains the superficial simplicity. A common bargaining counter makes possible the common trade in goods and services in an economy. But how it does so is best explained in terms of the bargaining counter constituting a credit accorded by society and redeemed by individual agents of the society through provision of goods and services. A sale of goods or services constitutes the redemption of the credit owing to the holder of the bargaining counter. The bargaining counter passes as a new credit to the seller. The bargaining counter thus moves through a society as credit to participating agents. Sellers of goods and services function as 'dependable debtors' in relation to the social credit. They assure the purchasing power of the bargaining counter. Money is then something like, as Ingham describes it, 'the pivotal institution of modern capitalism' (Chapter 6, Note 47). It is the bargaining counter of money-bargaining. It functions as a movable credit, accepted by all who engage in money-bargaining in the society of its adoption. Economic theory has to start with money, not scrabble to accommodate it as an awkward appendage.

The confusion of economists and economic anthropologists arises from the frames of reference they have established for themselves. It was seen in Chapter 4 that the assembly of support for interests, the essential purpose of support-bargaining, involves the assembly of support through intellectual support-bargaining for theoretical frames of reference that focus attention on observations and interpretations favourable to the interests of those formulating the theories. The frames of reference control the selection and interpretation of information. The idea of frames of reference is essential to a coherent account of the efforts of economists and economic anthropologists to provide theories of society and the origin of money. The frames of reference developed by both mainstream economists and economic anthropologists are formulated for the assembly of support for their interests, rather than to explain the workings of economies, whether ancient or modern. As a consequence, both have difficulty in explaining the nature of money. It is an awkward fit to either frame of reference.

DOI: 10.4324/9781003313472-14

Mainstream microeconomic theory, or neoclassical theory, is concerned to demonstrate the benefits to society of free individual initiative. The neoclassical model of the late-nineteenth century responded to extensions of the franchise, or in more alarmist terms the threat of 'mob rule' and a rising of 'the masses' to overwhelm the ruling elite of the time. In the aftermath of the Second World War, with the emergence of the Cold War between Western nations and the Soviet Union and communist China, the resource-based definition of economics provided by Lionel Robbins, a definition based on the neoclassical model, formulated in the context of factional disputes in the intellectual support-bargaining of professional economists, was adopted as the best means of assembling support for ideas of individual freedom and enterprise. Such ideas incorporated an appealing ethic of rugged self-reliance and independence, contrasted with the discreditable dependence of subordination to a group. Such a frame of reference for economic enquiry also offered security against a different sort of group when in the early 1950s Senator Eugene McCarthy launched an inquisition against communist tendencies in American society, including its intellectual society. A mathematical model could hardly be construed as subversive of the American way. Beyond the pale of the neoclassical model, life could be difficult. Moses Finley was obliged to leave the United States after a run-in with the McCarthy enquiry.[1]

Mainstream microeconomic theory developed its mathematical model of competitive dynamics in a limiting framework of assumptions about the agents involved (many small buyers and sellers), the products involved (standard homogeneous products) and the information available (perfect information about quantities, prices and anything else relevant to the market model). It incorporates no idea of spatial distribution of trade, or of time disparities and the budgets necessary to deal with them, or that needs and wants are dictated by situation, or of the importance of organisation and the role of companies, or of the manipulation of information, and no idea of the major role of the state in a functioning economy. All these deficiencies are the subject of 'modifications' to neoclassical theory, supposedly reconciling the model with observed realities. But the modifications do no more than confirm the deficiencies of the model.

Microeconomic theorists wholly reject the idea that their theory might constitute a frame of reference, constructed through selective observation and interpretation to advance their own interests. The mathematical formulation of the theory is regarded as giving it universal application, rather than constraining it to a narrow range of observations that can be treated mathematically, or reconceived in such a way as to permit mathematical treatment. It is mathematically simpler if transactions are distinct and of immediate completion, leading to neglect of time disparities, the need for credit and the use of budgets. Immediate transactions are also more private than those which involve credit. In the extreme form of the neoclassical model, the Arrow-Debreu model, once regarded as the definitive account, all transactions occur simultaneously.[2]

The microeconomic model is justified not on the basis of realistic representation of the functioning of an economy, but on the basis of resource allocation.

Strictly within the basic assumptions of the model, available resources are allocated mathematically in a way that is optimal – maximum output from given resources. Hence it was morally desirable that individuals should have freedom to trade. 'Optimal allocation' is a property only of the simplest version of the model, so that the argument requires justification of the simplest model. The neoclassical concept has no need for money, and no theoretical space to accommodate it. Neoclassical theory is concerned with resource allocation through an idealised model of exchange, with only a passing resemblance to the exchanges that actually take place in economies. Actual exchanges require money as a bargaining counter.

But even neoclassical economists have had to recognise the existence of money. It was excused, rather than explained, as a 'veil' overlying the real nature of material exchange – the barter of commodities. The model rendered in mathematical terms what was essentially a process of barter, with each commodity valued in relation to others. Money did not affect the valuations, but provided a common measure for the practical conduct of what was fundamentally barter exchange.

The management of actual economies required direct attention to many observable aspects of economic behaviour that appeared at best in modifications to the neoclassical model. Macroeconomic analysis developed as a basis for the management of economies. Understanding the practical functioning of economies opened up prospects of overcoming impediments to growth, establishing stable prices, maintaining levels of employment and responding to many other indications of national and international economic circumstances. A large part of macroeconomic analysis has used neoclassical theory as its frame of reference, because that is the accepted frame amongst economists – all economists are instructed in that frame of reference. But the neoclassical frame of reference has come to be acknowledged as incompatible with macroeconomic observation. The necessity of response to observation of the functioning of economies caused macroeconomic analysis to move substantially apart from neoclassical theory, recognising early on, for example, that 'free trade' did not necessarily promote competition. Companies did their best to minimise competition. The United States led in passing 'anti-trust' laws promoting competition. Polanyi concentrated on the 'self-regulating markets' of neoclassical theory that could be used to substantiate his case against capitalism; he was inclined to overlook the macroeconomic dimensions of economics. Macroeconomic analysis, at least that extensive part of it which pays little heed to neoclassical microeconomic theory, provides the essential information necessary to the management of economies. The idea of support-bargaining and money-bargaining fills the gap left by the failure of neoclassical theory. It provides a microeconomic explanation of macroeconomic behaviour.

Consideration of macroeconomic behaviour provided a more plausible account of the nature of money. Adam Smith described money as emerging from barter as a common commodity, a commodity in such common use as to have both value in use and value in exchange. Tokens were introduced to represent a common commodity for the facilitation of exchange. From these origins, money is naturally understood as a commodity, either an actual commodity or representative of a commodity. Barter is conceived as completed immediately, and the 'money commodity' is similarly conceived as settling transactions immediately. A 'money commodity' gives immediate satisfaction, just like an ordinary commodity. In Karl Menger's account of money, mentioned in Chapter 7, a commodity can function as money because of its 'saleability.'

Yet deferred barter has been widely practiced, accommodating in the barter process the time disparities that are inseparable from satisfaction of material needs. It introduces the idea of credit to transactions. The receiver of some commodity acknowledges a debt to the provider, to be repaid at a later date. A token provided in exchange for some commodity constitutes an acknowledgement of a debt to the recipient of the token. But in the case of the token, the debt can be a communal debt, rather than a debt to the individual provider of the commodity. A token recognised and accepted across a community is money, and represents a communal credit and debt of the community. Acceptance of the communal credit and debt is a condition of use of the token. The communal credit is redeemed by acceptance of the money token in exchange for goods and services from anyone in the community inclined to offer such goods and services for sale. So long as there are dependable debtors, a token has purchasing power and functions as a bargaining counter.

The neoclassical economic model suggests an 'optimal allocation of resources' as the natural outcome of 'free trade,' and hence good reason for allowing individuals maximum freedom to trade. It has thus assisted in the assembly of support for the 'individualist' side in the ongoing contention between individual and group which is fundamental to support-bargaining. The slow and reluctant acceptance amongst economists of the idea of money as credit is connected with this contention. Credit provision implies extended relationships with conflicting interests, and hence the necessity for regulation by the state. Acceptance of a credit theory of money implies acceptance of state intervention for the regulation of economic affairs.

Anthropologists have understandably scorned the mainstream economists' account of economic behaviour. They note that the conditions assumed in the microeconomic model, unrealistic in any age, are especially unrealistic in the context of ancient societies such as those of the Eastern Mediterranean and Near East. Their research suggests that the markets of 'supply and demand' portrayed in the neoclassical model did not exist in the ancient world. That, however, does not mean that there was not sufficient private exchange in the ancient world to give rise to price agreements and exchange. Around the world today people engage in exchange in circumstances far removed from those of neoclassical market assumptions. 'Money bargaining' catches the dynamic, and very likely the dynamic of ancient exchange – Heichelheim's account of behaviour in ancient economies is easily understood in terms of money-bargaining.

Anthropologists argue also that there is no evidence for the emergence of money from barter. Strictly defined, evidence of barter societies from which money did or might have emerged has been difficult to find. Anthropologists suggest a process of 'reciprocity and redistribution' as characteristic of ancient societies, in which material interests are accommodated in the course of establishment of social relations. 'Reciprocity' is gift-giving amongst members of a society. Transactions not conforming to a strict definition of barter are reckoned to be 'reciprocity.' 'Reciprocity and redistribution' are generally presented in terms of benign societies in which individual interest is subordinated to the group. 'Redistribution,' in this benign view, is the redistribution of material benefits from the rich to the needy through communal authorities. Most of those adopting the idea of 'reciprocity and redistribution' follow its instigator, Polanyi, in treating it not just as a description of ancient societies, but also as a prescription for the reform of modern societies.

'Money of account' economic anthropology derives from the left-wing and 'anti-capitalist' frames of reference used by Polanyi. It looks on the ancient world, and on neoclassical economic theory, with an eye to the assembly of support in opposition to ideas of competition and free trade. It advances the 'group' interest by portraying idealised societies based on group cooperation and harmonious group sentiment. It advances current interests through the adoption of frames of reference that impose certain interpretations on the limited evidence available concerning ancient societies. The political frames of reference are invariably associated with moral frames of reference, as a means of ensuring maximum assembly of support. Ethical codes derive mostly from religious teaching, based on the instruction of inspirational leaders. As was seen in Chapter 3, supernatural belief constitutes a major focus for the assembly of support. Polanyi's work, and that of his followers, is strongly imbued with ethical notions of the way humans should treat each other and the contention that in systems of 'reciprocity and redistribution' humans have actually treated each other in the prescribed manner.

Economic anthropologists have little use for money as a medium of exchange. Material interests in a system of 'reciprocity and redistribution' are accommodated by gift-giving and the distributions of a central authority. Nevertheless, the existence of money demands explanation. It is argued that money came into being as a 'money of account,' without reference to any role in exchange. The large temple and palace organisations of ancient Mesopotamia adopted a money-of-account as a means of controlling their affairs. Money originated as a matter of accounting or organisational convenience. The money-of-account is held to be valued through its acceptance by the state in payments due to the state, in particular acceptance in payment of taxes.

This account of the origin of money may originate in the lack of any understanding of time disparities and budgeting in neoclassical economic theory. If that concept had been present in economic theory, economic anthropologists might have put a different interpretation on the 'money of account' they conceive as arising as a matter of organisational expedience. The temple and palace accounts are clearly part of budgetary processes. But even given the economists' omission, economic anthropologists might have worked out for themselves the nature of the usage of money accounts by temples and palaces. Budgeting is not an obscure process. Heichelheim identifies it in ancient practices (Chapter 9, Note 55). The failure has to be connected with the choice of a frame of reference that tends to exclude private individual motivations, at least those of a constructive kind, and promote the ascendancy of the state.

Without reference to exchange means without reference to purchasing power. Acceptance by the state in payment of taxes provides no reference to purchasing power. The concept of money as a bargaining counter indicates that money has value for its users because of the existence of dependable debtors in its user community who will make good the social credit represented by the money through provision of goods and services in exchange for it. That is what gives it purchasing power, and is the foundation of public confidence in a bargaining counter. Valuation by acceptance in taxation implies quite the contrary – that people become indebted by virtue of their engagement with the state money, and are obliged to pay taxes to settle the debt. It is conceivable that a state money could be issued as a state credit, redeemable at state stores providing goods and services. This is analogous to the provision of tokens by companies for redemption at a company store. But such systems are nowhere apparent. It appears rather that the option providing extensive choice to people over how their credit will be redeemed has given bargaining counters involving that choice superior purchasing power. With that, such bargaining counters have generated greater confidence and become extensively used in societies. People will not willingly accept that what has been accorded to them as a credit for services rendered can be taken from them in repayment of a debt forced upon them. Geoffrey Ingham seems to acknowledge the weakness of the idea of a money-of-account given value by taxation when he affirms that the change to coin-money brought about a transition from money as a 'money of account' to money as a 'medium of exchange.'[3] A change in the form of money is held to bring about a radical change in the concept of money. There seems no reason why what was used as money before coinage should not be conceived also as a 'medium of exchange.' And beyond that, no reason to believe that money did not originate as a 'medium of exchange.' Or rather, as a bargaining counter, functioning as a credit to bridge time disparities. With that origin, the role of money as a unit of budgetary account becomes plain.

Anthropologists emphasise the failure of mainstream economic theory to recognise, either in the neoclassical model or in its account of money as deriving from barter, the importance of credit to the functioning of economies and the idea of money as credit. Economists have preferred to treat money as a 'commodity,' whereas economic anthropologists have affirmed the alternative view of money as 'credit.' Time disparities require the use of credit in some form. Under the benign view of 'reciprocity and redistribution,' money is intrusive. It subverts social justice and communal order. As state engagement, for a neoclassical economist, impedes the optimal allocation of resources, so the use of money credit in a system of 'reciprocity and redistribution' is detrimental to social justice. In the interpretations of economic anthropologists, debt is typically used by the rich and powerful to subordinate the weak and defenceless. Such interpretation fits neatly into an 'anti-capitalist' frame of reference, with modern resonance. Credit is the means by which the financial services industry, the iconic capitalists, gains its dominance of people, governments and Western society.

The idea of support-bargaining and money-bargaining thus suggests that the confusion over money in economic theory and amongst economic anthropologists arises from the frames of reference they have developed for the advance of current interests. Neither provides a satisfactory explanation of the evidence available, either with regard to the nature of modern usage of money or, more particularly, with regard to the origins of money. The debate over ancient societies and the origins of money reflects the modern contention between those who argue the importance of individual freedom of action and those who favour the ascendancy of the group. Money as bargaining counter provides a more consistent explanation of practices relating to money across the ages. It points to an origin in the various times and places where problems of barter were being resolved in different communities by the use of makeshift bargaining counters amongst ordinary people, with the most used of the bargaining counters becoming subject to communal administration through whatever there was of communal authority. The bargaining counters functioned as social credit, making possible the accommodation of the time disparities between revenues and expenditures that are inseparable from human affairs.

Authorities would be concerned primarily with their own maintenance of authority. Societies have historically been ruled mostly by autocrats or authoritarian regimes with preponderant capacity for violence. To such regimes, independent wealth would constitute a threat to their ascendancy. Whilst the threat might be manageable when money was cumbersome and in short supply, the wide circulation of coins would constitute a more significant threat. Money functions as an alternative bargaining counter to support. People will act to secure support, but they will also act to secure money. If people are not dependent for their security and prosperity on a ruling faction, the hold of the ruling faction on its people will slip. Hence autocratic rulers are likely to oppose or control very tightly the use of money. Given the potential of coinage, on account of its convenience, they would be unlikely to conceive of anything so subversive, and on being made aware of it, would be likely to oppose its introduction.

Coinage implied such convenience and flexibility as to offer to anyone, high or low in the established social order, the opportunity to become rich. Coin-money implied the capacity to buy services. It implied the potential to form organisations for the systematic and focused pursuit of interests. Thus whilst technology for minting of coins existed all across the Eastern Mediterranean and Near East in ancient times, it was not employed for minting until some time in the seventh century BCE. It is unlikely that people thought of making coins and rejected the idea as too dangerous; it is rather probable that the idea was beyond contemplation for those whose instincts were attuned to the maintenance of the support necessary to their continued ascendancy. Even when the idea was put into effect in Lydia, its usage was limited. It took the particular social order of the Greek *poleis* in the late sixth century BCE to adopt coinage for general usage. Some Greek states felt sufficiently secure to introduce coin-money.

As it turned out, whilst coin-money displaced support in some respects, it was also very prominently a supplementary bargaining counter. The character of coin-money, being portable, durable, divisible, countable, controllable, visible and tangible, gave it application in numerous transactions that were not possible with support as the bargaining counter or with the earlier cumbersome forms of money. The supplementary bargaining counter caught on in a big way.

Putting Bargaining Counters into Circulation

For something to be recognised and used as a bargaining counter, it has to have dependable value in exchange. It has to have purchasing power. People must be willing to accept it in exchange for goods, and be prepared to work for it. But such qualities only arise from usage in a money-bargaining system. Distributing a bargaining counter freely implies that it is of no value. Perennial shortages of money for the conduct of trade seem to originate in the difficulties of getting a bargaining counter into circulation whilst ensuring that it has recognised value.

Direct concern over the means of putting money into circulations has been largely subsumed under the question of 'what is money?' That determined, the issue of circulation seems settled. If money is a commodity, the circulation of money depends on the supply of the commodity. If a credit, the supply of money depends on the dispositions of those providing and accepting credit. But with money conceived as a bargaining counter, the means of putting the bargaining counter into circulation becomes a focus of attention.

Along with that issue, there arises the associated issue of ensuring that the right amount of money gets into circulation. Insufficient money in circulation constrains trade, obliging traders to make shift as best they can. Oversupply of a bargaining counter, in the absence of mitigating factors, causes rising prices and a fall in the purchasing power of money. 'Oversupply' naturally implies that the basic question of getting money into circulation has been resolved. The issue becomes that of 'money supply' and the control of inflation.

The Earliest Bargaining Counters

To gain initial circulation and function as a bargaining counter, a commodity needs some value independent of its use as a bargaining counter. Thus the earliest bargaining counters seem to have had value independent of their transactional value. They had value as utilitarian commodities, as foodstuffs and utensils are valued for their utility. They were adopted as 'makeshift' bargaining counters to reduce the inconveniences of barter.

In the understanding of support-bargaining and money-bargaining, these 'makeshift' bargaining counters were primarily valued by reference to their satisfaction of requirements related to the physical or social situation of those acquiring them (Chapter 6). Oil or honey would have primary valuation as food; utensils would be valued for their practical applications in the kitchen. But in addition to this primary valuation, they might come to be valued further by reference to the budgetary requirements of those acquiring them. With the observation that they were widely accepted in exchange for other items, they would be acquired with a view to later purchases of other items. They would bridge time disparities between current sale of goods and anticipated future requirements. The holders of such dual-value commodities could consume them, give them away or use them, or they could be exchanged at some time for other goods and services, according to circumstances.

The earliest forms of money, such as those listed by Heichelheim – honey, sesame, reeds, garlic, oil, etc. (Chapter 9, Note 32) – are mostly commodities that would be available in the common course of life. No special effort would be needed for them to be available as 'money.' Their value was conferred by their use value. They were so commonly used that they could take on a budgetary function. Heichelheim records that use of these commodities died away. They may nevertheless have been used, either intermittently or continuously, for long periods. Most of them clearly lack such qualities as dependable availability and durability that would be desirable in a permanent bargaining counter. Experience would suggest improvements. As trade and trading conditions changed, they would be displaced by other bargaining counters. They were part of the 'makeshift' of exchange at certain times and in certain places. They are the 'everyday' commodities that Karl Menger would understand as being functional as money because of their 'saleability'.

The use of commodities as bargaining counters that are available in the common course of life is apparent also in the use of utensils as money in pre-coinage Greece. Spits and other utensils were probably used as money. They had obvious use value as potential fallback if their effectiveness as bargaining counters fell away. The evidence is inconclusive, because the usage was probably not systematic, but a matter of local circumstances, local 'makeshift' and local understanding of the nature of a transaction.

Whether or not spits and other utensils functioned as money would be a matter of communal acceptance. Communities can also shape commodities for use as bargaining counters. Some commodities, being cumbersome and inconvenient, were adapted to improve their function as bargaining counters. Real knives and sickles became token knives and sickles. The items lost their valuation by reference to practical usage – they ceased to cut – and took on a valuation wholly related to their function as bargaining counters in money-bargaining. It is a valuation based on communal acceptance of such a role, or communal support for the role. So long as the costs of production in time and materials are adequately recompensed by their value in exchange, such bargaining counters can be traded into circulation.

Emergence of a commodity as the bargaining counter in common use gives rise to demands for communal regulation, to prevent counterfeiting, control supply and ensure accurate measures and appropriate quality. Hence the state becomes engaged in the management of a money. A 'primitive' or 'popular' money becomes a money 'managed' or 'regulated' by a state.

Utensils are durable but cumbersome – especially cauldrons. Shells and 'sparkling metals' are similarly durable and have aesthetic appeal. They are also fairly convenient, or can fairly easily be made so. They were widely adopted as commodity moneys. Shells were naturally a popular choice in maritime communities. People dived for certain types of shells in certain locations, and fashioned them to an acceptable form for use as bargaining counters. The effort involved in provision, and the natural limitation on where they could be obtained, provided some control on the supply of the bargaining counter.

Paul Einzig notes that *rongo*, a popular form of shell money, is produced on reef islets near Malaita, Solomon Islands, and has a wide sphere of circulation.[4] At Laulasi, an artificial island in the Are-Are Lagoon off Malaita, visitors can still watch local ladies operating 'string and stick' rotating drills, with flint drilling bits, to make holes in round shell pieces of different colours, which are then strung on twine for use locally in certain transactions, most importantly the payment of 'bride-price.' The shell-money is put into circulation by sale in exchange for the national money, the Solomon Islands Dollar. The value of the customary money is thus linked to the national bargaining counter. Visitors can also buy the hand drills used in making the money, so they can mint for themselves when they get home, if they have the shells, and the patience.

Gold and Silver

Some commodities were apparently valued on the basis of their decorative or aesthetic appeal, gold and silver being the prominent examples. They are often referred to as having 'intrinsic value,' thus avoiding specification of the mysterious means by which they have acquired and retained a general perception of their value. Their value is based partly, it seems, on their ornamental attraction, itself arising not just from their attractive appearance, but also from the ease with which they can be worked and, in the case of gold, its freedom from tarnish. Surviving artefacts suggest thriving workshops devoted to gold and silver ornamentation across many societies at many times. The attraction of gold and silver as bargaining counters is enhanced by their durability. Ornaments are the more valued for having long life. In a bargaining counter used to reconcile time disparities, durability is clearly advantageous. Durability has meant also that gold and silver exist in sufficiently steady volume in relation to trade as to give them sufficiently stable value for use as bargaining counters. In broad terms, they retain purchasing power as well as, and mostly better than, other commodities that might be adopted. Stocks of gold and silver survive whose value is for the most part little affected by increments from mining and panning. New supply has seldom been so large as to result in price rises and loss of purchasing power. Shortages, however, have not been uncommon, and trade has suffered as a result. Gold and silver are broadly manageable as bargaining counters in their natural state. They must, however, be weighed and assayed to be fully functional as bargaining counters.

Communities in many places at many times have regarded gold and silver as valuable, and that communal support has given them value as bargaining counters. The element of 'communal support' is particularly notable with regard to gold and silver, since it is so widespread and apparently so spontaneous. People need little prompting to recognise that gold and silver are valuable. The idea of an 'intrinsic' value of sparkling metals seems to relate partly to their ornamental qualities, but reflects also the spontaneous communal acceptance of their value. It is a phenomenon that advocates of state theories of money have had difficulty in accommodating. Popular recognition of the value of gold is apparent in its selection as one of the gifts given to honour the infant Christ. The value in exchange of gold and silver has made it possible for miners to trade them into circulation, sometimes with large profits. Discoveries of gold deposits, particularly alluvial deposits, have triggered legendary 'gold rushes.'

It is apparent that silver was widely used in the ancient Eastern Mediterranean and Near East as a bargaining counter. Its use was constrained by the necessity for weighing and assay. But certified bags of silver, and marked ingots, overcame some of the inconvenience. Silver seems to have dispelled some of the makeshift apparent in the use of less durable commodities as bargaining counters. It was used typically in communities of professional traders, which formulated their own rules and regulations with regard to what was acceptable in the community. The communities reached across political borders, making possible long-distance international trade.

Coin-money of gold and silver dominated exchange for centuries after the introduction of electrum (an alloy of gold and silver) coins in Lydia and the wide adoption of silver coins in ancient Greece. The value of gold and silver coins remained dependent on the communal sense of the value of the commodity they were made of, but the issue of shaped and stamped coins marked the management of the coinage by the state, and hence an enhanced element of security with regard to the continued purchasing power of the money. States widely took over the minting of coins, or officially contracted for minting, so that supply was given an enhanced measure of control. The money-bargaining counter was brought under the jurisdiction of the political support-bargaining system. The Athenian mint is thought to have been located in a corner of the *agora*.[5] Coins could be traded into circulation provided the value of the metal as bullion and the costs of production and provision were covered by the value accorded to them as bargaining counters in money-bargaining. Athens used its coins to pay public officials. Pericles called Athens, 'a salary-drawing city.'[6] Silver from the mine at Laurion financed the construction of ships that were used to defeat a Persian invasion at the battle of Salamis.[7] Material wealth was transformed into violent capacity.

The Spanish conquests of Mexico and Peru in the early-sixteenth century gave Spanish monarchs access to large amounts of gold. The Aztecs and Incas, to their misfortune, shared the European taste for gold as ornamentation, attributing to it also qualities associated with their religious beliefs. These tastes and local mines meant they were well supplied with it. Spanish monarchs found its value in Europe more than sufficient to cover the costs of acquisition, shipment, distribution and the security arrangements necessary to limit the depredations of pirates, plus the costs of minting gold coin when it arrived. Europeans willingly worked and soldiered for it, fulfilling the function of dependable debtors. With the proceeds from import of gold bullion in the sixteenth and seventeenth centuries, Spain exercised extensive power in Europe. Inflows of gold also brought rising prices to Europe, though the rates of inflation were modest compared with twentieth-century experience.[8]

In times of abnormal disruption the price of gold tends to rise. It is seen as a 'safe haven.' Gold is still regarded as a commodity that will retain purchasing power better than almost any other potential store of value. Gold is, for many, still the 'money of last resort.' This faith in the value of gold when the prevailing circumstances are such that the purchasing power of the ordinary managed bargaining counters of nation states is regarded as uncertain depends on the spontaneous popular recognition of the value of gold. If financial systems collapse, it is assumed that people will still value gold. The widespread communal sense of its value means that it can sustain its function as bargaining counter. Popular recognition of its value is reflected in some societies, most notably in Asia, in its prominent role in cultural traditions, especially with regard to betrothal and marriage. The cultural embedding helps also to sustain the popular perception of its value. The impulses that made sparkling metals an essential part of the provision of bargaining counters in earlier times are still apparent now.

People make shift with whatever is available to perform the functions of a money-bargaining counter. The settlement of much international popular and elite opinion on gold and silver as items of value reduced the 'makeshift' apparent in ancient trade. The introduction of coinage enhanced the convenience of the form in which gold and silver could be used as bargaining counters, further reducing the need for 'makeshift.' Nevertheless, people were obliged to make shift when gold and silver were in short supply. Even in the early years of the industrial revolution in England there were shortages of coin that were met by trading on credit, the issue of private tokens, being acknowledgements like those of Innes's brewer and baker, and use of bills of exchange.

Official detachment of the value of a bargaining counter from gold has brought spectacular failures of bargaining counters and resort to 'makeshift.' Germany replaced its Goldmark with the Papiermark in 1914, when it abandoned the gold standard on the outbreak of the First World War. After the War, Germany sought to pay reparations by printing Papiermarks. The resulting inflation went out of control, making the Papiermark all but worthless in the early 1920s. Germans had to carry currency in wheelbarrows, or otherwise make shift in their trading. 'Makeshift' today often takes the form of the adoption of a foreign bargaining counter, typically the US dollar, as a substitute for a local bargaining counter that no longer has communal support. Isolated communities may need to resort to 'makeshift.' The Red Cross and other charities provided cigarettes to allied prisoners in German camps in the Second World War. In an echo of what was very likely the origin of commodity money, cigarettes became makeshift bargaining counters. The satisfaction to be derived from smoking them gave them functional value. They were in wide demand, so they could function as a form of credit, with dependable debtors, giving them a budgetary function. Their supply was apparently sufficient to make possible their use as bargaining counters, but not so plentiful as to erode their purchasing power.

Paper Representing Gold

The link between the supply of a bargaining counter and the general level of prices in its user community has meant that the limited supply of a commodity such as gold has been reckoned an advantage. Limited supply means limited scope for rising prices and limited scope for the erosion of the purchasing power of the bargaining counter. In particular, control of money supply through the control inherent in the supply of a commodity removes from government the option of printing its own money for its own expenditure, whereby it can increase its support. Hence, until quite recently, a 'gold standard' was seen by many as essential to the control of inflation and the maintenance of a stable currency.

The problem is that the volume of gold available is not necessarily related to the level of trade that traders wish to maintain. Shortage of gold can constrain the level of trade. In the seventeenth century payment in silver bullion by the East India Company to Asian providers of tea, coffee, cotton textiles and silk, all in strong demand in Europe, left England short of silver coinage, with deleterious effects on the economy.[9] With silver in short supply, England adopted gold as the reference by which the value of its trade would be assessed. As noted above, the expansion of companies in Britain at the start of the industrial revolution was hampered by shortages of coins, causing companies to adopt various schemes to alleviate their difficulties, including the issue of tokens for work done, redeemable at the company store.[10]

The prominence of gold as a basic standard of value gave goldsmiths in London in the mid-seventeenth century an opportunity to derive income from the stocks of gold they held. They gave receipts for gold deposited with them, and found that the receipts were being used as bargaining counters for trade in goods. Since it was unlikely that everyone would demand their gold back at the same time, they issued receipts, at a charge, for rather more gold than they held. The receipts, payable to their bearers, continued to circulate as bargaining counters, though with reduced security.

Private banks also responded to the needs of their clients by issuing their own paper notes, with an assurance that they could be exchanged for gold on demand. Private banks maintained reserves of coin, but in an emergency a bank would seek the assistance of other banks, including correspondent banks in London. The issue of private paper bargaining counters, particularly those issued by private country banks, proved unsatisfactory. Country banks were always at risk from local panics. At times of national financial crisis, failures were common.[11] Legislation was passed in Britain in 1844 that conferred on the Bank of England exclusive rights to the issue of currency notes, with banks that had already issued notes forbidden to expand their issue. The issue of currency notes in England became wholly the prerogative of the Bank of England in 1921. The Bank of England, acting as an agent of the state, assumed sole responsibility for the issue of a national bargaining counter. The Bank was taken into public ownership in 1946.

Though they could only make available credit denominated in the national bargaining counter and issued by the central bank, private banks maintained their provision of credit. Such provision, in any period, less the withdrawals attendant on paying down of previous credit, puts the bargaining counter into circulation. Each bank puts the national bargaining counter into circulation through provision of credit. The provision becomes deposits in the provider bank and, through the expenditures of its clients, in other banks. Each bank becomes debtor for the deposits it holds, with its viability dependent on its ability, and that of other banks, to identify suitable clients for profitable credit provision.

Private banks issuing their own private bank notes provide credit and at the same time put a bargaining counter into circulation. Such private banks themselves must hold gold coin, or have access to gold coin, to cover issue of their own notes. When private banks can only issue notes of the central bank, they provide credit and put the national bargaining counter into circulation. They no longer need to hold backing in gold for the currency they provide as credit. The private bank is responsible for its own continued solvency. The stability of the national bargaining counter is the responsibility of the central bank, as agent of the state. Thus whilst the bank notes issued by a bank may display a 'promise to pay the bearer…,' sometimes understood as a promise of the credit-providing bank to exchange for gold, the bank will not provide gold to clients claiming from them. The bank note is a central bank note, and claims to payment in gold have to be addressed to the central bank.

The role of private banks in the provision of credit and the holding of deposits as commercial undertakings has to be distinguished from their role in provision of credit whereby the national bargaining counter is put into circulation. The credit itself does both – provides credit to a client and puts the national bargaining counter into circulation. But the former is the responsibility of the private bank, whilst the latter is the responsibility of the central bank. A central bank avails itself of the opportunity of private bank provision of credit to put into circulation the national bargaining counter. Although the national bargaining counter may involve a promise to redeem in gold, that is not part of the service provided by the private bank. Rather it is an undertaking by the central bank, on behalf of the state, given to sustain confidence in the national bargaining counter. The notion that 'banks create money,' with an implication that a function of such national social importance should not be entrusted to private agents, misses this distinction between the private provision of credit and the putting into circulation of a national bargaining counter. The double function of credit provision involves dual responsibilities.

The provision of the national bargaining counter, whilst assuredly a means of bridging time disparities, and hence a matter of credit, is a credit of a different kind to the credit provided by the private bank. Holders of the national bargaining counter hold a social credit, as opposed to an individual credit, that must be redeemed by the society on whose behalf it is issued by the central bank.

Under a gold standard, the credit is ostensibly redeemed through the provision of gold by the central bank. The national bargaining counter is then a matter of paper representing gold. The bargaining counter is still fundamentally a commodity. The implication is that gold has a more dependable purchasing power than the paper notes of the national bargaining counter, or deposits denominated in the national bargaining counter.

The option for redemption in gold from the central bank became increasingly a matter of form rather than a utilised facility. Various conditions were imposed regarding the obligation to meet that 'promise.' The promise nevertheless bolstered support for the national bargaining counter amongst those who only recognised gold as having fundamental value. It was seen, however, in Chapter 10 that sterling circulated in the nineteenth century to a value well beyond gold reserves, even allowing for any officially permitted fractional excess of currency in circulation over its backing in gold. Rather, according to Peter Mathias, trade was conducted on the basis of a 'sterling standard.' Trade involving the use of sterling as bargaining counter was so extensive that those using it had confidence in its purchasing power. In the twentieth century the need for even a formal peg to gold was increasingly questioned. John Maynard Keynes was amongst the most pressing questioners in the 1920s, with Friedrich Knapp in support, insisting on the prerogative of the state to declare what would be money (Chapter 10).

But still the nature of the credit that sustained the value of the national bargaining counter was not recognised. The implication of redemption in gold was that holders of gold would be able to acquire goods and services with gold, since many people would accept gold in payment for goods and services. But redemption in gold was not necessary and in many cases not possible. Redemption of the national bargaining counter could be made directly in goods and services, without the intermediation of gold. So long as there existed in the national community agents who would provide goods and services in exchange for the national bargaining counter, the national bargaining counter would maintain its purchasing power and maintain its function as a bargaining counter. So long as there were dependable debtors who would redeem the credit represented by the national bargaining counter through the provision of goods and services, the bargaining counter would fulfil its function. Dependable debtors are essential to maintenance of the purchasing power of the bargaining counter. They redeem the social credit represented by a national bargaining counter.

Maintenance of purchasing power requires also control of the aggregate supply of the national bargaining counter. Each private bank will provide credit so as to meet and exceed the viability condition. But they have no immediate interest in the aggregate value of credit provision, and even if they did, they would have no means of controlling it. That has to be the responsibility of the central bank. Too little, and business is deprived of the means by which it deals with time disparities between investments and returns from trade; too much and changes in the terms of trade across the money-bargaining system, arising from changes in bargaining positions, and the bargaining counter will lose its purchasing power. Central banks influence the supply of the national bargaining counter through the interest rates they charge private banks for the credit they extend to them, and adjustment of the amount of credit private banks can provide relative to their assets.

Credit, Purchasing Power and Dependable Debtors

Even in the earliest times the bargaining counter is best understood in terms of credit and the presence of dependable debtors. The metamorphosis of the value of a commodity from value in meeting general situation-related requirements – the value in use – to value by reference to budgetary requirements, or the accommodation of time disparities, implies a change in the nature of a transaction from a wholly complete transaction, such as is characteristic of simple barter, to an exchange in which on the one side a useful commodity is acquired whilst on the other a token or 'holding value' is accepted. It becomes more like a credit sale, with an assumption that there will be sufficient numbers in a community ready to redeem the credit later by acceptance of the tokens in exchange for goods or services. The communal bargaining counter involves the concept of money as credit, in the distinctive form of money as a credit accorded by society, with no specific individual debtor, but with confidence in the existence in the community of dependable debtors.

Whilst the 'intrinsic' value of gold and silver may appear to provide an alternative basis for valuation of a money, such commodities can, as was seen in Chapter 7, under the heading 'Commodity and Credit,' be understood as constituting credit tokens. The cultural embedding of gold in many cultures can be taken as implying the presence of dependable debtors across those cultures, ready to provide goods and services in exchange for gold. The 'intrinsic' value of gold and silver would surely be lost if it were found they could not reliably be exchanged for goods and services. Gold and silver, like other bargaining counters, need dependable debtors. They nevertheless display, like no other commodities, the strength of group support in determining value and ensuring that dependable debtors can be found to provide goods and services for something the group has agreed is valuable. Central banks continue to store large volumes of gold as 'reserves' in recognition of its continuing international hold on human minds as 'value.'

In the Innes example involving butcher, baker and brewer, in the provision of tokens by a company, and with a bill of exchange, there is only one debtor (or two, in the case of baker and brewer), whose dependability is essential to the use of the credits as money. There is a significant risk of default. With the multiple joint debtors of a national community, the chances of encountering dependable debtors are much higher, and the sustained purchasing power of a bargaining counter is better assured. Furthermore, the redemption of the social credit does not depend on the endurance of a single organisation. It was seen in Chapter 9, under the heading 'Organisations and Budgeting,' that a preference for multiple debtors may have prevented the emergence of money as organisational debt. The issuing organisation of such money has to be protected from alternatives, giving it a strong bargaining position. Hence societies have preferred that their social credits, their bargaining counters, be redeemable through many debtors. In modern banking systems, private banks can fail without threat to the functioning of a national bargaining counter.

The dependable debtors in a national community, as was seen in Chapter 7, will not normally see themselves as debtors for a social credit. They will not feel the burden of the social debt represented by the bargaining counter in circulation. They will have none of the reluctance normally associated with payment of a debt. Dependable debtors are motivated by their aspirations to earn money, to become creditors themselves. In the case of companies, they are motivated to sell goods and services to meet and exceed the viability condition. As private persons, they will commonly be looking for employment. These motivations give rise to reductions in unit costs and lower prices. They positively enhance the purchasing power of the bargaining counter they use. The purchasing power of the bargaining counters used in strong economies increases and their value appreciates relative to the bargaining counters used in weaker economies.

The money-bargaining counter is both alternative and supplementary to support, the counter used in support-bargaining. Part of the effectiveness of the money-bargaining counter is the physical characteristics listed earlier. But it can also be attributed to the dependability of its debtors. A holder of a well-managed money-bargaining counter can depend on getting value for it in goods and services. The returns to support are less dependable. In formal support-bargaining systems a majority vote normally determines outcomes, but majorities can be difficult to assemble and sustain. In informal support-bargaining treason and disloyalty on a petty scale are universal. People may not fulfil the obligations placed upon them by their engagement in support-bargaining. They may be punished by losing their friends, but they may get away with it by finding other friends. Money-bargaining is more precise and hence commonly more dependable. Money-bargaining can potentially be used for exchanges that would not be regarded as secure if conducted as matters of support-bargaining. The precision also facilitates the improvement in terms of exchange noted in the previous paragraph. The great growth of money-bargaining, albeit under regulation imposed through support-bargaining, reflects the enhanced scope for exchange through money-bargaining.

The function of money as credit provided by society and the use of bank credit to put it into circulation have confused the understanding of money. The straightforward credit–debt relationship between banks and their clients has to be distinguished from the social credit aspect of a bargaining counter. Private banks have a conventional creditor–debtor relationship with their clients. The credit provided by society is of a different kind. It is conventional in that it tides over time disparities in revenues and expenditures. But it is unconventional in that its redemption depends on no single identified debtor, but on the existence of many agents ready to accept the bargaining counter that denominates the credit in exchange for goods and services. It depends on the existence of a money-bargaining system whose agents are actively seeking to acquire revenues denominated in the bargaining counter. The social credit is distinctive also in that oversupply of the bargaining counter through provision of credit will potentially diminish the purchasing power of the bargaining counter. Its management has therefore to be entrusted to a communal agency, normally a central bank, that can control its supply. By these measures, a bargaining counter retains the support and confidence of a society.

Circulation of a 'Money of Account'

Central Banks avail themselves of the provision of credit by private banks to private borrowers to put a national money into circulation. They also provide credit to governments. The additional credit, less repayments of earlier credit, adds to the circulation of the national currency.

Money established as a 'money of account' and valued through acceptance by the state would appropriately be put into circulation by the state that creates it. Central banks are legally defined organisations, invariably owned and controlled by the state, so that the state can be regarded as lending to itself. How much the state lends to itself in its own money, and how much it repays, then appears as a matter of discretion. One pocket lends to the other, and the debtor pocket repays the creditor pocket, at the discretion of the owner of the trousers.

The principle that the state created the money as a 'money of account' and is consequently free to put into circulation what money it chooses implies disregard for the principles attaching to the circulation of a money based on exchange values. Under the latter principles, the supply of money has to be adjusted to the level of trade, in order to avoid inflation and a deterioration in the purchasing power of the money. A 'money of account' is held to be established without regard for exchange values, so that such considerations are irrelevant. The state-defined 'money of account' is established for the advance of state interests. As was seen in Chapter 6, advocates of a state theory of money, Geoffrey Ingham in particular, decry the importance of purchasing power.

Knapp's state theory of money is not concerned with inflation or purchasing power (Chapter 10).

Moses Finley's understanding of money as 'strictly political,' as summarised by Darel Thai Engen, was quoted in Chapter 11 (Note 106).[12] States mint coins not to facilitate economic transactions among their citizens, but for state purposes. Randall Wray's view of the origin of money in tax levies, not as a medium of exchange, was quoted in Chapter 9 (Note 71).[13] In his section on policy implications of his theory of modern money he remarks further:

> Governments issue money to buy what they need; they tax to generate a demand for that money; and then they accept the money in payment of the tax. If a deficit results, that simply indicates that the population wishes to hoard some of the money. The deficit is of no consequence to the government; it merely allows the population to save in the form of government money.[14]

Tax is imposed on people to generate demand for the money. Rather than a purchasing power based on the presence of voluntary 'dependable debtors,' value is established through the exaction of taxes. Wray makes prominent Keynes's early affirmation of a 'money of account,' but makes no mention of Keynes's subsequent emphasis on the importance of purchasing power.[15] Ingham emphasises the origin of money in social conflict: '…the value of money is the enacted outcome of social and political conflicts between the main interests in the economy.'[16] Money is, '…socially constructed as a reality in a process of conflict and struggle.'[17] According to Ingham, coinage 'escaped' from where it was rightfully held, within the confines of the state:

> Although coinage was a jealously guarded instrument of state, it inevitably enabled economic power to escape from state control through the massive injection of portable, abstract value into the relatively loosely integrated Greek and, later, Roman empires.[18]

Money is conceived in origin and usage as deriving from political conflict and fulfilling political functions. Tax impositions are the basis of its value. Its role in exchange is incidental, or even a matter of 'escape' from its proper place. These concepts of the origins of money reflect the group and anti-capitalist interests of economic anthropologists under the influence of Karl Polanyi.

Protagonists of the state theory of money do not entirely ignore the potential damage arising from inflation. Wray remarks, following shortly after the above quotation (Note 14), that, 'This does not mean that the deficit cannot be too big, that is, inflationary.'[19] But it is a concession against the theory. There is nothing in the theoretical exposition that gives grounds for concern over inflation and purchasing power. It is anomalous to the interpretations of the 'money of account' frame of reference. With much less theoretical prominence, the issue of purchasing power may be accorded much less practical prominence. There is a risk that inflationary effects will be overlooked in pursuit of support for the interests incorporated in the frame of reference. Frames of reference have powerful influence (Chapter 4). The arguments of mainstream microeconomists for 'free trade' and consequent 'optimal allocation of resources,' based on the core neoclassical frame of reference, have historically caused states to move more slowly than is desirable to regulate private trade. The 'money of account' frame of reference will potentially assemble support for monetary policies that expand money supplies beyond what is compatible with the stable purchasing power of currencies. The idea of a 'money of account' underpins Modern Monetary Theory, giving it a weak foundation that will potentially result in damaging monetary policies. In the bargaining frame of reference the purchasing power of the bargaining counter is of fundamental importance and has to be protected.

Whilst central banks are owned and controlled by states, their separation means that they operate in a different support-bargaining environment. State governments operate in a context of national support-bargaining formalised over a national territory, with engagement in money-bargaining through their budgets. Central banks operate under legislation in a more limited sphere of support-bargaining and money-bargaining, involving agencies closely concerned with credit provision and the conduct of monetary affairs. The division gives central banks interests distinct from those of their governments, enough to be a source of friction. The interests of a central bank relate particularly to the management of the national bargaining counter. It is an alternative bargaining counter to support, and its management potentially conflicts with the interests of those engaged in political support-bargaining. The immediate interests of governments can be detrimental to the functioning of a money-bargaining counter. In particular, whilst state governments will be keen to expand their expenditures so as to assemble the support necessary to electoral success, central banks will be keen to ensure that government expenditures are held to a level that maintains money supply at a level compatible with the stability of prices, to protect the purchasing power of the national bargaining counter.

Notes

1 Shaw, Brent D. and Saller, Richard P., 1981, 'Introduction' to Finley, M. I., 1981, *Economy and Society in Ancient Greece*, London: Chatto & Windus, pp. x–xii, xvi; Wikipedia contributors, 'Moses Finley', *Wikipedia*. Accessed 19 February 2021.

2 Arrow, Kenneth and Debreu, Gérard, 1954, 'Existence of an Equilibrium in a Competitive Economy', *Econometrica*, Vol. 22, pp. 265–90. The definitive account is recognised as Debreu, Gérard, 1959, *Theory of Value: An Axiomatic Analysis of Economic Equilibrium*, New York: Wiley. For comment see Spread, Patrick, 2016, *The Evolution of Economies: Money-Bargaining, Economic Change and Industrial Revolution*, London and New York: Routledge, pp. 49–55, drawing on Geanakoplos, John, 2004, 'The Arrow–Debreu Model of General Equilibrium', *Cowles Foundation Paper No. 1090*, Cowles Foundation for Research in Economics at Yale University, p. 122.

3 Ingham, Geoffrey, 2004, *The Nature of Money*, Cambridge: Polity Press, p. 99.

4 Einzig, Paul, 1966, *Primitive Money*, Oxford: Pergamon Press. First published 1949, p. 56. Einzig's reference: Schneider, Oskar, 1905, *Muschelgeld-Studien*, Dresden, p. 75.
5 Trevett, Jeremy, 2001, 'Coinage and Democracy at Athens', in Andrew Meadows and Kirsty Shipton (Eds.), *Money and Its Uses in the Ancient Greek World*, Oxford: Oxford University Press, pp. 23–34, p. 30.
6 Trevett, 2001, p. 24.
7 Schaps, David, 2004, *The Invention of Coinage and the Monetization of Ancient Greece*, Ann Arbor: University of Michigan Press, Kindle Edition, L3720.
8 Backhouse, Roger E., 1994, *Economists and the Economy: The Evolution of Economic Ideas*, New Brunswick: Transaction Publishers, pp. 109–10.
9 Coleman, D. C., 1977, *The Economy of England, 1450–1750*, Oxford: Oxford University Press, pp. 141–2. See also Spread, 2016, p. 26.
10 Ashton, T. S., 1947, *The Industrial Revolution*, Oxford and New York: Oxford University Press, pp. 80–1.
11 Mathias, Peter, 2001, *The First Industrial Nation: An Economic History of Britain 1700–1914*, London and New York: Routledge, pp. 148–55.
12 Engen, Darel Tai, 2004, 'The Economy of Ancient Greece', EH.Net, p. 33. https://eh.net/?s=the+economy+of+ancient+greece, Accessed 6 April 2021.
13 Wray, L. Randall, 2000, 'Modern Money', in John Smithin (Ed.), *What Is Money?* London: Routledge, p. 43.
14 Wray, 2000, p. 61.
15 Wray, 2000, pp. 53–6.
16 Ingham, 2004, p. 87.
17 Ingham, 2004, p. 203.
18 Ingham, 2004, p. 100.
19 Wray, 2000, p. 62.

References

Arrow, Kenneth and Debreu, Gérard, 1954, 'Existence of an Equilibrium in a Competitive Economy', *Econometrica*, Vol. 22, pp. 265–90.
Ashton, T. S., 1947, *The Industrial Revolution*, Oxford and New York: Oxford University Press.
Backhouse, Roger E., 1994, *Economists and the Economy: The Evolution of Economic Ideas*, New Brunswick: Transaction Publishers.
Coleman, D. C., 1977, *The Economy of England, 1450–1750*, Oxford: Oxford University Press.
Debreu, Gérard, 1959, *Theory of Value: An Axiomatic Analysis of Economic Equilibrium*, New York: Wiley.
Einzig, Paul, 1966, *Primitive Money*, Oxford: Pergamon Press. First published 1949, p. 56.
Engen, Darel Tai, 2004, 'The Economy of Ancient Greece', EH.Net, https://eh.net/?s=the+economy+of+ancient+greece, Accessed 6 April 2021.
Geanakoplos, John, 2004, 'The Arrow–Debreu Model of General Equilibrium', *Cowles Foundation Paper No. 1090*, Cowles Foundation for Research in Economics at Yale University.
Ingham, Geoffrey, 2004, *The Nature of Money*, Cambridge: Polity Press.
Mathias, Peter, 2001, *The First Industrial Nation: An Economic History of Britain 1700–1914*, London and New York: Routledge.

Meadows, Andrew and Shipton, Kirsty, (Eds.), 2001, *Money and Its Uses in the Ancient Greek World*, Oxford: Oxford University Press.
Schaps, David, 2004, *The Invention of Coinage and the Monetization of Ancient Greece*, Ann Arbor: University of Michigan Press, Kindle Edition.
Schneider, Oskar, 1905, *Muschelgeld-Studien*, Dresden.
Shaw, Brent D. and Saller, Richard P., 1981, 'Introduction' to Finley, M. I., 1981, *Economy and Society in Ancient Greece*, London: Chatto & Windus.
Smithin, John, (Ed.), 2000, *What Is Money?* London: Routledge.
Spread, Patrick, 2016, *The Evolution of Economies: Money-Bargaining, Economic Change and Industrial Revolution*, London and New York: Routledge.
Trevett, Jeremy, 2001, 'Coinage and Democracy at Athens', in Andrew Meadows and Kirsty Shipton (Eds.), *Money and Its Uses in the Ancient Greek World*, Oxford: Oxford University Press, pp. 23–34.
Wikipedia contributors, 'Moses Finley', *Wikipedia*. Accessed 19 February 2021.
Wray, L. Randall, 2000, 'Modern Money', in John Smithin (Ed.), *What Is Money?* London: Routledge.

Index